The Creation of Israeli Arabic

Palgrave Studies in Languages at War
Series editors: **Hilary Footitt**, University of Reading, UK, and **Michael Kelly**, School of Modern Languages, Southampton University, UK.

Languages play a crucial role in war, conflict and peace-making: in intelligence gathering and evaluation, pre-deployment preparations, operations on the ground, regime change, and supporting refugees and displaced persons. In the politics of war, languages have a dual impact: a public policy dimension, setting frameworks and expectations; and the lived experience of those 'on the ground', working with and meeting speakers of other languages.

This series intends to bring together books that deal with the role of languages in situations of conflict, including war, civil war, occupation, peace-keeping, peace-enforcement and humanitarian action in war zones. It will offer an interdisciplinary approach, drawing on applied linguistics, sociolinguistics, translation studies, intercultural communication, history, politics, international relations and cultural studies. Books in the series will explore specific conflict situations across a range of times and places, and specific language-related roles and activities, examining three contexts: languages and the military, meeting the other in war and peace-making, and interpreting/translating in war.

Titles include:

LANGUAGES AT WAR: Policies and Practices of Language Contacts in Conflict (edited by Hilary Footitt and Michael Kelly)

LANGUAGES AND THE MILITARY: Alliances, Occupation and Peace Building (edited by Hilary Footitt and Michael Kelly)

INTERPRETING THE PEACE: Peace Operation, Conflict and Language in Bosnia-Herzegovina (Michael Kelly and Catherine Baker)

'WARTALK': Foreign Languages and the British War Effort in Europe 1940–46 (Hilary Footitt and Simona Tobia)

THE CREATION OF ISRAELI ARABIC: Political and Security Considerations in the Making of Arabic Language Studies in Israel (Yonatan Mendel)

Forthcoming:

REGIONAL LANGUAGE POLICIES IN FRANCE DURING WWII (Amit Aviv)

LANGUAGES AT WAR AND PEACE: NATO Language Policy and Practice in Operations since 1994 (Ian Jones and Louise Askew)

TRANSLATING EVIDENCE AND INTERPRETING TESTIMONY IN WAR CRIME TRIBUNALS (Ellen Elias-Bursac)

Palgrave Studies in Languages at War
Series Standing Order ISBN 978–0–230–35516–3 Hardback
9780–230–35517–0 Paperback
(*outside North America only*)

You can receive future titles in this series as they are published by placing a standing order. Please contact your bookseller or, in case of difficulty, write to us at the address below with your name and address, the title of the series and the ISBN quoted above.

Customer Services Department, Macmillan Distribution Ltd, Houndmills, Basingstoke, Hampshire RG21 6XS, England

---

The Creation of Israeli Arabic

Political and Security Considerations in the Making of Arabic Language Studies in Israel

Yonatan Mendel
University of Cambridge, UK

palgrave
macmillan

Softcover reprint of the hardcover 1st edition 2014 978-1-137-33736-8

First published 2014 by
PALGRAVE MACMILLAN

Palgrave Macmillan in the UK is an imprint of Macmillan Publishers Limited, registered in England, company number 785998, of Houndmills, Basingstoke, Hampshire RG21 6XS.

Palgrave Macmillan in the US is a division of St. Martin's Press LLC, 175 Fifth Avenue, New York, NY 10010.

Palgrave Macmillan is the global academic imprint of the above companies and has companies and representatives throughout the world.

Palgrave® and Macmillan® are registered trademarks in the United States, the United Kingdom, Europe and other countries.

ISBN 978-1-349-46378-7 ISBN 978-1-137-33737-5 (eBook)
DOI 10.1057/9781137337375

A catalogue record for this book is available from the British Library.

A catalog record for this book is available from the Library of Congress.

Typeset by MPS Limited, Chennai, India.

Transferred to Digital Printing in 2014

إلى محبِّي اللغة وروحها

Contents

Documents

Appendices

Preface

Arabic, Security and Me

It was a conversation that I dreaded having. Up until that point, two months into my studies, my relationship with Professor Yasir Suleiman, my supervisor at Cambridge University, had progressed nicely. I had shared with him experiences from previous joint Israeli–Palestinian activities and protests in which I have participated in Israel/Palestine – a teacher at two different Arab schools, working in the West Bank with Physicians for Human Rights, my politically motivated refusal to participate in military reserve duty in the Occupied Palestinian Territories and my great interest in Arabic. Things seemed to be going really well; he was interested in the welfare of my family and I inquired as to the whereabouts of his sons. He seemed sufficiently impressed with me to introduce me to other related faculty and Arab intellectuals, who had previously seemed beyond reach to me. He even shared with them, with a measure of pride, the focus of my studies. Still, no matter how many times I thought about it in my head, I couldn't quite work up the courage to broach the subject.

Two months into my studies, on knocking on his door, I was not filled with pride and excitement, rather with trepidation. He said, 'Come in,' and was slightly confused to see me on the other side of the door. 'Did we set an appointment?' he asked, rather surprised, in that deeply British accent that scholars have there. Professor Suleiman lifted up his eyes from the pile of essays on his desk. 'No', I answered, 'we didn't set an appointment, but it is quite important.' Putting down his pencil, he switched to English–Arabic: '*Tfadal*, then, *Ustaz* Yoni,' he said. 'Come in and let me know *shu shaghel balak*.'

I stepped inside and sat opposite him. Professor Suleiman examined me carefully, perhaps noticing my discomfort. I did not know how to begin this conversation. Despite having planned this moment for two months, delaying it week after week, I still didn't remember how to begin. Eventually, as abruptly as the silence began, I broke the silence and just started speaking. And speaking. And I kept speaking for a long time, words coming out of me in waves, in broken English and broken Arabic, as broken words and broken sentences.

'My life didn't begin at the age of 23,' I said. 'I was also a 16-year-old once, and also 18 and 20. I am indeed interested in the archaeology of Arabic language studies in Israel, academically and intellectually, but not only. It is also because of my life experiences. I am not just interested in Arabic and security, you see. I know that this is a topic deserving of research.'

My sentences tumbled out, partially in the wrong chronological order. I felt incoherent at times but continued. 'I feel you treated me kindly without knowing the whole lot about me.' 'Everything I told you about myself was true, but I also omitted other pieces of information.' 'I feel I have a stone weighing on my heart.' I continued, 'I was not always very politically aware, you see. I was born to a regular Jewish family in Israel in a regular Jewish neighbourhood in Jerusalem. Not a right-wing-leaning environment but not a left one either. I studied Arabic in high school, and I also knew, like my classmates, that Military Intelligence is interested in pupils who study Arabic. At the time, I didn't have a problem with that and when I turned 18, I was recruited into the Navy.' The words kept on coming. 'But it was connected to the Arabic language, you see, and I wasn't a bad soldier. I was even recognised for outstanding service by the Chief of the Navy, the Chief of Staff and the President.' I stopped, and then continued. 'During the entire military period, I didn't ask too many questions, and the route I made from studying Arabic in school to my position in the army was commonsensical and unquestionable. At the time, even imagining that one day I might have an Arab-Palestinian supervisor with whom I would discuss the status of Arabic in Jewish-Israeli schools was out of the question. Even Palestinian friends at the time were not an option.' 'You know how it is', I said, 'Jews and Arabs don't really mix together in Israel and back then it was natural for me that Arabic will bring me closer to Military Intelligence than to Arab-Palestinian people.'

Professor Suleiman didn't twitch the entire time that I blurted out that emotional, broken confession. He didn't nod but didn't stop me either – he just kept looking at me. After I finished, when silence returned to the room, he waited a long minute before speaking. 'I think you did well telling this to me,' he said. 'Perhaps at an earlier stage it would have been better but, still, I think it is important that you decided to step forward and speak to me. It is important to understand each other as we will be working together.' A few more moments of silence passed before he started speaking again. 'As you can also imagine', he said, 'I am not surprised by what you just told me. After all', he didn't smile, 'how many Israeli men are there, who, in their twenties and thirties, know Arabic, and who were not a part of the security establishment?'

After a brief pause, he continued. 'But perhaps I should take advantage of this opportunity and tell you one thing. One thing that can make both of us feel better about the project that you are just beginning to embark upon. Perhaps this is a piece of advice that will be useful to you in later stages of your research.' 'Promise yourself', he said, 'that you will not hide behind your research anymore. Make a decision not to disguise the fact that your life didn't begin at the age of 23 working in Arab schools. Acknowledging your background may make your research more important and might encourage others to think critically and to speak out. Promise yourself, therefore, that if this work someday materialises into a book, you will not hide the fact that you have a personal connection to this topic. Instead, please tell your readers straightaway that you are not an external observer and that Arabic for the sake of security was at one point very much a part of your life. Perhaps this will help you to lift this stone from your heart.'

Acknowledgements

This book would not have been possible without the support and help of many dear friends and colleagues, scholars, interviewees, archivists, academic institutions and funders. While I am sure that there will be some oversights, I will do my best to thank everyone.

I would like to start by thanking Professor Yasir Suleiman, who supervised my work at the University of Cambridge and whose help and input cannot be understated. Perhaps the warm bond that developed between us was also due to the fact that we represent two very different sons of Jerusalem: he, a product of Al-Quds of the 1950s and I, a child of Yerushalayyim of the 1980s. His support and contribution towards my work have been invaluable and meaningful in so many different ways. *Alf shukr lak Ustaz Yasir.*

I would also like to thank the many additional individuals who advised me academically. Dr Lori Allen and Dr Basim Musallam from the Middle East Department at Cambridge read my work at an initial stage and made some valuable comments. I was also privileged to benefit from the insights of Dr Amira Bennison, Professor Elana Shohamy and Professor Re'uven Snir, who sat on my examination committee and whose key insights and input significantly improved my work. Special appreciation is due to Dr Tami Sarfatti, who read various sections of this book and provided me with vital critiques and profound support. Dr Jake Norris, Dr Adam Coutts, Dr Gregor Schwarb, Dr Ronald Ranta, Mr Bob Mark, Mr 'Eran Ḥakim, Dr Yuval Ivri, Ms Sandra Fine and Ms Naomi Mark, have also read different parts of this book and have given me important and helpful feedback. Lisa Richlen edited the final version of my work and did an amazing job in improving my English and saving me from falling into some serious language traps.

I was truly blessed and privileged to benefit from the warmth and support of a number of friends during my studies in England. Ignacio Sanchez, Manar Makhoul, Bruno De Nicola, Marta Dominguez Diaz, Ronald Klingebiel, Jess Johnson, Tarik Mouakil, Simon Ryle, Chloe Massey, James Weaver and Chaoqun Lian deserve endless gratitude. I would also like to express my thanks to dear family friends in England, including David Bernstein, Paul Zuckerman, Matt Murphy, Simon Hancock, Mary Kay Wilmers, Sam Frears, and the Conlin family, who – together with Norwich City Football Club – have all made my stay in the UK pleasant and who kept my spirits high.

During the long period of fieldwork conducted in Israel, I was surprised by the amount of help and information that I received from both interviewees and archivists. I would like to thank the more than 30 interviewees whom I met who shared their perspectives on the relevant Arabic-oriented issues. They greatly contributed to the research outcomes by opening their hearts to me and shared their opinions, knowledge and stories about their life experiences. No less important, I want to thank the archivists in the five Israeli archives that I visited for my research who gave me access to information despite the sensitivity of the subject.

This research was made possible due to a number of generous scholarships that enabled me to conduct my studies in the UK. I would like to acknowledge the British Council Chevening Scholarship, as well as the Council of British Research in the Levant, the Department of Middle Eastern Studies at Cambridge University, the AVI Fellowship, the Wingate Foundation, the Anglo-Jewish Association, the Anglo-Israeli Association and the B'nai B'rith organisation, all of whom provided me with support throughout the various periods of my studies. In addition, I want to acknowledge Palgrave Macmillan, the publishers of my book.

Lastly, I would like to thank my family in Israel, including my parents, two sisters, my brothers-in-law, an inspiring grandmother and five cheerful nieces, who were supportive from afar and made sure that I took breaks from time to time. An ultimate thanks goes to my dear Ella, whose encouragement, support and reminders to keep things in proportion were all precious assets during the exhausting process of researching and writing this book.

Abbreviations

CZA	Central Zionist Archives, Jerusalem
IDFA	Israel Defense Forces and Defense Establishment Archives, Tel ha-Shomer
ISA	Israel State Archives, Jerusalem
MoEA	Ministry of Education Archive, Jerusalem
YYA	Yad Ya'ari Archive (Archives of Ha-Shomer ha-Tsa'ir movement), Giv'at Ḥaviva

Note on Transliteration and Translation

This book uses the system of Arabic and Hebrew transliteration as outlined in the guidelines of the *International Journal of Middle East Studies* (*IJMES*). Where names of people and places have standardised spelling in English, the *IJMES* system of diacritics has been dispensed with. When citing books and articles written in Arabic and Hebrew, the footnotes include the original language while also providing an English translation. The full citations, including all diacritics, are found in the Bibliography. The Arabic letters *hamza* and *ʿayn* are written throughout this research as ʾ and ʿ respectively.

All translations in the text are my own, unless specifically stated otherwise. The particular style of language used by Israeli officials from the Ministry of Education, the IDF and the Prime Minister's Office is an important aspect of the analysis presented here. Therefore, when a translation from a Hebrew or an Arabic source is given in the text, I have included in parentheses certain key words, using the appropriate transliteration.

Introduction

Arabic and Security in Israel

The research presented here is about the history and politics of Arabic language studies in Jewish-Israeli schools and the extent to which political and security considerations have influenced Arabic language studies in Israel. It is primarily based on archival documents from the years 1935 to 1985, but also includes an analysis of the study of Arabic in Jewish-Israeli schools at the end of the twentieth and beginning of the twenty-first centuries. In so doing, this book aims to uncover the political history of Arabic studies in Jewish schools in the country, and to offer a new look at the ongoing issue of Arabic studies in Jewish-Israeli schools today.

This specific subject – of Arabic studies and security in Israel – is usually referenced in footnotes, mentioned as general themes that are 'beyond the scope of this essay' or noted euphemistically as 'national considerations', 'strategic concerns' or 'public matters'. The study presented here, therefore, which is based exclusively on an examination of publicly accessible material from official Israeli archives, military and civilian alike, focuses on this topic and exposes the scope of this open secret. It outlines the tremendous penetration of security and political concerns into Arabic studies, its impact on Jewish society in Israel, its influence on the pupils who studied and study Arabic and on the kind of Arabic that they were taught and are being taught. It also uncovers the methodologies for teaching Arabic to Jewish-Israeli pupils, including the 'silent' or unstated norms conveyed while studying it, and the influences that have established the nature of Arabic studies in Israel.

Even before conducting any research on this topic, a few contemporary examples come to mind that illustrate the scope of the military's influence on Arabic language studies: these include surveys that demonstrate that service in Military Intelligence is a primary factor motivating

Jewish-Israeli pupils to study Arabic; public projects implemented by the Military Intelligence in the field of Arabic studies, including the 'Oriental Youth Battalions' or 'Military Intelligence on the Horizon'; the insignificant number of Palestinian citizens of Israel who teach Arabic in Jewish-Israeli schools; and the intensive attempts by the Military Intelligence to increase the number of high school pupils learning Arabic. My own personal experience bears this out as well. As an Arabic-speaking Jewish-Israeli, Jews and Palestinians who meet me for the first time regularly ask me whether my Arabic skills were acquired through past or current association with Military Intelligence. In their view, this is the most obvious explanation for an Israeli-born Jewish person who can speak, read or write Arabic. Sadly, this view is, by and large, true.

While not openly stated, then, the influence of security considerations and military bodies on Arabic language studies in Israel is quite clear. This combination, between what we know and what we are unwilling to speak about and reflect on, makes security the 'elephant in the room' of the research and discussions on Arabic studies in Israel. This begs the question: Why are Jewish-Israeli academics and decision-makers unwilling to examine this issue from an in-depth and critical perspective? And why, despite the widespread assumptions and acknowledgement of this issue informally, scholars have not demonstrated an inclination to question the basic premises underlying this phenomenon in a meaningful or direct way through academic articles, educational panels and open debate dedicated to this topic.

I believe that this has happened, at least partly, due to a sense in the Jewish-Israeli reality that military expertise and involvement in Arabic studies is natural, a part of life, and even necessary for Jewish-Israelis. Such an approach finds its foundation in a general blurring of boundaries between the civilian and military spheres in the country. This, as I show in the research, resulted in the adoption of an all-encompassing 'peace and security' ideology that has obscured the extent to which military interests influence the civil sphere – with 'Arabic for peace and security' being a primary case study. In light of this national context, critical thinking regarding the way in which Arabic is being taught and the ideology, interests and actors behind its study has been lacking. As I demonstrate in the book, due to an absence of intellectual and cultural figures who question or oppose the 'peace and security' mantra – including, first and foremost, the absence of the Arab people themselves from all decision-making processes in the field – Arabic language instruction for Jewish-Israelis has shaped pupils' views about the language and its native speakers to the detriment of both.

Following Joshua Fishman's analysis of language, 'not only as a carrier of the message, but as the very message itself',[1] I will show in this book how focusing on Arabic studies can shed light on important ways in which Jewish-Israelis understand the region of the Middle East, and especially Israel/Palestine, and the people living in it. Following this, the extensive involvement of security actors in the teaching of an official language of Israel, one that is spoken by Palestinian citizens of Israel, which was a language spoken by a considerable percentage of Mizraḥi Jews (or Arab-Jews) who emigrated from Arab countries,[2] and which is the lingua franca of the region where Israel is located, is worthy of critical research and open discussion.

Unfortunately this line of thought, and more generally a critical examination of contemporary Israeli society and Israeli history – including language study – are considered, far too often and increasingly in the last decade or so, as being 'anti-Israeli' and, as such, illegitimate by Israeli decision-makers, the Ministry of Education, the security establishment and even elements of Israeli academia. 'Some things should be left un-researched,' a professor from the heart of the field of Arabic studies said to me on hearing about the subject of this book. My views are diametrically opposed to his; I believe that this subject is worthy of discussion precisely due to its controversial or even sensitive nature and the desire by many to keep it under wraps. As a matter of fact, a sense that there was a need to shed light on this subject and open it up for examination serves as the rationale for this publication, motivating me to conduct this study with an aim to 'take' the field of Arabic studies out into the 'sunlight' as one proven method for disinfection.

It is noteworthy that the framework of this book – one that concerns language and society – is an area of research ridden with theories. However, while much of the theoretical discussion is in the background of my research, here I chose a more empiricist, and rather 'old-fashioned', social and political approach that I hope will be as accessible, clear and reader-friendly as possible. Therefore I tried to restrict these theoretical conceptualisations to the notes or the bibliography.

A few leading questions have led me throughout the writing of this book and have helped me define the relationship between Arabic language studies and Israeli notions of security as well as those of geopolitics. These primarily focused on the 'why', 'who', 'how' and 'what' of Arabic language education in Jewish-Israeli schools. More specifically this book asks the following questions: *Why* was Arabic studied in Jewish schools during the British Mandate in Palestine, and from 1948 onwards, in Israel? *Who* directed Arabic language courses in civilian educational institutions and what were their motivations? *Who* framed the goals of Arabic language education in Jewish-Israeli society and what was the nature of their participation? *How* was Arabic as a topic of study constructed in the Israeli education system? *What* are the characteristics, limitations and dangers of this new 'type' of securitised Arabic language – which I refer to as 'Israeli Arabic' – that emerged as a result of the unique sociopolitical circumstances of the ongoing conflict in Palestine/Israel?

My primary focus of analysis is the Jewish-Israeli school system. However, as I wish to analyse *the field of Arabic studies*[3] in a broader way, the book also investigates two Jewish-Israeli educational institutions not affiliated with the formal educational system that placed peaceful coexistence as prime justifications for the study of Arabic. The investigation of these two institutions, Givʿat Ḥavivah and Ulpan ʿAḳiva, uncovers how the Arabic studies offered by them were often driven by – or were a by-product of – security considerations similar to those we see in the formal education system. Focusing on these two institutions – the first run by the socialist Kibbutz movement, and the second run by an extreme right-wing individual who was a former member of the Irgun, a paramilitary revisionist organisation – also reveals an overarching phenomenon in Israel and Arabic studies as these intitutions, located at the two Zionist political extremes, were actually doing the same thing.

This book is based on an investigation of historical events and decision-making bodies, including political transitions, military campaigns, educational committee decisions, personal careers of actors in this field, resource allocation and inter-organisational collaboration. The analysis and findings presented indicate how security-political considerations undergirded the motivations of the key individuals and organisations who initiated, supervised and funded Arabic studies in Jewish-Israeli society. This clear connection between Arabic studies and the Israeli security establishment was evident not only in the motivations of key actors but also in the contextualisation of Arabic studies as a subject that 'reacts' to political and military events and that 'fulfils' security and Military Intelligence needs.

Arabic for the sake of security

But was it always the case? What did Arabic symbolise for Jewish people before the conflict in Palestine? And what was the moment that made it desired by the military establishment?

As this book will show, when looking at the place of Arabic among Jews in Palestine/Israel over the last 100 years, a very different story than that of contemporary Israel emerges. During the pre-state period and prior to extensive Jewish immigration from Europe, Arabic was acquired by the Jewish community in Palestine, either in school or independently, because it was the lingua franca of the region. Proficiency in Arabic facilitated daily interactions between different sectors of the population in the region; therefore its study was utilitarian in nature and entirely lacking in security implications. The rise of Zionism in Palestine, as a European movement in the Orient, had a tremendous influence on the nature of Arabic language studies in the country. Different interest groups – including Jewish educators, political organisations and security bodies – began to emerge, each holding their own views about the necessity of studying the language. It was then, as a result of the arrival of new Jewish groups in Palestine and in light of deteriorating relations between Jews and Arabs, that knowledge of Arabic was no longer viewed solely as a means for daily interaction and integration into the region, rather it was harnessed for ideological reasons and for political and security-oriented purposes. In other words, this book will examine the process by which Arabic was transformed from the language of the neighbour to the language of the enemy.

As this book will demonstrate, Arabic studies in the Jewish-Israeli context has been reactive in nature; it has primarily responded to and has been driven by critical military and political events and junctures. While pedagogical and educational considerations were present, they have been subordinate to events and the perceived needs and priorities that arose from them. This phenomenon first came to light in the pre-state period and following the Arab Revolt of 1936–39 and the accompanying Jewish–Arab outbreaks of violence. The first signs of 'Arabic for the sake of security' appeared at this early stage.

During the same years, and as the conflict heated up in Palestine, the Zionist-Jewish community in the country made a clear push towards Hebrew studies, and gave preference in schools to 'the West' (English) over 'the East' (Arabic) or 'the Diaspora' (especially German and Yiddish). Arabic, in light of the geopolitical situation in Palestine in the 1940s, became significantly less desirable as a cultural language or as an integrative language, and as such the study of Arabic became increasingly associated with the Zionist movement's political and security considerations and was encouraged mainly for these reasons. This was the first inkling of the emergence of a new path for Arabic – a path that combined political and security needs with language instruction. Subsequent stakeholders in Israel, from 1948 onwards, further developed and widened this path, paving it with new methods and finding increasingly sophisticated rationales for its existence.

The 'entrance' of security considerations into the field of Arabic studies was also a function of changing demographics and sociological processes that took place during this crucial historical period. Jewish-Israeli society – and particularly its Ashkenazi-European elite – adopted an Orientalist[4] attitude towards Arab culture, countries and societies and began to reject elements considered to be 'too Arab'. However, while many of Edward Said's protagonists were safely situated, so to speak, in Europe and could afford wearing *jallābiyya*s and *kūfiyyā*s during their excursions to the East (Flaubert, Lawrence and others), the Zionist project led mainly by its Ashkenazi elite was engaged in actively differentiating itself culturally from the region in which it planned to stay.

As an outcome of this approach, in an attempt to distinguish and separate Israel from the Arab world, Arabic in the Israeli education system underwent an unofficial process of foreignisation and perhaps even Ashkenazisation and Europinisation. As this book will show, Arabic and Arab culture in the young state was only permissible as long as it operated within clearly defined Zionist boundaries and where it contributed to the state's pressing political and security needs. Indeed, an Arabic that related to culture, art, intellectual life, literature, identity, integration into the region or a deeper understanding of pivotal political events, fell outside of the boundaries of established discourse for the language and, therefore, was neither encouraged nor supported.

Such attitudes and approaches also extended to the Mizraḥi Jews. In order to be considered 'Israeli', by the Ashkenazi leadership and in the context of the discourse that it has established, Mizraḥi Jews, by and large, had to renounce the 'Arab' aspects of their identity.[5] In attempting to fit in, Arab-Jews in general, and the second generation in particular, emphasised their Jewish credentials, played down their Arab origins and culture and adopted Zionist ideology while distancing themselves from anything that appeared to be 'too Arab' – including studying Arabic in school. Thus, the larger story of Arabic was one of forgetting, neglect and denial.

In fact, the only recorded examples of the Zionist establishment encouraging Arab-Jews to consume Arab culture, listen to Arabic music and integrate with local Palestinian Arabs, was in relation to security: the training and activities of the undercover *Mistaʿaravim* Unit, in which Arab-Jews disguised themselves as Arabs and took part in the new demarcation of borders between 'Jews' and 'Arabs'.[6]

The partnership of 'peace and security'

But what forged the partnership between the military – as represented by Military Intelligence – and the civilian – as represented by the Ministry of Education? Was it an ideological collaboration or a temporary confluence of interests?

The answer, as will be shown in the book, is complex and multilayered. The book discusses how following the establishment of the State of Israel, there was a demand for individuals with knowledge about 'the Arabs'. This meant a need – primarily driven by the Israel Defense Forces (IDF) and especially the Military Intelligence and Military Government – for Jews who could understand or read and understand Arabic. As it was the Ministry of Education that administered Arabic studies in Israeli schools, the cooperation between the two sides almost 'had to happen' and indeed began at a very early stage. The book will trace the evolution of this cooperation, and will analyse its development and the special interests that brought each 'side' to collaborate with the other.

In this light, the Ministry of Education, along with Giv'at Ḥavivah and Ulpan 'Aḳiva, in collaborating with the military establishment accepted and even welcomed a growing military presence in their institutions and military involvement in their programmes, and it seemed 'natural' for them especially in relation to the militaristic characteristics of Israeli society.[7] One of the examples of this was the creation of a semi-military semi-civilian formula of 'Arabic for peace and security', which, as will be shown, enabled the blurring of boundaries in the field of Arabic studies between sectors and institutions and made the connections between civilian life and military bodies to be perceived as a matter of common sense.[8] To demonstrate this, I refer in the book to the terminology used in the correspondence between the two 'spheres', and also to the use of symbols. One example of the latter is in the extensive use – and even consecration – by the Haganah (the main Jewish paramilitary organisation in the pre-state period) and the IDF of the olive branch and the sword juxtaposed with each other. The 'peace and security' formulation, therefore, will be seen in this study as an extension of this, especially in Israel as 'a nation-in-arms',[9] and as part and parcel of a Jewish-Israeli narrative.

Furthermore, I will show the relationships created and connections made between different actors in the policy networks and social networks that shaped Arabic studies in Israel.[10] I will demonstrate that these networks were a product of the blurring of boundaries between the military and civilian spheres and will analyse how they made possible the constant intersection and overlap of ideas, knowledge, individuals and roles.[11] I will also reveal how in these networks, and in order to preserve their own power and status, a small clique of highly connected individuals acted as both protectors of this knowledge and as the authorities who certified it as legitimate. All in all, I will indicate how these patterns established the *securitisation* of the field of Arabic studies more firmly, and entrenched accepted boundaries within this field while making it almost impossible to challenge its main assumptions.[12]

A new 'type' of Arabic

But what kind of Arabic emerged as a result of these processes? And what 'kind' of speakers did it 'produce'? What skills did these pupils acquire from their teachers? And which tools were they equipped with?

As this book will analyse the construction of the field of Arabic studies in Israel, it will also shed light on a new 'type' of Arabic that took shape at the core of these studies. This was a new 'type' at least from the discursive viewpoint, but also in relation to the constructed associations of Arabic within the Jewish-Israeli context. I will highlight how this 'Israeli Arabic' was connected to earlier attempts to 'Eretz-Yisraelise' the Arabic language in Jewish-Israeli society, and will emphasise its uniqueness in relation to the 'horizons' of the pupils, the corpus of the language, the skills acquired by the pupils, the associations that they have with the language and the *hidden curriculum* that they study while studying Arabic.[13]

I will stress that this unique 'type' of Arabic served as a barrier that separated Jews who studied Arabic from the object of their studies – Palestinians and other Arabic-speaking communities. In other words, it was a new 'type' of language that did not bring its learners closer to those who speak the language, rather it was intended to help the learner comprehend 'the Arabs' in an impersonal and sterile way, or to decode 'what the Arabs want' without regard for the Arabs as their neighbours – not to mention as citizens of the same state.

A brief outline of the book's chapters will help trace the main processes that this book presents. The first chapter of the book, 'Rooting Security in Arabic Soil', starts with a brief historical overview of the relationship between Jewish people and Arabic prior to the rise of Zionism and the conflict in Palestine. It highlights the role that Arabic played in Jewish religious, cultural and daily life. However, the main focus of the chapter is Arabic studies in Palestine from the beginning of Zionism in 1882.

The chapter details how European Jewish immigration to Palestine and the political conflict between Jewish-Zionists and Palestinian-Arabs were reflected in the changing attitudes to Arabic and in the beginning of the politicisation and securitisation of the language in the Jewish context, and highlights internal Jewish debates about the Arabic language. The chapter also demonstrates how, during this pre-state period, and especially during the years 1936–48, the 'seeds' of using Arabic as a security tool for the Zionist cause were sown.

The second chapter of the book, 'Whose Language is it, Anyway?', analyses the forces that shaped Arabic studies in Jewish-Israeli schools from 1948 to 1967. This chapter looks at the way in which the processes of institutionalisation affected the study of the language. Concentrating on the nascent Jewish-Israeli school system, this chapter discusses the debate for and against the study of Arabic in schools. It shows that processes initiated prior to the foundation of Israel, most evidently the connection between Arabic studies and security were strengthened following the establishment of the state. Special attention is given to the creation of the programme of accelerated Arabic studies in the Israeli school system, titled 'The Oriental Classes' (lit. *ha-Megamah ha-Mizraḥanit*). Analysis of this flagship programme serves as an important case study for the embedded political and security orientations of Arabic studies in Jewish-Israeli society.

The third chapter, titled 'Recruiting Arabic for War', is concerned with the years 1967–76 in which two momentous security-political events took place: the 1967 and 1973 wars. This chapter examines in detail the connection between Arabic studies and the Jewish-Israeli security-political situation. It reveals how Arabic studies in Jewish-Israeli society are first and foremost shaped according to the needs of the political and military establishments and therefore are not a school subject per se. During this period, a combination of political, security-oriented and social processes exposed the connection between the Military Intelligence and Arabic studies in the educational system. This previously hidden relationship began to be perceived as both normal and urgent.

The fourth chapter, titled 'Israel's Army of Arabists', focuses on the years 1976–85, but also offers a brief overview of the 1990s and 2000s. This chapter analyses the various initiatives taken by the Israeli political, security and educational establishments to encourage the study of Arabic, which intensified over this period. The chapter explains the extent to which the Ministry of Education, in the aftermath of the 1967 and 1973 wars, was willing to accept the imperatives of the security establishment. It uncovers the projects initiated to encourage Arabic studies in Jewish-Israeli schools and shows that they were a continuation, or even a culmination, of processes that began developing in the 1930s.

The fifth chapter, 'Giv'at Ḥavivah and Ulpan ʿAḳiva', analyses the field of Arabic studies in these two institutions, in which 'peaceful Arabic' for understanding and coexistence, was almost their motto. The chapter examines the stated goals of the two institutions regarding the teaching of Arabic as the 'language of the neighbour' and analyses their work and evolution from the 1960s onwards. It reveals how similar security-education networks, evident in the school system, also emerged in the programmes of Arabic studies in these two institutions. In so doing, this chapter shows that the security connection has become part and parcel of Arabic studies in Jewish-Israeli society.

1
Rooting Security in Arabic Soil
When Zionism Met Arabic

Even a fist was once an open palm with fingers.
Yehuda Amichai, poet[1]

From the Arabic of ibn Maymūn to that of Unit 8200

The connection between Arabic studies and security considerations in Israel is an open secret widely shared by the majority of Israelis. Nevertheless, there is a lack of academic research on this specific topic, a fact that I find rather telling. An examination of the motivations of pupils for studying Arabic aptly demonstrates the explicit and straightforward nature of this open secret.[2] For example, research conducted in 1988 was done to assess the attitudes of Jewish-Israeli high school pupils towards Arabic studies. Specifically, the research inquired as to why pupils chose both to study Arabic and also elected to take the final exam on the subject on completion of high school. It found that 65 per cent of those who chose to study Arabic had a 'desire to serve in the army in a position that demands knowledge of Arabic'.[3]

Along the same lines, a different survey, conducted in 2006, found that 62.9 per cent of Jewish-Israeli pupils who sat for end-of-high-school exams in Arabic mentioned a desire to serve in Military Intelligence as a primary motivation for studying the language. This poll also examined teacher attitudes and found that 72.8 per cent of the Arabic teachers surveyed believed that a desire to serve in Military Intelligence was a leading factor in their pupils' decisions to choose Arabic. Strikingly, 'the wish to serve in Military Intelligence' was consistently at the top of the list of reasons for studying Arabic in Israel, as indicated by both pupils and teachers, in intermediate and in high schools alike.[4] These findings correlate with and support additional research that have highlighted the importance of instrumental considerations – including service in Military Intelligence – in motivating Jewish-Israeli pupils to study Arabic in school and the supremacy of such considerations over ones that are more integrative in nature.[5]

Security and Arabic are inseparable from general suspicious and negative attitudes among Jewish-Israelis in relation to Arabs and the Arab world. In 2003, a government-appointed investigation committee found that on the state level, and historically since 1948, 'the Arab citizens of Israel have lived in a reality in which they have been discriminated against just for being Arabs'.[6] A survey conducted in 2006 revealed that about half of Israel's Jewish citizens believe that the state should encourage Arab emigration. The same survey also investigated how people felt when hearing spoken Arabic. Some 50 per cent of respondents said that hearing Arabic makes them fearful, 43 per cent responded that they feel uncomfortable, and 30 per cent said that Arabic aroused feelings of hatred within them.[7] Another survey investigating the attitudes of 1600 Israeli high school pupils and conducted by the Center for Research on Peace Education (CERPE) at Haifa University found that 75 per cent of the Jewish respondents associated Arabs with being 'unclean, uneducated and uncivilised'.[8] These selected examples demonstrate that Jewish-Israeli views of Arabs are, by and large, negative, and that such attitudes have a profound effect on the way Israeli society relates to its Arab citizens and to the Arabic language.

These negative perceptions towards Arabic and its speakers that is pervasive among Jews in Israel, are also in evidence in the diminishing Israeli interest in knowing Arabic and in the low number of speakers of Arabic among Jewish-Israelis. Yossi Klein, for example, writes:

> Today it is hard to find Arabic-speakers in Israel who are not Arabs or who were not born in a Muslim country ... *only 3 per cent of Israeli-born Jews speak Arabic*. Last year [2012] only some 2000 Jewish high school pupils took the matriculation exam in the language of 20 per cent of their country's residents. The teenagers who took that test in Arabic did not see it as a bridge: they saw it as a weapon, and most of them, presumably, were inducted into [the Military Intelligence's] Unit 8200.[9]

Keeping Klein's quotation in mind, and in light of research and surveys that have taken place over the past three decades, one could get the impression that animosity between Jews and Arabs, or Jews and Arabic, has always been the case. The truth, however, is quite the opposite, and in order to grasp fully the abyss that has been created between the Jewish people and Arabic, it is important to gain some historical perspective. This section, accordingly, will demonstrate that Jews used to enjoy close ties to Arabic and that Arabic was a lingua franca for the Jewish people of the Middle East, serving as a daily language for communication and trade and as a Jewish language of culture, intellectual debate and also religion.

Indeed, for thousands of years, the Jewish world was centred in various parts of the Middle East. In pre-Islamic times, Jewish communities spoke the language of the ruling empire or regime of that period – primarily Greek, Aramaic or Persian. Hebrew was also prevalent during these periods, however, by and large, it was not the mother tongue or the dominant spoken language among the Jewish communities.[10] This gradually changed following the Arab conquests of the seventh and eighth centuries and a situation whereby Jewish communities were increasingly ruled by different Arab Islamic regimes. As a result, and similar to the acquisition of Greek, Jews of the region underwent a gradual process of Arabicisation that included their adoption of the Arabic language and its accompanying culture.

The new rulers related to their Jewish subjects in different ways, some better than others. In all cases, though, Jewish and Christian minorities were under special *dhimmī* status (a special protection pact with a number of restrictions), meaning that they were not privy to the same level of rights granted to the Muslim majority. While sectarian tensions did occur, Jewish communities enjoyed an official status, and using Lewis's words: 'A recognised status, albeit one of inferiority to the dominant group, which is established by law, recognised by tradition, and confirmed by popular assent, is not to be despised.'[11] This established status overall served as an asset and was advantageous for Jews in Muslim lands.

Despite some of the restrictions placed on Jews, they flourished during this period. Various scholars contend that from the ninth century onwards, 'the bulk of Jews lived and prospered among Arab Muslims, whether in Spain, North Africa, or the Middle East'.[12] This relatively positive experience was most famously exemplified in Abbasid Baghdad, Fatimid and Ayyubid Cairo, the city of Kairouan in Tunisia and Ummayad Spain (Al-Andalus) where Jews enjoyed a 'gracious productive and satisfying way of life they were not, perhaps, to find anywhere else until the 19th century'.[13] This was considered to be a unique period of harmony in relations between Jews and Muslims. Shlomo Dov Goitein, the great scholar of Middle East history at the Hebrew University, characterises this period as the pinnacle of Jewish–Arab relations. According to him, '[N]ever has Judaism encountered such a close and fructuous symbiosis as that with the medieval civilisation of Arab Islam.'[14] Lewis had similar feelings and believed that the Jewish–Muslim linguistic and cultural symbiosis surrounding Arabic was 'not merely a Jewish culture in Arabic, but a Judeo-Arabic, or one might even say a Judeo-Islamic, culture'.[15]

This period of stability and prosperity continued throughout the Middle Ages – especially in the Iberian Peninsula, Iraq, Iran and Central Asia, the Maghrib, Yemen and Bilād al-Shām (Palestine, Lebanon and Syria). Jewish communities prospered and enjoyed a relatively better situation – socially and financially – than during the preceding period and in comparison with those of their fellow Jews living in Christian areas. Undoubtedly, Jewish communities enjoyed a reasonably egalitarian and, for the most part, sustainable and productive relationship with their Muslim neighbours.[16]

Spain (Al-Andalus) is a particularly poignant example of the flourishing of Jewish life during this period. In Spain in the tenth and eleventh centuries, Jewish life and society thrived, with members of this community enjoying economic well-being and cultural prosperity. This place and period in time was later characterised in Hebrew as 'Tor ha-Zahav' or 'The Golden Age' of Jewish creation. In this significant era of Jewish thought and religious output, Arabic was the primary vehicle for the transmission of Jewish expression. Some of the most important historical figures of Jewish thought were from this period. They included the Jewish philosopher and physician Abū ʿImrān Mūsā ibn ʿUbayd Allāh ibn Maymūn al-Qurṭubī (also known as Maimonides, or in contemporary Hebrew as Ha-Rambam), the renowned and prolific grammarian and translator Saʿīd ibn Yūsuf al-Fayyūmī (in Hebrew, Rabbi Saʿadia Gaʾon), poets like Abū Ayyūb Sulaymān ibn Yaḥyā ibn Jabīrūl (in Hebrew, Shlomo ben-Gvirol) and scholars such as Abū Ibrāhīm Ismāʿīl ibn Yūsuf ibn Naghrīla (in Hebrew, Shmuʾel ha-Nagid); who were primarily active in Al-Andalus.

In a similar vein, out of the thousands of scholarly works created during this period by Jewish scholars, Arabic was by far the dominant language. Some of the texts were written in Arabic using Arabic script, some were written in Arabic using Hebrew script and some Jewish scholars wrote their studies in Hebrew using Arabic script. This dominance of Arabic not only influenced Jewish thought, but also Arab philosophy. Some of the more influential of these texts include Dalālat al-ḥāʾirīn (*The Guide for the Perplexed*; Hebrew translation, *Moreh ha-Nevokhim*); Kitāb al-Ḥujja wa-al-dalīl fī naṣr al-dīn al-dhalīl (*The Kuzari*; Hebrew, *Sefer ha-Kuzari*); Yanbūʿ al-ḥayāt (*The Source of Life*; Hebrew, *Meḳor ḥayim*); and Kitāb al-durar (*The Book of Pearls*; Hebrew, *Sefer peniney ha-musarim ṿe-shivḥey ha-ḳehalim*). These texts have had a profound influence on Jewish thought over the centuries and, to this day, remain central to Jewish religious tradition.

Increasingly, Jewish literary output during this period was written and consumed in Judeo-Arabic (Arabic written with Hebrew letters, known in Hebrew as *ʿAravit-Yehudit*). This specific type of Arabic, common in the Jewish community, often included consonant dots from the Arabic alphabet that helped to accommodate phonemes that did not exist in the Hebrew alphabet.[17] Interestingly, during that time, Arabic was a prime example of the Jewish language used by Jewish communities. For example, when analysing religious sources used during the twelfth century, the bulk of Jewish religious writing and literature – almost 90 per cent of the sources – were written Arabic.[18] Furthermore, Arabic translations of the Bible by rabbinic Jews were widespread within Jewish communities. This even extended to Muslim communities, and a significant work from this period was *al-Tafsīr*: Saʿīd al-Fayyūmī's translation of the Bible into Arabic (and in Arabic script) in the early tenth century.[19]

In addition to having a profound influence on Jewish thought and religion in the Middle East, North Africa and Al-Andalus, Arabic was also the language of Jewish scientific works outside these regions. Interestingly, Jewish scholars often used translations from Arabic in the development of scientific texts. Gad Freudenthal's analysis of intellectual preferences of Jewish scholars in Europe from the twelfth to the 15th centuries found that the overwhelming majority of Jewish philosophical writers were consistently more interested in Arabic than in Latin when borrowing, translating and using existing scientific knowledge.[20] Therefore, Arabic was widespread in secular and religious subjects alike among Jewish thinkers of this period.

The importance of this era for Jews and Arabic stems from the fact that the Jewish Arabic-speaking community that lived under Islamic rule in Spain, North Africa and the Middle East represented the largest, most active and most influential Jewish community in the world at that time. Arabic played a major role in this Jewish renaissance; it was the language of daily life and was the vehicle for Jewish expression of spiritual, literary and religious achievements. Lewis emphasises this point in his comparison of Jewish communities living under Muslim rule with those living under Christian rule during the Middle Ages. He noted that, 'The Jews who lived in Christian countries, that is in Europe, were a minority, and a relatively unimportant one ... With few exceptions, whatever was creative and significant in Jewish life happened in Islamic lands.'[21] The flourishing of Jewish life during this period is inseparable from the Jews' daily interaction with Muslim communities and regular use of the Arabic language.[22]

The 'Golden Age', as it came to be known, ended in the fifteenth century with the *Reconquista* of the Iberian Peninsula. As noted by Goitein, this development signified the end of 'the most important period of creative Jewish–Arab symbiosis lasting about 800 years'.[23] Like their Muslim neighbours, Jews were required to convert to Catholicism, or forced to flee, and they began to be haunted by the Inquisition. In 1492, following the surrender of Granada, and according to the Edict of Expulsion, Jews were no longer permitted to remain within the Spanish Kingdom. An occurrence of major import in Jewish history, most of the Jews affected by this edict relocated to Islamic-ruled regions such as those in the Middle East and North Africa that were amicable to Jewish communities. As *Spharad* means 'Spain' in Hebrew, this group of emigrants, and their offspring, would later be referred to as *Sephardim,* demonstrating the deep roots of these communities in Spain.

Some of these expelled Sephardic Jews immigrated to Palestine. There, they encountered a Jewish community that was only a few thousand in number[24] and that spoke a local dialect of Arabic.[25] Initially, the interaction did not go smoothly; the Sephardim and the local Palestinian Jews represented two different 'types' of Jewish life. The Sephardim, who within a short period of time outnumbered the locals, brought with them an air of superiority due to their Muslim-Spanish culture and its achievements. In what today can be viewed as almost an act of colonising arrogance, the Sephardim nicknamed the local Jews *Mustaʿribūn* (in Arabic, those who became Arab). This rather polemic term was intended to denigrate Palestinian Jews and was a way for the Sephardim to emphasise their Spanish-oriented superiority, including command of the Ladino language (a Jewish-Spanish religiolect).[26] As the years went by, however, and especially due to the numerical dominance of the Sephardim, the two communities merged. Gradually, the Mustaʿribūn adopted Sephardic customs in prayer.[27] Together, the two groups created a joint Oriental-Jewish community in Palestine – the Sephardim.

This community contrasted with another Jewish group in the country – the *Ashkenazim*. Originating in Central and Eastern Europe (*Ashkenaz* means 'Germanic-speaking areas' in Old Hebrew), Ashkenazim were considerably smaller in number than the Sephardim during the early Ottoman period. The arrival of Ashkenazi Jews in Palestine (or *Eretz Yisrael* in Jewish terminology) was primarily motivated by religious belief. They gradually increased in numbers throughout the seventeenth to nineteenth centuries, yet for the most part lived in Jewish-only enclaves while maintaining their traditional religious and cultural way of life and characteristics, including the use of Yiddish (Jewish-German) language.

These two groups – the Sephardim (those who emigrated from Spain and also the local 'Mustaʿribūn') and the Ashkenazim – together constituted the Jewish population of Ottoman Palestine, which Zionist historiography refers to as *Ha-Yishuv ha-Yashan* (lit. the Old Settlement). Their percentage in the overall population in the region was marginal: about 2 per cent in 1800 (5000 out of 250,000), and about 5 per cent in 1882 (25,000 out of 540,000).[28] Due to their distinct religious backgrounds and lifestyles, the Jewish communities were concentrated in four cities considered to be sacred, known in Hebrew as *Arbaʿ ʿArey ha-Ḳodesh*. These cities were Jerusalem, Safed, Tiberias and Hebron.

Despite their shared religious beliefs, the communities remained culturally and socially distinct and employed different means of supporting themselves. Socioeconomically, the Sephardic community was quite independent, with its members working and living in Jewish neighbourhoods as well as in mixed Jewish–Muslim areas. The Ashkenazi-European community, on the other hand, maintained a more conservative way of life, and was more dependent on donations from Jewish communities in Europe who sent money in order to support their Jewish brothers and sisters in *Eretz Yisroel* (Yiddish pronunciation).[29]

Consistent with this separation, the Sephardic and Ashkenazi communities also maintained separate school systems. Schools catering to the Sephardic community, in addition to Jewish studies, also included the study of professional and non-religious subjects. By the early nineteenth century a number of schools of this nature were in operation, while by the middle of the nineteenth century Literary Arabic (also known as Modern Standard Arabic) was being taught in a considerable number of Sephardic community schools. Due to the nature of their education and the immigration of Arabic-speaking Jews to Palestine, knowledge of Colloquial Arabic in this community was not at all unusual.[30]

The same was not true of Ashkenazi schools. Not only was Arabic not included as a topic of study in the education system, but it was also actively rejected. The study of Literary Arabic was viewed as a secular and everyday subject not in line with the religious nature of these schools. An anecdote demonstrates the active rejection of Arabic: in 1879, the British Jewish philanthropist Sir Moses Montefiore offered to pay £200 to promote the employment of an Arabic teacher in an

Ashkenazi religious school. He believed that literacy in Arabic would benefit pupils who were not likely to succeed at religious studies but may be able to acquire a profession. His initiative was soundly rejected by leaders of the Orthodox Ashkenazi community, who even created a religious ban 'against the study of any external wisdom'.[31] In comparison, the leader of the Sephardic community praised attempts to increase the study of Literary Arabic, which by then was popular with his community.[32]

Beyond the learning and teaching of Arabic, the language was also dominant in the general public space in which Jews in Palestine lived. As highlighted by several researchers, Arabic was the lingua franca of the region, and proficiency in it – even on a basic colloquial level – was necessary for working, transactions and socialising outside the confines of the Jewish community and, in particular, in relation to transportation, trade and professional skills. Therefore, by the end of the nineteenth century, a considerable number of Jews in Palestine – mostly Sephardim but increasingly Ashkenazim as well – had proficiency levels ranging from basic communication to full fluency and mastery of the Arabic language.[33]

Despite their principled rejection of Arabic, the Ashkenazi community was slowly forced to recognise the utility of knowledge of Arabic. As in the eighteenth and nineteenth centuries they made up about 1 per cent of the total population of Palestine and were also smaller in size than the Sephardic community, it was nearly impossible for their members to segregate themselves completely from the rest of society. Occasionally they were forced to communicate with the majority of those surrounding them in Arabic. Therefore, even though Yiddish remained their primary language, they began to acquire Arabic 'for intercommunity purposes'.[34]

This is somewhat surprising and runs counter to the widespread perception that the Ashkenazi community of Palestine was a segregated, Yiddish-speaking society, which hardly had any contact with their Muslim or Christian neighbours. But this situation was not frozen in time; it can be compared to that of contemporary Yiddish-speaking communities in Israel or the United States. While Yiddish-speaking Ashkenazim live in Orthodox Jewish areas, members of this community speak the majority's language as well – either Hebrew or English, respectively – at proficiencies that rage from basic to full mastery. Then as now, some knowledge of the dominant language is unavoidable.

Another reason for language integration among the Ashkenazi community is related to the special characteristics of Yiddish. The language was described by Max Weinreich as a 'fusion language'; it combines aspects of Germanic, Slavic, Semitic and other languages.[35] The historically flexible nature of Yiddish facilitated the absorption of vocabulary and new linguistic structures from 'hosting' languages and societies. Even today this is the case: in the United States, for example, Yiddish has transformed into *Yinglish*.[36] Similarly, it is clear that contemporary Yiddish in Israel has been influenced by Hebrew.[37]

This relationship between Yiddish and Arabic, while under-researched, is described in Mordecai Kosover's *Arabic Elements in Palestinian Yiddish*. The author writes about the gradual increase of Arabic words that entered Palestinian Yiddish, in the seventeenth, eighteenth and nineteenth centuries. According to Kosover, this process began in the early seventeenth century when Ashkenazi community leaders realised that the lack of Arabic prevented them from participating in various trades. This was highlighted in *Ways of Zion*, a book written by Moshe Porges in 1650, where the author writes that, 'Some Sephardic Jews own shops and stores, full of all kinds for sale ... Only we, Ashkenazim, do not know the languages to converse with various people, and we are therefore unable to trade with them.'[38] Kosover, therefore, explains the penetration of Arabic elements into the Yiddish language in Palestine as 'mainly *economic* in nature' and describes the economic incentive for proficiency in Arabic.[39]

For the period from the nineteenth century onwards, Kosover increasingly identified signs that the community acquired knowledge of Arabic, even if external to the school system. He cites a book, *Ḳoroth ha-ʿIttim li[Ye]shurun b'Erec Yisrael*, written by Rabbi Menaḥem-Mendl of Kamenitz in 1839, following his immigration to Safed. One chapter, dedicated to *Lashon ʿAravit* (Arabic Language), mentions the crucial importance of Arabic. Menaḥem-Mendl concludes the chapter with probably one of the first Yiddish–Arabic dictionaries. He wrote:

> Jerusalem is called in their language '*ʿIr Ḳuds*' [*ʿIr* means 'city' in Hebrew], Nablus is *Nablāt*, Safed is *Sāfāt* ... When one inquires about the price, he says *ḳadesh hadā*... money is *mesāri*, and when one asks for money he says *hati mesāri* ... *bācīl* [means] onions, *mīzan* means the scales, *zeit* is oil ... and *ḥubzeh* is bread'.[40]

During the second half of the nineteenth century and at the dawn of the twentieth century, Arabic gradually became more common among Ashkenazi Jews. While still not taught in school, this was related to socioeconomic developments locally and to influences of the

Enlightenment in Europe. In his memoirs, Abraham Frumkin, who was born in Jerusalem in 1873, recalls the multilingual reality in which he grew up and specifically mentions his command of Arabic. According to him, 'I spoke [Arabic] very fluently while still a child. I acquired it without the slightest effort on my part ... The times were different then. No one knew yet of an Arab–Jewish problem.'[41] Similar sentiments were expressed by Ephraim Cohen-Reiss (born 1863). He reminices that 'the Ashkenazi Jews of Safed generally spoke Arabic far better than the Jews of Jerusalem ... Even in their way of living, as well as in the attire, they were closer to the Arabs.'[42]

Various parts of Kosover's book point to the relationship between Arabic and Yiddish among Ashkenazi Jews and the entry of Arabic words into Yiddish in Palestine during the period under discussion. Some examples from the world of food include the Yiddish-sound *kuselakh*,[43] which means courgettes (and comes from *kūsā* in Arabic with the 'akh' Yiddish diminutive plural) and kaftele,[44] which means meatballs (*kufta* in Arabic). He also points to the Yiddish-Arabic word *koyes*[45] (with its Yiddish sound, and based on the Colloquial Arabic term *kweyyis* that means alright) or to the expression *'Allah karim, Got vet helfn'* (God will help) in both Arabic and Yiddish,[46] which seems to indicate that symbiosis took place on a number of levels.

This background sets the sociolinguistic stage in Palestine on the eve of the rise of Zionism in the country in 1882. It introduces some of the processes, definitions and social groups addressed by the research and points to the depth of the change that occurred in the twentieth century. This context and sociolinguistic background is a reminder that at the close of the nineteenth century, the Jewish community in Palestine was a small minority that lacked contemporary nationalistic sentiments and did not have a standing army, a national anthem or a national language. The Jewish community in Palestine during this period integrated Jewish religious practice with everyday life while also maintaining generally good relations with its neighbours and a basic-to-high-level proficiency in Arabic. Unlike today, violent incidents between Jews and Palestinians were infrequent and dissimilarities between the communities were not a source of tension or an excuse for conflict. In Frumkin's words, during the middle of the nineteenth century, 'No one yet knew of an Arab–Jewish problem.' In light of this, the gradual change in the study of Arabic in Jewish schools will shed light on much greater and more powerful processes that transformed the face of the country and the relationships between its people forever.

Between three conquests: labour, land and language

The year 1882 was an important landmark in the history of Palestine, given the arrival of the first wave of Zionist immigrants from Europe. These immigrants, and those that followed, were infused with national aspirations embedded in Zionism. As events would demonstrate, the dominant Zionist political line positioned Jewish national interests in Palestine in stark opposition to those of Arab-Palestinians. This brought about the beginning of a zero-sum process that eventually changed the demographic, social and political situation in Palestine. Its most obvious outcome was the creation of the State of Israel in 1948 and the expulsion of approximately 700,000 Palestinians.[47]

Similarly, also in relation to Arabic, Zionist immigration to Palestine from 1882 onwards signalled a gradual change, which gained pace as nationalistic tensions in the region increased. The shift, as demonstrated in this book, was reflected in the trend of studying Arabic for the purposed of daily communication, regional integration and labour market considerations to goals driven by political separatist aspirations and Zionist leadership in Palestine's security considerations.

But in 1882, it was still too early to identify this impending change. The first Zionistically inspired immigrants had a variety of different associations with Arabic. Generally speaking, they did not have a unified idea about the local Arab-Palestinians or their language. Therefore, their perceptions of the local Arab population and language were mixed and ranged from admiration to disgust: some found positive aspects in the study of Arabic, whilst others intentionally ignored the language and considered it unworthy of attention.

One of the first groups to come to Palestine was the *Bilu*, a small group of Ashkenazi secular Russian Zionists, who fled anti-Jewish pogroms and dreamed of establishing a Jewish home in Eretz Yisrael. Despite the small size of this group, it is important to examine their perceptions of Arab-Palestinians and their language; this movement symbolises some of the most significant first 'seeds' of political Zionism, as well as the Zionist idea of 'pioneers, blazing the path for the Jewish masses that would follow in their footsteps'.[48] Furthermore, the Bilu serve as a good demonstration of Zionism's ambivalent attitudes towards the local Arab-Palestinians, a dual sentiment that accompanied later stages of Zionist institutions and thought.

The first Bilu arrived in Palestine during the summer of 1882, and in their desire to become locals in Palestine and to shake off their Diaspora characteristics, they imitated and romanticised the Arab-Palestinians. Working in the fields like the local *fallāḥs* (peasants), wearing black and white *kūfiyyā*s on their heads and chatting in Arabic were some of the adaptations made by these Ashkenazi Jews.[49] They believed that their 'return' to Eretz Yisrael presented an opportunity for a historic meeting with 'the Arabs', not as enemies but as 'two brothers of the Semitic family, the children of Abraham'.[50] Accordingly, Palestinian *fallāḥ*s or local Bedouins were seen not as the ultimate 'other', but as a romantic reflection of the primaeval Jewish 'self'.[51]

'Romantic' could also describe the way Theodor Herzl, the founder of Zionism, viewed the local Arab-Palestinians. In his utopian novel, *Altneuland* (The Old-New Land) published in 1902, he outlined his vision for a socialist Jewish life in Eretz Yisrael. The prototypical Palestinian depicted in the book was Rashid Bey, an educated man from Haifa, who surprisingly enough, spoke fluent German.[52] The national Palestinian–Zionist tension that was about to materialise in the 1920s and more so in the 1930s and 1940s, bothered Herzl insofar as he viewed it as a potential future obstacle. We know this because he made sure that the Palestinian character in his book addressed this matter. According to Rashid Bey, the Palestinians were 'not at all angry about the increased Jewish immigration to the country'. 'What kind of stupid ideas do you have in your mind?' Bey replied in German to the protagonist who asked him about the Zionist immigration, 'Would you call someone who never took anything from you, and kept giving you more and more, a thief?!'[53]

In terms of language, while Herzl's book does not mention that the local Palestinians spoke Arabic, in reality the practical question of studying the language became increasingly important to early immigrants. Some Zionist groups, including the Bilu, made an effort to learn the language independently. This effort resulted from the ambivalent 'triangle' that seems to have shaped mainstream Zionist thought in the pre-state period: a mixture of admiration for the Arab *fallāḥ*s (although rarely for the urban Arab-Palestinians); a wish to be connected to the land like them; but also a desire – hidden or overt – to take their place. This desire can be seen, for example, in the idea of 'creating' a Jewish peasant that looks like the Arab *fallāḥ*. However, the means of subsistence for Arabs and Jews were different as Jewish workers received 'European wages' through *subsidisation* from Zionist institutions, which was intended to attract Jewish peasants to do the work, with the aspiration of ultimately excluding the Arab *fallāḥ*s from the field.[54] This same desire and ambivalence is evident in two additional Zionist groups, whose members came to Palestine during the second wave of Zionist immigration: *Ha-Shomer* (The Watchman) and *Ha-Ro'eh* (The Shepherd).

The origins of the Ha-Shomer movement, established in 1909, stretch back to 1907 when a group of Jewish activists from *Po'aley Tsiyon* (Workers of Zion) created a Jewish watchmen's organisation called *Bar-Giyora*. The main aim of this group was to serve as guards in new Jewish settlements. Interestingly, the movement was named after Simon Bar-Giyora, a Jewish military leader who fought against the Romans in Jerusalem in 69 CE. This demonstrates the use of another Zionist 'principle': a dual act of 'return' to the land with another 'return' to the desired powerful and brave historical Jew through the creation of the 'new Jew'. Another interesting point, which signifies the 'admiration and exclusion' mentioned earlier, was the context for the creation of Bar-Giyora. The decision to establish this group followed a couple of decades where local Arab-Palestinians were hired in order to serve as guards for Jewish settlements.

Interestingly, in the act of creating a Jewish watchman, one had to go through a period of 'Arabicisation', a stage of training in which they learned required skills from local Arab-Palestinians. This served as required preparation which made it possible to replace Arab-Palestinians and complete a Jewish 'return'. Ha-Shomer's acceptance tests, therefore, following from those of Bar-Giyora's, required proficiency in the use of guns, horsemanship and Arabic.[55] As mentioned before, the members of this organisation, who were in contact with local Arab-Palestinians, had an ambivalent attitude towards the latter: they admired them, sometimes even eroticised them, but they also wanted to usurp them. Ha-Shomer member Zvi Nadav's fantasy was 'to marry four Bedouin women, who will give birth to many strong and healthy boys'.[56] This serves as a glimpse into the world of Ha-Shomer, in which Oriental eroticism, admiration and perhaps also 'improving' the Jewish national and physical strength, were intertwined.

The selected watchmen who successfully finished their training were hired to protect the new Jewish settlements, a job that had previously been done by Arab-Palestinians. The Jewish watchmen rode horses, spoke Arabic and wore *kūfiyyā*s and *jallābiyya*s (an Arab dress).[57] However, this should not be understood exclusively as romantic imitation. Aspects of admiration of the Arab's appearance and a wish to be *like* him were indeed present, but, even more, the watchmen wanted to be the perfect Jewish *replacement* for the Arab.[58]

Likewise, the Ha-Ro'eh (The Shepherd) organisation had its own romantic-Orientalist approach. This group, created in 1914, was one of the notable offshoots of the Ha-Shomer movement, and its members had to learn the art of shepherding from local Bedouin. Gershon Fleischer, one of the members of 'The Sheperd' remembers that the movement was created when members of Ha-Shomer concluded that in order to improve, they 'must be mobile like the Bedouins, live in tents like them, herd sheep and cattle like them ... We decided to go to the Bedouins and learn the art of shepherding from them.'[59] Indeed, during their apprenticeship period, wearing a long Bedouin sword under their white *jallābiyya*s, the Jewish shepherds learned Arabic, how to watch over and raise a flock of sheep and how to make a tent from their Bedouin teachers. They also accustomed themselves to goat-milk products and to the difficult living conditions outdoors.[60] However, and this is the important principle, when this period of practice ended, they returned to their settlements and gradually replaced the Palestinian shepherds whom they had previously employed.

By imitating some of the indigenous population's customs, the Zionist pioneers created the desired 'new Jew': a type that made a clear break with the European past. The 'new Jew' had local Oriental characteristics but was not identical to the local Palestinians and emphasised separation from them. This phenomenon was connected to a leading Zionist concept of promoting Jewish labour in Palestine – eventually known as 'Conquest of Labour' (lit. *Ḳibbush ha-ʿAvodah*).[61] The creation of a 'new' *Jewish* shepherd, therefore, or a 'new' *Jewish* watchmen, served as an example of, and explanation for, the Zionists' general aim of firmly establishing themselves in the country on the one hand, and separating from the local Palestinian population on the other. Imitation in this case should be understood as an intermediary step towards separation, since it first allowed the new Jewish immigrants to gain the required skills, but then led to the creation of a Jewish *alternative* to Palestinian dominance.

A linguistic insight into Hebrew and Arabic seems to complement and correspond well with this notion. Arabic, as noted, was needed by the 'new Jew' in Palestine, even on the most basic level. However, it was Hebrew, and its revival, that became the symbol of the Jewish 'return' to the Orient. Starting in the last decade of the nineteenth century, the modern revival of Hebrew gained prominence and popularity and was led, among others, by Eliʿezer Ben-Yehuda. The revival of Hebrew played a prominent role in Jewish national aspirations, as well as in the desired transition from an old Jewish European-Diaspora identity, associated with German, Yiddish or Polish, to the status of the 'new' Hebrew person.[62]

Interestingly, similar to the behaviour of Ha-Shomer and Ha-Roʿeh, Ben-Yehuda found great significance in the study of Arabic as the basis for 'return' and for 'reviving Hebrew' and, in a metaphorical way, for the replacement of Arabic. Ben-Yehuda noted that Arabic had a rich and ancient vocabulary, unlike Hebrew that was 'dead' as a spoken vernacular and did not have the same continuity. Therefore, and since both languages are Semitic, Ben-Yehuda perceived Arabic as a reservoir of words that could be used in Modern Hebrew. His explanation is based on the similarity of the root system on which both Arabic and Hebrew are based.[63] Strikingly, by referring to the similarities between the structures of the two languages, Ben-Yehuda linked the Hebrew *linguistic root system* to the *national roots* of Zionism in Palestine. As Ben-Yehuda states:

> Only those who, like me, compare words between these two languages [Arabic and Hebrew] can feel how little difference there is between them. You can actually decide that every root in Arabic also exists in Hebrew ... We are allowed to rule that most of the words found in the Arabic vocabulary also existed in the Hebrew vocabulary, and that therefore these are not foreign roots. They are even not Arabic roots. They are our roots. They are the roots that we lost, and that now we are coming back to find them ...[64]

This fascinating approach draws similarities between the 'imitation and replacement' method vis-à-vis the training of members of Ha-Shomer and Ha-Roʿeh to that of the revival of Hebrew. Moreover, it demonstrates that, in all cases, the connection to Arab customs and culture was made on the basis of a Jewish 'return' – as well as on principles of separation through integration. Furthermore, all of the projects shared an almost military-like element of conquest: from *Ḳibbush ha-ʿAvodah* (Conquest of Labour) through *Ḳibbush ha-Adamah* (Conquest of Land) to *Ḳibbush ha-Safah* (Conquest of Language).

These 'conquests' corresponded with broader sociopolitical Zionist justifications and rationalisations for the displacement of the Palestinians. Along this line of thought, the Zionist movement needed to be 'grateful' to the local Arab-Palestinians who fulfilled their 'historical role' by preserving the alleged Jewish customs, place names and values that were all 'waiting' to be 'redeemed' or at least 'relearned' and reconstructed by the Zionist movement.[65] This period of hybridisation, therefore, was much more a mask than an internal and integrative change, and the Hebrew and Jewish separatist national identity became increasingly evident as contact with the local population continued.

The question of Arabic

During the same period, the question of Arabic studies was discussed at the highest levels of Zionist leadership. One of its primary supporters was the philologist Yitzḥak Epstein, considered one of the first Zionist thinkers of the period to deal publicly with the question of Jewish–Arab relations in Palestine. In 1905, together with the Jewish educator and publicist Dr Yosef Lurya, he spoke at the Jewish Congress in Basel about the need to study Arabic as a means of rapprochement between Jews and Arabs, and as a way to learn Arab customs and culture.[66] In 1907, Epstein published an article called 'The Forgotten Question' in the Jewish journal *Ha-Shiloʾaḥ*. According to him:

> We have forgotten that there is in our beloved land an entire nation that has been there for hundreds of years and who never intended to leave ... We must get to know the Arab people properly, their ambitions and literature ... It is a disgrace that nothing has been done on that matter yet.[67]

Similar views were voiced by Dr Nissim Malul, a Palestinian-born Sephardic Jew who later played an important role in the world of Zionist Arabic publications. In an article he published in *Ha-Ḥerut* (The Freedom) newspaper in 1913, he argued that integration into Arab culture is essential for the revival of a Hebrew culture. The article, which was entitled 'Our Position in the Country', was based on his great knowledge of and proximity to the Arabic language and culture and stated that: 'we must consolidate our Semitic nationality and not obfuscate it with European culture. Through Arabic we can create a true Hebrew culture.'[68]

However, despite the desires of Lurya, Epstein and Malul to become acquainted with the Arabic language, they faced strong opposition. Many other Zionist leaders thought that there was no need to familiarise themselves with either Arab-Palestinians or their language. Scholars such as Asher Ginzburg and Yosef Klausner believed that 'in studying Arabic there is an unnecessary Levantinisation of the Jewish people'.[69] This contempt towards the local Palestinians and their culture was not rare, and some of the most important Zionist leaders expressed similar patronising attitudes towards them.[70]

It is unclear whether the trend in teaching Arabic in Jewish schools in Palestine, which gained momentum at the beginning of the twentieth century, stemmed from a mostly integrative or instrumental orientation, to use Robert C. Gardner and Wallace E. Lambert's concept.[71] Either way, over the course of time, and for a number of reasons – among them the practical need to know Arabic in a country with a majority of Arabic speakers, pressure from parents to teach the language, the establishment of new European schools in Palestine or the belief that studying Arabic would support the study of Hebrew – Arabic studies were included in the curriculum in many of the Jewish schools in Palestine from 1911 onwards.[72]

The collapse of the Ottoman Empire in 1917 – which signalled the disappearance of Ottoman Turkish from all institutions – enhanced the status of Arabic in Jewish schools in Palestine and reinforced it as the second foreign language, after Hebrew and English. Furthermore, the establishment of British rule in Palestine signalled the beginning of a period of increased institutionalisation and standardisation in all aspects of social life. This can also explain the concurrent increase in discussions within the Zionist movement for the need for Arabic studies.[73] During this period, and in parallel with the intensifying conflict with the Palestinian community, somewhat contradictory aims of Arabic studies were prominent. These included getting to know the language of the *neighbour* in order to promote peaceful relations, along with studying the language of the *enemy* in order to fulfil Zionist security needs as well as a separatist political agenda.

An important watershed with regards to the status of Arabic in Jewish schools during the period under consideration came in 1935. Avinoʿam Yellin of the Jerusalem Committee for the Teaching of Arabic, who encouraged the study of the language and criticised the incoherence in its teaching in different schools, outlined a programme of study for Jews and highlighted the importance of making it a mandatory school subject. The document that outlined this vision, subsequently referred to as 'Yellin's Memorandum' (lit. *Tazkir Yellin*) asserted that the most obvious reasons for the study of Arabic were 'practical reasons and general education reasons ... we need to teach Arabic as a living language, and we need to highlight two goals: (1) to train the students to *understand* Arabic; (2) to train the students to *express* themselves in Arabic'.[74] He then elaborated on these categories:

> *From the practical point of view*: 1. Daily needs (speaking, writing and reading); 2. Clerical work, trade, etc. (reading, translation, speaking, writing); 3. Reading newspapers in Arabic; 4. Fostering social relations with the Arabs of the country, and [the Arabs] of the neighbouring countries.
> *From the general educational point of view*: 1. Studying one of the world's most important literatures and cultures; 2. Developing the ability to use its linguistic structure; 3. Comparison between the mother-language [Hebrew] and another Semitic language [Arabic] for a better understanding of the former; 4. Creating appreciation of the

> mutual relations between the spiritual assets of the people of Israel and to those of the Muslim people.[75]

Yellin's Memorandum is an interesting document as it is one of the last educational papers written by a Jewish intellectual working on Arabic studies in Jewish schools that does not include and does not hint at a connection between Arabic studies in school and the political or security needs of the Zionist movement. As a matter of fact, its very uniqueness lies in its formulation as a purely educational document with an exclusive focus on integration and educational considerations.

Yellin's integrative goals, however, had little chance of being implemented in light of the growing hostility between followers of the Zionist movement who continued to immigrate in growing numbers and local Arab-Palestinians who feared for their homeland. It is perhaps overly metaphoric, but two years after Yellin wrote his memorandum, his city, Jerusalem, was at the forefront of the 1936–39 Arab Revolt and at the heart of the clashes between Jews and Arabs. During these events, Yellin was murdered by a local Arab-Palestinian outside his office. To a certain extent, the period in which Yellin was murdered, which saw many Palestinian and Jewish casualties in Jerusalem and around Palestine, signalled a shift in relations between the communities – a shift reflected in Arabic studies as well. To a certain extent, then, Yellin's Memorandum can be considered to be the swan song of Arabic studies as a school subject that was educational in nature. From this point onwards, Arabic gradually became associated with the 'hostile other'.

In 1938, a first assessment of the Yellin Memorandum was carried out during an assembly of the Arabic Teachers Committee of the Education Department of the Jewish Agency. Committee members noted that most schools did not fully implement the report. Only the Hebrew Reali School in Haifa taught Arabic as a mandatory subject; 'the rest of the schools [taught] Arabic, French or Italian, according to the will of the pupils'.[76] Moshe Sharett, at the time Director of the Political Department of the Jewish Agency in Palestine, attended the meeting indicating an emerging realisation that Arabic had become more than a regular school subject in light of the conflict in Palestine. Sharett expressed his discontent at the situation, saying:

> Arabic teaching is a big failure in Hebrew schools. If before the [First World] War we had a limited number of pupils who knew Arabic, today this number is zero ... Some of the reasons for this are objective, which we cannot do anything about: the Hebrew Yishuv is now

> living in united blocs, and the number of Jews who need Arabic on a daily basis is becoming smaller and smaller ...[77]

In September 1939, the Arabic Teachers Committee met in Tel Aviv to discuss the development of Arabic studies during the preceding year. According to renowned Orientalist and historian S. D. Goitein, who attended the meeting, there was still 'a real disorder (lit. *ʿirbuviyah*) in the way in which we teach [Arabic] ... Out of 33 institutions that responded to our survey, there are 15 different Arabic timetables.'[78] Goitein also mentioned that only half of the Jewish schools use Arabic language textbooks written by Jewish authors (mentioning Yosef Rivlin, Yoḥanan Kaplivcky and Eliyahu Ḥabuba) and the rest use textbooks written by Arab scholars (including *Al-Jadīd* of Sakakini and *Darajāt al-Qirāʾa* of Baydas), and that out of 42 Arabic teachers in Jewish schools there are '18 Sephardic teachers, 11 Jewish-Iraqis, 10 Ashkenazi teachers from abroad and three local Ashkenazi teachers'.[79]

Goitein's comment about the textbooks is most probably connected to a process that began to accompany the study of Arabic in Jewish schools at the time, and that can be seen as a political 'Judaisiation' of the language, both in terms of teachers and of textbooks written mostly by Jewish scholars. This process was basically completed following 1948 when Jewish pupils were to study Arabic from textbooks written, by and large, by Jewish authors only.

A parallel transition that became very clear in the 1930s was the straightforward preference for Jewish teachers of Arabic. This is not only evident based on Goitein's description, but was also emphasised in a statement made a year later by Dr Yisrael Ben-Zeʾev, the first full-time supervisor of Arabic studies in the Jewish school system in Palestine and who was then also a leading figure in the Arabic Teachers Committee. Ben-Zeʾev mentioned the dominance of Jewish teachers of Arabic and the complete lack of Arab teachers, saying:

> All of the teachers in our institutions are Jews. The reasons for this are that Arabic teachers must know Hebrew ... They also need to have the proper training for teaching as is customary in European schools ... Thirdly, the Arabs' teaching methods are not appropriate for the nature and cultural level of our pupils.[80]

Ben-Zeʾev's remarks and, in particular, his comments regarding differences in 'nature' and 'cultural level' suggest the emergence of a rather bleak attitude towards the local Palestinians and their place in the emerging field of Arabic studies. Regarding the preference for Jewish labour, either as textbook writers or as teachers, Goitein's and Ben-Ze'ev's comments may suggest several explanations. First, it could have been due to a desire to employ Hebrew-speaking Jewish teachers, in keeping with the Zionist ideology of the time. Second, it may be related to the hostility between the two communities that prevented them from cooperating in educational endeavours. Third, it may be connected to pedagogical considerations. Fourth, it might have stemmed from security-oriented considerations.[81]

From the various archival documents, however, it seems that especially following the 1936–39 Arab Revolt and as violence in Palestine increased, the study of Arabic and how Arabic was perceived became more politically and security oriented in the Zionist movement and school system. Gil Eyal, who studied the Zionist perceptions of the local Orient, also believed that the Arab Revolt represented a watershed moment in regional history:

> There is no doubt that as the years passed, especially after 1936, when the conflict with the Palestinians intensified and the separatist institutions of labour Zionism gained dominance, the emphasis on the negative valuation of [Jewish–Arab] metamorphosis, on the dangers inherent in the Orient and the need to separate from it, grew as well.[82]

Oren Barak and Gabriel Sheffer, who have studied contemporary Israeli 'security networks', also argue that their roots are found in the pre-state period. Specifically, they conclude that during the post-1939 years, especially 1940–48, such networks were created and subsequently spread throughout Israeli society.[83] As I will highlight, during the same period Arabic language studies also became more associated with security and political considerations, linking educators and security personnel, as well as the political and military wings of the Zionist administration.

The growing political connotations of Arabic in Jewish schools are demonstrated by Moshe Brill's book, *The Basic Vocabulary for Daily Arabic Newspapers*, written in 1940. In an article about the book, Brill wrote:

> [The] results of the final examination in Arabic prove that the ability to read and understand an Arabic newspaper, one of the targets of teaching Arabic, is still lacking among many pupils ... most of them cannot understand an article in Arabic with simple political content.[84]

As a result of this, and the 'dangers' of not being able to understand 'political content' in Arabic newspapers, the directors of Arabic studies in the Jewish education system launched a project called 'Selection from the Arabic Press' (in Hebrew, *Leḳeṭ min ha-ʿItonut ha-ʿAravit*). This was a brief newsletter, published monthly, which was distributed on a regular basis to Jewish pupils.[85] In 1941, a letter from four prominent Arabic scholars and language teachers said that this was not sufficient and asked the editors of the *Selection* to publish it every two weeks.[86]

The *Selection*, as well as Brill's book, was part of a pattern that began in the 1940s that directly and increasingly linked the geopolitical and security situation to the study of Arabic in Jewish schools, and was a central element in the creation of 'Israeli Arabic'. This linkage was expressed by Ben-Ze'ev himself, who was appointed Supervisor of Arabic Studies in 1941. In a letter to the Director of the Education Department of the Jewish Agency, Ben-Ze'ev linked immediate and practical political needs to the educational aims of the study of Arabic. According to Ben-Ze'ev, the Hebrew Reali School in Haifa was the only one worthy of mention, yet:

> Even in this institution the direction of studies must be changed: the current direction has scientific and research characteristics, but not practical ones. This way of teaching might be suited for Arabic studies in a European university, but we need Arabic for specifically practical needs (lit. *tserakhim maʿasiyyim shel mamash*).[87]

It is unclear what Ben-Ze'ev meant by 'practical needs'. However, in all likelihood, he was referring to a series of politically oriented projects and activities that the Jewish Agency began to implement during that very same period. His conception of necessary skills was probably shaped by the perceived security needs of the Zionist leadership. These projects took knowledge of Arabic in a new direction – new, anyway, to scholars and teachers of Arabic – a direction that included propaganda, surveillance, security and politically oriented projects and psychological warfare. All of these projects were initiated by the Political Department of the Jewish Agency, which in the 1940s was headed by Moshe Sharett (Shertok) and Golda Me'ir (Meyerson). As will be shown – and at least in relation to Arabic studies from that particular moment – the division between the educational, political and military spheres was on paper only.

The Arabic-oriented projects that were initiated during this period by the Political Department included, among others, the dissemination of Zionist information in Arabic through covert and overt means. This included two news agencies that operated in Arabic in order to emphasise the 'growing strength' and successes of Zionism in the country: the *Arabic Palcor* (operated from Jaffa) and the *Agence d'Orient* (operated clandestinely from Cairo).[88] Other projects focused on Arabic studies but had heavy political and security implications. For example, in 'Arabic Teaching at the Border Villages' (lit. *Limud ʿAravit ba-Neḳudot*),[89] Arabic teachers were sent to Jewish border villages in order to train two or three members in Arabic in order to ease tensions with the local Palestinians and enable the continuation of the Zionist project. A similar project, 'Courses for Jewish *Mukhtārs*' (*lit. ha-Ḳurs le-Hakhsharat Mukhtarim*) had an obvious intelligence angle.[90] The 'Good Neighbour Committees' (lit. *Ṿaʿadot le-Shipur Yaḥasey Shekhenim*) was a project sponsored by the Arabic *SHAI* (*Sherut ha-Yediʿot*; in English, the 'Information Service'), the Arabic branch of the main Haganah intelligence wing (established in 1940) and was a project that aimed to reduce tensions in heatened conflict areas in Palestine and minimise the number of Jewish casualties.[91] Other Arabic-oriented projects that were created by the Haganah during the same period had even more straightforward security implications – primary among these projects were the Mistaʿaravim Unit of the Palmach established in 1943.[92]

The 'practical needs' mentioned by Ben-Zeʾev, therefore, should be read in the context of the increasing friction in the 1940s in Palestine and in light of a dramatic increase in Arabic-oriented projects for *practical* political and security concerns. This new take on 'practicality' meant that knowledge of Arabic was required for education and integration but, more primarily, in order to provide services for the political and security establishments. In a debate in the Education Department of the Jewish Agency held in 1944 about Arabic studies in Jewish schools, Ben-Zeʾev again noted the importance of Arabic language studies to the greater needs of the Zionist movement. According to him, at the time Arabic was being taught in 37 Jewish schools in the General Stream in education (lit. *ha-Zerem ha-Klali*), while in the Workers' Stream (lit. *Zerem ha-ʿOvdim*) the vast majority did not teach Arabic. According to Ben-Zeʾev, 'Even though I am doing my best to encourage them to recognise that there is a national need in that, my attempts were unsuccessful.'[93]

This does not mean that the rationale behind Arabic studies changed completely, but only that due to the growing tension, the educational motivation to teach Arabic was combined with a much more urgent 'justification', as well as with much more powerful actors. This change was reflected in the coalitions that were formed surrounding Arabic studies in the Yishuv, as will be shown. As a result, during that period, a dual attitude towards Arabic studies was established in which 'national', 'political', 'security-oriented' and 'peaceful' elements were paired with each other while the relative weight ascribed to them varied according to context. This was a crucial period as the principles of Arabic studies were crystallised through the creation of networks that exist to the present day.

Early examples of the crystallisation of this civil–security network were previously given in the discussion on different Arabic-oriented projects that blurred the lines between the military, political and educational spheres. Another one relates to an Arabic teachers' summit held in 1945, in which Yehoshafat Harkabi – who, after the creation of the State of Israel became the IDF Chief of Intelligence – said: 'I used to be an Arabic teacher myself, and worked so hard in order to acquire this rich language. Knowing the language helps to establish contacts with the Arabs, and to live peacefully with them.'[94] Harkabi's words, and his military background, can be seen as just another example of the formulation of Arabic for 'peace and security' that became prevalent at the time. Another report, which the Jewish Agency asked Ben-Ze'ev to write for the Anglo-American Committee of Enquiry on Palestine of 1946, focused on the question of Arabic studies in Jewish schools. In the report, there is no mention of political or security agendas regarding the teaching of Arabic. Rather, Ben-Ze'ev stressed the peaceful element of Arabic studies:

> Today we teach Arabic in 72 schools ... and we have 55 Jewish teachers of Arabic ... Alongside the teaching of Literary Arabic, we started teaching Colloquial Arabic in 1940. [We did this as] our goal was to give to the people of the Yishuv who live in the homeland (lit. *bney ha-Yishuv ba-moledet*) the opportunity to live as proper good neighbours [with the Arabs] ... We see this as a sign of [the] maturing of the Hebrew school in the land of our forefathers, without going into the regretful fact that the Arab educators did not find it necessary to teach Hebrew not even in a single Arab school ...[95]

Ben-Ze'ev's prominent linkage between Arabic studies and good neighbourly relations with the Arab-Palestinian population was perhaps due to the fact that the report was to be submitted to an external committee investigating the question of Jewish immigration to Palestine. However, he did not write this cynically. Ben-Ze'ev, who was a Jewish educator, a fluent Arabic-speaker and a scholar who taught Arabic at several academic centres in Egypt, was probably torn between the initial (both scholarly and integrative) instinct to teach Arabic and the insistent needs of the Zionist movement in the context of the worsening Arab–Jewish conflict. In all likelihood, other scholars were probably faced with similar conflicts of interest. Goitein, for example, who in 1944 helped to establish the curriculum for the Arabic studies of the politically oriented 'Courses for Jewish *Mukhtārs*',[96] did not see any contradiction between the Zionist idea and the study of Arabic for integration. He actually saw the two as one; 'teaching Arabic is part of Zionism', wrote Goitein in 1946, 'it is part of our return to the Hebrew language and to the Semitic East ... [We teach the language] as we want our children to feel at home in the Arab East and to be able to work in it ...'[97]

The mixture of perceptions towards the Arabic language was evident in the attitudes of the different actors but also within each of them. In other words, debates at the time were typically characterised by competing interests. The balance between integrative and security focused rationales for teaching Arabic were most likely tipped in one direction or the other according to the strength of the conflict or the personality of the actor. The political situation, therefore, and its deterioration in the 1940s, can explain the increasingly political orientation of Arabic studies. For example, while in the late 1920s and during 1930s the study of Arabic was, by and large, in the hands of the Education Department of the Jewish Agency, during the 1940s we can gradually observe the entrance of senior Zionist political leaders into the Arabic arena. This could explain a transition from more peaceful justifications of Arabic studies to more instrumental, political and security-oriented rationales for the study of the language.

One indication of this 'politicisation' of Arabic studies is the changes in personnel involved in Arabic language studies. In the 1940s, Yitzḥak Ben-Zvi, the then head of the Jewish National Council, and Moshe Sharett, the head of the Political Department of the Jewish Agency, started to take vigorous and influential roles in educational conversations regarding Arabic studies. As a matter of fact, from the beginning of the 1940s it became clear that Arabic teaching was not solely in the hands of the Education Department of the Jewish Agency, but a cooperative project with the Political Department.

A letter written by Arabic Supervisor Ben-Ze'ev in 1942 to the Deputy Director of the Education Department clearly demonstrates this. Ben-Ze'ev complains about the 'insulting' attitude in which the Education Department treats the Political Department in relation to Arabic studies. His letter hints at the convergence of political and educational interests during that period surrounding the teaching of Arabic. This is how Ben-Ze'ev put it:

> As you know, we owe our thanks to the Political Department for having a full-time Supervisor for Arabic Studies in the Jewish school system. The Political Department also follows very carefully the teaching of Arabic ... And for the Arabic project they are willing to put much more money than what [Ben-Tsiyon] Mossinson [head of the Education Department] has asked ... They [the directors of the Political Department] are providing us with their contacts, their money and the services of [Eliyahu] Sasson [the head of the Arab Bureau] ... Therefore, when you asked [for their support] in our new Arabic programme they were utterly offended ... They see themselves as important initiators and producers of these programmes, and therefore would like to appear as [equal] partners ... The Political Department has a national-political interest in our Arabic studies foundation, while we have only an educational-cultural interest. It is the other side of the same coin, and this is a completion that we see as appropriate ...[98]

This is a revealing letter, which shows the place of Ben-Ze'ev, the Jewish school system's Arabic Supervisor, within the power structure of the Zionist establishment. Ben-Ze'ev probably knew better than others how crucial the support of the Political Department was for the teaching of Arabic in schools, on different levels. He also emphasised that the Political Department and figures like Eliyahu Sasson – with his overt security interest – were inherent to the teaching of Arabic in Jewish schools, or, in his words: *the other side of the same coin*. This insight, together with his apologetic inference of 'we have *only* an educational-cultural interest', proves that the merging of interests was not only due to financial considerations but also to the legitimacy provided by the Political Department and the shared ideological beliefs between the Political Department on the one hand, and the Education Department on the other. It can also be argued that during that period of time Ben-Ze'ev had realised that, like it or not, Arabic studies would no longer be considered purely educational in nature.

A memorandum from the same year reveals the involvement of the Political Department in another aspect of Arabic studies: the training of Arabic teachers for Jewish schools. Addressed to the Political Department and Education Department of the Jewish Agency, the memorandum noted that 'during the summer, training courses for Arabic language teachers for Hebrew high schools took place in Tel Aviv and Jerusalem. These courses were initiated and supported by the Political Department of the Jewish Agency.'[99]

The 1942 annual review of the Education Department reveals the continuation of this educational-political partnership, as well as the place of the security-oriented Arab Bureau (affiliated with the Political Department) in it. According to the review:

> When Dr Ben-Ze'ev became the Arabic Supervisor there was a huge shortage of Arabic teachers, of textbooks for teaching Literary Arabic and of textbooks for teaching Colloquial Arabic ... He needed to launch exclusive courses for the [training of] Arabic teachers. These courses were supported by the Arab Bureau [lit. *Ha-Maḥlaḳah ha-ʿAravit*] of the Jewish Agency. During five years, about 40 teachers were trained in these courses, most of them graduates of the Hebrew University.[100]

The Arab Bureau, which as noted was part of the Jewish Agency's Political Department, was in charge of both Arab and intelligence affairs in the Agency, and was also the predecessor of SHAI, the intelligence branch of the Haganah.[101] The fact that this unit – mostly populated by Jewish men with an interest in Arab affairs and security issues – was the primary body to allocate money for Arabic textbooks and Arabic teachers is important in our understanding of the way in which Arabic studies in Jewish schools was shaped, the power relations that shaped its creation and the departments that cooperated publicly and privately to create the field. It is also an indication of how Arabic studies came to be seen by the establishment: not primarily as an educational school subject with integrative aims to live with the 'Arab neighbour', but gradually – and as clearly demonstrated in the 1940s – as a political and security interest of the national Zionist project in combatting the 'Arab threat'.

From 1944, the Political Department and its Arab Bureau frequently participated in educational meetings and conferences. Its members were not external initiators or supporters, rather, an important component of the discussions, or the Education Department's 'partners' in the words of Ben-Ze'ev. For example, minutes from the 1944 Education Department's 'Committee for Training Courses for Arabic Teachers' demonstrates that five people took part in the meeting: three prominent scholars from the Institute of Oriental Studies at the Hebrew University (Goitein, David Zvi Baneth and Yitzḥak Shamoush); and two officials, one representing the Education Department (Ben-Ze'ev) and one representing the Arab Bureau of the Political Department (Sasson).[102]

A month later, a meeting initiated by Ben-Ze'ev and titled, 'By Invitation Only: On the Question of Teaching Arabic', again demonstrated the convergence of the two departments. At the meeting, Miriam Glickson, Sasson's deputy, represented the Arab Bureau. On the question of how to approach the teaching of Colloquial Arabic, Literary Arabic and general knowledge of Arabic taught in the curriculum of the Jewish school system, Glickson stated that:

> Colloquial Arabic has a practical goal and therefore it needs to be made mandatory ... Literary Arabic [is important] since it widens the horizons in Arabic language ... However, on teaching values of general knowledge [in Arabic] there is nothing to say, since these values are so few in the Arabic language.[103]

Again, Glickson's words seem to indicate new attitudes that had began to be openly articulated in the study of Arabic: as instrumental for practical needs, and certainly not a scholarly, intellectual or integrative school subject with 'so few values' for general knowledge.

In the summer of 1944, the Education Department held its annual meeting of Arabic teachers. Again among the participants was a representative of the Arab Bureau: Yitzḥak Navon, who later served as the head of the Bureau, but is most known as serving as President of Israel in the 1980s. In the meeting, probably due to the presence of Navon, Ben-Ze'ev felt that it was important to thank the political and security-oriented 'patrons' of this school subject. He said: 'I would like to thank the Director of the Political Department of the Jewish Agency, Moshe Shertok [Sharett], who shows great interest in our institution, and to express special gratitude to Eliyahu Sasson who did the utmost in helping me to obtain the funding.'[104]

The financial support given by the Political Department and the Arab Bureau was most probably very crucial. We can learn this from a meeting dedicated to the training of Arabic teachers, which took place a year later in the offices of the Political Department. Minutes of the meeting demonstrate that, by this point, the Education Department had become dependent on help provided by the Political Department. The meeting was attended by two members of the Arab Bureau (Sasson who headed the Bureau, and Yitzḥak Shim'oni who was leading the Bureau's research team), two scholars from the Institute of Oriental Studies at the Hebrew University (Jacob Landau and Shamoush) and a single representative of the Education Department (Ben-Zeʾev). In the meeting, Sasson started by noting that:

> This is the fourth year that we maintain these courses [Arabic teachers training] paid for by the Political Department ... I would like to note that this will be the last year that we will do so. We [the Political Department] wanted only to give a push to this important project, but we are not going to maintain it forever. I hope that we will succeed in convincing the Education Department to be ready to take charge of these courses beginning from next year ...[105]

In his response, Ben-Zeʾev did not hide his disappointment:

> Eliyahu Sasson's announcement is very sad [lit. *ʿagumah*] ... in the last three years, with the help of the Jewish Agency's [Political Department] we trained 23 teachers, and thanks to them we introduced Arabic studies to 35 more schools. Four years ago only 34 schools taught Arabic, but today we have 69 ... In my opinion, the training course is one of the most positive projects of the Political Department of the Jewish Agency, and I do not understand how it can say that its mission has ended. The Political Department should at least put its efforts into influencing the Education Department to give us the needed funding for next year ... I would like to emphasise that the Political Department must help us to find a way to continue with these courses ...[106]

Ben-Zeʾev's words are worthy of further examination. First, they indicate that there was a huge increase in Arabic teaching between the years 1941–45. Second, based on previous insights, it is clear that this increase was a result of the involvement of the Political Department in the field of Arabic studies, including the appointment of Ben-Zeʾev as supervisor and the creation of the Arabic teachers' training course. Third, it is interesting to note the emerging power relations within this group of decision-makers. After all, Ben-Zeʾev concluded his statement by asking Sasson and the Political Department to 'put its efforts into influencing the Education Department to give us the needed funding for next year', while he himself is employed by the Education Department. This request, therefore, is rather telling, indicating that despite Ben-Zeʾev's senior position in the Education Department, he required the head of the security-oriented Arab Bureau to speak with his own department to convince its directors to allocate more funding for Arabic studies. This indicates the 'weight' of political and security actors in the field of Arabic studies in the 1940s, as well as the security-political orientation, even a certain de-educationalisation, of Arabic studies at the time, even in the eyes of one of the most senior Arabic language officials in the Jewish sector.

There is no clear indication as to whether the Political Department actually halted all financial support for the teachers' training courses. It definitely did not cease its ongoing general support for programmes of Arabic studies in the Jewish school system. For example, in October 1947, when Gymnasia High School in Jerusalem requested financial support for an enhanced Arabic programme – quite integrative in nature that, unlike the regular programme, it included Arab folklore studies and meetings with Palestinian youths, a programme that was supported by Goitein – it addressed the head of the Political Department, Golda Me'ir. The response was rather dry:

> The Political Department believes that this programme should be encouraged, but it needs to be addressed to the appropriate educational authorities [and not to us] ... Due to a limited budget we will not be able to give you financial support, *on top of the funding that you already receive from us.*[107]

This correspondence illustrates that the Political Department supported, at least at a basic level, Arabic studies in Jewish schools. Moreover, we can also assume that the decision not to increase its support stemmed from the rather 'naive' intention of this school, in the midst of the Palestinian–Zionist conflict, to teach Arab folklore and bring Jewish and Palestinian youngsters together. Arguably, at the time, these aims were not part of the Zionist movement's milieu. Perhaps the years 1940–48, a period of emergent nationalistic feelings mixed with the realisation of an inevitable violent conflict, symbolised the countdown to the creation of a Jewish state in Palestine, and signalled as well the gradual forgetfulness of the Jewish people of the hyphen that connected the Arab-Jewish identity and Arabic more specifically.

Paraphrasing Goitein's immortal and over-quoted prose, Arabic was indeed 'part of Zionism', but probably not in the way in which he aspired it to be. Rather, Arabic served the movement in its political goal of expanding its influence over Palestine, facilitating its campaign and enabling its successes with as little rejection as possible from the local

Arab-Palestinians. In this process, Arabic within Jewish society gradually became a tool in the stockpile of devices employed by the Zionist movement, on a par with land acquisition and the 'conquest of labour', and somewhere between the symbol of the Haganah (the sword and the shield) to a midpoint between military force and political establishment. All in all, and as the years passed, it became clearer that Arabic studies were devoid of serious consideration of peace and integration with the Arab neighbours.

2
Whose Language is it, Anyway?
Arabic in Jewish-Israeli Schools, 1948–67

> In Israel, the civilian is a soldier on 11 months' annual leave.
>
> Yigael Yadin, former Israeli Chief of Staff[1]

Arabic language in a new country

The 1948 War represented a watershed period in the sociopolitical reality of Palestine. The tension between Jewish and Palestinian communities, which had transformed into overt hostilities following the 1947 United Nations Partition Plan for Palestine, peaked with the 1948 War. Throughout the war and in its aftermath, more than 700,000 Palestinians fled or were expelled from their homes, and were not allowed to return to them.[2] The events of 1947–48 dramatically altered the demographic balance in the region – to the detriment of its indigenous Arab-Palestinian inhabitants. In the newly created Jewish State of Israel, Jews were a significant majority, comprising some 716,000 people while Palestinians under Israeli rule were a minority comprising only 92,000 individuals.[3]

Israel, as a nascent country, also enjoyed expanded territorial control. Postwar, the newly born 'Jewish and democratic state' controlled 78 per cent of Mandate Palestine, as opposed to the 55 per cent allocated to it in the context of the 1947 UN Partition Plan.[4] The Israeli sociologist Baruch Kimmerling argued that the 1948 War and its consequences embedded notions of security in the heart of Israeli society. He wrote:

> Since the birth of the country it strived to protect its borders, especially from attempts by Palestinian refugees to penetrate its borders and return. These attempts kept the state in a constant border war ...

> The continuous skirmishes, even though low in intensity, caused damage to life and property, but it also rebuilt the army around small but high-standard units. This constant battle situated national security and militarism at the centre of the collective consciousness from very early childhood, and contributed to the creation of strong social solidarity through the construction and illustration of Israel as a society under siege.[5]

This 'siege' mentality was combined with militaristic values. Not only did this affect territorial, demographic and militaristic aspects of life in the new state, but it also influenced the language and its instruction. As will be demonstrated, the post-1948 situation in Israel stimulated the formation of new networks and introduced new actors into the field of Arabic language studies. While there were some differences, these changes also reflected a certain continuation of processes that had begun during the pre-state period, and these patterns became more pronounced in the new state.

In order to understand fully Arabic language studies in Israel, it is important to survey briefly the standing and legal status of Arabic, along with its political and social significance. Interestingly, Arabic has become an official language in Israel, but it was not an active and inclusive decision, rather, it was a passive acceptance of the status quo. During the British Mandate in Palestine, by virtue of Article 82 of the 'Palestine Order in Council' (1922) there were three recognised official languages: English, Arabic and Hebrew. The Article states that:

> All Ordinances, official notices and official forms of the Government and all official notices of local authorities and municipalities in areas to be prescribed by order of the High Commissioner shall be published in English, Arabic and Hebrew.[6]

In 1948, during the process of decision-making regarding legislation and regulations governing the new state, the legislature decided to incorporate the legal norms of Mandatory rule into the nascent Israeli legal system, unless it specifically ruled otherwise. The one relevant exception was the status of English: Section 15(b) in the Israeli decision on its official languages noted that, 'it was decided that the Order for the Arrangements of Government and Law cancel all commands which demanded the use of English'.[7] Therefore, the decision to remove English as an official language maintained the status of Arabic as an official language in a somewhat indirect way.

Irrespective of the legal status of Arabic, Hebrew was, of course, the primary official language of the country – even from the very beginning. The Declaration of Independence, for example, only references Hebrew, and says as follows: 'In recent decades the Jewish people returned in masses to their ancient homeland ... they made deserts bloom, *revived the Hebrew language,* built villages and towns, and created a thriving community' (my emphasis). Furthermore, following the creation of the state in 1948, officials from the Hebrew Language Committee decided to establish a language academy for Hebrew. Subsequent legislation reinforced this; for example, the 1952 Nationality Law states that a person needs to have 'some knowledge of the Hebrew language' in order to obtain Israeli nationality by naturalisation. Daily norms also favour Hebrew: the language of instruction in all Israeli universities is Hebrew and Hebrew is a mandatory subject in all state schools (Jewish and Arab alike). On top of this, it goes without saying that Hebrew is integrally connected to the concept of Israel as a 'Jewish state' according to modern interpretations of Zionism.

While it is understandable – from the new political hegemony point of view – that Hebrew became an official language in Israel, it is less clear why Arabic was not demoted along with English. Ilan Saban notes that in cases where countries have two official languages they are usually binational states or civic nation-states with multicultural orientations. Given its overt and intentional Jewish orientation, however, Israel is anything but a binational state. Israel is also far from reflecting an intentional model of a multicultural society. In fact, Israel is an ethnic nation-state and, as such, should be expected to promote one official language. The status of Malay in Malaysia and Slovak in Slovakia are more accurate indicators of the preferred model in Israel. As a matter of fact, the official status of both Hebrew and Arabic in Israel does not accurately reflect the politics and identity of the country; the present legal situation in relation to language in Israel – which has two official languages – is common to the identity of very different case studies and much more inclusive in nature.[8]

Various explanations have been given in an attempt to make sense of this anomaly. Some scholars, such as Alexander Yakobson and Amnon Rubinstein, argue that granting Arabic official status in 1948 – even if this status is not equal to that of Hebrew – is an indication of Israel's liberal approach towards its Palestinians citizens. Indeed, Arabic script is found on stamps and printed currency that Yakobson and Rubinstein term one of many 'meaningful acts that has special significance for the identity of a national minority'.[9] Other, more critical, scholars have argued that considerations of realpolitik played a central role in the Israeli decision. Muḥammad Amara and ʿAbd al-Raḥman Marʿi posit that the new state maintained Arabic as an official language for reasons of public policy; it did not want to provoke further confrontation or be viewed globally as a 'culture destroyer'. They also believe that internal political reasons played a role in this decision: Israeli decision-makers felt that by allowing Arabic to exist, this would ensure separation between Jews and Arabs in Israel.[10] In a similar vein, Saban and Amara suggest that in revoking Mandate legislation regarding Arabic, Israel would have been severely criticised by the international community.[11] The logic underlying their reasoning can be found in the Zionist movement's acceptance of the 1947 UN Partition Plan that states that 'the preservation of minorities' rights to use their own language' will be respected in the newborn Jewish state.

Saban and Amara posit the idea that the solution adopted by Israel reflected a 'gap between rhetoric and practice ... instead of taking the problematic step of annulling the official status of Arabic, Israel settled for a unilingual practice among its official bodies in the country'.[12] Or, in the words of Saban:

> Rather than annul the official status of Arabic, Israel settled for unilingual practice among all governmental bodies ... and counted on the dominance of Hebrew in the Israeli labour market to further marginalise Arabic. Such factors compelled the Palestinian minority to adopt bilingualism, and thus the hegemony of Hebrew was ensured.[13]

Irrespective of the reasoning of Israeli decision-makers, many researchers have investigated the gap between the official legal status of Arabic and its inferiority in practice.[14] In my view, this somewhat awkward reality of Arabic as an 'official–non-official' language, has allowed official institutions in Israel and the majority of Jewish-Israelis to maintain a perception of itself as a country that upholds the values of democracy, including demonstrating a concern for its minorities, while not really having to become a more egalitarian, and inclusive, society. Indeed, it has proved to be a winning strategy for Jewish Israel; the country can claim that Arabic is an official language – with all the liberal connotations and international acclaim that accompanies this position – while not being forced to make significant efforts and concessions in practice in light of the fact that the official status of Arabic is certainly not evident in higher education, nor in the public or diplomatic sectors. In actuality, Arabic is *official* for the Palestinian population of Israel only, but is *foreign* to Jewish-Israeli society. This ambiguity has maintained and supported the unclear 'official–non-official' status quo for Arabic. Some researchers maintain that this should lead to the erasure of the official status of Arabic in Israel, not to the strengthening of its status in the country.[15]

From the perspective of linguistic rights, Palestinian citizens have been forced to engage in an ongoing war of attrition aimed at actualising this right from 1948 to the present day. The main battlefield for securing individual and collective linguistic rights has been the judicial system, and there are many examples for this.[16] A well-known one demonstrates this when in 2005 a new terminal at Ben-Gurion Airport in Israel was unveiled with signs that were only in Hebrew and English. Only following the intervention of Arab parliamentarians in the Knesset (the Israeli Parliament), was Arabic given its rightful place in this important public building.[17]

'Teaching Hottentot on the moon': Arabic in the Israeli education system

The post-1948 situation had an obvious demographic difference in comparison to the preceding period: there were very few Arab-Palestinians left within Israel's postwar borders. Indeed, while Palestinians had attempted to return to their homes and land after the Nakba (lit. the 'disaster' or 'catastrophe'[18]) they encountered numerous difficulties. Those who succeeded in staying or who managed to return found that overnight they had become 'Arab-Israelis'. As such, they lived in isolated areas under Military Government control and suffered restrictions on their daily life and freedom of movement. This new situation also meant that Palestinians who had fled the country were now living 'behind enemy' lines – according to Israel – while those who had managed to stay and were awarded citizenship found themselves behind military lines. While interaction between Jews and Arabs may have decreased in the 1940s due to the conflict, in the post-1948 period the two societies were far more separated than they had ever been previously. Furthermore, in light of the conflict, there was a common perception that Palestinians outside of Israel were aligned with the Arab enemy while Palestinians in Israel were a 'fifth column'.[19] Understandably, this did not contribute to tendencies towards integration among pupils and teachers of Arabic and served as a major disincentive to studying the language.

In the post-1948 period, a number of influential people increasingly argued that the new sociopolitical reality necessitated the weakening of Arabic in Jewish schools. This was due to several factors, including the lack of social contact between Jewish-Israeli civil society and Palestinian citizens of Israel and growing animosity between the groups. In 1949, for example, Shlomo Morag, a promising scholar at the Hebrew University and a student of Goitein, argued that the new political state of affairs necessitated the cessation of the teaching of Colloquial Arabic completely. Morag's reasoning was as follows: 'the opportunities of true contact between the Hebrew citizen of the country and the Arab citizen are significantly fewer than those which existed during the British Mandate'. He also noted that even if these interactions were going to take place, due to the new political and demographic situation, they were most likely to be conducted in Hebrew.[20]

The Hours Committee (lit. *Ṿaʿadat ha-Shaʿot*) of the Ministry of Education, which was responsible for establishing and coordinating the number of hours dedicated to each topic of study in each stream of education, expressed conflicting views on the topic. Yaʿacov Halpern, who was the supervisor of the Workers' Stream of education (lit. *Zerem ha-ʿOvdim*) argued that 'Arabic should be taught [from intermediary level] since we are neighbouring Arab countries, due to the Semitic proximity between Hebrew and Arabic that is beneficial pedagogically, and since we want the Hebrew child to become a son of the Orient.'[21] His views were challenged by another member of the Committee, Moshe Dafna, supervisor of the General Stream in education, who took issue with Halpern's views on the geographical necessity of studying Arabic. According to Dafna:

> If we want to take into consideration that we neighbour Arab people, then we should put more emphasis on sport and physical exercises. We will always be fewer than them [the Arabs]. And we will always need to stand guard, and to be unable to dedicate too much time for study [of Arabic]. Today, in the era of airplanes, our closeness to the West is not more distanced than the East. Arabic is not an easy language, and it cannot be studied in two years' time ... I believe that instead, they [the Arab people] should adapt to us and study Hebrew. We must free ourselves from the Diasporic inferiority.[22]

Based on this exchange, it is clear that while Arabic suffered from some serious difficulties in the pre-state period, post-1948 teaching and studying of Arabic was even harder to justify because the language had lost some of its practical relevance. Together with Dafna's Western orientation (common during that period), and a general Israeli belief in the importance of promoting Hebrew culture in the Jewish state, interest in studying Arabic in wide swathes of Israeli society was very low indeed. Simultaneously, English was much more popular and prestigious and also perceived to be far more 'practical' than Arabic. Therefore, following the recommendations of the 'Hours Committee', English became a mandatory school subject, and was given the status of 'first foreign language'. The Hours Committee's decisions, which highlighted the difficulty of studying both English and Arabic, reflected these attitudes. Consequently, the protocol of the meeting of the Hours Committee stated that it would be 'impossible to study them both'.[23] In another indication of its inferior position, Arabic was assigned the status of an *elective second foreign language* – the name, which speaks for itself, hints at the low rank and foreignness of the language and acts as a proxy for the similar status of its speakers in Israel.

In September 1949, Supervisor Ben-Ze'ev, who was almost a decade in his position, again attempted to advocate the relevance of Arabic language studies in the Jewish school system. In a letter addressed to Dr Barukh Ben-Yehuda, the Director of the newly established Ministry of Education, Ben-Ze'ev referred to an official committee that created a plan for the teaching of 'Arabic Language Studies in High Schools'. According to Ben-Ze'ev, the plan was to teach Arabic from the 9th to the 12th grade, four hours per week, and to focus on 'basic vocabulary and simple Arabic sentences that comprise the *practical* usages of the language ... while emphasising *daily* language materials reflecting the language of Arabic *newspapers* and *radio* stations, social and financial life, and Colloquial Arabic'.[24]

A few months later, and still in the context of moulding Arabic studies in the post-1948 period, Ben-Ze'ev sent another letter to Ben-Yehuda, this time with a tentative plan regarding the teaching of Arabic in junior high school (7th and 8th grade). Ben-Ze'ev defined the aims of studying Arabic for this age group as such:

> [T]o provide *practical* knowledge of Colloquial Arabic together with basic reading and writing skills of *practical* Literary Arabic based on a limited number of *key words* and Arabic accent. Studying Arabic will allow [the pupil] to read materials that relate to the contemporary *Arab way of life* in Israel [lit. *nos'im min ha-hayay ha-'Aravi bi-Medinat Yisra'el*] and the neighbouring countries ... On graduating from junior high school, the pupil will be able to use his knowledge of

> Colloquial Arabic for *practical* needs and Literary Arabic for reading and translating easy and short sentences ...[25]

As can be seen in both of the educational plans outlined by Ben-Ze'ev above, Arabic language studies was viewed as having obvious *practical* implications such as gaining the ability to understand contemporary items in the print media and on the radio, to acquire Colloquial Arabic skills and to gain knowledge of the Arab people's 'way of life'. Thus, during this period, the acquisition of Arabic language skills was meant to serve 'contemporary matters'. These 'contemporary matters', as will become more evident when examining the 1950s, linked the study of Arabic with serving Israeli *official* needs, which were more often than not political and security-oriented in nature, and took part in shaping related policies towards the Arab-Palestinian people and the Arab world. This, of course, is far from being a new phenomenon. In line with Pierre Bourdieu's insights regarding the connection between education and regimes, official education systems are not democratic, equitable or intended to facilitate social and political mobility. Rather, they strive to replicate the ideologies of the regime and reproduce knowledge that supports the political and ideological 'pillars' on which the establishment stands.[26]

Gradually, in fact, the regime's ideology filtered down into the rationales and justifications employed by various figures in the field of Arabic language studies. This is clearly demonstrated by a report on Arabic studies in Tel Aviv written in 1951. Ben-Ze'ev expressed frustration, most probably due to the slow acceptance of his educational plans in the school system and the relative lack of motivation in relation to pursing Arabic studies. Ben-Ze'ev opened the report with a critique of the Israeli notion that Arabic studies should be weakened, justifying its study as follows:

> There are parents and school administrations in Israel, especially in Tel Aviv, who believe that Arabic studies should be diminished as there are no Arabs among us anymore. They don't get that the educational and national needs [in Arabic studies] that were required before [in the pre-state period], did not dissipate with the creation of the state.[27]

Following this, Ben-Ze'ev made a more direct case for the need for Arabic-speakers in advancing matters of state. Ben-Ze'ev wrote:

> The study of Arabic in high schools is needed in relation to Hebrew cultural matters but we have also a need for hundreds of

> Arabic-speakers for our government offices, different activities of the IDF, and [other state activities] related to the direct contact we have with the Arabs, who are not as few in number as many imagine.[28]

This citation clearly demonstrates Ben-Ze'ev's increasing use of the 'political card' to promote Arabic language studies. Indeed, gradually references to the pedagogic virtues of the study of Arabic decreased while there was an increase in the emphasis on the *practical* need for Arabic through inferences to challenges posed by the Arab world, including urgent military and political challenges and the Israeli need for Arabic-speakers for the services of the IDF, governmental offices and Military Government. His views reflected a new and emerging understanding of 'practical' Arabic, very different from that mentioned only 15 years previously by Avinoʿam Yellin. Clearly, the passage of time and the conflict had changed the Jews' perception of Israel/Palestine, along with their priorities and thus influenced the motivations undergirding the study of the language.

Not only was this change reflected in the education system, but it was also evident in the appointment of manpower. For example, in 1946, Yitzḥak Navon and Moshe Piamenta went from being Arabic teachers to working in the SHAI Unit of the Haganah, while in 1942 Shimʿon Somekh, also a teacher of Arabic, began work with the Mistaʿaravim Unit of the Palmach.[29] They were not the only ones: in the 1940s, young orientalists from the Institute of Oriental Studies at the Hebrew University 'crossed the boundary between academia and officialdom and took positions in the intelligence services of the Jewish community'.[30] Similarly, and according to Ben-Ze'ev, 'prior to the War of Independence [1948 War] and following it, many fine teachers left to join the different government offices, the Ministry of Foreign Affairs and the IDF'.[31]

This shift from 'Arabic in school' to 'Arabic for intelligence' not only reflects a changing orientation by individuals, but also was in line with a general set of priorities established by the state and present in its discourse. During this same period, and independent of the Ministry of Education, numerous discussions took place noting the growing shortage of Arabic-speakers in the Military Government and Military Intelligence. In line with a number of suggestions, the Prime Minister's Office made a decision to create a new stream of Arabic studies in the school system called the 'Oriental Course of Study' or the 'Oriental Classes' (lit. *Ha-Megama ha-Mizraḥanit*). This was an intensive Arabic programme, taught in a few Jewish schools only, which pupils participated in during their final two years of high school. The programme created a linkage between Arabic studies in school and the need of the state for a reservoir of 'Arabists' who could then be appointed to positions in the Military Government, Military Intelligence and other official bodies. A separate section below titled, 'A Sentiment-Free Arabic: The Creation of the '"Oriental Classes"', will be dedicated to this course of Arabic studies as it requires special analysis.

In the context of the general education system in Israel in the early 1950s, 'Arabic for security' increasingly proved to be relevant and practical in terms of Arabic studies in schools. Some of this change was in response to articles published in the *Ha-Boḳér Newspaper* (The Morning), which proposed halving the hours allocated to Arabic in high school and asserted that it was a pity that Arabic had been taught in Jewish schools during the British Mandate in the first place. Ben-Ze'ev reacted publicly and with tremendous fury to these articles. He attacked the idea of reducing Arabic teaching hours in the curriculum and countered that the study of Arabic was important in order to gain a fuller understanding of Hebrew. Specifically in relation to the reference of Arabic study during the period of the British Mandate, and fully aware of which direction the winds were blowing, Ben-Ze'ev decided to respond by using the 'security card':

> Thanks to the sufficient hours of Arabic taught during the Mandate, our brave youth succeeded in studying the Arab problem in our country ... part of our victory in the War of Independence needs to be credited to the study of Arabic [in the 1940s] and the perfect use of it in the days of the War of Liberation.[32]

While it is not completely clear what Ben-Ze'ev meant when referring to the 'perfect use of Arabic' studied in the pre-state period, it most likely refers to the various activities and achievements of the Arab Bureau of the Haganah, and the Arab Bureau of the Political Department mentioned briefly before. They both played an active role in gathering intelligence during the war by employing and activating Jewish individuals with a good command of Arabic.

Even though Ben-Ze'ev shrewdly played the 'security card' in a national newspaper, his arguments failed to improve the status of Arabic in the Jewish-Israeli school system. The Arabic language as a school subject continued to languish due to a lack of interest. This was exacerbated by a focus on the teaching of Hebrew and English, a lack of trained Arabic teachers and the ongoing association of Arabic with the hostile 'other'.[33] One of the outcomes of these difficulties was the Prime Minister's Office's decision to increase the emphasis on 'Oriental Classes' in some schools. In the rest of the education system the 'hardships' faced by Arabic studies brought the Ministry of Education closer to a new partner, which had previously been outside of the debate: the IDF.

The relationship between the Ministry of Education and the IDF was first outlined in a letter sent by Dr Michael Ziv, the Director of High School Pedagogy in the Ministry, to the Ministry's General Director, Professor Eliʿezer Rieger. In the letter, Ziv highlighted the importance of cooperating with the military, and emphasised the IDF's increasing interest in Arabic studies:

> A few months ago, senior authorities in the IDF contacted me and asked me to pay special attention to the teaching of Arabic in high schools. They said that the army has many reasons for expressing its need for pupils with knowledge of Arabic. During conversations we had with representatives of the army it was suggested that we arrange meetings with head teachers of high schools, in which Arabic is being taught, in order to discuss the question: *What can be done in order to fulfil the desires of the army?* I spoke about that with [Supervisor] Ben-Ze'ev and he sees these meetings as highly essential.[34]

The 'desires of the army' (lit. *mish'alot ha-tsava*) and the enthusiasm of Israeli educational officials to 'fulfil them', was the impetus for meetings between representatives of the IDF and Arabic teachers a couple of months after Ziv's letter was written. At the meetings, Arabic teachers complained about the decreasing number of Arabic teaching hours in schools and about a 'general diminishing of this subject in most [Jewish-Israeli] schools in the country'.[35]

While the IDF became increasingly aware of the situation, Jewish-Israeli society continued to reject the study of Arabic en masse – a trend that mainly emanated from the grassroots: pupils and parents. Nevertheless, Ben-Ze'ev believed that the decline was also due to a lack of genuine support from top officials in the Minister of Education. This lack of support left a 'gap' that was later to be filled by the IDF. These feelings were expressed in a furious letter written in 1956 that Ben-Ze'ev sent to Yoseph Shoḥat, the head of the Pedagogical Secretariat in the Ministry of Education. According to Ben-Ze'ev:

> Over the last couple of months I have asked several times ... to authorise the teaching of Arabic in 20 elementary schools in the districts of

> Jaffa, Ashkelon, Be'er-Sheva and the border villages in Upper Galilee. *All of my requests were rejected.* Is it possible that throughout Ashkelon and Be'er-Sheva there is not one school in which Arabic is taught? Is it possible that in border areas, such as next to Gaza and the Upper Galilee, Arabic – which is part of our children's security needs – is not taught even at a minimal level in a single school? On top of this, Arabic was removed from some of the schools in which it was taught ... a decision made without consulting the professional experts. *This attitude is very disturbing.*[36]

Based on the content of the letter, it can be deduced that Ben-Ze'ev believed that the Ministry of Education actually preferred not to expand the study of Arabic into more schools. In all likelihood, the Ministry wanted to focus on and promote Arabic in a limited number of educational institutions (such as those with the 'Oriental Classes') instead of encouraging its study nationally.

Despite Ben-Ze'ev's clear disagreement with the decisions of the Ministry of Education, his influence on the situation was seemingly limited. It continued to deteriorate, with 1957 marking a new low. An article written by Y. Ophir and published in the *Ḥerut* newspaper entitled, 'The Youth in Israel does not want to Study Arabic', notes that, based on Ministry of Education statistics, only 90 pupils out of all of those studying Arabic in the 7th and 8th grades chose to continue to study the language in high school, and that only 60 pupils studied Arabic as part of the 'Oriental Classes'. Ophir pointed to a shortage of trained teachers; in fact, 50 per cent of Arabic teachers did not have an academic education. He also indicated that the motivation to study Arabic was low as he wrote that in the few schools that offered a choice between Arabic and French as a second foreign language, '[t]he vast majority of pupils choose to study French'.[37]

The rejection of Arabic studies emphasised by Ophir probably coincided with pressure from within the Ministry of Education to decrease the number of hours allocated to it. In a report written in 1957, Ben-Ze'ev stressed that pressures from the Pedagogical Secretariat in the Ministry had the aim of actually cancelling Arabic as a school subject in all Jewish-Israeli schools.[38] The decline of Arabic, therefore, stemmed from a number of factors: it was not only rejected by pupils but also lacked support from the Ministry of Education and from head teachers. To add insult to injury, there were also diplomatic reasons for the ever-decreasing status of Arabic: in 1959, Israel and France signed a mutual cultural agreement, according to which there would be an increase in Hebrew taught in universities in France and also an optional examination in Hebrew in French schools. For its part, Israel agreed to promote the study of French in the Israeli school system and even committed to establishing French as a *first foreign language* in a few French-oriented schools and as a *second foreign language* in the vast majority of Jewish-Israeli schools. This presented a clear alternative and threat to Arabic, and an almost impossible challenge for Ben-Ze'ev and other Israeli advocates for Arabic.[39]

Ben-Ze'ev's relentless efforts to introduce Arabic studies into more schools, therefore, faced a seemingly endless array of challenges. Various reports and archival documents attest to the ongoing decrease of Arabic language studies in the general education system between the years 1957–59.[40] Ben-Ze'ev's inability to change the language situation in most schools in Israel generated substantial desperation and prompted his use of increasingly direct and dire language. In 1960, he wrote the following to Naḥum Gavri'eli, the head of the Pedagogical Secretariat:

> Since 1957, the Secretariat has applied incessant pressure in order to cancel the study of Arabic [lit. *laḥats bilti posek̩ levaṭel et hora'at ha-ʿAravit*] ... This has brought us to the current year of 1960, in which only 39 elementary schools all over Israel are teaching the language ... This [deterioration] will lead us to the complete elimination [lit. *anaḥnu holkhim lik̩rat ḥisul sofi*] of Arabic in our institutions [schools] ... In border villages, a negligible knowledge of Arabic is a security problem [lit. *beʿayah biṭḥonit*]. Moreover, we should not discount the international political factor: external bodies like UNESCO [United Nations Educational, Scientific and Cultural Organization] will consider [our] cancellation of Arabic studies not only as an extreme nationalistic step, but also as a complete lack of sociopolitical understating of our reality in a country surrounded by millions of Arabic-speakers. We should not reach a point in which the curriculum in Jewish schools will be 'clean' of Arabic ... The Arabic language will also be beneficial for the study of Hebrew grammar.[41]

It is interesting to note the sheer variety of justifications mentioned by Ben-Ze'ev in such a short letter: he uses the *security* argument on referencing the border villages; the *international* argument in the context of UNESCO; a *geopolitical* argument when writing about Israel being surrounded by millions of Arabic-speakers; and an *educational* argument while emphasising the contribution of Arabic to the study of Hebrew grammar. Lastly, he includes a *moral* argument as well; he argues that Jewish-Israeli schools should not be cleansed of Arabic (lit. *tokhnit limudim neḳiyah me-ʿAravit*) – a thinly veiled reference to cultural ethnic cleansing, or even to the Nazi concept of *Judenrein*, 'a land clean of Jews', to which Jewish-Israeli society is naturally very sensitive.[42] Ben-Zeʾev had reached a point of such desperation that he sought any and all justifications in order to make his voice heard.

In November 1961, Ben-Zeʾev reached a level of desperation so severe that he initiated direct personal contact with Abba Eban, the Minister of Education, himself. In a letter entitled, 'Arabic Language in our Institutions', he suggested a number of options that could improve the status and teaching of Arabic in schools pointing to the regions in Israel where Arabic was not taught, and the lack of institutionalised training of Arabic teachers. According to the letter, '[d]uring the British Mandate, we had seminars for Jewish teachers of Arabic as well as Arabic training courses, but now there is no institution that trains Arabic teachers'. Ben-Zeʾev also noted that the entire education stream of 'Agricultural Schools' had ceased to teach Arabic.[43] Unfortunately, there is no record of a response from Eban to Ben-Zeʾev. Nevertheless, existing correspondence indicates that Ben-Zeʾev's efforts were unsuccessful and that Arabic in Jewish-Israeli schools had declined dramatically, reaching a nadir in the late 1950s and the early 1960s.

Perhaps as a direct outcome of Ben-Zeʾev's endless campaigning or due to a confluence of internal needs, the Israeli army reappeared in the picture around this time. The IDF, which took an active role in the development of 'Oriental Classes', probably shared Ben-Zeʾev's concern regarding the decline of Arabic studies, although most likely for different reasons.

Bernard Spolsky and Elana Shohamy make a similar suggestion; they argue that by 1961, 'the Israeli army was starting to recognise a shortage of people who could speak the language'.[44] Archival documents examined in the course of the research support this view and shed light on its depth and intensity. Strikingly, from 1961 onwards, the majority of the documents found demonstrate that the military played a prominent role in the debate on Arabic studies in schools, with security arguments at the forefront.

Internal correspondence from the Prime Minister's Office is a good starting point for this discussion. In October 1963, Ori Stendel, a senior and energetic official in the Bureau of the Adviser on Arab Affairs in the Prime Minister's Office, wrote a summary report to his superior, Reḥavʿam ʿAmir, entitled 'Arabic in [Jewish-]Israeli High Schools'. The first section, called 'General Background', included the following:

> In the past few years, there has been a worrying decrease in the hours allocated to teaching Arabic in high schools. This is mainly

> due to two reasons: (1) Pressure from the Ministry of Education to introduce French, which displaced Arabic ... (2) Requests from parents to have their children taught French instead of Arabic ... This double pressure causes head teachers, even if they themselves believe in the importance of Arabic, to give it up ... The situation is getting worse and it seems that the day will soon come when there will be no appropriate institution [lit. *misgeret mamashit*] to train the next generation of experts for positions that require Arabic knowledge ...[45]

Following on from this, and mentioning that his ideas were based on discussions held with Lt Col. Avraham Sharoni from Military Intelligence, Stendel made a number of recommendations for improvement as follows:

> (1) Creation of an Arabic training seminar in the army, following which the graduates will teach Arabic in Israeli elementary and high schools. (2) Encouragement of the study of Literary Arabic in the military academy from which teachers for higher classes will be selected. (3) Arabic in schools should start in 7th grade. (4) More Oriental Classes in high schools should be launched. (5) Pupils of Oriental Studies [in schools] should be given greater leeway in their final exams [in other school subjects]. (6) Budgets given to schools in which Arabic is taught should be increased. (7) Scholarships should be given for excellent pupils of Arabic who choose to continue studying it in high school. 8. Scholarships should be given for graduates of the Institute for Oriental Studies [at the Hebrew University] who decide to teach Oriental Classes in schools.[46]

Stendel, who also sent the letter to Sharoni, ended by stating that 'in order to discuss these options further, and to find ways to implement them, I believe that we need to initiate an urgent meeting with the Chief of Staff, the Director of the Ministry of Education and the Supervisor of the Oriental Classes'.[47]

This letter is striking not only in its demanding tone, but in the Prime Minister's Office's perception of itself as a mediator, or a bridge, between the needs of the army and the pupils. Stendel's recommendations note and link several different 'actors' in the field of Arabic within Jewish-Israeli society: the IDF (military training seminar), the school system (Oriental Classes and regular schools) and the higher education system (the Hebrew University). Furthermore, his recommendations are multifaceted and involve the school system, the army, academia and schools offering Oriental Classes. Thus, he outlined a network of actors with interests in Arabic and various roles to play in its promotion. At this stage, this network was coordinated by the Prime Minister's Office and based on interests shared by various Jewish-Israeli institutions in charge of Arabic studies. Indeed, the 'networked structure' and linkages outlined here facilitate efficient flow of information, in line with Bourdieu's notion of 'reproduction of knowledge' as well as with the idea of the 'circulation of knowledge'.

Despite its importance, and even with Stendel and Sharoni on board, the educational–political–military alliance continued to face strong opposition from other facets of Jewish-Israeli society who did not agree with them on the importance of Arabic. The tension between those defending Arabic studies and the masses who found it irrelevant came to a head in 1964. In February of that year, the Ministry of Education announced that Arabic would cease to be a school subject that involved final exams in Jewish-Israeli schools, and that its study in high school would only be conducted in the context of the few schools offering Oriental Classes. This immediately prompted an angry reply from the National Committee of Israeli Arabic Teachers, who wrote to Ben-Zeʾev as follows:

> Is not it enough that we are surrounded by Arabic-speaking countries? Is not it enough that a few of these Arab countries, even if they do not have a border with us, are our enemies? Is not it enough that amongst us there is a big and agitating [Palestinian] minority [lit. *miʿuṭ gadol ṿe-toses*] that speaks Arabic? Is not it enough that our Hebrew language is studied and researched in relation to Arabic? ... Are not these political, security and scientific reasons enough to justify the study of Arabic, or at least to prevent further damage to its status? If the suggestion [to cancel Arabic as a subject for final exams] is accepted, we will not hesitate to go on general strike in all schools.[48]

Following this correspondence, the head of the Arabic Teachers Committee, Avraham Lavi, who was probably the country's most senior Arabic teacher at the time, wrote a personal letter to the Director of the Ministry of Education, Ḥanokh Rinot. In his letter, Lavi noted that: 'the decision to cancel Arabic final exams ... is an elimination of the study of Arabic ... this decision represents an official authorisation of the negative attitudes of the Israeli public towards Arabic'.[49] In order to demonstrate the importance of the Arabic language and culture, Lavi used what was probably the most convincing rationale in his arsenal: the 'security card'. 'Attached is a letter I received from the IDF', wrote

Lavi to Rinot, 'which proves that the level of the pupils reaching the army is high and that they fulfil the most important national and security tasks ... and that the numbers of pupils are already [before the new decision] not sufficient for the IDF.'[50]

Both correspondences – Lavi's and that of the Committee of Arabic Teachers – demonstrate the strong military and security-oriented discourse surrounding the study of Arabic during this time. Indeed, it overshadowed scientific, educational and pedagogic considerations. While one could argue that teachers of Arabic employed these justifications exclusively to bolster their position, this is unlikely. First, many of these teachers were serving – or had already served – in Military Intelligence and were therefore less likely to find the link between military needs and the teaching of Arabic in their civilian lives objectionable. Second, *personal* and *direct* connections and correspondence between a distinguished educational figure, such as the Arabic teacher Lavi, and a senior Military Intelligence officer, such as Sharoni, highlights the strong alliances and common interests shared by these very different actors. Therefore, even if Arabic teachers had used the military justification in order to rescue Arabic from near certain death, the consensus around Arabic and national security cannot be viewed in purely pragmatic terms.

Irrespective of this, the Arabic teachers' direct correspondence with senior intelligence officer along with their use of political and security-oriented arguments proved to be more effective than the relentless efforts of Ben-Ze'ev. An analysis of a series of meetings that took place between representatives of the Ministry of Education and Military Intelligence as well as a committee appointed to review the teaching of Arabic in Jewish-Israeli schools during this period demonstrate this. As Military Intelligence officers were involved in these meetings and in the committee, it is clear that the Ministry of Education viewed the IDF as a partner in the context of Arabic language studies.

Several weeks later, the committee – comprised of representatives from the Prime Minister's Office, Military Intelligence and Ministry of Education – published its recommendations. Its primary recommendation involved strengthening Arabic studies in schools. As a means to increasing the popularity of Arabic, it suggested the 'use [of] publicity and persuasive means [lit. *emtsa'ey hasbarah ve-shikhnu'a*] and to give financial, organisational and psychological incentives in order to broaden the teaching of Arabic in the country'.[51]

Gen. Aharon Yariv, who served as Chief of Intelligence and participated in the committee's discussions, formulated a series of specific recommendations intended to support the committee's findings.

These included a *hasbarah* campaign (the Israeli concept of 'public diplomacy' or 'propaganda'), the expansion of the 'Oriental Classes' programme and the granting of IDF-funded scholarships to pupils who chose to study Arabic and committed to serving in Military Intelligence. Yariv's summary of this process also called for continuing discussion on issues raised by the committee in a similar format but also including the Manpower Directorate of the IDF in the committee's work.[52]

Indeed, the committee's recommendations, as reflected in Yariv's summary, were similar to those put forward by Stendel in October 1963. A general consensus emerged amongst members of this network that favoured improving the status of Arabic studies and also enhancing cooperation between the IDF and the Ministry of Education. It is clear from this interchange that the Adviser on Arabic Affairs in the Prime Minister's Office had a central and highly regarded role in this process. Furthermore, this indicates a gradual shift whereby responsibility for Arabic education moved from being the exclusive province of the Ministry of Education to a shared endeavour between the Ministry, the Prime Minister's Office and Military Intelligence. Lastly, the involvement of the Manpower Directorate of the IDF in this matter was also significant as it signals the perceived direct connection between the study of Arabic and future 'employment' in the IDF. This process also points to a key administrative change: instead of being the province of 'education', Arabic language studies was now at least partially overseen by the army.

In 1964, another significant change in manpower took place. Ben-Ze'ev, who by then was 65 years old and had served as Supervisor of Arabic studies for 23 years, announced his intention to retire at the conclusion of the school year. In response, the Ministry of Education announced that it was looking for a *part-time* candidate to fill his position. The call for a part-time employee, as opposed to seeking a full-time worker, indicated that despite IDF involvement, Arabic studies continued to rank as a low-status subject in the eyes of Israel's educational decision-makers.[53]

As previously noted, one further significant and distressing development for supporters of Arabic took place in 1964 with the introduction of another proposal, which called to cancel Arabic as a subject for final examinations. That summer, Member of Knesset (MK) Shmu'el Mikunis submitted proposed legislation entitled, 'Cancelling the Status of Arabic as a Subject for Final Examinations', in response to the ongoing unwillingness to study Arabic among Israeli youngsters. As the proposal received initial authorisation from the Ministry of Education, it triggered another round of battles between proponents and opponents of Arabic studies in Jewish-Israeli schools. In favour of Arabic and against this proposal were Arabic teachers, Military Intelligence and the Prime Minister's Office, while many in the Israeli public, including prominent figures in the Ministry of Education, stood on the other side of the debate hoping to weaken the study of the language. Gearing up for what was perceived to be their last opportunity to rescue Arabic, the National Committee of Israeli Arabic Teachers sent a public letter to all MKs asking them to vote against the law:

> The importance of Arabic is well known to all of you, due to our life in the region, the Arabs present here, the Arab [Jewish] immigrants [lit. *ʿolim*] and the significance of [studying] Arabic for Hebrew studies. But words and action are two different things. Out of tens of thousands of pupils who took the final exams last year, only 300 were examined in Arabic. In cities like Jaffa and Beʾer Sheva, Arabic [studies] has been totally absent. On top of this, following the retirement of Supervisor Ben-Zeʾev in August 1964, the Ministry of Education is looking for a part-time position only, rather than a full-time one ...[54]

The Knesset's Education Committee, which was asked to discuss the merits of Mikunis's proposal, decided to invite representatives of the Israeli Arabic Teachers Committee to explain the need for Arabic and the challenges that it faced. First to speak was Avraham Lavi, the head of the Teachers' Committee:

> Many should be blamed for the current situation, including head teachers, students and municipalities ... At the Ministry of Education, for example, we were told that we cannot swim against the tide [of public opinion]. But are we going to wait for the students to educate the Ministry? We demand the calling off of this 'cancellation decree' [lit. *gzerat ha-biṭul*], and, in the long run, seek to have a much more reasonable division between Arabic and French in schools.[55]

Lavi's words were supported by Meʾir Abulʿafia, a leading Arabic teacher who was invited to participate in the same meeting. According to Abulʿafia, Arabic was under constant attack:

> In the 9th grade Arabic needs to compete with French, and in the 12th grade it needs to compete with history ... and this is in the only

> 16 [high] schools that offer Arabic in the first place ... We [Arabic teachers] are being treated as if we were teaching Hottentot on the moon. This school subject is suffering since the perception is that everything that is Oriental is also Arab, and everything that is Arab is also dirty.[56]

Lavi and Abulʿafia, each in his own way, made it clear that Arabic was not only crucial to Jewish-Israeli society, but also that its status was very low. They pointed to a number of reasons for this: the language's poor social capital, the preference for European languages like French over Arabic and the general anti-Arab sentiments in Israeli society. 'The pupils will not educate the Ministry,' said Lavi, indicating strong opposition to Arabic studies among pupils while the reference to 'teaching Hottentot on the moon' is perhaps indicative of the Arabic teachers' low standing in the eyes of their colleagues and education officials.

Lavi and Abulʿafia's efforts – which were joined with pressure exerted by external bodies and particularly the Prime Minister's Office and IDF – bore fruit. A few days later, the Knesset Education Committee announced that, 'following the summaries that we heard on this topic, we recommend that the Ministry of Education reconsider its decision and not follow the cancellation proposal'. Instead, the Education Committee recommended taking active measures to strengthen the place of Arabic studies in schools.[57]

The Ministry of Education accepted the recommendation of the Committee, however it continued to be indecisive about the future of Arabic. As the teachers' letter stated, 'words and action' – at least in relation to the Ministry – were indeed two different things. For example, in December 1964, four months after Ben-Zeʾev's departure, the Ministry of Education still had not hired someone to replace him. In a letter to Rinot who was the Director of the Ministry, Lavi complained on behalf of the Arabic Teachers Committee:

> we do not know anything about the promised increase in Arabic hours in schools ... what we do know is that Supervisor Ben-Zeʾev retired from his position on 10 August 1964, and since then there has been no announcement regarding the future Supervisor of Arabic Studies ... We demand, for the sake of education, the appointment of a new supervisor as soon as possible.[58]

The year 1965 represented a continuation and intensification of trends from previous years: pressure on Arabic studies from below and above continued while the alliance between security and educational bodies intensified in response. Early that year, the Ministry of Education – following the efforts of the emerging 'Arabic lobby' composed of actors from Military Intelligence, the Prime Minister's Office and the Arabic Teachers Committee – established a committee called 'The Awareness Committee' (lit. *Ṿaʿadat ha-ʿEranut*). Its goal was to develop strategies for promoting the importance of studying Arabic in Jewish-Israeli schools. Clearly, this committee believed that studying Arabic was vital and that its status was in need of rehabilitation. Similar to previous committees, the members of this committee included representatives of the Ministry of Education, the Prime Minister's Office and the IDF. Appointed on the 22 January 1965, the Committee members met a number of times over the course of three months.[59] Their final report called for the establishment of Oriental Classes in more schools and they also advocated the instruction of Arabic as an obligatory subject in the regular school system.[60] Similar to such previous initiatives in relation to Arabic, the Committee's recommendations were not implemented. Indeed, the more things changed, the more they stayed the same.

In 1965, a new Arabic supervisor, Yaʿacov Eyal, was appointed. Previously, Eyal had served as supervisor of 'Oriental Classes' that, as noted, were established with clear political and security emphases. Eyal's promotion, therefore, further strengthened the securitisation of this subject, as will be seen. Eyal's more immediate and pressing concern, however, related to the low number of Jewish pupils studying Arabic in Israel. Soon after his appointment, the Deputy Director of the Ministry of Education – who was supportive of Arabic studies – sent Eyal a letter in which he highlighted this. Titled 'The Status of Arabic Language Studies in High Schools', the letter said:

> During meetings conducted in March 1965 with representatives of the Ministry of Education, the Prime Minister's Office and the IDF, an evaluation of previous decisions was made. It was highlighted that the attempt to encourage Arabic studies in the 9th grade and to establish new Oriental Classes was not successful ... This was also the case with regards to meetings with [the] head teachers ... It was then decided that only an administrative ordinance that will enforce Arabic studies in some of the schools will bear fruit ... I would like to re-emphasise that Arabic studies in Israel are in the midst of a very serious crisis [lit. *limud ha-ʿAravit ba-Arets natun be-mashber ḥamur*] and that only an energetic, comprehensive and speedy act may help us to rectify this situation ... If, God forbid, we will not be able to do

> so, we will soon be facing a situation in which the Israeli intellectual will be disconnected from the Arab reality that surrounds us, and we will not be able to fulfil the cultural, political and civil positions that require the knowledge of the language and culture of the Arabs.[61]

Copies of the letter were also sent to the Director of High School Pedagogy in the Ministry, the Adviser on Arab Affairs in the Prime Minister's Office and to Sharoni in Military Intelligence. It is striking to see this emerging network of Arabic education experts, and how decisions regarding Arabic studies – which were necessary for 'cultural, political and civil positions' – were taken by officials in education, politics and security. Even more striking is the complete absence of Arab-Palestinian intellectuals or pedagogues. This point will be returned to later in the book; however, it is important to note that in the pre-1967 period, Arabic no longer bore any association with Hebrew and the Jewish experience. Rather, in the best case scenario it was 'the language of the Arabs', and in the worst case the 'language of the enemy' and, as such, it seemed natural that it was managed and guided by experts who were exclusively Jewish and Israeli.

Arguably, the link between Arabic, security and politics was fully established and concretised in the general education system in 1965. In November of that year, the Director of the Ministry of Education asked his deputy, Shoḥat, to continue discussions on Arabic in Jewish schools and, similar to previous processes, he recommended that this take place 'through coordination with the military bodies involved'. Significantly, Shoḥat was asked to ascertain 'the levels of Arabic studies that the army needs' (lit. *Levarer mah ha-yediʿot ha-derushot le-tsarkhey ha-tsava*].[62] The army, for its part, was pleased to share this information with the education system and organised a meeting at the Ministry of Education for this purpose. Three Military Intelligence members (Lt Col. Pinḥas Ostrovsky, Sharoni and Maj. Y. Bar-Yehuda) and one member of Ministry of Education (Dr Michael Ziv, the Director of High School Pedagogy) attended this meeting. According to Ostrovsky, '[w]e emphasised during the meeting, over and over again, the importance of making Arabic an obligatory high school subject ... and that the matter is indeed very urgent'.[63] A similar sense of urgency was expressed in another letter that he wrote, in which he stressed that 'our most important demand is that the Ministry of Education make an immediate intervention to influence head teachers to prevent a further decrease in Arabic studies'.[64]

The military–education relationship emerging from Ostrovsky's letters, and from those of Shoḥat and Rinot from the Ministry of

Education, highlights a shared concern between the Ministry and Military Intelligence regarding Arabic teaching. Both sides (and in the Ministry, at least some of the officials) believed that urgent steps must be taken, and both acknowledged the significance of military involvement in this process.

Indeed, it seems that education officials and military officers working together during this period enjoyed a shared vision of Arabic and their work was characterised by cooperation, mutual regard and a crystallisation of the network of Arabic expertise. A letter from Supervisor Eyal to Sharoni sent in April 1966 gives a similar impression. In light of the upcoming final exams in Arabic, Eyal invited the senior Military Intelligence officer to accompany him on visits to schools; he wrote, 'I will be very happy if you could join me this year as an observer in the final oral exams in Arabic.'[65] To facilitate this cooperation, Eyal included the dates of all oral exams in Jewish-Israeli schools, asking Sharoni to select a date that was convenient for him. 'On any of these dates', wrote Eyal, 'I will be welcoming you with *Ahlan wa-sahlan*.'[66]

Sharoni's views display this relationship in a slightly different light. In an interview that he gave following his retirement from the standing army, he said:

> Since I was also an Arabic teacher [in the army] I have contacted [Arabic] teachers in schools and asked them to recommend to me good pupils who will fit Military Intelligence. Usually they would invite me to come to the class so that I can get a personal impression of the pupils. When I sat in the class, I endeavoured not to make any professional comment so as not to embarrass the teacher.[67]

Sharoni implies that he was invited to schools even though he himself never requested this. Moreover, he was treated like a guest of honour, evaluating pupils with the Supervisor of Arabic Studies prior to their transition into the military. This implies that, at least from the perspectives of Eyal and Sharoni, Arabic in school and Arabic in Military Intelligence no longer were separate entities, rather, they were a logical continuation of each other.

Notwithstanding the growing closeness between the Military Intelligence and Arabic teachers, the rejection of Arabic amongst Jewish-Israeli children, parents and head teachers continued to strengthen. Plummeting levels of Arabic in schools resulted in despair within the professional ranks of the Ministry of Education and this probably paved the way for the Military Intelligence to take the initiative. In

January 1967, Rinot, the Director of the Ministry of Education, held a high-level meeting to discuss the future of Arabic studies in high schools. 'Egalitarian' in nature, the meeting included three participants from each of the two bodies in attendance – the Ministry of Education and Military Intelligence. Representing the Ministry were the Director (Rinot), the Deputy (Shoḥat) and the Deputy Director of the Ministry (Dr Ya'acov Sarid), while the Military Intelligence was represented by the Chief of Intelligence (Yariv) and two senior officers (Col. Yitzḥak Bar-On and Sharoni). The meeting was dominated by Yariv, who in all likelihood, established the agenda and tone of the meeting. He was very straightforward in his summary of the situation, which he characterised as follows: 'the diminishing number of pupils who graduate with Arabic as a school subject has resulted in an evident shortage [of manpower] in military positions that require knowledge in Arabic'.[68]

As a result, the participants came to the conclusion that 'presenting a demand that would make Arabic obligatory in all high schools is not necessary; instead the Ministry of Education and the IDF will work together to focus on a few selected high schools that will agree to teach the language'.[69] The six attendees agreed that the IDF and the Ministry should jointly approach high school teachers in order to convince them that the study of Arabic was crucial to Israel. Moreover, each side agreed to present Arabic as an option of study in the boarding schools under their respective auspices.[70] These reciprocal relations – both in the context of working with boarding schools and in the 'joint effort of the Ministry and the IDF' – serve as a good example of the cooperation and complementary visions shared by the Ministry of Education and Military Intelligence.

The meeting strengthened the bonds that had developed during this period between the military and the education system in relation to Arabic. Within two months, Sarid, the new Director of the Ministry, established a 'Committee for the Advancement of Arabic Studies' (lit. *Ha-Va'adah le-Ḳidum ha-'Aravit*) to follow up on and reinforce the suggestions put forward by previous committees. The newly established Committee had four members and, like the previous committee, there was equal representation by the two partner organisations. The Ministry of Education was represented by Supervisor Eyal and Ziv (from the Directorate of High School Pedagogy). Bar-On and Sharoni participated on behalf of the Military Intelligence. Supervisor Eyal suggested adding another member to the Committee: Shmu'el Toledano, the Adviser on Arab Affairs in the Prime Minister's Office.[71] While there is no evidence as to whether Toledano actually participated in the discussions, it is worth highlighting this recommendation. Indeed, neither Eyal nor anyone else considered the appointment of a different 'kind' of figure to the Committee such as an Arabic teacher, a senior professional of the Ministry of Education or certainly not an Arab-Palestinian scholar. The request to include Toledano was a strategic choice: he was a senior figure from the Arab Bureau in the Prime Minister's Office who had formerly served in the SHAI Unit of the Haganah and subsequently (from 1953 to 1965) had served in the Mossad. Eyal's suggestion supports the argument that at this point, the teaching of Arabic was viewed as a security and political project even from the perspective of the Ministry of Education. The latter actively encouraged this development; in all likelihood, they realised that in order to support Arabic studies, they would need to build alliances with powers greater than themselves – be it the Prime Minister's Office or the IDF.

The nature of such collaboration is supported by the documentation. For example, in the conclusions published by the 'Committee for the Advancement of Arabic Studies', its members discussed how to overcome the problem of providing Arabic language classes in a situation of insufficient demand. The Committee decided that:

> If the number of pupils is not sufficient to open a class of Arabic studies in the school, these pupils will study as a special group ... and the expenses for this will be paid for jointly by the Ministry of Education and the IDF ... The estimated expenses are 20,000 Israeli Pounds in the first year of the project, 40,000 in the second year, 60,000 in the third, and 65,000 from then on ... the IDF will pay half of the sum, and the Ministry of Education needs to find a way to cover the other half ...[72]

This equal division of expenses is a good indication of the nature of the collaboration between the military and the education system, and most likely reflects the way in which they viewed their partnership. Apparently, by the middle of 1967, a formula to rescue Arabic studies from its crisis had been found. The agreement reached on this subject was due to a confluence of interests between the Ministry of Education and the Military Intelligence and was also made possible by the financial resources and increasing public regard for the military establishment. The IDF had proven to be a reliable 'partner' in the educational-military-political battle to keep Arabic studies alive.

As mentioned previously, these developments took place in parallel to the establishment of a unique programme of Arabic studies called the 'Oriental Classes'. This programme was implemented in a very different manner to that of the study of Arabic in the general education system. Furthermore, it was implemented in only a handful of schools. Therefore, it will be analysed separately.

A sentiment-free Arabic: the creation of the 'Oriental Classes'

As previously demonstrated, following the establishment of the State of Israel, the study of Arabic in Jewish-Israeli schools went through a period of crisis. One of the clearest and most obvious reasons for this crisis was the perceived lack of practicality in studying Arabic in the post-1948 era. In part, this was related to an almost complete separation between Arabs and Jews: Palestinian citizens of Israel lived under Military Government control that restricted their freedom of movement and confined them to specific geographical areas while Arabs in neighbouring countries such as Jordan, Egypt, Syria and Lebanon were behind *enemy* lines as far as officials in the state were concerned. Therefore, it should not come as a surprise that the lack of Jewish-Israeli Arabic-speaking personnel, and the urgent need to train and teach future experts in Arabic in Israel, was most strongly expressed by the two bodies that had contact or 'tasks' that involved interaction with Arabs: the Military Government and Military Intelligence. Indeed, they were the driving force behind the decision to create a separate format for Arabic studies that envisioned these studies taking place in a very small number of schools and having a course content that would address security, political and practical needs. This special course of study was meant to be the standard-bearer for Arabic studies in Jewish-Israeli schools. Called the 'Oriental Classes', this programme was known in Hebrew by three similar names: *Ha-Kitah ha-Mizraḥanit, Ha-Kitah ha-Mizraḥit* and *Ha-Mégamah ha-Mizraḥanit.*[73]

The first correspondence regarding the creation of these classes was in the form of a letter drafted by the Prime Minister's Adviser on Arab Affairs, Yehoshu'a Palmon. He sent it to three senior officials – Gen. Ḥayim Laskov, the head of the Department of Training and Courses in the IDF, Moshe Sharett, the Minister of Foreign Affairs, and Zalman Shazar, the Minister of Education. An analysis of his letter can shed light on the narrative, roots and initial rationale for the creation of the Oriental Classes. Titled 'Employee Training for the Arab Sector', Palmon wrote:

> The tasks that are required from us regarding the Arab minority in Israel, and the duties that are linked to our relations with neighbouring

> countries, necessitate a large number of [Arabic-speaking] employees. The current manpower that we have is not enough ... and those who in the past were [trained] to be in contact with the Arabs, such as [Arabic experts carrying out] anonymous intelligence tasks [lit. *'avodot almonim*], are now not suitable to represent the country. Signing peace agreements or a second round of war will require trained people. Already today, ministerial offices, the Military Government, the Arab Education [Department], the security services, the intelligence forces and the police are suffering [from a lack of trained personnel]. I therefore suggest the following: to select pupils in the 10th, 11th and 12th grades, and to give them throughout the course of their studies theoretical training in the Arab problems in Israel and in the Middle East, as well as Arabic language instruction. On graduating they will serve as Hebrew teachers in Arab schools, and so enhance their knowledge and contacts with the Arabs ... later to enter the military or civilian branches dealing with Arabic.[74]

Palmon's proposal to create an Arabic course that directly addressed the need for Arabic-speakers in the political and security establishments was discussed by Laskov and the officers in his department. Their response, submitted to Mordechai Maklef, the Deputy Chief of Staff, and signed by Laskov, was as follows:

> The arguments of the Adviser on Arab Affairs seem valid to me. I therefore suggest calling a committee, represented by the IDF, Ministry of Foreign Affairs, Ministry of Education and Ministry of Defence, to discuss this problem and to find ways to solve it, as well as to coordinate our work.[75]

Laskov continues:

> At the most immediate level, we need to help and support the Arabic classes that are currently taught in schools ... and to assign the graduates of these [Arabic] courses to appropriate positions in the IDF, ministerial offices and schools.[76]

Palmon's letter and Laskov's response raise a number of interesting points. First, they believe, rather simplistically, that knowledge of Arabic would help Israel in the pursuit of *peace* and *war*. This notion framed the teaching and learning of Arabic in political contexts and related fields rather than education and culture. Their viewpoint was supported by the idea of assigning pupils to 'appropriate positions in the IDF'. Last, the fact that the IDF's Department of Training and Courses offered its Arabic expertise to the Ministry of Education further signals the penetration of military matters into the field of Arabic studies.

Following from Laskov's letter, selected Jewish-Israeli high school pupils who had studied Arabic were sent to Palestinian areas in Israel to teach Hebrew. According to correspondence from 1950, following an order from the Ministry of Defence, 30 Jewish-Israeli high school graduates of Arabic from the Hebrew Reali School in Haifa were sent to teach Hebrew in Palestinian schools.[77] The security establishment viewed this initiative as an important opportunity to improve these pupils' command of Colloquial Arabic. Col. Binyamin Gibli, who then served as head of IDF Military Intelligence, pointed to the importance of this initiative. In a letter that he sent to his counterpart in the General Security System (Shabak), Gibli wrote: 'I believe that sending [Jewish-Israeli] Hebrew teachers to Arab schools will [also] be utilised by you in the future ... and, therefore, I think you should support it.'[78]

Despite its security importance, the initiative was limited in scope. The Prime Minister's Office sought a more comprehensive programme that, they believed, would fulfil Israel's 'national needs' regarding Arabic studies. In August 1950, Palmon sent Laskov another letter, this time titled, 'Training Senior Staff for the Arab Sector'. Palmon sought to answer the question 'what do we need?' as follows:

> We are in need of personnel for the Military Government, including [military] governors, representatives of [military] governors, district officers, staff officers ... and [military] governing units for territories that may be occupied by the IDF ... We are also in need of personnel in the Arab education system ... the General Security System[Shabak], the police and foreign affairs services ... and perhaps with possible stabilisation of peaceful conditions there may be a demand for professional [Jewish-Israeli] experts by countries in the Middle East.[79]

It is interesting to note the rationale 'peaceful conditions' that appears at the end of the list, behind the Shabak, the Military Government and the police. This may be an indication of how peace was perceived at the time – as low in priority and low in likelihood. The Military Government, and Palmon who was in close contact with its directors, identified more pressing needs that, among other things, related to controlling and administrating the Palestinian population in Israel.

As a result of Palmon's letter and his department's ongoing efforts to identify a more comprehensive and 'practical' programme of Arabic studies, the Hebrew-teaching project was in decline while use of the Oriental Classes was re-evaluated. In 1951, the Ministry of Foreign Affairs became involved in the matter; the Middle East Department of the Ministry of Foreign Affairs sent a letter to the Prime Minister's Office on this subject. Re'uven Shilo'aḥ, the head of Mossad (then called the Central Institute for Coordination of Intelligence Activities), also received a copy. The letter said the following:

> *Concerning Middle Eastern Studies in High Schools*: The Minister of Foreign Affairs gave his support for Palmon's programme ... and as an initial step we joined the experimental programme initiated by Dr Biram, Dr Ayalon and Mr Palmon in the Hebrew Reali School in Haifa ... The Ministry of Foreign Affairs took it upon itself to organise the curriculum and to find appropriate teachers ... Among them are Mr Shim'oni, Mr 'Ezra Danin and Mr Ya'ari ... It is important to note that the responsibility of the Oriental Classes in schools will be shared by the following institutions: the Prime Minister's Office, Ministry of Foreign Affairs, Ministry of Education, the IDF, universities and schools ... The assistance and interest shown by the army are highly important, especially since practically all graduates of the Oriental Classes will go to the IDF, and it will be an advantage to use their Arabic skills [taught in the Oriental Classes] for their military duties.[80]

The first point of interest regarding this correspondence is the name of the programme, 'The Oriental Classes' (lit. *Ha-Kitah ha-Mizraḥit*) – terminology that was first used in this letter in this context. This was the same name given to Haganah military units in charge of patrolling kibbutzim close to Arab-Palestinian population centres in the 1940s.[81] Indeed, the term 'class' (lit. *kitah*) in Hebrew has a double meaning: it can refer to the physical classroom in a school but is also used to indicate a military unit or a 'squad'. Perhaps metaphorically, perhaps not, this could indicate the military-educational weight of the word in Hebrew, but even more so regarding the explicit expression 'Ha-Kitah ha-Mizraḥit'. Thus, use of this term may suggest an ideological link, or association, between the 'Oriental Classes' of the Prime Minister's Office and the pre-state 'Oriental Classes' of the Haganah.

Also worth noting is that the six 'founding fathers' of the Oriental Classes mentioned in Ministry of Foreign Affairs letter, for the most part, shared a vision about the role of Arabic in serving the political needs of the newborn state. The letter, which also noted different spheres (academic, political and security-oriented), indicates an increasing tendency to demarcate the boundaries and borders of the discourse surrounding Arabic studies in Israel. Arabic studies were viewed as a Jewish enterprise and the different interest groups involved (school, university, IDF, Military Intelligence, Prime Minister's Office) were understood as complementing each other.[82] All six of the figures noted were Jewish men, primarily of Ashkenazi descent; all were prominent Zionist figures who supported Jewish–Palestinian separation; and all were part of, or had at least served in, military or security apparatuses connected to the Zionist movement. Representing different areas of expertise vis-à-vis Arabic, their roles served to define the limits of the field of Arabic studies. Their involvement, and the kind of group-think that accompanied it, also solidifies the acceptable boundaries of discourse surrounding Arabic thus serving as a bulwark against the entrance of other more integrative ideas and participants.

Irrespective of this, suggestions presented by the Ministry of Foreign Affairs were subsequently modified and their vision did not materialise until 1954. During the years 1951–53, the 'Oriental Classes' were not an organised programme; they were only implemented in the Hebrew Reali School in Haifa. As a project of the school and the Military Government, pupils studied Colloquial Arabic and Modern Standard Arabic and subsequently taught Hebrew and visited the Palestinian areas, which were under the control of the Military Government. Nevertheless, throughout this period, a process was taking shape whereby the field gradually became more organised and the central players – including the Prime Minister's Office, the Ministry of Education, the Military Government and Military Intelligence – began to define the nature of their cooperation.

A breakthrough took place in 1954; at that time the Prime Minister's Office – on identification of appropriate personnel and budgets – pushed the idea of the Oriental Classes forward. Early that year, the Adviser on Arab Affairs in the Prime Minister's Office asked Meʾir Kister to create a pilot programme for Oriental Classes that could be implemented more widely. Kister was a former presenter on the Haganah's Arabic Radio station who, at the time of his appointment, was in charge of Arabic language studies at the Reali School. Kister's programme, entitled 'The Oriental Classes', included Arabic studies, extracurricular lectures about the contemporary Middle East and annual visits to Palestinian cities and villages in Israel in order to practise Colloquial Arabic, familiarise themselves with Palestinian society and better understand the work of the Military Government. The pilot programme took place in 1954 in the

Hebrew Reali School in Haifa, a pilot that was judged to be a tremendous success by the Prime Minister's Office. Kister was thus officially appointed to supervise the programme that he had established and to oversee its implementation in additional schools. By 1956, it was in three schools: the Hebrew Reali School along with two schools in Tel Aviv – 'Ironi Alef and 'Ironi Dalet.[83]

The Oriental Classes came to fruition due to the close cooperation and shared interests of five different bodies: the Military Government, Prime Minister's Office, Military Intelligence, Ministry of Foreign Affairs and Ministry of Education. Their division of roles can be seen in relation to the arrangement and execution of a visit of the boys' group of the Oriental Classes (all the boys who studied in the three schools) to Nazareth at the end of the same school year. Laskov, who finished his term as the head of the Department of Training and Courses in the IDF and was appointed the Deputy Chief of Staff, wrote a letter to the head of the Military Government and the IDF Northern Command requesting assistance in arranging this endeavour. Under the title, 'Assistance of the IDF to the Oriental Class Pupils', Laskov wrote:

> Following a request I received from the Adviser on Arab Affairs in the Prime Minister's Office, I am asking you to help accommodate in a military camp 16 young men and one instructor of the Oriental Classes, who will stay one month [in the Palestinian areas] in order to study and get to know the customs of and conditions in the Arab village and surrounding ...[84]

Another letter about the same event was sent by Col. Gibli, the Chief of Intelligence, to the Northern Command. His letter, classified as 'restricted' and headed 'The Oriental Classes – Assistance', noted that:

> At the end of July a group of apprentices [lit. *ḥanikhim*] of the Oriental Classes will go out on a practical educational programme in the Arab area of the Command. *Responsibility*: the headquarters of the camp will be directly responsible for the administrative needs of this group. *Method*: the group will be accommodated in Nazareth in buildings designated by the [Military] Government and authorised by the Adviser on Arab Affairs ... The Military Governor, in coordination with the representatives of the Adviser on Arab Affairs, will issue written instructions about the customs and manners of Nazareth and the surrounding Arab areas.[85]

An analysis of both letters exposes some of the rationale underlying the programme. Both writers characterise accommodation of the pupils as 'assistance' (lit. *siyuʿa*) given by the IDF. Thus, it was clear that the IDF viewed the programme as a partner or satellite group, to which it offered assistance. In addition, while Laskov headed his letter 'Assistance to the Oriental Classes Pupils', he termed the pupils 'young men' (lit. *naʿarim*) and referred to their teacher an 'instructor' (lit. *madrikh*). Gibli neither used 'teacher' nor 'pupils' in his letter; rather, he referred to them as 'instructor' and 'apprentices' (lit. *ḥanikhim*). These terms indicate that the trip was viewed – at least by the army – through a militaristic rather than educational lens. The tone of the letters also indicates the seniority of the two officers involved. Involvement by the head of the Department of Training and Courses in the IDF implies that there was a close coordination between the education and military instruction units while the active participation of the Chief of Intelligence is indicative of the military orientation of this endeavour. It is important to note that as Palestinian villages and towns were controlled by the Military Government, scheduling any kind of visit required coordination with them. Nevertheless, the involvement of the Chief of Intelligence rather than an administrative unit in the Military Government in facilitating the visit demonstrates that the visit had an intelligence aim.

The group of pupils visited the 'Arab area' during the summer of that year. Soon thereafter, in late August, an evaluation was made of their visit. To this end, the Ministry of Foreign Affairs scheduled a meeting that included Emmanuel Marx who worked in their department of the Adviser on Arab Affairs, Nuzhat Darwish, a young Jewish-Iraqi woman who worked at the time for the Arabic Radio of the Israel Broadcasting Authority (IBA) and Avraham Yinon who was the teacher in charge of the boys' group. The evaluation developed by attendees at the meeting was forwarded by Marx to the Chief Military Governor, Col. Mishaʾel Shaḥam.[86] Marx's summary notes that in addition to the boys' group, which was supervised by Yinon, there was also a girls' group participating in the Oriental Class. The girls stayed in the Druze villages of ʿUsfiyya and Dalyat al-Karmel and were supervised by Darwish.

The evaluation prepared by meeting attendees defined the goal of these two one-month trips as follows:

> To get to know the surroundings and the way of life of the minorities ... to acquire confidence [for future tasks] from contact with the sons of minorities, and to recognise the significance of working among them. A secondary target is of course studying Colloquial Arabic.[87]

The meeting record also included a section entitled 'The Connection to the Military Government, and the Responses of the [Local] Population'. It contained the following:

> The connection to the Military Government and to the military authorities was an element that helped the young boys, and that ensured that no problems arose ... The Military Government willingly gave a hand to this project, in the belief that in the future it will be aided by those pupils ... The connection [of the pupils] to the Military Government did not result in the pupils being rejected by the [Palestinian] inhabitants ... Some argued that this is a project of the Ministry of Foreign Affairs, or that they are linked to some military project, but most of the [Palestinian] inhabitants accepted the explanation that these pupils were sent by the Ministry of Education ... All in all, the connection to the Military Government definitely promoted the aims of the project since it enabled accurate planning and supervision. It also prevented the pupils from developing a one-dimensional perception of the [Arab] problem, and helped them maintain an objective attitude, doing so without [establishing] an emotional relationship ... Regarding the girls: there was no way to prevent an emotional relationship, but one should not look at this negatively, since they were with Druze girls ...[88]

This summary highlights some of the main goals and concerns of the organisers. Concerns were mostly related to the possibility that the Palestinians would refuse to cooperate with the pupils, especially if they found out that the Ministry of Foreign Affairs and the Prime Minister's Office, not the Ministry of Education alone, were behind the initiative. They were also concerned that the pupils would establish friendships with the Palestinians and that, as a result, they would sympathise with their political oppression thus adversely affecting the structured way in which these pupils, the boys in particular, were meant to learn about the Palestinian 'other' as defined by members of the Israeli establishment. An indication of this can be seen in Marx's explicit wording, where he notes that they should study the Arabic language and Arab people and culture 'without [establishing] an emotional relationship'. Furthermore, Marx's summary indicates that the army was viewed as an objective balancing power, which could help the pupils achieve impartial and unbiased knowledge of Palestinian life and society.

Strikingly, Marx's comment 'regarding the girls' suggests a rather male-oriented attitude towards Arabic expertise. He seems to believe that the girls almost had a different nature – one that would make it hard for them to develop detached relationships with the Palestinians. Furthermore, his comments should be understood in light of the different ways in which the Israeli authorities perceived the Palestinians and the Druze. Because the Druze were viewed as being friendlier and more trustworthy, it is reasonable to assume that it was less risky for the Jewish and Druze girls to develop relationships; in all likelihood, this was part of the rationale for the selection of Druze villages as the target of their visit.

The final part of Marx's summary relates to the activities in which the pupils participated during their trip to the Palestinian areas. According to Marx, the pupils were matched with different Palestinian workers every day in order to become familiar with their jobs, families and opinions. Marx mentions the importance of dressing in an appropriate way; he notes that girls should avoid wearing trousers or short-sleeved shirts, and that the boys should not wear khaki-coloured clothes. Considerations of modesty drove this directive for the girls, however the explicit recommendation to avoid 'khaki-coloured clothes' indicates that the organisers' sought to diminish any association between the programme and the military.

At the conclusion of the first complete year of the Oriental Classes (including the visits to Palestinian areas), a summary was prepared. It was written by the Director of the Ministry of Foreign Affairs, Walter Eitan, further highlighting the political motivations behind the project. In a letter sent to the Director of the Ministry of Education, Eitan expressed his satisfaction with the programme to date and mentioned that he had been advocating for this project since 1950.[89] Eitan then elaborated on the reasons for his support, mentioning that 'during the last five years, the number of [Jewish-Israeli] Arabic experts has fallen, and the shortage in civil servants with proper training for Arab affairs has become severe'.[90]

Accordingly, Eitan asked the Director of the Ministry to ensure that Kister, the Supervisor of the Oriental Classes project continues to function in this role. He wrote:

> The establishment of the Oriental Classes has become a reality due to the efforts by Mr Kister, who was co-opted from the Hebrew Reali School in Haifa by the Adviser on Arab Affairs in the Prime Minister's Office, in order to head this programme ... Mr Kister is supposed to go back to the Reali School this coming school year. However, I am sure that you will find a way to continue his services.[91]

The Ministry of Foreign Affairs' efforts were successful and, following a few more such letters, advocates on his behalf managed to ensure that Kister continued to serve as Supervisor of the Oriental Classes project.

In September 1956, the beginning of the second academic year in which Oriental Classes took place as a structured programme, Shmu'el Divon, the Adviser on Arab Affairs in the Prime Minister's Office, wrote a letter to the Director of Ministry of Education. The letter, which was copied to Eitan and the Chief of Intelligence, sought to maintain the momentum generated during the pilot year of the Oriental Classes. Divon began the letter by explaining that the creation of the Oriental Classes was in response to the 'evident shortage of Arabic language experts within the Ministries and the IDF'.[92] He then briefly listed the subjects covered in the classes as follows: 'extensive studies of Colloquial Arabic, Modern Standard Arabic and Classical Arabic; information about the countries and people living in the Middle East; lectures on contemporary events in the Arab world; and a one-month stay during the summer in an Arab area aiming at studying the Arab mentality and way of life'.[93] Divon continued by describing the rationale and logic behind the programme:

> Our aim is to continue training the pupils of the Oriental Classes following their graduation from school. Therefore, during their service in the IDF, they will receive further training on Arab affairs and they will be allocated to military positions relating to Arab affairs. On finishing their military service, the gifted graduates of the Oriental Classes will continue their training in the Institute for Oriental Studies at the [Hebrew] University.[94]

This description could be described as 'the life cycle of the Israeli Arabic pupil', and could be seen as the roots of 'Israeli Arabic'. This 'life cycle' starts with pupils studying Arabic in school from a teacher who had previously served in Military Intelligence. They then complete basic studies and continue on to Military Intelligence followed by studies at the Institute of Oriental Studies of the Hebrew University in order to become Arabic experts. The final stage is a return to the education system, as teachers or Arabic experts, in order to prepare the next generation to follow in their footsteps.

The 'life cycle', as depicted by Divon, also indicates the shared perceptions of the dominant actors in this programme regarding the ultimate aim of training – to create a cadre of Jewish-Israeli Arabic experts. Furthermore, it exposes the way in which the military, academia and the school system worked together to advance this aim and the supremacy of political and military actors in this equation. Financial arrangements between the partners are also indicative of the nature of the partnership. According to Divon:

> Our office [the Prime Minister's Office] gave its [financial] support to all three schools, and was in charge of the lectures and the visits to the [Palestinian] villages ... Our office will carry on supporting the Oriental Classes financially during the next school year [1956–57]'.[95]

Regarding Supervisor Kister's salary, Divon highlighted the point that:

> Kister needs to be released, at least partially, from the Hebrew Reali School in Haifa, so that he can continue in his position as the Supervisor of the Oriental Classes. If this happens we will be ready to pay his salary and all further expenses.[96]

Indeed, the Prime Minister's Office played a central role in promoting the Oriental Classes. Supportive from the very beginning, the Office facilitated cooperation between the various actors and lent financial, administrative, ideological and educational support to the endeavour. Notwithstanding current levels of support, the Adviser on Arab Affairs in the Prime Minister's Office aspired to create an even more comprehensive Arabic scheme. In a letter to the Chief of Intelligence, Divon shared his vision about an intensive and multi-staged Arabic training programme. According to him, such a programme would begin in high school, continue through Military Intelligence and university and conclude with Arabic-oriented positions in Israeli society. In his letter, classified 'secret', Divon highlighted the importance of the Oriental Classes in filling gaps in 'all the positions related to Arab affairs in the political and administrative fields ... I am sure that the IDF generally, and Military Intelligence particularly, feel these shortages at least as much as we do.'[97] Following this opening, Divon presented his vision for the Oriental Classes:

> There is a need to develop cadres [of Jewish-Israeli pupils of Arabic] to fill these [Arab affairs] positions. This is a long-term plan that demands serious effort, as well as adjusting the system [lit. *hat'amat ha-manganon*] to these specific needs ... A plan has been prepared according to which future [Jewish-Israeli] personnel in the Arab field will go through a seven-year training programme ... During the first

> stage, the pupils will dedicate the last two years in school [Oriental Classes] to intensive Arabic language studies. During their [two-year] military service the pupils will be appointed to Arabic-oriented positions, where their previous training will be used. These positions will help them develop and gain further experience. At university, they will study for three years aiming at Oriental positions.[98]

This correspondence outlines the Prime Minister's Office's long-term vision for Arabic studies. Divon pointed out that it may be necessary to *adjust* the educational system in order to accommodate it to the needs and requirements of the Israeli political establishment. This would involve *diverting* Arabic studies in Jewish-Israeli schools into a more political, or at least 'national', direction. Furthermore, Divon created linkages between Arabic in schools, military service and academia, indicating the networked relationships between them and their joint goal of working together to create *experts* who can fulfil the needs of the state.

Towards the end his letter, Divon made another important reference to the connection between 'different' sources of knowledge in the Jewish-Israeli Arabic network:

> Currently, the Oriental Classes are implemented in four schools[99] and 65 pupils take part in the programme ... This could not have been done without the army's help ... Between the two stages [school and university] military service constitutes a connecting link [lit. *ḥulyah meḳasheret*] with fundamental importance, since only there can a man [lit. *ʾish*] acquire experience in practical positions, and only there can his character be evaluated.[100]

In this section of the letter, Divon notes the 'role' that the IDF plays in the creation of Israeli 'experts' on Arab Affairs; he terms it 'a connecting link'. It is also worth mentioning his emphasis on *men* studying Arabic. This may have been related to a number of factors, including a shortage of males studying the subject, the fact that the military was and continues to be dominated by men and that there was a greater need for men in Arabic-oriented positions within the IDF.[101]

The increasingly militarised and male-dominated tone of the Oriental Classes was reflected in preparations leading up to the second cohort of pupils visiting Arab areas in 1957. Emmanuel Marx, who worked at the office of the Adviser on Arab Affairs, used military terminology to describe the programme to the Northern Command's Military Governor. Indeed, he referenced the 'rear base' (lit. *basis ʿorpi*), a term heavily associated with military connotation and values, when describing the boys' meeting place. While the visit clearly had an educational purpose, this was embedded in a dominant political and military framework. Marx also referenced the military connection to the visit when he asked the military governor '*to assess and approve our programme ...* as well as to choose the final village [in which the programme will take place] ... and to prepare the families with whom the boys will stay'.[102]

Following from Marx's letter, the Military Governor selected Peḳiʿin (Al-Buqayʿā), a village mostly populated by Druze, as the location for the visit.[103] The programme, which lasted three weeks, concluded in August 1957. Avraham Yinon, who again accompanied the boys as their teacher, submitted a comprehensive summary of the event. Titled 'Summary of the Colloquial Arabic Course', his report highlighted a number of important issues. First, Yinon noted that some of the Palestinians made the connection between the pupils of the Oriental Classes and the Military Government:

> Our connection with the army is rather essential, but it gives rise to questions [being asked] among the inhabitants. Since we cannot deny this connection, and since it has been revealed to be very useful ... I recommend acknowledging the truth. I cannot see any civilian body that can replace the army.[104]

The last sentence suggests that, if asked about the visit, participating pupils were instructed to deny its connection to the Military Government. Elsewhere in his summary, Yinon indicated satisfaction with the visit to Peḳiʿin. He mentioned that the boys visited 'local workshops, garages, and the cigarette factory ... the Military Governor's Office, reception [and] ... the District and Military Court'.[105] This, according to Yinon, provided the pupils with the opportunity 'to get to know the nature of the local Arab and to understand his mentality'. Immediately after writing 'Arab mentality', Yinon added in brackets: 'I hate to use this term.'[106] His awareness regarding the problematic nature of essentialising the Arab 'mentality' did not prevent him from doing this.

The final part of Yinon's summary focused on how the programme gave him a chance to learn a great deal about his pupils. He wrote:

> I got to know them extremely well ... Therefore, and if we want to use them in the security establishment later on [lit. *laʿasot bahem shimush biṭḥoni*] ... I recommend observing [their behaviour while staying in

the Arab villages] carefully in a way that will help us evaluate their skills ... I will send a separate report about this subject.[107]

Yinon finished his summary by noting that 'some of the boys displayed a serious attitude to the Arab problem in the country. It was their first experience with it and it seems that some would like to see it as part of an ongoing, *sentiment-free,* relationship' (lit. *roman be-hemshekhim, bli senṭimenṭim*).[108]

The explicit mentioning of the *sentiment-free* relationship that the pupils were meant to develop in relation to Arabic is telling. Indeed, it echoes Yinon's statement a year earlier where he hoped that the boys who visited Nazareth would do so 'without establishing an emotional relationship' with local Arab-Palestinians. Clearly, Yinon, along with other officials, feared that study of Arabic and an encounter with its speakers would result in the creation of positive emotional and ideological bonds. Yinon's words were a warning to educators and others in charge of the Oriental Classes, indicating that they should take measures to *tame* the study of the language. Perhaps this is why officials demonstrated a clear preference for Jewish-Israeli officials and the IDF in Arabic studies; only they could model an appropriate and 'objective' attitude towards this topic. This *tamed* version of Arabic, which has to be kept sentiment-free and shared with IDF experts, was the beginning of the 'Israeli Arabic' that took shape in the country.

As graduates of the Oriental Classes entered the army, the IDF – including the Military Government – took on an increasingly central role in evaluating the programme. This was in evidence when graduates of the first year of the programme (beginning in 1955) entered the army in 1958. In January 1958, an officer in the Military Adjutancy to the Adviser on Arab Affairs sent a letter to all Oriental Classes teachers titled, 'Recruitment of the Graduates of the Oriental Classes'. The military noted that, 'As we want to recruit the Oriental Classes' pupils into the Military Intelligence Directorate, we will be grateful for your help ... Please forward us details of the Oriental Class graduates, including their names, father's names, dates of birth, ID details, school and home addresses.'[109] Similar letters can be found relating to subsequent years, which indicates that the sharing of such information had become routine.[110]

Also beginning in 1958, the IDF started requesting pupil evaluations from teachers. For example, in a letter classified 'secret', the Adviser on Arab Affairs wrote to Lt Col. Yitzḥak Halperin from Military Intelligence as follows: 'I forward you a list of all pupils finishing their studies in the Oriental Classes this year, and whose knowledge [of Arabic] seems to be adequate for service in Military Intelligence ... I attach also the [Arabic] teachers' evaluations of pupils.'[111] Thus, schools routinely shared information about pupils with Military Intelligence, either directly or through the mediation of the Adviser on Arab Affairs.[112] Moreover, the monitoring of pupil progress continued during their IDF service. This was the subject of correspondence between Stendel from the Office of the Adviser on Arab Affairs and Sharoni from Military Intelligence. In a letter titled, 'Graduates of the Oriental Classes at the Military Intelligence Directorate', Stendel wrote to the senior Military Intelligence officer, Sharoni, that:

> Following our conversation ... I would like to know the scale of annual recruitment of Oriental Classes graduates to Military Intelligence, and how successfully they have adjusted ... I would like to know if there are enough graduates [for Military Intelligence] ... and whether it is necessary to expand the Oriental Classes in Israeli high schools according to the needs of Military Intelligence ... (lit. *be-het'em le-tserakhaṿ shel ḥeil ha-modiʿin*) ...[113]

In this correspondence, the army emerges as the ultimate recruiter of pupils from the Oriental Classes, with the Prime Minister's Office serving as the 'connecting link' between the education system and the IDF. The army, accordingly, was an actor whose 'needs' must be reflected in the size and activities of these classes. The same mediator role is evident in IDF support of extracurricular educational activities. A letter that Marx in the Prime Minister's Office sent to schools with Oriental Classes is consistent with this pattern. According to Marx:

> The IDF has recently published the *Middle East Book* that contains an account of contemporary Arab countries as well as a report regarding the general problems of the region. This book was originally written for internal IDF use, but the military authorities have approved the Prime Minister's Office's request and will be happy to provide the Oriental Classes with a few copies of it.[114]

Another letter sent by the Office of the Adviser on Arab Affairs to Military Intelligence reveals similar cooperation, but in this case relates to acquiring Arabic newspapers. The Adviser on Arab affairs asked Maj. Noʿam Ṭal 'to provide us with Jordanian newspapers to be used in Arabic language studies of the Oriental Classes'.[115]

The alliance between the Oriental Classes and the Military Intelligence was based on financial, administrative, pedagogical and ideological grounds. Strikingly, partnerships in this field were so strong that Kister was able to correspond directly with Military Intelligence units and to recommend specific pupils to them. An example of this was found in a letter sent from Intelligence-5, an Israeli OSINT (Open Sources Intelligence) Unit, to the IDF adjutant, which stated that: 'Mr Kister recommended [candidate's name] to the post of ... in the unit. We therefore intend to integrate him [the candidate] as an [Arabic] newspaper analyst.'[116]

The education system and IDF actively cooperated in implementing the Oriental Classes programme, thus strengthening the sense that this was a joint endeavour. Indeed, the two agencies, together with the Military Intelligence and the Prime Minister's Office organised annual gatherings whereby graduates of the programme who had subsequently completed their military service in Military Intelligence, met with the programme initiator, the Adviser on Arab Affairs, senior Military Intelligence officers and Arabic teachers. These meetings focused on the importance of the way in which participation in the Oriental Classes contributed to future service in Military Intelligence.[117]

A summary of the 1958 annual gathering demonstrates that it aimed 'to understand to what extent the knowledge of the graduates in Arabic is being used ... and what their plans for the future are'.[118] This same document also mentioned that the 'majority of the soldiers expressed their desire to continue their studies following the completion of their service, and some of them have mentioned specifically the humanities: Middle Eastern and Arabic studies'.[119] These annual gatherings were usually held at the military headquarters in Tel Aviv (Ha-Ḳirya) and often in the presence of senior military officials. Indeed, meetings such as the one noted here are an additional indication of the central role that the IDF played in what others would have considered to be a strictly educational matter.[120]

The increasing importance of this programme in the name of security is also demonstrated by the fact that Oriental Class teachers were given an exemption from reserve service due to them accompanying pupils on their annual visits to Palestinian areas.[121] A number of documents note that Military Intelligence recognised 'educational' visits to 'Arab areas' as an alternative to active reserve service for Arabic teachers in Military Intelligence. For example, a letter sent in June 1958 by an officer in the Chief of Intelligence office to the Adviser on Arab Affairs included a confirmation note saying: '[f]ollowing my conversation with you, I would like to inform you that we have spoken with the commander of the [reserve] unit in which the three teachers accompanying the Oriental Classes serve ... and it was agreed that they will not be called for duty this year'.[122] According to a letter written by Divon, the Adviser on Arab Affairs, and sent to Lt Col. Ya'acov Ḥefets, the Commander of the Planning Department of Military Intelligence, the practice was repeated the following year. Divon wrote:

> This year, as every year, pupils in the Oriental Classes will spend three weeks in Arab villages, in order to study and practice their Colloquial Arabic and to gain familiarity with the Arab way of life. The pupils are being accompanied by their teachers ... In previous years, there was an arrangement with Military Intelligence whereby these teachers, who are part of the reserve force of Military Intelligence, will accompany the pupils and this will be considered as their reserve duty. I would therefore be grateful if you could make sure that this arrangement maintains its validity during this year. If this does not happen, the whole project [of visiting Arab areas] will be put into doubt. It is perhaps unnecessary to mention the significance of this project for the pupils, who by and large will be serving in the IDF, mainly in Military Intelligence ...[123]

Indeed, there was a clear connection and strengthening of relations between participation in Oriental Classes and Military Intelligence, along with a 'closed circuit' of connections and expertise between Military Intelligence, teachers of Oriental Classes and their pupils. Teachers, who had already served in Military Intelligence, benefited by being excused from reserve service and their exemption was directly related to their work in preparing pupils for future service with Military Intelligence. While it is well established that the school system plays an important role in encouraging pupils to serve in the military,[124] in the specific case of Arabic the nature of this service was virtually synonymous with Military Intelligence.

In June 1958, two additional groups of pupils from the Oriental Classes spent time in Arab areas. One group visited the Triangle region, near the centre of the country, while the second went to Nazareth in the north. The group in the Triangle region visited both Ṭayyiba and Al-Ṭīrā – but only during the day. Overnight, participants were housed in the nearby kibbutz of Ramat ha-Kovesh (meaning, Height of the Conqueror) and their activities were based in this location. Some 50 pupils from six different schools running the Oriental Classes took part in the programme that summer, in both locations.[125]

In a change from previous years, and according to available documentation, pupils were given very specific instructions on how to behave and what to wear. This, as will be now shown, indicates an increased awareness of the politically sensitive topics that the organisers believed that pupils may have to deal with and how to prevent them from coming up. It also signalled attempts by the military to control even more tightly the information that pupils could be exposed to during their visit.

The instructions that pupils received from the office of the Adviser on Arab Affairs prior to the visit are telling. Pupils were instructed to 'behave in a polite and courteous manner. It is forbidden to get involved in political debate, or to voice political opinion ... Clothing must be clean and tidy ... It is better if clothes do not have any military implications (e.g., khaki colour, military belt, etc.)'.[126] Another letter, titled 'Restricted', mentioned that weapons (most likely carried by teachers) should be inside their rucksacks and that each group should have at least one weapon.[127] Furthermore, the organisers tightly controlled and restricted methodologies for gaining information about Palestinians. In accordance with a pre-set time frame, the project started with 'a guided tour given by an official representative of the [Military] Government, who will provide information on the area and will explain about the people living in it to the pupils' (lit. *ʾish ha-mimshal she-yasbir et ha-ʾezor ṿe-et toshavaṿ*).[128] The fact that the Palestinians were not given an opportunity to speak about themselves at this initial stage of the visit is indicative of the attitude towards them. The Palestinian citizens of the state were viewed as a subject of study and, ultimately, control. Thus, in quite a poetic way, the answer to Gayatri Chakkravorty Spivak's question, 'Can the subaltern speak?' was, in this case, and according to the Israeli Military Government, a decisive 'No.'[129]

Indeed, in the eyes of the organisers of the Oriental Classes, Palestinians were to be accessed and understood through the mediation of Israeli officials. As such, Military Government soldiers were in possession of 'all' relevant knowledge. While the visit was supposed to give pupils the opportunity to meet the Military Governor and the Military Government's staff and learn about their work as well as about 'the [Palestinian] coffee house, selling and buying, the waiter, the merchant ... the barber, the carpenter, the farmer ... manners, politeness',[130] the Military Government was firmly in control of the agenda and framed the nature of the knowledge that pupils were meant and encouraged to acquire from the very beginning. As such, those in charge – especially Military Government and actors associated with it – were considered to be experts and objective mediators between Jewish pupils and Palestinians. By creating highly supervised and structured visits, the military created a filter through which Jewish-Israeli pupils understood and analysed Palestinians during the course of their three-week visit. Arguably, this strictly regimented study experience also cemented the pupils' – if not the teachers' – perspective that the IDF was an expert authority on Arab affairs, including Arabic studies.

The schedule of activities for pupils visiting the Triangle region also reflects the militarily-orientated nature of the programme. Pupils began their daily routine by 'waking up at 6, followed by morning exercises between 6:05 to 6:15, washing and polishing [their shoes] between 6:15 to 7:00 (lit. *raḥatsah ṿe-tsiḥtsuʾaḥ*), then cleaning their rooms'.[131] This timetable, which looks suspiciously similar to an IDF basic training course, strongly hints at the connection between the two experiences.

Summaries produced by accompanying teachers further reflect the militaristic nature of this endeavour. The three teachers with the group in the Triangle region wrote that, for the first time, accommodation was not divided into a boys' camp and a girls' camp, but that there was one camp that included both boys and girls. According to the teachers, this 'helped create an atmosphere of a youth labour camp, and not a pre-military course, as experienced in previous years'.[132]

This same document also notes the use of Arabic media as a means of study during the visit. The teachers wrote that 'From 16:00 to 18:30 daily the pupils received lessons in Colloquial Arabic, then listened to the radio newscast in Arabic and discussed in Literary Arabic the themes mentioned. They then read the Arabic newspaper *Al-Yawm*.'[133] These activities are significant as the learning of contemporary Arabic vocabulary of political issues and the understanding of news items (particularly in order to be able to translate them from Arabic to Hebrew) is a feature of Arabic studies in Jewish-Israeli schools today, and is related to the work of the open-source intelligence (OSINT) units of Military Intelligence. This stands in contrast to the study of other languages in Israel, such as English or French, which do not place the same emphasis on newscasts, newspapers and political vocabulary. Indeed, the Oriental Classes had very specific instrumental and political purposes that only became more pronounced as time passed.

The sources of information chosen were not coincidental; pupils learned Arabic from a specific newspaper, *Al-Yawm*, and listened to Arabic via a specific radio station, *Ṣawt Isrāʾīl* (The Voice of Israel).

Both of these media outlets were officially approved Israeli 'hasbarah' ('propaganda' or 'public diplomacy') outlets whose primary purpose was to influence Palestinian discourse and politics via the dissemination of Israeli-run programmes in Arabic.[134] Indeed, pupils could have read *Al-Ittiḥād*, the communist party newspaper, which, at the time, was the most influential Arabic media outlet in Israel.[135] Likewise, they could have also listened to *Ṣawt al-ʿArab*, broadcast from Cairo, which was highly popular among the Palestinian citizens of Israel.[136] However, this would have exposed the pupils to genuine Arab and Palestinian national discourse and voices representing the Palestinian street. Instead, organisers relied on *Al-Yawm* and *Ṣawt Isrāʾīl* that were initiated, headed and edited by Jewish-Israeli experts, and were therefore an extension of the permitted discourse of the field of Arabic studies. This was one more avenue by which pupils were exposed to knowledge sources approved of by the Israeli military establishment both in the summer programme, and in general.

This trend of military dominance in and control over the summer programme continued into 1960. That year, 90 participants visited Nazareth.[137] In a slight change, in addition to the Military Government, the governmental 'Hasbara Department' was also involved – at least in selecting speakers and lecture topics for the visit. The choice of topics is telling; one Palestinian was invited to discuss 'youth criminality in the Arab community' while the Deputy Mayor of Nazareth at the time was asked to speak about 'the Arab tradition' (lit. *ha-masoret ha-ʿAravit*). Pupils also watched a film in Arabic and a dance performance by an 'Oriental group' (lit. *lehaḳah Mizraḥit*).[138] This programme of activities seemingly reflects the specific messages that the establishment wanted pupils to be exposed to and the Orientalist discourse that contextualised such studies.

Prior to the visit, pupils spent time studying the Palestinian community in Israel and, in particular, Arab values. Barukh Mazor, a teacher of Arabic in the Oriental Classes, emphasised the importance of understanding the specific value of honour and respect. He noted that, 'when the Arab respects you, he actually respects himself'.[139] In an article dedicated to the required preparations for a visit to the 'Arab areas', Mazor stressed the importance of studying the masculine ideals of 'murūʾa' (an Arabic concept of virtues) that originates in the pre-Islamic *Jahiliyyah* (the 'Age of Ignorance', which refers to the pre-Islamic period in Arabia). He concluded that 'these ideals are still the ones that guide the Arab in the present day, in his house, in his society and when meeting outsiders'.[140] Among other topics that Mazor also recommended in preparation for the visit was the study of 'the Arab *ḥamūlā* [extended family], its origins and status'.[141] Mazor's views on the matter present us with a glimpse into the way in which Palestinian society was perceived and studied by Israeli pupils in the Oriental Classes. It was presented as traditional, static or 'frozen in time' and driven by archaic and different concepts. This viewpoint echoes those of Arab experts with Orientalist orientations along with general Israeli conceptions whereby Arab-Palestinians were considered to be culturally inferior.[142]

Following this period of preparation, the pupils visited Nazareth in July 1960. At the time, the Oriental Classes programme was at its zenith, thus there is a significant amount of documentation regarding this particular programme. Perhaps the most interesting piece of documentation was a list of 13 'Rules of Behaviour in Nazareth' drafted by the Adviser on Arab Affairs. Pupils and teachers were required to carry this list with them at all times as these rules were of primary importance. Due to the centrality of this document, a translation of it is presented in full here as Document 2.1.[143]

Document 2.1 Rules of Behaviour

1. Nazareth is an Arab city. The customs of its people, and the way they think, do not match the [situation in] Hebrew cities in Israel. Remember that not everything that is acceptable in your society is also acceptable here.
2. The Arabs generally, and the people of Nazareth in particular, are sensitive to your responses, even if they do not articulate it. Therefore, be careful with your words.
3. It is forbidden to be within the boundaries of Nazareth and be scruffily dressed. Therefore, pay attention to your cleanliness and dress.
4. While passing through the city streets behave in a civilised manner, avoid shouting or speaking loudly. While talking to a [Palestinian] inhabitant [lit. *toshav*] listen to him patiently, and answer politely and succinctly.
5. Accept in a democratic spirit any opinion that will be voiced to you, even if this opinion is most unacceptable to you.
6. You are ordered not to enter into any political debate, and not to voice any opinion regarding Israeli–Arab relations (lit. *yaḥasey Yisrael–ʿArav*) and the minority problem in the country. On these topics, listen carefully but do not join in the argument.

(continued)

Document 2.1 Continued

7. You need to reject politely any request voiced by a [Palestinian] inhabitant who wants you to help him, in writing or orally, with any matter involving public or private bodies. Remember, you are not a channel for any requests or complaints.
8. While exploring the city with your friends do not respond to any possible irritations.
9. The status of the woman in Arab society is very different from that in Hebrew society. Therefore, avoid joking about this matter, or behaving in a free manner, as you would allow yourself in your society.
10. Stress the fact that you are a pupil, and that your visit to the city is not intended to educate the [Arab] public. Stress your attitude regarding the Arabic language as a bridge for building relations.
11. You are not allowed to visit [Palestinian] inhabitants without receiving permission from your instructor. Moreover, you are not allowed to invite guests from outside during the study period [in Nazareth] unless you received permission to do so from your instructor.
12. It is forbidden to receive any kind of inducement from inhabitants, either through gifts or any other way. It is forbidden to be a burden on the guest and to eat at his table.
13. Be careful not to offend Muslim or Christian religious values or holy sites.

Source: 'Rules of Behaviour in Nazareth', attached to the letter from Na'im Sofer, Bureau of the Adviser on Arab Affairs in the Prime Minister's Office, to the teachers of the Oriental Classes in the Israeli education system, in preparation for their visit to Nazareth. The letter is dated 8 May 1960, ISA/GL-13919/10 (Hebrew).

This fascinating document demonstrates that the Israeli separatist establishment was driven by the belief that there were fundamental differences between Arabs and Jews. Furthermore, Jewish values were presented as being modern while Arab values were believed to be outmoded. The document is also another concrete demonstration of the role that the military and political establishments played as mediators of officially sanctioned knowledge about the Palestinians and how this knowledge pervaded Jewish-Israeli society to such an extent that it was regarded as common sense.

The style and tone of the document is bureaucratic and institutional, resembling military orders. Thus, in all probability, the military government formulated the rules. The central message of the document is that

Arab/Palestinian areas or cities are very different from those inhabited by Israeli Jews and that the people who live there also behave differently. Expressions such 'the way they think', 'the Arabs generally' and 'the people of Nazareth in particular' indicate that the Jewish-Israeli side held an essentialist perspective of the 'Orient'. This perspective is further reinforced by the following statements: 'do not match the [situation in] Hebrew cities in Israel'; '[This] is very different from that in Hebrew society'; 'acceptable in your society'; '[Avoid] behaving in a free manner, as you would have allowed yourself in your society.' All such statements serve to accentuate the differences through essentialism and simplification. Pupils are induced to be: 'careful with [their] words'; and that ' It is forbidden to be [in Nazareth] scruffily dressed. Pay attention to your cleanliness and dress'; to 'avoid shouting'; 'accept ... any opinion'; 'reject any request'; '[y]ou are not allowed to visit'; and 'you are not allowed to invite'; are all also integral aspects of this perspective.

Another interesting characteristic of this document is the preference shown in it for the term 'Hebrew' over 'Jewish'. Concepts such as the Hebrew man, the Hebrew language or Hebrew work are central to Zionism. Not only does the document reinforce Zionist thought, but it also further solidifies points of difference between the two societies. By emphasising the *Hebrew* nature of Jewish-Israeli society, the writer presents the Hebrew language and culture and its speakers as the antithesis of Arabic and Arab culture, and the way in which the two are viewed as binary and unbridgeable.

The conceptualisation of Arab-Palestinians is also worth noting. They are referred to generically as 'the Arabs' or as 'the minority problem'; in a particularistic way as 'the Nazareth people in particular'; or in a non-descriptive manner as 'inhabitants'. Notable for its absence is the fact that at no point are Arabs described or referred to as *citizens* of the State of Israel. Furthermore, the word 'Palestinian' does not appear in the document as this term would conjure up notions of national identity, the history of the group and their legitimate rights and aspirations. Paradoxically then, while the Oriental Classes brought the pupils physically closer to Palestinian society, their political knowledge and aim only distanced them from the Arab-Palestinian people. This, as will be argued later, is a central characteristic of 'Israeli Arabic'. In other words, through a process of defamiliarisation, anonymisation and exclusion, Palestinian citizens of Israel were turned into 'inhabitants' of 'Arab areas'. This pattern remains consistent to this day in Jewish-Israeli society; by and large, Jewish-Israelis ignore or downplay the extent to which Arab Palestinians are citizens, are a Palestinian national group or 'Palestinian citizens of Israel'. Instead, they tend to emphasise the Arab-Palestinians' general and undifferentiated *Arabness* using the term 'Israel's Arabs'.[144]

A final observation regarding the document relates to a seeming desire to remove political elements from contact with Palestinians. When it instructs its readers: 'You are ordered not to enter into any political debate' and '[do] not voice any opinion regarding Israeli–Arab relations', it is making a deliberate attempt to prevent discussions on probably the most important subject for Palestinians: namely their political situation, discrimination against them in Israel and their restricted life under the Military Government. This restriction most likely aligns the pupils' experience with established Military Government and military goals and was consistent with the military's political goals, fears and aspirations. Indeed, this is probably the real rationale for the comprehensive ban on being hosted by Palestinian families and on receiving gifts from them. While the Israeli security establishment would claim that these rules were designed to protect the safety of the pupils, perhaps, in fact, the organisers hoped to eliminate the possibility that pupils would 'owe' anything to the Palestinians and would develop relations of reciprocity, or that such encounters would engender positive feelings. Indeed, in the words of Avraham Yinon, relationships formed during the visit were intended to be 'sentiment-free'.

In the 'Rules' list, the phrasing of the ban on receiving gifts and eating in Palestinian homes is also telling. Pupils and teachers were instructed not to 'burden' Palestinian hosts. However, the text in Hebrew features a linguistic mistake: instead, it says that one should not burden the Palestinian 'guest'. The Hebrew word for guest (*ore'aḥ*) was interchanged with the Hebrew word for host (*me'are'aḥ*). While this may have been an innocent oversight, when examining this rule in context, and especially in light of an ongoing attempt to erase Palestinian feelings of belonging, the 'mistake' could be understood to mean that the Military Government and the Oriental Classes instinctively perceived themselves as the real 'hosts' while the Palestinians, even when residing in their own villages, were actually viewed as 'guests'.

The visit to Nazareth and its accompanying list of rules was the focus of a newspaper article written by ʿAtallah Mansour, a Palestinian citizen of Israel. At the time, Mansour was working for *Haaretz* newspaper and served as its first Arab-Palestinian journalist. In an article that he wrote titled, 'The Oriental Classes Pupils in Nazareth', Mansour gave an overview of the pupils' visit and, following from interviews conducted with some of the pupils, shared his impressions of the project.

He wrote: 'Most of them said that they were surprised when they met with Arabic-speakers ... and when I asked them what was most surprising they said: that they are like us.'[145] According to Mansour, 'One of the boys took a piece of paper out of his rucksack on which was printed the 13 rules of behaviour ... the boy told me: "had we been to Netanya [a Jewish-Israeli city] we would not have been given this".'[146] At that point, Mansour asked the pupil to give him the piece of paper and quite spontaneously decided to read the rules out loud in front of the boys. Having the Palestinian 'other' read the rules and regulations in Hebrew – guidelines that indicated how they should behave when approaching people like him – in the presence of the Jewish-Israeli youths was most likely a powerful experience for the boys. Mansour summarised their reactions as follows:

> I read all of them [the rules] out loud, and the boys looked down. Nobody wanted to look me in the eye. I asked them: what do you think of these? One of them told me that from these rules we understand that we are in a hostile environment. His friends were silent ... Hundreds of people visit Nazareth every day. No one harasses them. No one attacks them ... Is the aim of Arabic studies in Israel to intimidate the pupils in order to prevent them from being in contact with the Arabs? Naʿim Sofer from the Prime Minister's Office has told me that the rules were written in order to prevent inconveniences.[147]

Mansour's report, rather moving indeed, raises a number of key points. First, the rules gave the pupils the impression that they were in hostile territory and that they needed to exercise caution in order to protect themselves. Second, in light of the fact that the pupils were amazed to find out that the Arabs that they met were much more 'like us' than they had imagined, it is reasonable to assume that the Oriental Classes studies impressed upon them that Arab society and culture were very different from anything else.

It seems that despite the pupils' personal interactions with Arab Palestinians and due to the impressions that they formed as a result of these experiences, their trip was still dominated by a pervasive sense of fear. This fear was a natural and logical outcome of the educational content of the programme. So while the trip enabled physical proximity, in actuality its outcome was intercultural distance. Mansour's question, 'Is the aim of Arabic studies in Israel to intimidate the pupils in order to prevent them from being in contact with the Arabs?' is one that continues to resonate throughout the pages of this book.

In my view, the Oriental Classes established a clear boundary dividing Jewish-Israelis and their Palestinian neighbours; as such, it did everything but serve as a 'bridge'. Sitting at the fault line between those two groups, and serving as a kind of mediating force were Jewish-Israeli Arabic experts and Orientalists (*Mizraḥanim*). They functioned as guards whose aim was to maintain and promote the ongoing segregation between the groups. Gil Eyal believes that while this process began prior to the founding of the state, it intensified in 1948 and subsequently. He characterises it as follows:

> The cognitive territory of the 'Orient' was carved into different and separate jurisdictions, each claimed by a different group of experts: intelligence, government, *hasbara* (propaganda) and the absorption of immigrants. The Orient was disenchantment, while *Mizraḥanut* (Oriental studies) became separatist, no longer straddling the seams of Jewish–Arab symbiosis but occupying a watchtower, overlooking the hardening boundary between [Jewish] Israelis and Arabs. A younger generation of Israeli-born Orientalists have applied themselves to this disenchanted and fragmented universe, no longer seeking there the secret of Jewish renewal but rather searching for 'overt intelligence on the intentions, plans and deeds' of Arab leaders and regimes ...[148]

Oriental Classes visits to the 'fragmented Orient' – within the boundaries of Israel – was, without a shadow of a doubt, an indication of the emerging discourse driving Arabic and Oriental studies in Israel. All aspects of the programme pointed to the increasing role of the military in shaping this programme, including annual visits to the 'Arab areas,' yearly gatherings held at IDF headquarters and military and civilian evaluations of pupils in the programme. These elements served the additional function of ensuring the continuation and preservation of networked institutions involved in this endeavour – the Ministry of Education, Military Intelligence, the Military Government and the Prime Minister's Office. As a single closely linked unit, they unequivocally established the security-political aims of Arabic studies.

Despite the strength of the relationships between this network of actors and the resources that they invested in the Oriental Classes, the programme underwent a slow decline. Its problems reflected the larger context of Arabic studies, generally speaking, in Jewish-Israeli schools. As noted previously, despite the centrality of Arabic to the security-political establishment, it was being rejected by Jewish-Israeli society. Substantial written evidence demonstrates that pressure from head teachers and parents and pupils' dissatisfaction and a pervasive anti-Arab and anti-Arabic sentiment, all contributed to the weakening of Arabic studies in the general education system and in the Oriental Classes. Indeed, many in Jewish-Israeli society were questioning the practical value of Arabic in comparison with globalised languages such as English and French. Thus, fewer and fewer pupils elected to study Arabic.

This weakened status of Arabic language studies was a cause for concern for the Ministry of Education, the Prime Minister's Office and Military Intelligence. Such worries were featured in documents written by Ministry leaders during 1961–62 and peaked in 1963. While the programme that took place in Acre in the summer of 1963 seemed to reflect business as usual,[149] correspondence between the various figures involved reveals an entirely different picture. Ya'acov Eyal, who had succeeded Me'ir Kister as the new Supervisor of the Oriental Classes in 1963, began his term by sending two identical letters: one to Uri Lubrani, Adviser on Arab Affairs at the the Prime Minister's Office, and the second to Michael Ziv from the Department of High School Education at the Ministry of Education. Both letters were titled, 'The Oriental Classes', and began with general information about the programme. In a following section of the letter, Supervisor Eyal outlined his reasoning for writing the letter:

> The Oriental Classes programme, which was operated through ongoing cooperation between the Ministry of Education and the Prime Minister's Office, is currently fighting for its life [lit. *ne'eveḳet 'al ḳiyumah*] ... Its difficulties begin at the pre-Oriental Classes stage, when pupils do not have the option of studying Arabic [during intermediary school] ... In many schools parents object to the study of Arabic and are not willing to listen to [our] explanations regarding the country's need for Arabic-speakers ... Another element that diminishes the role of Oriental Classes as a future reservoir [for Israel's Arabic language positions] is the fact that most of the pupils are girls, and, as you know, most of the positions within the Oriental field [lit. *ba-teḥum ha-Mizraḥani*] are not for them ... All in all, in its current scope, the Oriental Classes just cannot fulfil the needs of the country with regard to the training of a reservoir of pupils who have a good education in Arabic, the history of Islam and the problems of the region. The question of Arabic studies should therefore be raised with an authorised governmental body ...[150]

Eyal's letter did not clarify which 'governmental body' he thought should be responsible for dealing with the question of Arabic studies.

He also did not specify positions within 'the Oriental field' that required filling and why most of them are 'not for girls'. His use of this 'coded language' most likely indicates that his meaning was clearly understood by the various actors, a notion that will be elaborated on later in the book. In all likelihood, his reference to a 'governmental body' indicated either the Prime Minister's Office or the IDF (and Military Intelligence in particular).

Indeed, during this same period, the IDF significantly increased its efforts to promote the study of Arabic in general in Israel and the Oriental Classes specifically. Evidence for this comes from a letter written by Stendel of the Prime Minister's Office to Chief of Intelligence in Military Intelligence, Gen. Meʾir ʿAmit. Stendel's letter focuses on the situation of Arabic studies in Tel Aviv; he notes that the 'negative attitude of head teachers' was one of the biggest obstacles standing in the way of expanding the Oriental Classes programme. To deal with this, Stendel wrote, 'We are going to gather all head teachers in the high schools ... and I believe that if Military Intelligence is represented there it will give a further push for our demand. The importance of the matter is obvious.'[151] Interestingly, Stendel prefers to say that '[t]he importance of the matter is obvious' without specifically elaborating on his meaning; probably one more example of 'coded language' used by different actors in the field of Arabic studies whose meaning was clear too all.

The army's more intensive involvement was in evidence late in 1963. At that time, the Chief of Military Intelligence wrote a letter classified as 'restricted' and titled, 'Arabic Studies in High Schools', which was sent to the Director of the Ministry of Education, the Adviser on Arab affairs, the head of the Military Adjutant and the head of Unit 515 (the Signal Intelligence Unit).[152] In the letter, he invited addressees to a 'discussion in my office that will deal with the topic [of Arabic studies in high schools]'.[153] In the second part of the letter, the Chief of Intelligence outlined a few possible subjects for discussion – listing the Oriental Classes first. He then articulated the main challenge facing Arabic studies in Jewish-Israeli schools as he saw it:

> There is solid contact between Military Intelligence and the teachers [of Arabic] ... and we position Arabic studies graduates according to recommendations we receive from their teachers ... from several discussions we had with head teachers we learned that most of them support extending Arabic studies ... However, the main obstacles that we face are a result of pressures from the parents who would prefer that their children study French and not Arabic.[154]

Indeed, the decision to introduce French language studies in 1959 and the ongoing anti-Arab sentiments in Jewish-Israeli society had a determinatively negative impact on the study of Arabic.[155] The Chief of Intelligence as well as the IDF, the Prime Minister's Office and the education system realised this and, given the importance of Arabic to Military Intelligence, they became increasingly involved in the issue. A discussion titled, 'The Oriental Classes', which took place a week later, on 7 January 1964, clearly indicated the centrality of Military Intelligence in decisions involving Arabic education. The meeting was hosted by the Office of the Chief of Intelligence and was attended by four representatives from the army, including the Chief of Intelligence and three of his senior officers. This heavy military presence was augmented by an adviser on Arab affairs from the Prime Minister's Office.[156] The final participant was the head of the High School Department in the Ministry of Education. The discussion opened with the Chief of Intelligence noting 'the growing need of Military Intelligence and all of its branches for high school graduates who know Arabic'.[157] He continued:

> Military Intelligence has a special interest in graduates of the Oriental Classes due to their [high] level [of Arabic linguistic ability] ... but the number of pupils [graduating annually] is not growing in accordance with [military] needs ... The ways that the IDF can help are: (1) Awarding scholarships for excellent pupils. (2) Supporting the budgets of Arabic teaching in schools. (3) Offering financial support to pupils of Oriental Classses who want to join the standing army. (4) Establishing Arabic Studies in a military academy. (5) Making our utmost efforts to ensure that all graduates of Arabic studies will be positioned in Arabic-oriented military positions.[158]

Ziv from the Ministry of Education, who was at the meeting, echoed the points raised by the Chief of Intelligence when he said that 'there is indeed cause for concern'.[159] To address this problem, he proposed increased investment in the Oriental Classes such that the programme would be 'our only and most central source [of pupils who know Arabic]'.[160] Following a discussion on the issue and an evaluation of different options, participants agreed that 'the Chief of Intelligence will send a letter to the Director of the Ministry of Education and will ask him to assemble a committee that will study the different options for increasing the number of pupils taking Arabic'.[161]

This meeting indicates a gradual evolution whereby Military Intelligence became the guiding hand behind Arabic studies. All elements of the meeting point to this: its location, the roles of the participants, the power relations between the various bodies involved and the conclusions reached. Further supporting this point was the decision to have the Chief Intelligence Office send a letter to the Director of the Ministry of Education, as opposed to having the representative of the Ministry of Education in attendance at this meeting take over this function. Indeed, the decision reached here echoes another one, taken two decades prior – Supervisor Ben-Ze'ev's decision in 1944 to seek financial support for Arabic studies from Eliyahu Sasson at the Arab Bureau of the Political Department as opposed to approaching his supervisor in the Ministry of Education for this purpose. These two events, while separated by 20 years, suggest that in all matters related to Arabic in the Zionist Israeli context, it was always advantageous to advance the topic via the political and security establishments. Here again, the more things change, the more they stayed the same.

However, during the 20 years spanning 1944–64, some new patterns emerged and solidified, in particular the nature of military involvement. For example, while in 1944 Arabic was important for educational and political ends, in 1964 it was clear that interest in Arabic and motivation to study the language were much more strongly connected to security-military needs and purposes.

Based on developments in the field, it may appear that the Ministry of Education was ceding control of Arabic studies to the military. However, when viewed in context, the decision to let Military Intelligence take the lead was probably logical. The Ministry knew that it was facing a serious problem in promoting Arabic studies and identified a potential lifeline in the form of Military Intelligence. Supervisor Eyal had articulated this very clearly the previous year when he wrote that the Oriental Classes programme 'is currently fighting for its life.' Indeed, his letter was a plea for outside assistance and a clear indication that the Ministry was ready to grant control of Arabic studies to the IDF and the Prime Minister's Office. Therefore, the growing role of Military Intelligence should not be understood as an unwelcome intrusion into educational matters, rather – at least in the eyes of Arabic teachers and the Ministry of Education – it should be understood as a last desperate attempt to keep Arabic alive.

The Oriental Classes programme continued to operate on a similar scale, and with similar security-educational goals, throughout 1964–67.

In May of 1967, one month before the 1967 War, 115 pupils from the 12th grade were enrolled in the programme.[162] While classes also continued to operate following the war, the field of Arabic studies in general, and the Oriental Classes specifically, underwent a dramatic transformation. Eventually, the Oriental Classes were merged with a different course of studies, which eventually came to be known as Five Units Arabic (in Hebrew, *Ḥamesh Yeḥidot ʿAravit*).

The notion that the Oriental Classes were intended to promote military aims, or that the programme was of a security nature, is not generally discussed in Israel. In an interview with Professor Reʾuven Snir, an Israeli scholar who teaches Arabic poetry and literature at the University of Haifa, he said that, in his view, the Oriental Classes were indeed 'Military Intelligence oriented', and were also the vehicle with which 'many of the professors of Middle Eastern Studies, in all the universities, emerged'.[163] Eyal and other scholars have expressed similar views. Eyal posited that even in the 1990s, 'The explicit purpose of the study of Arabic [in Israel] was to allow pupils to continue working on this issue also during their army service.'[164]

However, Professor Aryeh Levin, who served as the head of the Arabic language School Subject Committee (lit. *Vaʿadat ha-miḳtsoʿa*) in the Ministry of Education during 1986–2000, offers a dissenting view. In an interview, he supported the notion that the intensive programme of Arabic studies currently offered in Israeli high schools (Five Units Arabic) is based on experience accumulated in the Oriental Classes,[165] but believes that the Oriental Classes were strictly educational and that their relationship to the army was exclusively administrative in nature. According to Levin, 'The Oriental Classes were just like any other course of study taught in high schools, except for the fact that this one was called Arabic.'[166]

In my view, Levin's comment reveals the depth of denial regarding the profound role of the military and the political echelons in the Oriental Classes amongst senior officials in the Israeli Ministry of Education. It is also indicative of the dominant discourse whereby some topics were open for discussion and some modes of thought were acceptable while others were not. Drawing on archival research carried out for this book that is presented in this chapter and introduced in subsequent chapters, this kind of denial – or perhaps a conscious decision to downplay military elements, possibly due to considerations of national interest – can be understood as a convenient veil of ignorance regarding the obvious cooperation between the Prime Minister's Office, the Ministry of Foreign Affairs, the Ministry of Education and Military

Intelligence in positioning the Oriental Classes as the driver of Arabic studies in Israel. These networks led to further militarisation of the Arabic language in Israel, and created a new 'type' of Arabic, which I call 'Israeli Arabic', which was associated with the security needs of Israel, and served to distance Jewish-Israeli pupils of Arabic from the Arab people and from the region.

3

Recruiting Arabic for War

The Influence of the 1967 and 1973 Wars on Arabic Studies in Jewish-Israeli Schools

> Wars do breakout sometimes, don't they?
> For us they go with the seasons:
> Winter, spring, summer, war.
>
> Hanoch Levin, playwright[1]

The Jewish-Israeli school system: in the aftermath of the 1967 War

The 1967 War had a tremendous influence on the geopolitical and social life of millions of people in the Middle East. Much has been written about the impact of the war on Israeli society and the way in which it was perceived by Arab countries.[2] During the war, Israel occupied vast territories, including the West Bank, the Gaza Strip, the Sinai Peninsula and the Golan Heights, and when those six fateful days in June were over, the area under Israel's jurisdiction had tripled.

Interestingly, the war and its aftermath were also influential in the teaching of Arabic in Jewish-Israeli schools. In fact, the importance of Arabic studies was clear within a matter of days following the war; military battles ended on 10 June and by 29 June, steps had already been taken to increase the number of pupils studying Arabic in a direct connection to postwar Israel. At that time, the Ministry of Education released an announcement that was published in national newspapers and also distributed personally to all head teachers of Jewish-Israeli high schools. It read as follows:

> **A Call to High School Head Teachers Regarding Arabic Studies**
>
> The Ministry of Education is calling on all high school head teachers whose schools are not teaching Arabic to systematically increase

> efforts to teach the language during the next school year. According to a special announcement by Dr Ziv, the Director of the Department for High Schools in the Ministry, the new reality requires a new examination of our hitherto insufficient efforts to teach Arabic in our schools. There is no doubt that the need for people with general education in and proper knowledge of Arabic is now of paramount importance. These people are needed to act in all walks of life. Therefore, the high schools are instructed to do their utmost to help train the reserves [of Arabic-speakers] needed [for the country] as soon as possible and with the maximum efficiency. The Ministry of Education will support any institution that decides to teach Arabic, and will help it find knowledgeable teachers with proper pedagogic training.[3]

This announcement and the decision to publish it in national newspapers indicated the importance that the developers of this document gave to the subject. It also exposed the extent of the decline of Arabic language teaching in Israel on the eve of June 1967. While not spelled out directly, 'the new reality' referred to in the document most likely related to the new geopolitical situation whereby Israel controlled and occupied hundreds of thousands of Arabic-speaking communities, such as the Syrian Druze community in the occupied Golan Heights and the Palestinian community in the occupied West Bank and Gaza Strip. This set off warning bells and renewed the Israeli decision-makers' determination to ensure that they had access to the appropriate manpower required in order to manage and administrate these vast new territories and the Arabic-speakers who lived in them.

Indeed, the goal of ensuring that there was a sufficient pool of Arabic-speakers was now elevated to the level of a national mission. This is indicated by the urgent tone in the announcement, the decision to publish it widely and its timing. The announcement entreated Israelis to study Arabic in order to serve the state and to contribute to its national interests. It can be argued that, in postwar Israel, Arabic was viewed as a national priority – and even necessity – with widespread implications for Jewish-Israeli society as a whole, and was no longer regarded as the exclusive province of a select group of educators, scholars and security experts.

It is important to note that the call was positively received in Israel. Figures released during the initial postwar years point to an increase in the number of pupils learning Arabic. In parallel, the rejection of Arabic by parents, teachers and pupils that had been so pronounced during the years 1948–67, declined significantly following the war. The increased motivation to study Arabic along with more willingness to embrace it stemmed from a confluence of factors in Jewish-Israeli society. First and foremost, the increase was an indication of the need for speakers capable of serving in political- and security-oriented roles necessary for administering the newly occupied territories and controlling populations perceived to be hostile to the interests of the state, or at least 'not loyal' to it. However, alongside these considerations, other factors of a more instrumental and civilian nature were also at work. In light of the euphoria following the war, many in the Israeli society – including potential pupils and their parents – now believed that not only was knowing Arabic a national obligation but it was also a tool for a better and more promising future.

Financial considerations played a substantial role in this change of attitude. Many figures in civil society viewed the capture of these new territories as an opportunity for work and profit and that knowledge of Arabic would make entering the Palestinian market easier for Israeli businessmen and entrepreneurs. In search of cheap labour and goods, they envisioned opportunities for increased prosperity through the exploitation of the Palestinian economy. In other words, the occupation introduced Israelis to opportunities for investment and access to a cheap labour force, and opened for them a world that was unreachable until that point. As such, the rejection of Arabic, which was based on the argument that it lacked practical significance in the global marketplace, was no longer valid; Arabic was increasingly associated with economic opportunity.[4]

The way in which Jewish-Israelis perceived Israel's standing in the Middle East – in light of its victory in the war – was another factor contributing to the study of Arabic. During this period, there was a widespread belief that the future was bright for Israel; the 1967 War was definitive proof to the surrounding Arab nations that Israel was a fact on the map and that they would have no choice but to recognise its existence and negotiate with it. In fact, many Israeli publications maintained that a central factor contributing to the increase in Israelis studying Arabic was a genuine belief that the end of the war would improve Israel's status in the region and eventually result in *peaceful relations* with its neighbours. Uri Rubin, a professor emeritus at the Department of Arabic and Islamic Studies at Tel Aviv University, recalls these times. According to him, 'Following the 1967 War there was a blossoming in the study of the Arabic language and culture ... Following the occupation of the territories we came into direct contact with the Arab population, and there was an illusion that from now on, coexistence would prevail.'[5] Similar sentiments were voiced by Avraham Lavi, the head of the Arabic Teachers Committee. Sensing that history was on his side, in an interview conducted in 1968, he said that 'the Six Day War changed the attitude of many Israelis to Arabic and currently there are many who show interest in studying it'.[6]

In retrospect, given that the occupation has now entered its fifth decade in light of the fact that relations between Jewish-Israelis and Palestinians in territories occupied in 1967 are far from being 'peaceful,' these views may appear to be naive. However, throughout the first two years after the 1967 War, they were repeatedly voiced, which had important implications for the study of Arabic. The prevailing discourse very much reflected a question that was at the forefront of the minds of Israel's political establishment at the time: whether to swap the Occupied Territories for peace. In the end, and as highlighted by Raz, Israel chose occupation over peace.[7] Interestingly, Arabic studies seemingly went down the same path; instead of being used to promote peace, instrumental, political and security-oriented considerations prevailed.

Nevertheless, when examining the school system in 1967 and in the years immediately after that, it was still too early to know whether Arabic studies were on the cusp of radical change or whether this was just post-war caprice. Irrespective of this, following the Ministry of Education's announcement, and in light of 'the new political reality', the Ministry genuinely encouraged more schools to teach Arabic. In a parliamentary question submitted in July 1967, MK Shlomo Cohen-Tsidon asked the Minister of Education to elaborate on the steps that they were planning on taking to achieve this goal. Deputy Minister of Education, MK Aharon Yadlin, answered on behalf of Minister Zalman Aran as follows:

> In light of the new reality, the Ministry of Education is in the process of exploring options of how to enhance Arabic studies, and is planning new programmes in this regard. We are focusing our efforts on producing a large and appropriate cadre of Arabic teachers, and currently only hope that the desire to study Arabic will emerge among pupils and parents.[8]

Soon thereafter, the Ministry of Education unveiled its new course of action; this was a widespread campaign to encourage Arabic studies in the 7th and 8th grades. To support this, Shraga ʿAdiel, the head of the Pedagogic Secretariat in the Ministry, wrote a letter to all the head teachers in all the schools nationally outlining the urgency of Arabic studies:

> The new reality that was created in Israel following the Six Day War increased the importance of and the need for Arabic studies. The

> encounter with the Arab public and social and economic contact with Arabic-speakers require that a considerable number of [Jewish-Israeli] citizens will study [the] Arabic language and culture, and will get to know different matters related to the minorities in our country ... Some schools have already announced that they will establish Arabic classes starting from the next school year, and others announced that they will widen their already existing provision. I would therefore urge the head teachers to look into the possibility of teaching Arabic in the next year.[9]

This view was reflected in administrative decisions as well. Three months later, in October 1967, ʿAdiel mentioned that the Ministry of Education had decided to hire a new staff person to fill the newly created position of part-time Supervisor of Arabic Studies for primary and intermediate schools. This person would work alongside the preexisting full-time position of Supervisor of Arabic Studies for high schools.[10] This renewed emphasis on supporting Arabic studies reflects the importance of the language in the post-1967 period and stands in stark contrast to its decline prior to the war.

The sense of urgency regarding the need to promote Arabic continued. At the beginning of the 1967 school year, Minister of Education Aran asked the Director of his Ministry to make another announcement underlining the importance of teaching Arabic in Jewish-Israeli schools. Aran asked that the announcement be sent to 'all high schools, mayors, head teachers and general supervisors'.[11] It confirmed that the urgent call to increase Arabic studies had been received positively and stated that in two months' time, 'the number of schools in which Arabic is being taught has already increased'.[12] However, the Director of the Ministry also noted that many schools were still not teaching Arabic and encouraged them to devote their attention to the matter 'both for educational-cultural reasons and for reasons that were caused by time' (lit. *mi-ṭeʿamim she-ha-zman gramam*). The ambiguity of this terminology is noteworthy; it was not the first or last time that Israeli officials avoided mentioning the Israeli *occupation* by name. Instead, they used euphemisms such as 'the new reality', 'the new status' and a new situation that was 'caused by time'. Perhaps this is indicative of an overall trend whereby Israelis attempted to avoid the term *occupation*, a political and linguistic manoeuvring that remains dominant in present-day Israel.[13]

Soon afterwards, the Ministry released new figures regarding the status of Arabic studies in the aftermath of the 1967 War. Yoseph Shoḥat, the

Deputy Director of the Ministry sent a letter to the Minister of Education, where he mentioned that 'following the actions initiated by the Ministry, about 20 more schools decided to teach Arabic'.[14] This number indicates that efforts made by Ministry officials were received positively by schools, pupils and parents. However, another, more important, fact 'hides' between the lines of the letter. According to Shoḥat:

> The decision to send the calls to all head teachers followed the recommendations of the joint committee of the IDF and the Ministry of Education that was established two months ago (in July 1967) ... in which participated Ya'acov Sarid [Director of the Ministry], Ya'acov Eyal [the Supervisor of the Oriental Classes] and two representatives of the IDF: [the Chief of Intelligence Gen. Aharon Yariv] and Lt Col. Sharoni [from Military Intelligence] ... The committee discussed the options regarding introducing Arabic in more schools, and based on its recommendations, Dr Ziv sent the call to all head teachers ...[15]

This rather straightforward description of the process pulls the rug out from under the feet of those who had the impression that the Ministry of Education acted alone and in accordance with exclusively civilian considerations when promoting Arabic in the postwar period. Importantly, the Ministry was not the only body to take action immediately following the war; rather, action was taken by two bodies – the Ministry of Education and Military Intelligence. The two worked jointly to identify common interests, define cooperation and achieve joint goals vis-à-vis the committee established jointly by of the IDF and the Ministry of Education. In other words, while civilian concerns were certainly important, at its core other forces were at play.

In October 1967, the Ministry of Education published a third special announcement, most probably in response to another joint IDF–Education Committee recommendation. This time, the Ministry of Education announced that, following discussions regarding the status of Arabic studies in high schools in the postwar era, a decision had been taken according to which, 'for cultural, educational and practical-state reasons [lit. *mi-ṭe'amim tarbutiyyim, ḥinukhiyyim, u-mamlakhtiyyim-ma'asiyyim*] the teaching of Arabic and Islamic culture ought to have a substantial place in high school syllabuses'.[16] Again, the announcement was vague as to what exactly 'practical-state' reasons meant, instead letting the readers interpret this for themselves.

In November 1967, four months after the end of the war, Aran addressed the Knesset to elaborate on his Ministry's activities in the field of Arabic studies. In mentioning the postwar situation, Aran noted that:

> The 1967 War and the political and demographic change that came immediately afterwards have caused a considerable change in public awareness regarding the teaching of Arabic. Therefore, we have witnessed interest and aspiration to study the language and we hope that this pattern will gain pace. Following on from our continuous efforts, especially our direct calls to the schools, we expect a rise of 35 per cent in Arabic teaching during the next school year ...[17]

Aran's prediction came true, and quite imressively, and in 1969 the Ministry of Education announced that the number of classes in which Arabic was taught had 'almost doubled'.[18] Yet, the increased motivation to study Arabic, especially in light of the military–civilian joint committee, presented just another opportunity to deepen the alliance between the Military Intelligence and Ministry of Education, at least as far as the security establishment understood it. As demonstrated in the preceding chapter, the two sides regularly cooperated prior to the 1967 War in the context of joint meetings whereby they strategised the increase in Arabic studies in Jewish-Israeli schools. However, in the prewar period, and in the face of the rejection of Arabic by pupils, parents and head teachers, the dominant feeling on both sides was tremendous despair. In contrast, in light of the renewed motivation to study the language in the postwar period, the cooperation between the two sides was efficient and generated better results.

Indeed, the joint committee, involving the Chief of Intelligence, was only one example of such cooperation. In 1968, the IDF's involvement and influence in Arabic studies became more pronounced when in July of that year, an IDF delegation consisting of two Military Intelligence officers (Lt Col. Pinḥas Ostrovsky and Maj. Y. Bar-Yehuda) and one officer from the IDF's Manpower Directorate (Lt Col. Aryeh Zamiri) met with two senior officials from the Ministry of Education (Yaʿacov Sarid, the Director of the Ministry, and Yaʿacov Eyal, the Supervisor of Arabic Studies). The officers, who had initiated the meeting, bluntly told Sarid and Eyal that despite their efforts over the previous year 'the number of graduates in Arabic does not meet the growing needs of the IDF'.[19] In response, the Military Intelligence officers asked the Ministry to proclaim Arabic a compulsory subject. The Director of the Ministry responded, saying that there were 'political, public, pedagogic and financial difficulties' to overcome before making Arabic compulsory, and in light of this suggested that Arabic classes should be offered in as many schools as possible. The participants – from both the IDF and the Ministry – also recommended that the IDF and the Ministry of Education arrange a seminar with 100 to 120 head teachers of primary and intermediate schools, in order to encourage them to initiate Arabic studies, which 'in the long-term would increase the number of pupils who also choose to study Arabic in high school'.[20] The IDF officers realised that if they wanted a larger number of new recruitments with knowledge of Arabic, they would have to assure that more pupils took this subject in high schools, and that in order to achieve this they would have to increase the number of pupils taking Arabic at earlier stages: in both intermediate and primary school education.

The IDF's recommendation is notable in that it stands in stark contrast to the position held by the Chief of Intelligence and Ministry of Education prior to the war. At the time, they recommended establishing Arabic as an elective subject and proposed that the language was studied in a small number of schools only.[21] Undoubtedly, the general perception of Arabic as a national priority from June 1967 onwards, and the growing alliance between the Military Intelligence and the Ministry of Education, was the impetus behind the IDF's new set of demands. What had seemed overly ambitious just six months earlier was now deemed to be realistic.

In light of the post-1967 situation, the IDF's efforts to convince senior officials in the Ministry of Education to make Arabic a compulsory school subject continued. During 1969, for example, ʿAdiel, the head of the Pedagogic Secretariat in the Ministry, wrote an op-ed for the daily newspaper *La-Merḥav*, entitled 'Arabic Studies Should be Compulsory.' His claims in the article were very similar to those made by the army; he simultaneously advocated for 'Arabic for peace' and 'Arabic for security' and supported his position as follows:

> [T]he results of the Six Day War changed the map of the country, but also created a new reality in the Middle East ... We must train the young generation in Arabic studies, for understanding and cooperation with the Arabs, either if peace is close or far away, as well as in order to open a network of new Arabic course for the soldiers of the IDF ...[22]

During the same year, MK Nissim Eliʿad from the Independent Liberal Party, tried to promote a parliamentarian bill that aimed at making Arabic a compulsory school subject. The bill, which was never actually legislated, held that Arabic should become a compulsory subject in all

Israeli schools and a mandatory subject for final exams.[23] While it is unclear whether Eli'ad included military or security-oriented justifications in his bill, such considerations were a permanent feature of other initiatives relating to Arabic during that period. For example, Eliyahou Mansour, the Supervisor of Arabic Studies in primary and intermediate schools, wrote in a report that the study of Arabic should be mandatory in 5th and 6th grades as 'the child is still capable of acquiring new languages at this age ... and due to the security situation' (lit. *ha-matsav ha-biṭḥoni*).[24] Similar recommendations were made by the Yadlin Committee (headed by the Minster of Education, Aharon Yadlin), which was dedicated to attempts to encourage Arabic studies in schools. One of Yadlin's primary recommendations was to promote the study of Arabic by 'hasbarah activities' in the 6th grade, which were to be conducted by university pupils and Military Intelligence officers.[25]

An even clearer example of the increasingly close relations between the Ministry of Education and Military Intelligence – and the people sitting at the top of the two systems – was their in-depth cooperation regarding every aspect of Arabic studies. A letter sent by the Chief of Intelligence, Yariv, to the Director of the Ministry of Education, El'ad Peled (who was himself a retired IDF general) demonstrates the extent of their partnership. Yariv opened the classified letter to Gen. Ret. Peled with the words, 'Hello my friend El'ad', and then outlined his reason for writing the letter:

> In another check that we conducted in Military Intelligence regarding our need for Arabic experts, it was found that we have a quantitative problem, and an even more acute qualitative problem. I would therefore like to meet you again as soon as possible to discuss the following subjects: the planning of Arabic language instruction [in schools]; the writing of new school textbooks; preparing the Arabic language curriculum; discussing continuing education programmes; recruiting new teachers; increasing the number of Arabic hours [in schools]; discussing the teaching of Colloquial Arabic; increasing the number of Arabic teaching schools; and making Arabic studies in intermediate school a compulsory subject ...[26]

The comprehensive, almost endless, list of subjects for discussion is not only indicative of the IDF's increasing demands and involvement in Arabic studies but also of the wider scope of action that became feasible – and justified – following the 1967 War. The letter gives a good indication of the depth of the relationship between the two bodies and the full extent of their cooperation with each other. For example, the phrases (my empahsis), '*another* check we conducted in Military Intelligence' and the request to meet '*again* and as soon as possible', are indicative of ongoing relations and regular contact. Furthermore, Yariv addressed the Director of the Ministry of Education, a retired IDF general, as 'my friend Elʿad' (lit. *Shalom Elʿad yedidi*), thus pointing to a degree of intimacy between these two men. This closeness was probably borne out by their long-standing friendship but may very well reflect their shared beliefs vis-à-vis Arabic language education and the militaristic discourse of the debate.

Concerted action to promote Arabic continued with the establishment of the Shoḥat Committee in 1973. Committee members were appointed by the Ministry of Education while the committee was chaired by the head of the Pedagogical Secretariat, Shoḥat. Not surprisingly, it was comprised of civilian scholars – representatives from the Ministry of Education, scholars from the Hebrew University and Tel Aviv University – as well as military experts from the IDF. Its mandate was to investigate the status of Arabic in Jewish-Israeli schools. In February 1973, the committee published its findings. It recommended that: 'Arabic studies will become a compulsory school subject, for all pupils from the 5th to 9th grades.'[27] The committee further decided that the transition of integrating Arabic into more schools and classes would be gradual, with implementation taking place in the majority of Israeli schools over the course of six to eight years, a decision that – as with similar decisions in the past – was never implemented.[28]

Despite the relatively significant decision taken above, some still felt that more action was needed in order to assure a real impact. A few weeks after the committee released their findings, Maj. Aharon Hadar from Military Intelligence sent a letter to Shoḥat on behalf of the Chief of Intelligence. In the letter, in addition to pupils in grades 5 to 9 studying Arabic, the officer also advocated making Arabic compulsory for pupils in grades 10 to 12. Hadar justified this on the grounds that increasing the intensity and length of the studies would consolidate the pupils' knowledge of the language, bring their fluency to a higher level and also 'prevent a situation of forgetfulness'.[29] Hadar also noted the Military Intelligence's readiness to assist the Ministry of Education in the research and production of Arabic textbooks. The letter was copied to Col. Yo'el Ben-Porat, the commander of the Signal Intelligence Unit of the IDF, presumably in order to bolster the credibility of the military request.

Hadar's letter points to efforts by the Military Intelligence to make Arabic a compulsory subject from the 5th to 12th grades. His choice of words is also telling; when Hadar strove 'to preserve the knowledge of Arabic and prevent a situation of forgetfulness', he was most likely concerned that the time delay between Arabic studies in the lower grades and army service would weaken their mastery of the language. He seemingly sought to recruit soldiers whose knowledge of the language was 'fresh', and preferably pupils who took Arabic in high schools. The use of indirect language such as this was rife in similar documents from the period, and were one more indication of the way in which political and security considerations were pervasive in driving Arabic language studies.

In order to contextualise developments that took place during this period, they should also be examined through the lens of Israeli militarism. According to Uri Ben-Eliezer, '[t]he evolution of Israel as a nation-in-arms attained its zenith in the aftermath of the Six-Day War of 1967'.[30] The notion of Israel as a nation-in-arms has been the focus of substantial research, with a general consensus that IDF involvement in civilian matters peaked in the post-1967 period.[31]

Consistent with this general trend, during the same time period and due to similar civil-military power relations, the relationship between the Ministry of Education and Military Intelligence was strengthened. Indeed, the power that the military held sway over Israeli society during this period gave the IDF and Military Intelligence unprecedented influence over Arabic language studies in schools at all levels. This influence was further enabled by a broad-based consensus in Israeli society regarding the need for Arabic in guaranteeing state security. This emerging consensus only intensified following the next military event that took Israel by surprise. The 1973 War thoroughly shook Israelis and pushed Arabic studies even further into the sphere of the military and intelligence.

The 1973 War: the catastrophe of Israeli Arabists and its aftermath

On Saturday 6 October 1973, during the Jewish holy day of Yom Kippur, at 13:55, sirens began wailing throughout the streets of Israel. The Egyptian and Syrian armies, with perfect timing and coordination, had launched a war on a completely unsuspecting and unprepared Israel. Only the previous day, the Research Department of the IDF Directorate of Ministry Intelligence had published a top secret nine-page report that surveyed the current situation on the Egyptian and Syrian borders. It had concluded that there was a 'low probability of a renewal of fighting'.[32]

By the war's end, Israel had over 2500 casualties. While the IDF eventually managed to push back the invading Egyptian and Syrian armies, it left behind a nation in shock. Although the Egyptians and Syrians did not reconquer territories captured from them in the war of 1967 – the Sinai Desert and Golan Heights, respectively – the war generated a tremendous panic in Israel and demonstrated that both Egypt and Syria were willing to undertake great military risks to regain their land. In taking Israel by surprise, by crossing the Suez Canal, by breaking through the Bar-Lev Line of fortifications and in gaining temporary control of the post on Mount Hermon, the joint attack also demonstrated that Israel was not omnipotent.

Following the euphoria generated by the 1967 War, the 1973 anticlimax was devastating. Israeli political leaders such as then sitting Prime Minister Golda Me'ir and the former Minister of Defence Moshe Dayan lost the support of a large strata of the Israeli public. Postwar, they were held responsible for the significant number of causalities on the Israeli side. Widespread civil protests led to the resignation of these two leaders and the tarnishing of the image of the IDF. A national investigation committee, the Agranat Commission, was established. Among other findings, they concluded that the conduct of Chief of Staff David El'azar, Chief of Intelligence Eli Ze'ira and the Commander of the Southern Command Shmu'el Gonen had led to operational and intelligence failures leading to the disastrous results of the war. Although the Commission recommended the dismissal of these officers, all of them resigned before the recommendations were put into place.

To date, the full deliberations of the Agranat Commission have yet to be published in their totality. However, in all likelihood, their recommendations also influenced the teaching of Arabic, even if indirectly. Therefore, it is worthwhile to present an overview of the Commission's work and its subsequent influence on Military Intelligence.

The Commission was tasked with investigating the circumstances that led to the outbreak of the 1973 War. Headed by Shim'on Agranat, the Chief Justice of Israel's Supreme Court, the Commission listened to 90 different testimonies. Its first report, published on 1 April 1974, vindicated Prime Minister Me'ir and Minister of Defence Dayan, but public pressure led to their eventual resignations. The report held six people accountable, all of whom were IDF officers. Four of the six were Military Intelligence officers; they included Chief of Intelligence (Ze'ira), his deputy (Aryeh Shalev), the head of the Egyptian Desk, and the Chief of Intelligence of the Southern Command. The Commission's recommendations focused primarily on Israel's secret services – Military

Intelligence, Mossad and the Research Department of the Ministry of Foreign Affairs, who were all criticised for their lack of coordination and information-sharing. The Commission also highlighted the importance of creating alternative intelligence assessments and analyses while harshly criticising 'the concept', a mistaken assumption by which Israeli intelligence officers were 'trapped'. According to this 'concept', which was proven wrong by the joint attack of Egytpian and Syrian forces, Egypt was not going to initiate an attack on Israel before achieving air superiority.

Due to the harsh criticism levelled at the intelligence institutions in place during this period, the Commission recommended establishing a special ministerial committee for security affairs along with the post of a special intelligence officer for the Prime Minister. They also instituted several reforms in relation to the division of authority within the Military Intelligence. One of the most pronounced reforms, which were carried out a few years later, involved the creation of the Military Intelligence Directorate (*Ḥaman* in Hebrew). This body, which was directly accountable to the Chief of Intelligence, was responsible for identifying and evaluating appropriate candidates for work in intelligence prior to their army service and their subsequent training once they had joined the IDF.[33]

Declassified sections of the Agranat Commission's Report note that senior Israeli intelligence official's command of Arabic was insufficient. For example, Ya'ir Algom, who served as the Director of the Research Division in the Ministry of Foreign Affairs, testified to the committee that 'The Egyptian Desk [in the Research Department of the Ministry of Foreign Affairs] was run by an experienced woman ... but the Syrian and Iraqi desks were run by a person who, as far as I know, does not know Arabic.'[34]

Shmu'el Divon, considered to be an expert in Arab affairs and who had served as the head of the Middle East Department of the Ministry of Foreign Affairs, admitted that there was a shortage of fluent Arabic-speakers in his department.[35] The following segment of the interview demonstrates Divon's embarrassment in acknowledging this fact:

> *Investigator*: I wanted to ask you something about the directors of the Middle East Desks. These people, they have key positions in the assessment of these countries. Do you know these people well?
> *Divon*: I do, and I think that their standards should be raised.
> *Investigator*: Why? For what reason?
> *Divon*: Because some of them, not all, are not at a sufficient level.
> *Investigator*: In what way ... what do you think they lack at their level?

> *Divon*: Some of them are lacking knowledge.
> *Investigator*: But knowledge of what?
> *Divon*: Knowledge of the subject. For example, someone who is in charge of Lebanon, or Syria, might lack education or expertise in subjects related to the Middle East, or perhaps even in their specific country of expertise.
> *Investigator*: We were actually told yesterday [by Algom] that the person who is in charge of Syria and Iraq could not even speak Arabic.
> *Divon*: Yes, this is what I meant to say. That there is a lack of general knowledge, and also lack of knowledge of Arabic ...[36]

Divon's evident discomfort when answering the investigators' questions reveals that he was attempting to hide a problem that arguably extended beyond the Ministry of Foreign Affairs. Despite the fact that he was speaking on behalf of the Ministry of Foreign Affairs, the problems concerned other agencies involved with security and, therefore, the Agranat Commission's recommendations were relevant across the board. As demonstrated in the previous chapter, while the number of pupils studying Arabic grew between the years 1967 to1973, officials from the Military Intelligence continued to be very unhappy about the pace and scope of studies. Since the 1950s, senior officials had advocated the teaching of Arabic on a much wider scale and believed that study of the subject should be mandatory. They wanted more pupils to take Arabic in high school and more recruits to enter the IDF with a stronger command of the language and at a level that would enable them to serve in Arabic and security-oriented positions.

Due to testimony by Divon, Algam and others, the Commission became aware of the critical shortage of Jewish-Israeli personnel with a mastery of Arabic. This brought them to advocate changes in the way that the Military Intelligence selected and trained its soldiers, an act that had a direct influence on the field of Arabic studies. Therefore, it is logical to assume that changes that came about due to the Agranat Commission's findings also influenced the subsequent teaching of Arabic in schools. This was evident in the energetic work of the new Chief of Intelligence Shlomo Gazit (appointed in 1974), the reorganisation of Military Intelligence and the establishment of Ḥaman (1976), all connected to the Agranat Commission's recommendations. All of these factors – coupled with the increasing influence of the Military Intelligence in Arabic language studies – had a decisive impact on the way in which Arabic was taught, studied and perceived within the school system.

As will be seen below, in the aftermath of the 1973 Yom Kippur disaster, knowledge of Arabic was no longer considered to be a broad educational, political or national issue. Rather, it was regarded as a national imperative that was almost exclusively a military project – and quite urgent. As such, 1973 represented a critical turning point, which was connected to the gradual strengthening of the military–educational relations.

Personnel changes were one of the results of postwar introspection. Following Eli Ze'ira's resignation as Chief of Staff, in early 1974, Gen. Shlomo Gazit was assigned to the post. Not only did this change of manpower have important ramifications on the army, but it also deeply impacted on the Jewish-Israeli school system. In addition, an entirely new unit – that of the Unit for the Encouragement of Oriental Studies (*Ṭelem*, the Hebrew acronym for *Ṭipua'ḥ Limudei Mizraḥanut*) – was established in Ḥaman.[37] One of the officers who was associated with this unit was Ephraim Lapid, a senior Military Intelligence officer. The fact that this unit did not exist before 1973, as well as the connection to Lapid, points to the wide-ranging fallout of the Agranat Commission. It is also indicative of the tremendous importance that the Military Intelligence attached to influencing Arabic studies in the education system. In an interview conducted with Lapid, the former officer noted that, despite strenuous efforts taken prior to 1973 to increase the number of pupils studying Arabic, these efforts had not sufficiently filled the shortage facing Military Intelligence needs. Lapid said:

> Already in 1970, Military Intelligence started operating pre-army service courses [under military supervision], which aimed at teaching Arabic to pre-conscription youngsters ... We did so because there was a growing shortage of Arabists created in the education system, which peaked, both in numbers and in our awareness, following the 1973 War. These efforts received assistance from the new Chief of Intelligence Shlomo Gazit [appointed 1974] who had a genuine national vision. Professor Yehoshafat Harkabi [a retired Chief of Intelligence, who at the time was a professor teaching at the Hebrew University] also supported this process as he helped to bring scholars from academia into the debate, and emphasised the place of the research division in the process of evaluation in Military Intelligence.[38]

Lapid also noted the enthusiasm displayed by Gazit and concluded that:

> During the term of the new Chief of Intelligence, [Gen.] Shlomo Gazit, four main things changed: a real joint effort – even if unsuccessful – by

> him and the then Minister of Education, [Gen. Ret.] Yigal Allon, to make Arabic a compulsory school subject ... the training of Arabic teachers through the Soldier-Teachers [lit. *Morot Ḥayalot*] project that was then established in cooperation with the Ministry of Education ... the founding of Military Intelligence's Oriental Youth Battalions [lit. *Gadnaʿ Mizraḥanim*] around 1975–76 ... and, lastly, the creation of the Sharoni [Arabic–Hebrew] dictionary to the service of the civil education system. These actions were his [Gazit's] special contributions to the civil sector.[39]

The projects mentioned above are outlined in greater detail later on in this chapter, in accordance with research conducted at the Israeli State Archives and the IDF Archives. However, at this juncture, it is important to point out that Lapid's account supports the notion that following the 1973 War, and as the archival documents indeed reveal, the Military Intelligence felt deeply frustrated by the state of Arabic language studies and attempted to institute meaningful changes.

One example of the overlap between the military and civilian realms was the creation of the Sharoni Arabic–Hebrew dictionary in the post-1973 period. The dictionary was meant to serve the education system, but it stemmed from the military dictionary and expertise. At the time, its developer, Avraham Sharoni, held a very high-ranking position as an expert in Arabic in Military Intelligence. He was involved in pre-state intelligence activities (for example, the undercover Mistaʿaravim Unit of the Haganah that was active in Beirut and Damascus, as well as in the Arabic SHAI of the Haganah) and served as a leading expert in Arabic in Military Intelligence during the 1948 War and following the establishment of the state and of the IDF. Notably, based at the Arabic SHAI and later at the Arabic Department of the IDF, one of his most crucial contributions was eavesdropping on members of the Arab-Palestinian leadership during the war in 1948. He also headed the training section of the Military Intelligence's Communication Intelligence from 1963 to 1971. With relation to lexicography, from 1963 to 1969 Sharoni, together with ʿEzra Mani, created an Arabic–Hebrew military dictionary. In 1963, Sharoni won the Israeli 'Security Prize' for his special contribution to Military Intelligence, which included his work on the dictionary.[40]

In 1976, Sharoni, who had by then retired from Military Intelligence, was contacted by Lapid with a request to formulate what was later referred to as the Sharoni Arabic–Hebrew dictionary. Sharoni agreed to take on the task. The new dictionary, intended for civilian use, included some 1000 words and definitions that were featured in his previous military dictionary. One of Israel's most famous dictionaries, it was published in 1978 for the first time by the Ministry of Defence publishing house. That same year, it was presented to the public in the presence of Minister of Defence Yizthak Rabin, Israeli President Chaim Herzog (formerly the head of the Intelligence Department of the IDF) and Jerusalem's Mayor Teddy Kollek.[41] Even today, the dictionary is widely used in the Israeli school system and, arguably, it strengthens the link – even an unconscious one – between Arabic and the Military Intelligence among teachers and pupils, due to its promotion and development by actors associated with the military establishment.[42]

As previously indicated, given the national trauma caused by the war in 1973 and the panic in the military regarding their shortage of qualified Arabic-speakers, military involvement in Arabic studies became even more pronounced in the post-1973 period. Indeed, relations between the Military Intelligence and the Ministry of Education became crucial and so close and direct that the intervention of the Prime Minister's Office was no longer necessary and, in fact, almost disappeared completely.

Archival research supports this point. In 1974, for example, a meeting was held between Minister of Education, Aharon Yadlin, the Chief of Intelligence, Shlomo Gazit, and the Ministry's Supervisor of Arabic Studies, Ya'acov Eyal. Following this meeting, Eyal send a letter to the Minister of Education in which he stated that:

> Subsequent to our meeting with the Chief of Intelligence, I am sending this memorandum for you to authorise the implementation of the following steps: teaching Arabic as a compulsory school subject in [Jewish-Israeli] primary schools in Jerusalem; [and] forcing *all high schools in Israel* to teach another foreign language [other than English] ... The scope, direction and level of Arabic are disturbingly low for the needs of state. Immediate and decisive action is required [lit. *drushah pe'ulah miyadit ve-nehretset*] to fix the problem at all levels of education, from primary school to tertiary education.[43]

This letter shows the decisive role of the Military Intelligence in influencing the discourse surrounding the teaching of Arabic in Jewish-Israeli school. The decision to write this summary was most likely taken jointly by the Military Intelligence and Supervisor Eyal, and expresses the concern and urgency that both felt towards Arabic teaching at the time. Eyal advocated 'decisive action' in order to rescue Arabic from its perceived state of crisis. He sought to transform Arabic language studies into a tool to meet the 'needs of the state'; presumably he was referring to strategic, security and political needs. Due to all this, the military presence – and influence – at this meeting is indicative of a growing securitisation of Arabic studies in Israel.

Two months later, in another letter to the Minister of Education, Supervisor Eyal again referenced political and military considerations. In a summary of a meeting that he had held with Military Intelligence representatives, Eyal wrote to Minister Yadlin as follows: 'the meeting was held under the chairmanship of the Chief of Intelligence, and with the participation of his officers and myself'.[44] Eyal then elaborated on various solutions proposed at the meeting and said that: '[F]ollowing the recommendation of Military Intelligence, I suggest not teaching Arabic as a mandatory school subjects in all schools, but to focus on 25–30 intermediary schools that have good conditions for success.'[45] Eyal concluded his letter by noting that there was a shortage of Arabic teachers and institutions for Arabic teacher training, suggesting that 'Due to these circumstances, I see no other way but to establish a special institution, under the auspices of the Ministry of Education, the universities and the IDF, to increase the number of experts in modern and practical Arabic, for teaching needs, but for other national positions [lit. *tafḳidim mamlakhtiyyim*] as well.'[46]

Importantly, not only did the army offer the Ministry of Education advice, but it also took the initiative by inviting the Ministry's Supervisor of Arabic Studies to discuss the state of Arabic in the education system at a meeting 'under the chairmanship of the Chief of Intelligence'. Indeed, the meeting, which took place at a military base, was attended by a single representative of the Ministry of Education, who was surrounded by a general, the Chief of Intelligence and other Military Intelligence officers. Arguably, this scene – an education figure surrounded by four Military Intelligence officers in an office inside a military base – best exemplifies the new nature of the relationship between the two bodies and the balance of power between them in the post-1973 era.

A few months after the most recent correspondence (November 1974), the Chief of Intelligence initiated contact with the Minister of Education. In his letter to the Minister, Gen. Gazit summarised the activities that had taken place since their previous meeting and also outlined vigorous Military Intelligence efforts to encourage Arabic studies in Israel following the 1973 War. Under the title 'Enhancing Arabic Studies in Israeli High Schools', the Chief of Intelligence wrote:

> Subsequent to our meeting a few months ago, we in Military Intelligence, in coordination with your Ministry, launched a campaign for

> the encouragement of the Arabic language in Israel [lit. *masaʿ le-ʿidud limud ha-safah ha-ʿAravit ba-medinah*] ... Among the activities undertaken were creating incentives to study Arabic within the Ministry of Education ... widening the project of training new Arabic teachers ... and the allocation of a group of Military Intelligence officers to be in contact with pupils, teachers and head teachers who teach or study Arabic. Each officer was assigned to a different school ... Obviously, we are only at the beginning of the way [lit. *anu rak̩ bi-reshit ha-derekh*]. We still need to have numerous and continuous activities before we reach the required deepening of public awareness, which will increase the number of pupils who select Arabic willingly. Unfortunately, I believe that we must continue with these activities, and others, for many years to come, before we see true results. Currently, our situation is very gloomy: in the 12th grade level, we have only 68 men. The quota of men has a decisive importance for the IDF ... We therefore believe that it is absolutely essential, in the light of the situation, and in order to prevent an avalanche [lit. *im anu rotsim limnoʿa mapolet*] to take the following steps immediately: (1) Until Arabic is determined as a compulsory language, attempts should be made to force all pupils who start studying Arabic to continue with their studies up to their final year. (2) In those schools where pupils can choose between different subjects, Arabic will receive a higher mark, which will serve as an 'inducement' [lit. *tamrits pituy*] for the pupils to choose this subject. (3) We need to organise an expedited training system of Arabic teachers, to enable the teaching of as many Arabic classes as possible ... I suggest that you arrange a follow-up meeting in your office soon, in which we will determine the continuation of the activities of the Ministry of Education on this subject, together with the coordination of the efforts of Military Intelligence.[47]

This particular letter elucidates the state of Arabic studies in Israel at the time. In describing the military and educational establishments as equals working towards a common goal ('a campaign for the encouragement of the Arabic language'), the letter underlines both the confluence of interests between the two sides and the securitisation of Arabic as a school subject. Further evidence of this was the role played by Military Intelligence officers who interfaced directly with specific schools to encourage Arabic studies. According to the Chief of Intelligence, the dearth of Arabic pupils graduating with the requisite linguistic skills was a cause for concern as it left the country vulnerable from the security point of view. Lastly, the reference to *male pupils* is indicative of the security-focused nature of the letter.

Other archival files expose the unprecedentedly close cooperation enjoyed by Military Intelligence and Ministry of Education officials during the period under investigation. In a letter sent by Emmanuel Yaffe, the Deputy Director of the Ministry, to Lapid, the former stated that:

> Following our conversation with Maj. ʿAtsmon, I acted as promised (and even much faster than promised) and had consultations with Yaʿacov Eyal, the Supervisor of Arabic Studies, and other officials in the department ... In these consultations I found almost full consent, and therefore there is no need for further consultations. The decision of if and when to carry out our plans depends on us only.[48]

The subsequent section of the letter – which includes vague terminology and very little details – consists of an update regarding an expected increase in Arabic teachers' seminars and an Arabic teacher training course that was expected to start for soldiers who had finished their service in Military Intelligence. This demonstrates, once again, the cooperation and mutual dependence between the Ministry of Education and Military Intelligence.

The last document examined in this series of military–educational correspondence was written by Lapid and sent from the Chief of Intelligence to the Minister of Education in February 1976. It was entitled: 'The Status of Arabic Teaching in the Education System: The Point of View of Military Intelligence – A Headquarters Proposal for the Minister of Education'. This document, later referred to as the 'Lapid Report', reinforces and summarises many of the points raised here. As it is key to this research, the text is included here almost in full in Document 3.1.[49]

Document 3.1 The status of Arabic teaching in the education system: the point of view of Military Intelligence

Restricted

The status of Arabic studies in Israel is found to be in decline. Quantitatively, numbers of male pupils have decreased. Qualitatively, Military Intelligence's needs are not met by a sufficient number of pupils who took Arabic in schools ... This report will survey the following: 1. The main reasons for the decline in Arabic. 2. Actions taken by Military Intelligence for the encouragement of Arabic studies. 3. Suggestions for improvement ...

(*continued*)

Document 3.1 Continued

1. According to our understanding, the main reason for the decline in the teaching of Arabic is related to the fact that it is still an optional school subject ... with no inspiring teachers, and with no prestige [lit. *miḳtso'a ḥasar yoḳrah*] ...
2. The actions taken by Military Intelligence to address this situation were: in January 1975, Military Intelligence decided to embark on an intensive operation of encouraging the study of Arabic, raising the level of teaching, and improving its image and prestige ... *This mission was seen as a national project and we did not limit ourselves to the needs of Military Intelligence only*, and therefore, we introduced to the Ministry of Education our demand to make Arabic studies – in the long term – a mandatory school subject in all high schools ... The same national considerations led Military Intelligence to enhance the awareness regarding the importance of Arabic and Oriental studies among the public ...

To achieve this, Military Intelligence initiated different activities on four levels:

At the organisational level: A special team of dedicated and visionary officers [lit. *tseṿet shel ḳtsinim meshuga' im la-davar*] was established to navigate the activities of Military Intelligence towards the fostering of Arabic and Oriental studies ... A special department in Military Intelligence is intensively recruiting new candidates for positions in the security services that demand knowledge of Arabic ...

At the Ministry of Education level: There is continuous cooperation with the Ministry of Education, at all levels, in order to emphasise the importance of the subject ... Military Intelligence maintains close cooperation with the Ministry of Education regarding the updating of the [Arabic language] curricula, and the training of Arabic teachers ...

At the school and pupil level: About 30 high schools were chosen by us [Military Intelligence] as suitable for a special encouragement programme. A Military Intelligence officer was placed in each of these schools and he has continuous contact with the school regarding the study of Arabic ... We started the project of Military Intelligence's Oriental Youth Battalions (lit. *Gadna' Mizraḥanim*) as a cooperative linking of Military Intelligence and the Youth Battalions. This project aims to improve Arabic studies and to

(*continued*)

Document 3.1 Continued

nurture 'a pride in this school subject' [lit. *ṭipuaʾḥ 'gaʾyat miḳtsoʿa'*] ... Military Intelligence is also transferring large quantities [lit. *mazrim*] of contemporary materials to schools, including maps, Arabic newspapers, Arabic radio broadcasts, news and updates about the Middle East, and a conversation manual in Colloquial Arabic ...

At the public level: A strong public campaign [lit. *peʿilut hasbarah ʿanefah*] encouraging Arabic studies was conducted in the Israeli media ... Colloquial Arabic programmes were started on the Israeli Army Radio station [*Galei Tsahal*] and the military newspaper [*Ba-Maḥane*] ... Military Intelligence also maintains a tight cooperation [lit. *Ḥaman ʿomed be-ḳesher haduḳ*] with the Hebrew University in Jerusalem and Tel Aviv University in order to integrate professors in the Arabic and Middle East departments in our activities ...

3. Suggestions for Improvement: (a) Developing a new curriculum for Arabic studies, which will include different Arabic skills, including listening to radio broadcasts, translation skills and speaking. (b) Increasing the number of Arabic Studies Supervisors ... (c) Improving the current infrastructure of Arabic textbooks ... (d) Including Arabic progression lessons in Israeli Educational Television ... (e) Encouraging cooperation between university lecturers of Arabic and Middle Eastern Studies and the school system ... (f) Training Arabic teachers who will be in charge of the pupils taking Arabic – from primary to intermediate schools. (g) Trying to recruit Arabic-speakers from different activities to the field of Arabic studies. (h) Continuing the Eretz Yisraeli Colloquial Arabic seminars in Umm al-Faḥm, as started in 1975 ...

Note: Emphasis in point 2 is mine, to indicate that this was also the title of the document.
Source: The Lapid Report, attached to the letter sent by the Chief of Intelligence to the Minister of Education, 16 February 1976, ISA/GL-13133/8 (Hebrew).

The Lapid Report is of primary importance as it vividly demonstrates the high-level involvement of the Military Intelligence in every aspect of Arabic teaching in the post-1973 era. As evidenced by the report, during this period, Military Intelligence dominated the field of Arabic studies and was its very heart: it asks questions and provides answers; it defines needs and determines solutions. Indeed, the document deals with administrative questions, educational dilemmas, moral and motivational difficulties and the involvement of the media. During this period, Military Intelligence initiated and supported existing projects, proposed new programmes and spearheaded cooperation with civilian bodies, including schools, universities and the public. Furthermore, Military Intelligence framed the perception of the subject in society and engaged in activities intended to make Arabic more attractive to prospective pupils. To do this, it referenced the security connotations of Arabic such as the Youth Batallions that – using Lapid's words — can help 'to nurture a pride' in Arabic studies in schools. Perhaps this security orientation 'rescued' Arabic from public disinterest and from the widespread perception that the study of the language was impractical, however it also consigned Arabic to the realm of non-civilian, non-integrative and non-Arab.

The Chief of Intelligence sent the report to the Minister of Education along with a letter where he wrote the following:

> I attach to this letter a report prepared by Lt Col. Lapid, who serves as the Military Intelligence's Director of [the unit] in charge of activities to encourage Arabic and Oriental Studies. I do not want to delay preparations for the next school year. Therefore, I would appreciate it if we can set a meeting soon to coordinate and finalise the work plan for next year. I recommend that for this meeting you invite [from the Ministry of Education] Dr Dan Ronen, Mr Emmanuel Yaffe, Dr Karmi Yogev and Mr Y. Eyal.[50]

A letter sent by Minister of Education Aharon Yadlin to the General Director of the Ministry of Education, Gen. Ret. El'ad Peled the following week, indicates the dominance of Military Intelligence in Arabic studies. Strikingly, Yadlin echoed the words of the Chief of Intelligence almost verbatim. This points to the ascendency of the military over the Ministry of Education in relation to Arabic studies and decision-making in the field. According to Minister Yadlin:

> I attach to this letter a report prepared by Lt Col. Lapid, who serves as the Military Intelligence's Director of [the unit] in charge of the activities to encourage Arabic and Oriental studies. I do not want to delay the preparations to the next school year. Therefore, I would appreciate it if we can set a meeting soon with the Chief of Intelligence and his people, in order to coordinate and finalise the work plan for the next year. I recommend that for this meeting we [the Ministry of Education] invite Dr Dan Ronen, Mr Emmanuel Yaffe, Dr Karmi Yogev and Mr Y. Eyal.[51]

In explaining this convergence of interests, it is instructive to examine a project headed by Maj. Nissim ʿAtsmon. ʿAtsmon was a Military Intelligence officer and one of the first officers to serve in Ṭelem, the unit in the Military Intelligence dedicated to promoting Arabic and Oriental studies. From 1976 onwards, ʿAtsmon initiated a number of joint activities that brought together head teachers and Military Intelligence and aimed to highlight the importance of Arabic studies for Israeli national security.

In March 1976, for example, ʿAtsmon organised a trip whereby Israeli head teachers visited Gaza. Some 130 head teachers and senior Arabic teachers were invited, with 85 attending, a level of attendance that pleased ʿAtsmon. The programme included a tour of Al-Dahniyah and Al-Shāṭīʾ refugee camps; a tour of Yamit, an Israeli settlement in the northern part of the Sinai Peninsula; a lecture by Brig. Maymon, the Commander of the Gaza Strip area; and, finally – the cherry on top – a lecture given by the Chief of Intelligence, Gen. Shlomo Gazit.[52] According to ʿAtsmon, 'the event was a great success ... The visit impressed on them [head teachers] how important Arabic is ... Therefore, it is recommended to organise such a tour every year.'[53]

ʿAtsmon continued to expose head teachers to military uses of Arabic as well as to lectures by the Chief of Intelligence in military zones the following year. In February 1977, he sent head teachers an official invitation for the second such tour.[54] Rather symbolically, the letterhead of this invitation did not feature logos of the Military Intelligence or of the Ministry of Education. Instead, the new letterhead combined both: Military Intelligence was represented by the Ṭelem Unit, while the Ministry of Education was represented by its Youth Department. This new letterhead is indicative of two things: first, that in 1976, Military Intelligence – and probably soon after the reorganisation of the Military Intelligence (following the Agranat Commission) was made – had a unit to encourage Arabic language studies in Israeli schools that was already active.[55] It also demonstrates in a graphic and unequivocal way the extent of the cooperation between Military Intelligence and the Ministry of Education.[56]

In the letter, head teachers were encouraged to participate in 'the activity of the Military Intelligence and Ministry of Education for the encouragement of Oriental awareness in the education system [lit. *ṭipu ʾaḥ todaʿat ha-Mizraḥanut be-maʿarekhet ha-ḥinukh*]'.[57] Similar to previous correspondences in which 'coded language' was used, this letter also does not clarify what 'Oriental awareness' really means. This was the case as most likely the meaning was clear to the reader – that the nature of the trip was military–educational. According to the invitation, the 1977 trip took place on the Israeli–Lebanese border. The programme notes that head teachers met with the brigade commander of Division 300 at Biranit headquarters and received an explanation from the officer in charge of the Dovev Passage. It concluded with two more lectures; the first given by a Military Intelligence officer with the Northern Command and the second by the Chief of Intelligence himself.[58]

While it is clear that security considerations were involved in Arabic language studies, they also influenced what were seemingly purely educational discussions. For example, the Gargir Committee, which was established by the Ministry of Education in 1975, also referenced the military implications of studying Arabic. Named after Moshe Gargir, the committee's chairman, its goal was to improve Arabic studies, in particular by focusing on teacher training and textbooks. The committee began meeting late in 1975 and submitted its recommendations in April 1976. In the committee's final report, Gargir wrote:

> Following the 1967 War, and mostly after the 1973 War, there has been an awakening in the field of Arabic studies – after many years of stagnation – and more [Jewish] Israelis are interested in learning about the Arabs, their language, way of life, etc. ... The needs of our country have also evolved, especially the need for Arabic experts who would serve the country in the public domain ... including security, education and research ... and the demand is larger than the supply [lit. *ṿe-ein ha-heitsaʿ madbiḳ et ha-biḳush*] ...[59]

Gargir then noted that, owning to an increased interest and efforts invested in promoting the study and teaching of Arabic, between the years 1970 and 1976 there was a *sixfold* increase in the number of Arabic language pupils in primary schools. Gargir praised the IDF 'for sharing with the Ministry of Education their rich experience in training Arabists', and thanked Military Intelligence for its readiness to offer its services and expertise to the educational authorities.[60] In addition to suggesting that Arabic should become a compulsory subject of study, the committee also recommended that the Ministry of Education incorporate Military Intelligence teaching aids and experience into their educational programme.[61]

The Knesset's Education Committee also discussed Arabic language education – with clear security connotations – over two separate meetings in 1976. Specifically, members examined a bill proposed by MK Nuzhat [Darwish] Katsav, an Israeli parliamentarian of Jewish-Iraqi origin. Katsav, whose first language was Arabic, called her bill, 'Encouragement of the Study of the Arabic Language Due to its Importance for Security and Peace'. The bill explains that:

> Arabic is certainly needed for coexistence [with the Palestinian citizens of Israel], but it is also needed for security, since we [Jewish-Israelis] are an island in a sea of hate [lit. *anu 'i boded be-yam shel eivah*] ... Due to several failures, Arabic is not learnt sufficiently, and the quality of pupils is low ... This causes a real shortage in Arabic-speakers for the IDF.[62]

To support her position, Katsav referenced Hebrew language teaching in Arab countries. According to her, 'The Arabs in Arab countries teach Hebrew as a security need, unlike us in Israel who teach Arabic as a step towards peace ... Also their broadcasts in Hebrew do not serve the causes of peace, unlike our broadcasts in Arabic.' Katsav was making two arguments. First, she portrayed Israel, in contrast to its neighbours, as a peace-loving country that used the Arabic media to promote the aims of peace and brotherhood. However, her main point was that, in light of the political situation, the Ministry of Education should prioritise the teaching of Arabic in schools.[63]

In support of her argument, Katsav brought to Members of Knesset the 'usual suspects' of expertise in Arabic studies: representatives from the Ministry of Education and Military Intelligence, and she also presented them with relevant reports. Eventually, the Education Committee of the Knesset, in its summary on the matter, 'call[ed] on the Ministry of Education to declare immediately that the teaching of the Arabic language as a second foreign language will be a compulsory school subject in both primary and high schools'.[64] The Committee also decided that Arabic studies should include a general introduction to 'Arab cultural assets.'[65]

The bill of MK Katsav is noteworthy for it interesting juxtaposition of 'peace' and 'security' and, indeed, it seamlessly integrates Military Intelligence reports on the one hand, and 'Arab cultural assets' on the other. As indicated here, Arabic was increasingly viewed as both the 'language of the enemy' and the 'language of the neighbour', even when the initiator of the debate was a Jewish-Iraqi person who was not part of the security establishment. Mixed messages of this nature were not new; its seeds were sown in the field of Arabic studies from the very early days of Zionism in Palestine. However, the juxtaposition of 'security' and 'culture' alongside each other and presented as two complementary aims began to appear more frequently in the post-1967 period and intensified following the events of 1973. Even the official title of the bill, 'Arabic for Security and Peace', reflected this dual perspective. As will be demonstrated later, this way of conceptualising Arabic continued to be prominent throughout the 1980s, 1990s and also in the twenty-first century.

Unquestionably, the 1973 War ushered in a period of cooperation between the Military Intelligence and Ministry of Education that, in depth and intensity, far surpassed the previous period of 1967–73. This way or another, from 1967 to 1976, officers from Military Intelligence – up to and including the Chief of Intelligence – almost took over control of Arabic language studies. Gradually, they began to participate in all aspects of the field, including recruiting pupils, training teachers, developing teaching programmes, marketing and outreach and organising trips for head teachers to military zones. All of this took place with the blessing of the Ministry of Education, which probably realised that Military Intelligence adds prestige, as well as experience, to the study of Arabic. This close cooperation was due to an understanding that Arabic was not an ordinary school subject, rather its was an issue of national concern with security as a crucial consideration.

According to official figures released by the Ministry of Education, during this period there was a tremendous increase in the number of Jewish pupils electing to study Arabic. At the primary level, for example, the number of schools teaching Arabic rose from 80 in 1969, to 153 in 1972 and further increased to 265 in 1975. Likewise, the number of pupils increased as well: while 6900 were studying Arabic in 1969, by 1972 that number had risen to 20,150 and then jumped to 41,800 in 1975. The number of teachers also grew from 72 to 135 to 250, respectively.[66]

The growing influence and involvement of Military Intelligence and their personnel in the field of Arabic studies can be correlated with general changes in Israeli society after 1973. Uri Ben-Eliezer, in his study of Israeli militarism, helps us to contextualise these developments, as he identified the post-1973 period as a watershed in Israeli history:

> The Yom Kippur War not only did not challenge the hegemonic perception of Israel as a nation-in-arms, but did exactly the opposite. The war strengthened the feeling of Israeli people that they are the sons of one nation and that they have one destiny. Furthermore, the lesson that Israeli society learned from the failures of the Israeli army in the 1973 War, which were highlighted by the Agranat Commission, was a process of over-militarisation of society, its

> comprehensive recruitment [to the national cause] and a constant state of alertness.[67]

The preceding discussion supports the argument that this ethos was an integral part of teaching Arabic in Jewish-Israeli schools. The 1973 War represented a turning point in terms of the intensity of the securitisation of Arabic in the Israeli educational system. In spite of the discourse about peace and neighbourliness, the Arabic taught in Israel, which I call 'Israeli Arabic', was gradually dominated by and associated with one primary concern: security.

One other factor pushed Military Intelligence and the Ministry of Education into the same camp. Quite silent in nature, and sometimes only indirectly alluded to, it was central to the Military Intelligence's promotion of Arabic studies. Around this period of time, Military Intelligence came to the realisation that the second generation of Mizraḥi Jews neither studied nor were interested in studying Arabic. Thus, the IDF understood that the education system was the last remaining reservoir of potential soldiers who would have a knowledge of Arabic. This increased the urgency of the mission, as the next section reveals.

The 'disappearance' of Arab-Jews

> My father's colleagues were a 'nature reserve', as the Israeli expression goes: they spoke Arabic, read the Arabic press, and listened to Arabic radio stations; some of them spent time in other countries and identified themselves as Arabs. They eavesdropped on the famous radio conversation between Egypt's President Abd al-Nasser and Jordan's King Hussein a few days prior to the outbreak of the June 1967 War, in Arabic of course. How ironic that their very entry into the Israeli collective, which was made through their intelligence work, demanded that they remain part of the Arab world against which they worked. Such is the logic of the Israeli state: top-heavy with contradictions. On the one hand, it wants to strip its Arab Jews, citizens of Israel known as Mizraḥim, of their Arabness, while on the other, it implores some of them (like my father and his friends) to go on living as Arabs by license.[68]

This quotation, by Israeli scholar Yehuda Shenhav, provides an interesting glimpse into the reality of the Arab-Jews, following their arrival in Israel. In their countries of origin – primarily Iraq, Egypt, Syria, Palestine, Yemen, Morocco, Tunisia and Algeria – the Arabic language and its accompanying dialects were an essential part of their lives.[69] Israel, which considered Arabic to be an official language mostly in theory, did not encourage them and, to a certain extent, put them off maintaining Arabic as a fully functioning language, unless they were part of the security establishment.[70]

Coming back to 1948, it is important to note that following the creation of the state, the number of employment opportunities involving Arabic in the public domain was small. Not surprisingly, they were mostly directly or indirectly connected to Israel's political interests and security needs. The bodies where Arabic was in demand included Military Intelligence, the Department of Arab Affairs in the Prime Minister's Office, the Military Government, various security services, the Israeli media in Arabic, the education system for Palestinian citizens of Israel in the Military Government areas, and the teaching of Arabic in the Jewish education system. What all these job opportunities had in common was the close connection between Arabic and national concerns, not to say national security needs. Therefore, the Arabic of Arab-Jews – with its everyday human and cultural elements – was primarily confined to the private domain. It was only socially acceptable (or as Shenhav termed it, 'living as Arabs by license') in the realms of politics and security. In other words, Arab-Jews, who immigrated to a country dominated by Ashkenazi Jews, were exposed to a dominant social attitude that patronised Arab culture and people. Arab-Jews, who had a natural affinity to the Arab world, now spoke the 'language of the enemy' and were living in a country that idealised 'the West' and so prevented them from associating themselves with the politics, identity, culture and societies of the 'the East'. This paradox shaped the lives of Arab-Jews, influenced their attitudes towards their own culture, and completely transformed the experiences of their children.

Second-generation Arab-Jews who were born in Israel sought to distance themselves from their 'Arab' roots. They did not speak Arabic and did not associate with realms that were considered to be 'too Arab'. It was clear that being Arab – at least in the context of the Zionist European hegemonic discourse – meant being a non-Jew and an enemy of the state. Furthermore, from a socioeconomic perspective, Arabs and those associated with Arabs, found themselves in the lower rungs of the social hierarchy – something to be avoided at all costs. In light of this reality, the new generation decided – consciously or not – that accentuating one's 'Jewish-Israeli' identity meant diminishing his or her Arab characteristics. As if that was not enough, quite frequently, Arab-Jews were encouraged to 'prove' their Israeliness. This took place in a number of ways, including changing their family names, via service in the IDF and the Israeli police, by adopting a Western, non-Arab, pronunciation of modern Israeli Hebrew and more.[71]

The second generation's alienation from the first language of their parents was due to a number of factors. As noted, some of these were socioeconomic. Furthermore, Arabic was considered to be both the language of 'the enemy' and the language of the Diaspora. On the level of ideology, Arabic was associated with exile in a country dominated by a discourse that encouraged 'negation of the exile'.[72] Second, full entrance and acceptance into Israel society was conditioned on 'forgetting' one's foreign language – and Arabic most evidently and urgently as it included also disguising one's Arab cultural origins. The uniqueness of the Mizraḥi experience in Israel, and the pressures put on the Mizraḥi, can be demonstrated in the fact that even the second generation of these communities were considered by the Israeli establishment – Ashkneazi in nature – as keeping their 'Mizraḥiyut' (Mizraḥi orientation) and as such not becoming plain 'Israelis'.[73]

Thus, once in Israel, Arab-Jews were forced to make a choice: they were either Arabs or Jews. Being both was not an option – particularly outside the confines of their specific communities. Thus, those who wanted to succeed in Israeli terms were forced to become Jewish-Israeli. While similar processes influenced other immigrant communities, factors of class and sociocultural identity created the specific context and put pressures on members of this group in an acute way. Therefore, due to the Israeli establishment's adoption of an Orientalist approach, immigrants from countries considered to be Israel's 'enemy' faced unique dilemmas and challenges to their cultural identity.

Many were forced to prove their Jewishness through a process that has been termed *religionisation*. According to Shenhav, who coined the term, 'If the Ashkenazi entrance ticket to Jewish-Israeli nationalism was through secularisation, the Mizraḥi entrance ticket was by the strengthening of their Jewish religious beliefs.'[74] According to this theory, their religious identity served as a 'safety net', demonstrating that they would not slip back into Arabness. The desire to negate their 'Arabness', according to Ella Shohat, was also the reason why the term 'Arab-Jewish' fell out of favour and instead 'softer' expressions such as *Mizraḥim* (Orientals), *Sephardim* (descendants of the Jewish community that was expelled from Spain) and *'Edot ha-Mizraḥ* (the Oriental groups) were adopted.[75]

Indeed, as has been emphasised throughout this book, the separation of 'Arab' and 'Jewish' is analogous to the separation of the Arabic language and the Jewish people. The historic connection between the two, which was outlined in the first chapter, was intentionally denied or, at the very least, ignored. In Israel, Arabic became associated exclusively with Arab, non-Jewish communities, thus guaranteeing its rejection by those who strove to prove their Jewishness and their belonging to the Israeli collective. Strictly speaking, Arabic ceased to be Jewish the moment that Zionism's separatist principles – in language, land and labour – gained pace and tabooed the notion of Jews being Arabs.[76]

In 1970, Elie Eliachar, a prominent Sephardic leader, published a seminal article on the subject. Eliachar, who was born in Jerusalem in 1899 during Ottoman rule and studied medicine at the American University of Beirut and Law at the University of Cairo, had very different ideas regarding the connection between the Jewish people and the Arab world and between the Jewish people and Arabic. Observing the changes taking place in this group in Israel, he wrote:

> In schools, the children were made to believe that the culture of Israel should be that of a small town in Europe ... the rich culture of ʿEdot ha-Mizraḥ, which is intimate with Arab culture, was forced to be forgotten ... A kind of schizophrenia was then created among the Mizraḥi youth: on the one hand they respected their home, but on the other hand they were distanced from their home's culture while in school ... and as they wanted to be 'accepted' and integrated [to Jewish-Israeli society] ... they needed to deny themselves and to deny their past ... Psychologists and sociologists who will study this phenomenon in the future will realise the extent to which we have vandalised the souls of this generation and how much blind hate we have injected into their hearts towards anything that is Arab.[77]

Researches examining attitudes towards the study of Arabic and Arab culture among children of Arab-Jewish families in Israel have, indeed, uncovered low levels of motivation and some even display outright hostility towards Arabic and Arab culture. Eliezer Ben-Rafael and Ḥezi Brosh's research demonstrated that both Ashkenazi and Mizraḥi pupils perceived Arabic as a 'low capital language', whose speakers 'alienate the Jews'. However, they claimed that Mizraḥi pupils tended to have even more negative opinions about Arabs than Israelis of Ashkenazi origin. The research assumed that this was because Mizraḥi children were trying to differentiate themselves from the Arab people and culture by minimising the symbols that they had originally shared, including the mutual connection to Arabic.[78] Roberta Kraemer analysed this phenomenon employing Tajfel's Social Identity Theory:[79]

> The desire of the Mizraḥi Jews to integrate into the mainstream modern Jewish state and to shape their identity in terms of its dominant culture and language fosters psycholinguistic distinctiveness from the 'significant other' Arab group, which presents a negative social identity.[80]

Yasir Suleiman has argued that this Arab-Jewish alienation from Arabs and Arabic stems from the close proximity of the two communities. According to him, Mizraḥi youth try to differentiate themselves from Arabs because they are similar linguistically, culturally and socioeconomically.[81]

Returning to the school system in the 1970s, understanding the social situation and political oppression that the Arab-Jews were experiencing, helps to explain the strengthening of the partnership between the Ministry of Education and Military Intelligence. In other words, the second generation of Arab-Jews developed feelings of alienation vis-à-vis Arabic, a fact that made them more 'Israeli' according to the sociopolitical definitions of Israel, but posed a challenge to the Military Intelligence and the Israeli security establishment. Therefore, and as the first generation of Arab-Jews were now passing away, the natural reservoir of Jews who could speak Arabic and serve the Israeli security system was becoming depleted, with no clear replacement in sight. Arab-Jews – who had taken a decisive role in the relevant political- and security-oriented positions during the first two decades of the state, serving in fields such as education, Military Intelligence, politics, the media and the foreign service – were in the 1970s approaching the age of retirement. Prominent individuals included: Eliyahu Ḥabuba, who was born in Damascus in 1882 and served as an Arabic teacher at the Hebrew Reali School in Haifa; Avraham Sharoni, born in Baghdad in 1918 and served as the head of the Communication Intelligence Unit in the 1960s); Avraham Toledano, born in 1921 in Tiberias to a Moroccan-Jewish family and was the Adviser on Arab Affairs in the 1960s); Nissim Malul, born in Safed in 1887 to a Tunisian-Jewish family, who translated the Israeli official gazette in the 1950s; and Ephraim Dowek, born in Cairo in 1930 and served as an Israeli ambassador from 1963. They are all examples of individuals who were from the first wave of immigration to the country, who served in the above mentioned fields and who had no clear successors.

This 'shortage', unsurprisingly, was felt most acutely in the areas of Jewish-Israeli society where Arabic was most frequently used. It was especially pronounced in Military Intelligence, where proficiency in Arabic was crucial. Therefore, and as before, Military Intelligence officials were the first to notice this trend regarding Arabic and sound the warning bells. The new reality, whereby first-generation Arab-Jews began to reach retirement age, was a huge source of concern for the Military Intelligence. Consequently, they felt that they had no choice but to use all means at their disposal to create a pool of Arabic specialists who could satisfy national security needs. This also helps to explain their vigorous involvement in the field of Arabic studies throughout the 1970s, alongside the obvious reasons such as the 1973 War and its aftermath. In this way or another, it was again evident that in the process, Arabic was no longer the sole and primary preserve of the Ministry of Education, rather it became a joint endeavour between the state security apparatus and the Ministry of Education.

Evidence for this comes from a letter sent by Ya ʿacov Eyal, the Supervisor of Arabic Studies at the Ministry of Education, to Aharon Yadlin, the Minister of Education in 1974. In his letter, Supervisor Eyal noted the 'Arab-Jewish disappearance' and its impact on Arabic studies. He mentioned that he was prompted to write the letter by a meeting with Shlomo Gazit, the Chief of Intelligence, and said that he recognised the need for a national institution to train Arabic language teachers. According to Eyal:

> Such an institution is crucial to the field of Arabic studies in Israel, since those speaking the language, and who come from Arab countries, are getting closer to the age of retirement. If we do not train a reserve of Arabic experts, in a few years we will be facing a hopeless situation [lit. *naʿamod mul shoḳet shevurah*]. If this happens, we will not be able to allocate knowledgeable and authoritative people to national and sensitive duties [lit. *lo nukhal le-ʾayesh tafḳidim mamlakhtiyyim ḥashuvim ṿe-regisihim*] ...[82]

Here again, Eyal employs the 'coded language' of the security-oriented network of Arabic studies in Jewish-Israeli society. He notes the importance of Arabic in 'national and sensitive duties' with no clarification about what these duties actually entailed. Also of interest in this letter is Eyal's sense of urgency – which was prompted by his meeting with the Chief of Intelligence.

This same prognosis was offered two years later, in 1976, by Chaim Basoḳ, at the time the Deputy Mayor of Tel Aviv. Basoḳ wrote a letter to the Minister of Education in the context of a decision by the city of Tel Aviv to initiate a project supporting Arabic language teaching and learning. Basoḳ stated:

> The teaching of Arabic today is more important than ever for three main reasons: first, since it improves the chances for dialogue between us and our Arab neighbours, and this could help ease the hostilities. Second, due to the great interest that the IDF has in the language, e.g. Military Intelligence and the military units that operate in the [Occupied] 'Territories'. Third, since we are no longer experiencing ʿaliyah [Jewish immigration] from Arab countries, the Israeli Arabic-speaking intelligentsia is getting smaller and smaller, and filling in this gap is vital.[83]

Basoḳ also employed the well-known formula of 'Arabic for peace' (dialogue with our neighbours) and 'Arabic for security' (Military Intelligence's need for speakers of Arabic). However, his third rationale – the falling number of Arabic-speaking Arab-Jews – is significant.

Interestingly, the same three rationales were used by Avraham Kats, the head of the Knesset Education and Culture Committee. In the evaluation made in 1976 of MK Nuzhat Katsav's legislative proposal, Kats outlined the reasons why the Committee decided to support Katsav's bill. Following a reference to the importance of Arabic in serving national security, Kats added that:

> The meaningful numbers of Jewish immigrants coming from Iraq and Egypt are getting smaller and smaller ... Lt Col. Lapid from Military Intelligence explained to us the current needs of the IDF for Arabic experts, and the things are indeed clear [lit. *ṿe-ha-deveraim muvanim*].[84]

At the same meeting, in response to Kats's advocacy, the Committee also initiated a discussion focused on making Arabic a compulsory subject. Lapid, who supported the proposal, shared the IDF's views on the matter. He also highlighted the need to find an alternative for Arabic-speaking Jews:

> Contemporary needs force us to make Arabic a compulsory school subject ... We [the Military Intelligence] suffer from an acute problem: the presence in the intelligence community of the first generation of serious Arabists [lit. *ha-dor ha-rishon shel ha-ʿArabisṭim ha-retsiniyyim*], who immigrated to Israel from Arab countries, is getting smaller and

> smaller among the intelligence community. We need 250 [new] men every year in active service who have a good knowledge of Arabic. Remember that in these positions, confrontations with the enemy can last merely a matter of seconds. We are in need of Arabic-speakers who understand in a few seconds what the enemy says ...[85]

Lapid's explanation for the tremendous importance of Arabic-speaking Jews is very straightforward. In his conceptualisation, knowledge of Arabic can make the difference between life and death. Consequently, and according to Military Intelligence, the retirement of Arab-Jews and the dearth of Arabic-speakers among the younger generation was a serious and alarming *security* problem.

Indeed, archival documents demonstrate that the increasing involvement of Military Intelligence in areas under the purview of the Ministry of Educations following the 1967 and 1973 wars and throughout the 1970s was motivated by a number of factors, not least of which were demographic changes in the Arabic-speaking Jewish community in Israel. In an interview with him, Sasson Somekh, Professor Emiritus at Tel Aviv University, made a joke that referred to Arab-Jewish dominance in Israeli Military Intelligence in the 1950s and 1960s. His joke focused on Unit 8200, the Central Collection Unit of the Israeli Intelligence Corps and the largest unit in the IDF: 'Do you know why it was called 8200?' he asked me. Seeing that I was not familiar with the joke, he said smiling: 'Since in the 1960s, for every eight Ashkenazi Military Intelligence soldiers of this unit, you had 200 Iraqis.'[86]

This joke provides a glimpse into the world of the Israeli intelligence community. While there are no statistics regarding the exact number of Arab-Jews who served in Military Intelligence, or even about their relative proportion to Ashkenazi Jews, and even if Somekh's joke is only half-true, the retirement of Arab-Jews from security-oriented positions left a large gap in the Israeli intelligence world. This only further motivated the Israeli Military Intelligence – which following the 1973 War was already committed to the idea – to take more steps to encourage Arabic studies in schools.

4
Israel's Army of Arabists
1976 and Beyond

First comes the band, then the machine guns
From the military headquarters to the municipality hall
Let's wave hello to the parade

Habiluyim[1]

A lifelong journey: the Ministry of Education and Military Intelligence

As was demonstrated in the preceding chapter, the 1967 War and especially the 1973 War had decisive impacts on Jewish-Israeli society generally and specifically on the field of Arabic studies. The wars bolstered connections between those in charge of Arabic in Jewish-Israeli schools and the military establishment. Indeed, the IDF – especially in the aftermath of the 1973 War – due to a widespread feeling of panic and a sense of national mission, had more opportunities to increase its influence on Arabic language studies. This influence reached unprecedented levels in subsequent years. In other words, the wars had two related outcomes: first, they highlighted the importance of having sufficient numbers of Arabic-speaking military personnel working for the Israeli security establishment in order to prevent another Yom Kippur War and serve the Israeli security system; and, second, with regards to the anticipated shortage of manpower due to the imminent retirement of Arab-Jewish Israelis, they created a sense of emergency in the field. These trends strengthened the association between Arabic and security while pushing Military Intelligence even deeper into the realm of education. As a result, as this chapter will demonstrate, there was a marked increase in military–educational programmes and involvement in the Jewish-Israeli school system in the 1970s and the 1980s.

One of the first programmes to be created during this period was Ṭelem (the Hebrew acronym for *Ṭipua'ḥ Limudei Mizraḥanut*: Unit for the the Encouragement of Oriental Studies, which in Israel is associated with Arabic studies). Created in 1976 and implemented by Military Intelligence soldiers and officers,[2] Ṭelem's aim was to promote the study of Arabic among pupils while providing support to Arabic teachers. Ṭelem, which remains active to this day, will be discussed in this chapter in more detail.[3]

Another outcome of the 1973 War was the creation of the Oriental Youth Battalions, the *Gadnaʿ Mizraḥanim*. Founded in 1973 and, like Ṭelem, still operative, the project aims to familiarise Jewish high school pupils studying Arabic with the work of Military Intelligence and its personnel, and to boost their motivation to take Arabic in high school while understanding its relevancy to Israel's national security. Since 1976, the project has implemented one-week seminars whereby pupils are given the opportunity to learn about the various intelligence units and are encouraged to continue studying the language. This project closely aligns pupils' studies in the school system with their hoped for future service in Military Intelligence. The programme and the Military Intelligence mentors who run it, emphasise the important role that Arabic plays in guaranteeing Israeli security and they encourage potential conscripts to view Arabic as a pathway to service in the IDF. They bolster pupil motivation to continue studying the subject in light of the competition proffered by the study of other elective subjects in school, and they try to counter the stereotypes of Arabic as being low status, difficult to learn and not useful. Accordingly, the Oriental Youth Battalion notes the practicality of Arabic for security purposes while also strengthening the association between Military Intelligence and the education system, as the pupils leave their school, sometimes with their teacher, join the military-oriented Arabic week and then return to school to continue their Arabic studies. This way, the military serves as an injection of motivation for the pupils taking Arabic in school. Furthermore, from the perspective of the IDF, the programme is also an assessment tool that facilitates the ability of Military Intelligence to identify appropriate candidates for future recruitment and to strengthen the relations between Military Intelligence and the schools and classes where Arabic is taught, and with the pupils and teachers of Arabic.[4]

An interesting, even if indirect offshoot of the 1973 War, was the establishment of the Piamenta Committee. Set up in 1976, it was headed by Moshe Piamenta, an Arabic language professor at the Hebrew University who, at the time, was serving as the General Supervisor of Arabic Studies at the Ministry of Education. Committee members were drawn from the Ministry of Education and Military Intelligence. It is worth mentioning that the connection between Arabic and security was not new for Piamenta. In 1967, while working as a scholar at the Hebrew University, he participated in a committee called the 'High Committee for the Assessment of the Needs of Military Intelligence'.[5]

The aims of the 1976 ommittee echoed those of previous committees established by the Ministry of Education to assess Arabic, and it was tasked with examining the state of Arabic language teaching in the Jewish-Israeli school system and identifying strategies to strengthen and promote it. The establishment of the committee was driven by the intense need for Arabic-speakers in the military in the post-1973 era. A letter sent by Emmanuel Yaffe, the head of the Teaching Division at the Ministry of Education, attests to this. Addressed to Lt Col. Ephraim Lapid from Military Intelligence, Yaffe stated that the committee was nothing less than 'intensive care for Arabic teaching in Jewish-Israeli schools'.[6]

The Piamenta Committee published its findings and recommendations in June 1977, and there was indeed something unique in its conclusions. Interestingly, and unlike previous committees, it phrased its recommendations in civil, as opposed to military, terms. The Piamenta Report concluded that Arabic studies in Jewish-Israeli schools 'should familiarise the pupils with the sociopolitical entity of the Arabs [lit. *hakarat ha-yeshut ha-ḥevratit-medinit shel ha-ʿAravim*] and their cultural legacy'.[7] The document then identified 'the ability to understand contemporary Arabic newspapers and literature, and the development of listening skills [lit. *kosher haʾazanah*] to radio and television broadcasts' as a priority.[8] The committee also believed that pupils should be capable of 'face-to-face conversations in Colloquial Arabic'. The most profoundly civil aim, though, was kept for last: to educate pupils 'for a respectful coexistence with Arabs'.[9]

The recommendations, interestingly, and especially the emphasis on Colloquial Arabic, were based on a combination of political and security concerns along with the need to create dialogue, respect and coexistence. With regards to this, also the conceptualisation of Arabic studies by the committee reflected a dualistic understanding of the need for Arabic – Arabic for peace and Arabic for security. This duality, as I will explain, only served further to militarise – not civilianise – the subject. Although peace was a stated goal, the committee only consisted of Jewish-Israelis and was headed by a former Military Intelligence personality (Piamenta served in Military Intelligence during the 1948 War, and beforehand worked in the Arab Bureau of the Haganah in Jerusalem). In its work, the committee combined the civil and military expertise of Arabic studies, and at least in this dimension was no different to other committees.

It is likely that the relatively conciliatory direction of the committee's recommendations reflected the background of Piamenta himself. Piamenta, who grew up in Jerusalem in the 1920s and 1930s, spoke Colloquial Arabic fluently and was an Israeli academic and pedagogic authority in this vernacular. His specific realm of expertise in Colloquial Arabic was probably behind the committee's emphasis on Colloquial Arabic. Indeed, the committee recommended the teaching of Colloquial Arabic in grades 4 to 6 and then continue with instruction in Literary Arabic in grades 7 to 9.[10] This decision, which was approved by the Ministry of Education, was considered to be a major departure from the way in which Arabic had been taught until then. For the first time, Colloquial Arabic was introduced into the programme of study at an early age (grades 5 and 6), followed by the study of Literary Arabic in the intermediate school.

This decision was not only based on civilian and pedagogic considerations, it also stemmed from a confluence of interests of those in charge, and from the same mixture of 'peace and security'. In 1968, Piamenta published an influential book on Arabic language studies that hints at its Jewish perception and orientation. The book was titled *Speak Arabic: An Introduction to Eretz-Yisraeli Arabic.*[11] But this was only half of Piamenta's sides. Interestingly, the recommendation to introduce Colloquial Arabic to Israeli school children was made with the support of the IDF. In fact, the IDF probably suggested it as it reflected the way of thinking of another individual, the then Chief of Intelligence, Gen. Shlomo Gazit. Evidence of his interest in Colloquial Arabic can be found in the foreword written by Gazit to a 1976 textbook authored by Avraham Ḥakim entitled *Colloquial Eretz-Yisraeli Arabic.*[12] As expected, Gazit viewed the twin concepts of peace and security as compatible and, as such, envisioned Military Intelligence as a source of both. He wrote as follows:

> We see Arabic as an important and essential tool to be used in three fields. First, in a professional-military capacity. Who knows better than us in Military Intelligence how necessary it is, during peace and war, to have an increasing number of speakers of Arabic who will serve the network of [Arabic] experts, as researchers, translators, eavesdroppers, investigators of prisoners and more. Second, Arabic is important to understanding the Arab world that encircles us. Israel is located in

> the centre of the Middle East and is surrounded by Arab countries. Understanding this world, its customs and its way of thinking,[13] can enable us to confront the problems, the challenges and the threats created by this [Arab] world. Third is creating discussion, since a settlement of the Arab–Israeli conflict will not come out of nowhere ... A system of dialogue and discussion, as broad as possible, continuous and comprehensive, will lay the foundation for peace-making. I hope that the initiative to publish this book on teaching of Colloquial Arabic will contribute to finding solutions in these three areas.[14]

Both Ḥakim and Piamenta's *Eretz-Yisraeli Arabic* books, and certainly Gazit's introduction, point to the increased popularity of Colloquial Arabic following the 1967 War. This provides an important context for the Piamenta Committee's emphasis on Colloquial Arabic and the adoption of the recommendation to increase its study by the Ministry of Education. In fact, Piamenta's and Ḥakim's books reflected a general increase in publications about and interest in Colloquial Arabic in Israel during that period.[15] Furthermore, Gazit notes the close connection between Arabic studies and Military Intelligence while also pointing to the superiority of the IDF in assessing the field of Arabic studies. After all, according to him, 'Who knows better than us in Military Intelligence how necessary it is, during peace and war, to have an increasing number of speakers of Arabic.'

In the text quoted above, Gazit emphasises the need for dialogue in order to reach a peaceful settlement of the Arab–Israeli conflict. This view is reflected by Ḥakim himself. In answer to the question, 'why do we need to study Arabic', Ḥakim notes in the book that, 'even if we cannot reach an understanding with the Arabs who surround us, we need to study Arabic so that we can learn about their intentions'. He then finishes with a proverb, whose origin I was unable to verify, which goes as follows: 'A wise man once said, the Arabic language in Israel is a bridge for peace or a bridge to war' (lit. *jisr li-al-salām aw li-al-ḥarb*).[16] The views of the 'wise man' seem suspiciously similar to those expressed by Gazit in the foreword that he had written as the Chief of Intelligence. It can be argued that the wise man in this case was also the Military Intelligence one.

Irrespective of this, the dual notions of 'peace and security', mentioned here and before, were a convenient rationale for the need for Arabic languages studies in Israel, and are therefore a core value of 'Israeli Arabic'. This formulation gained traction following the 1973 War and remains prevalent to the present time but, interestingly, this trend is not unique to the field of Arabic. Rather, it reflects similar trends taking place in other areas of Jewish-Israeli life. Just as an example, I will mention that in the political arena in Israel and in other institutions of state, 'peace and security' were and continue to be recurrent themes. Many Israeli electoral campaigns are driven by the imperatives of 'security and peace' and 'peace and security'. For example, the Likud Party's political campaign in the 1996 elections featured two main slogans: 'No Peace, No Security, No Reason to Vote for Peres' and 'Likud: We Make a Secure Peace'. The Labour Party's slogan for that same election was 'Peace with Security'. In the Likud's 2001 campaign, Ariel Sharon's slogans included: 'Peace and Security, Security and Peace' and 'No Security without Peace'. A similar example comes from the late Prime Minister Yitzhak Rabin. Regarding negotiations with the Palestinians in the 1990s, he famously commented that: 'We will fight terror as if there are no negotiations and conduct negotiations as if there is no terror.'[17] Indeed, these two notions are central to Jewish-Israeli discourse and are viewed, naturally, as being complimentary.[18]

To conclude this argument, I will say that the military sphere, like the political sphere, adopted a similar outlook. This is evident in the symbols employed by the Haganah and the IDF. Both military bodies adopted the symbol of a sword wrapped in an olive branch.[19] The sentiment of 'security and peace' in Israeli discourse can, therefore, be regarded as a central characteristic of Jewish-Israeli society, especially in the political and military arenas, and to the 'Israeli-Judaisation' of any concept – including Arabic studies – that was considered equally important 'for peace and security' and so kept these fields, just like that of Arabic studies, Jewish-Israeli in nature and hardly open to Palestinian citizens of the state.

In his groundbreaking book *The Iron Wall*, Avi Shlaim examines Israeli decision-making at some of its most crucial decision-making junctures. He analyses a concept that is widespread among Jewish-Israelis, according to which the Israeli leaders – military and political alike – were always willing to stretch their hand out in peace. Shlaim finds this belief to be without basis, and I consider his findings to be supported by the arguments presented here. While the rhetoric of peace is prevalent in Israel, it is undergirded by a militaristic discourse and can serve as a justification to a 'defensive', 'last resort' war (in Hebrew: *milḥemet ein breirah*). Thus, the juxtaposition of the olive branch with the sword and the role of Arabic as a bridge for both war and peace gains a renewed clarity.

Back to the field of Arabic studies, I believe that in relation to this field, the notion of 'peace and security' has influenced the wider discourse surrounding conflicts between Jews and Palestinians. For example, Jewish-Israelis regularly place 'conflict' and 'coexistence' next to each other. The definition of an Arabic expert falls in Israel along similar lines. It has always been a Jewish person (and almost always a male) who embodies both the *civilian* and *security* orientations towards the language. People with these character traits, particularly in the post-1967 and 1973 eras, came to be regarded as the most 'objective' and 'professional' of Arabic language educators and experts. They were viewed as combining the Israeli concepts of *self-defence* with the Jewish-Israelis' perceptions of the country as *peace-seeking*. Thus, there is a high esteem for an Arabic professional who can serve in both capacities – promoting peace while guaranteeing security. They are viewed as the embodiment of war-and-peace and the holders of both the sword and the olive branch.

In the context of Piamenta's and Ḥakim's Arabic textbooks, and in light of the importance of Colloquial Arabic during this period, both authors employ a similar politically loaded term to define the Arabic dialect in their textbooks: *Eretz-Yisraeli Arabic*. In this definition, which is featured in the titles of both of their books, notably absent are references to Palestinians, Palestine or the Arab people, and in this way it can be seen as part of the creation of 'Israeli Arabic'. The choice of terminology was not accidental; it was consistent with Zionist ideology that denied the right of the Palestinians to land that it considered to be unequivocally Jewish. This is reminiscent of Eliʿezer Ben-Yehuda's conceptualisation of Hebrew as containing Jewish 'roots'. David Ben-Gurion, the Zionist statesman, political leader and Israel's first prime minister, also displayed similar themes in this thinking – he characterised Palestinian peasants as Jews who were forced to convert. Similar trends can be discerned in the selection of place names by Jewish-Israelis; these almost universally reflect a Zionist ethos.[20] Similarly, referring to Palestinian citizens of Israel as 'Israeli Arabs' is not accidental; it is a choice that attempts to rewrite their identity in ways that reflect Zionist thought.[21] Therefore, it is important to understand the term *Eretz-Yisraeli Arabic* – and Arabic in Israel in general – in the appropriate ideological context. The study of Arabic became an extension of a multifaceted national project whereby Jewish-Israelis asserted their political rights at the expense of and in order to displace Palestinians and to deny their narrative.

While the Piamenta Committee's recommendations were officially endorsed and garnered widespread approval, their implementation was slow. Perhaps support for the recommendation to add Colloquial 'Eretz-Yisraeli' Arabic was widespread due to its emphasis on Arabic as a means of achieving both 'peace and security' and because it reflected a culmination of the mutual interests and pedagogical views of both the Ministry of Education (represented by Piamenta) and Military Intelligence (represented by Gazit). However, despite the importance of this decision and this convergence of interests, operationally it required training new teachers and the development of new curriculums. Furthermore, it did not have either a direct or an immediate impact on the number of high school pupils studying Arabic. The IDF, not surprisingly, was displeased with the pace of progress.

Therefore, a year after the publication of the Piamenta Committee's recommendations, Gen. Rafael Vardi, the IDF Commander of the Manpower Directorate, asked to meet with the newly appointed Minister of Education, Zevulun Hammer. Following the meeting, in a letter sent by Vardi to Hammer, the former outlined the IDF's concerns:

> Without a significant change regarding the development of Arabic studies in schools, we may find ourselves facing a new fact: that the young [Jewish] generation in the country will have no fluency in Arabic ... in parallel with the low numbers of pupils, we experience, year after year, a depletion of [Jews] who came from Arab countries and who are fluent in Arabic. The needs of Military Intelligence are growing annually and we are therefore calling for urgent measures in order to improve the situation ... We therefore recommend turning Arabic into a compulsory school subject in all high schools, and to do so as soon as possible ...[22]

Vardi's letter outlined at least five more IDF-generated recommendations for the Ministry of Education – all of which were intended to increase the number of high school pupils studying Arabic. In all likelihood, the IDF strove to integrate 'peace and security' into its agenda and so to 'prove' that it was aware of the national discourse and belonged to the field of Arabic studies. The linkage that Vardi made was very telling and, as will be now shown, the IDF was definitely part and parcel of the 'peace-and-security' notion.

Indeed, the connection between security and peace became even stronger during this same time period. In 1977, in a truly historic event, Egyptian President Anwar al-Sadat, with the blessing of Israeli Prime Minister Menachem Begin, came to Israel to facilitate a peace treaty between the two countries. In November 1977, Sadat addressed the Israeli Knesset, an act that surprised many Israelis – and most probably Hammer among them. This event represented in the clearest way the new opportunities to use Arabic as a vehicle for peace, and to the

Arab world that could be opened up to Israel. This moment ushered in one of Israel's most ambitious Arabic educational programmes: a five-year plan aimed at doubling the number of Jewish-Israeli pupils studying Arabic. However, and despite being related to a peaceful, civilian event, even this plan was to be financed – rather unsurprisingly – by the security establishment.

The first inklings of this plan came to light two months after Ṿardi and Hammer met and a month after Sadat's speech to the Knesset. It was discussed at a meeting that took place between the Minister of Education and the Supervisor of Arabic Studies, Moshe Gargir. The plan, according to the Minister of Education, aimed to 'double the number of Arabic pupils within the next four–five years'.[23] The target of doubling pupil enrolment in Arabic appears repeatedly and by May 1978 had evolved to include specific numerical targets. According to the Ministry of Education, '[T]he management of the Ministry decided to double the number of Arabic pupils, from 100,000 to 200,000 within five years, and the Ministry has since worked on an operative plan to meet this target.'[24]

Following this, throughout 1978, officials at the Ministry prepared the first year of the five-year plan, which was scheduled to start being implemented at the beginning of the following school year, in September 1979. Even though the security establishment was probably happy with the established targets, the Ministry of Defence saw this moment as an opportunity to maximise its interests by being involved at the very early stages of the planning. Therefore, Minister of Defence Ezer Weizman tried to convince Hammer not only maintain the aim to double the study levels but also to add a goal – which had been reiterated many times in the past, yet always left unimplmented – of making the teaching of Arabic compulsory in all Jewish-Israeli schools. Weizman outlined his ideas in a letter as follows:

> For years there has been public activity in Israel, by Knesset committees, public figures, educators, *and especially by Military Intelligence and the IDF*, together with the Ministry of Education to foster Arabic studies in the school system. Regrettably, these actions have not been successful. Despite growing public awareness of the importance of the subject, the number of pupils was reduced ... we have now reached the stage where the number of graduates of Arabic studies does not meet the needs of the IDF ... Therefore, we [the Ministry of Defence] believe that only an unequivocal solution can promote this school subject: instituting Arabic as compulsory. We are aware of

> the difficulties in implementing this status ... and will be happy to continue with the practical collaboration that we have had with the Ministry of Education regarding the advancement of Arabic studies, and where possible also to increase our actions in the field.[25]

Hammer responded to Weizman's letter by pointing to actions that had already been taken to enhance Arabic studies. He mentioned the Piamenta Committee, the decision to teach Colloquial Arabic starting in the 4th grade and, above all, the ambitious five-year plan aimed at doubling the number of pupils taking Arabic. Regarding instituting Arabic as a compulsory school subject, however, Hammer argued that this would effectively be the case since the vast majority of pupils – 80 per cent according to his estimation – would choose Arabic and not French on being given the option in the 7th grade. In the conclusion to his letter, Hammer referred to Weizman's comment regarding cooperation between the Ministries:

> The supervision team of Arabic studies [in the Ministry of Education] maintains a strong connection with the IDF officers responsible for the subject of Arabic, and every effort will be made to encourage this connection so that the needs of the IDF will be taken into consideration when planning the new programme of Arabic studies and when implementing it.[26]

The correspondence between the ministers speaks for itself. It seems that this period was characterised by an acute sense of urgency, indicated by the fact that the ministers of the relevant government agencies were communicating with each other directly. Correspondence at the highest levels continued to take place into 1979, and as the planning of the five-year plan began to take shape. In February of that year, Hammer again facilitated cooperation between the agencies by initiating a meeting that included a group of officers headed by Chief of Staff Lt Gen. Rafael Eitan (Raful) and Gen. Moshe Nativ, the Commander of the Manpower Directorate of the IDF.[27] While their motivations may have varied somewhat, all of these high-ranking figures shared a single goal – to increase the number of pupils taking Arabic. In order to advance this goal, the Ministry of Education did not hesitate to take advantage of assistance offered by the Ministry of Defence. Indeed, advancing this goal and implementing the five-year plan required the training of new teachers and this necessitated additional budgetary allocations. To secure these funds, and rather naturally in the Israeli field of Arabic studies, the Ministry of Education turned to the Ministry of Defence. One could have expected that as the five-year plan was connected to a peace treaty, and to a possible opening of Israel to the Arab world, that it would be the dramatic moment in which the direction of Arabic studies would change, a moment that would signal the creation of new and original Arabic networks, more inclusive towards the Arab-Palestinian citizens of Israel and less militarily oriented. Yet again, in the teaching and study of 'Israeli Arabic', this was not even an option.

As a matter of fact, throughout this entire process, the Palestinian citizens of Israel – whose first language is Arabic and who are culturally connected to the Arab world with which Israel allegedly wanted to reconcile – continued to be marginalised by the Jewish-Israeli establishment. Not only were they not viewed as partners or consultants, but officials involved in both education and security also viewed them as a potential security risk in general and specifically in relation to the teaching of Arabic.

This attitude was evident in a letter sent by Professor Yoseph Ben-Shlomo, the head of the Teaching Division in the Ministry of Education to Supervisor Gargir. In the letter, Ben-Shlomo writes about the security examination that Palestinian citizens of Israel were required to undergo in order to be considered for positions that involved Arabic language instruction in Jewish-Israeli schools.[28] Supervisor Gargir's response indicates that there were only a small number of Palestinian teachers in Jewish-Israeli schools and also points to the ambivalence about this. He wrote that throughout the preceding year 'I did not recommend, and did not assign, even one [Arabic] teacher from the sons of minorities [Palestinian citizens of Israel] to any Hebrew school.'[29] Research conducted by Allon Uhlmann in 2008, 2010 and 2011, echo this. Uhlmann noted that the number of Palestinian teachers of Arabic in Jewish schools was marginal – less than 5 per cent. Strikingly, Uhlmann quoted a senior Supervisor of Arabic Studies who attempted to explain why over 95 per cent of Arabic teachers were Jewish even though, for the most part, the Jewish teachers were unable to speak Arabic or read and write the language fluently, let alone consume Arabic culture and literature. In relation to Palestinian teachers, the senior supervisor mentioned that although they were native speakers of the language, '*Arabic is the toughest subject for an Arab to teach in a Jewish school*'.[30] This is a striking explanation for the lack of Arab-Palestinian teachers of Arabic in Jewish-Israeli schools, and it can shed light on the rationale that shaped the creation of 'Israeli Arabic'.

The lack of native Arabic-speakers in the teaching of Arabic is in contrast with the English language teaching force in Israeli schools and is very stark, indeed. According to Uhlmann, native speakers of English in the country makes up almost 50 per cent of the teaching force, not to mention the rest of the teachers who can express themselves in English and communicate in writing with English-speaking colleagues.[31]

Given the prevalent attitude whereby native Palestinian Arabic-speakers were deemed unsuitable to teach Arabic, the military was viewed as being able to best provide a solution for the dearth of Arabic teachers. Accordingly, in 1978, Military Intelligence initiated the *Morot-Ḥayalot* (lit. 'Soldier-Teachers') project. This project focused on the training of young women who had studied Arabic and were recruited to do their mandatory army service as Arabic teachers in civilian schools. They received specialised training and were then sent to Jewish-Israeli schools in the periphery and in border settlements where the shortage of teachers was particularly acute.[32] Soldier-Teachers underwent eight to twelve months of intensive training at Ulpan ʿAḳiva and Beit-Berl College. The course was supervised by Military Intelligence and the soldier-teachers were instructed by IDF soldiers. The project was considered by the Ministry of Education to be a great success and an efficient solution to the problems of teaching Arabic in schools. In a meeting held at the Knesset in 1976, for example, Lapid from Military Intelligence reported that, 'We took 20 soldiers and we are now training them to be Arabic teachers in schools.' Emmanuel Yaffe, the Head of the Pedagogical Secretariat at the Ministry of Education, answered him without thinking twice: 'It is a pity that you took only 20 and not 200.'[33]

A few years later, similar satisfaction at the project was expressed by Eliʿezer Shmuʾeli, the Director of the Ministry of Education. In a letter that he sent to Chief of Staff Lt Gen. Moshe Levy, Shmuʾeli wrote:

> [Over the last few years] the IDF had provided the education system with 20 soldier-teachers who were trained in a one-year intensive course of Arabic for elementary and intermediary schools. The contribution of the soldier-teachers was very big, especially in the north and south of the country where there is an evident shortage of teachers ... The importance of the project is clear, as from experience, only increasing the number of Arabic pupils in primary schools and intermediate schools can assure a growing number of pupils who take their final exam in Arabic. And this will increase the main reservoir of candidates for IDF service positions that require Arabic.[34]

This project not only provided a solution for the lack of Jewish Arabic teachers in the educational system but was also an attractive army assignment for the soldiers themselves. The women participating in this programme had the rare opportunity to serve out their full term of army service in a completely civilian setting. Furthermore, on completion of the programme, the women were granted a teaching diploma recognised by the Ministry of Education.[35] While the Ministry of Education's stated goal for the project was to increase the number of pupils studying Arabic,[36] in all likelihood it also resulted in the further militarisation of the Arabic language among pupils and teachers and in the education system at large.

This project was initiated in the wake of the panic caused by the events of the 1973 War, but was contextualised in the goal to double the number of pupils studying Arabic following the peace with Egypt. The Soldier-Teachers project represented the ideal outcome for both the Ministry of Education and Military Intelligence: the Ministry was able to bring Arabic studies into more schools and reach more pupils, and so support the 'aim of doubling the number of pupils', and this aim was appealing to the IDF. Therefore, and while the influence of the IDF and Military Intelligence on Arabic increased, so did the association between Arabic and security became more evident.

Not surprisingly, and as mentioned above, given the military's intense interest in Arabic language studies and their support of the five-year plan, it was also financially involved. Doubling the number of pupils from 100,000 to 200,000 required the recruitment and training of new teachers, paying more salaries, publishing new textbooks and any attendant administrative work. While the Ministry of Education was highly motivated to implement this ambitious plan, it lacked the necessary funds to do so. Available documentation indicates that, from the very beginning, from 1978 onwards, the IDF supported the Soldier-Teachers project. From 1979, the IDF also financially supported other aspects of the five-year plan. Evidence of this comes from correspondence between the Ministry of Education and the IDF Manpower Directorate. In March 1979, during the first year of the five-year plan, the Director of the Ministry of Education, Eli'ezer Shmu'eli, sent a letter to the Commander of the IDF Manpower Directorate asking the Ministry of Defence for financial support. Shmu'eli wrote:

> If the Ministry of Education does not receive the required budget, of 25 million Israeli pounds, we will not be able to extend the teaching programme in the way we described ... If [financial] participation [of the IDF] is lower than this amount, the Ministry of Education will have fewer opportunities to implement the [five-year] programme as planned.[37]

Towards the end of that first year, Shmu'eli initiated a meeting with Gen. Moshe Nativ, the Commander of the IDF Manpower Directorate, where he again requested financial assistance from the IDF. At the meeting, Nativ emphasised how important Arabic language studies was to the IDF and added that the army and the Ministry of Defence were willing to support financially the teaching of Arabic in Jewish-Israeli high schools.[38] While the protocol of the meeting did not outline the sum that the Ministry of Defence, or the IDF, would allocate for this purpose, Nativ promised to speak to the Chief of Staff regarding the budget and to give the Ministry of Education an answer within a week.[39]

Most probably, and due to the sensitivity of the issue, the available documentation is insufficient to ascertain the exact details of the negotiations and sums transferred from the IDF to the Ministry of Education. However, a letter sent three weeks later indicates that a compromise was reached and elucidates the sum agreed upon. The letter, drafted by Uri Marom, the Director of the Budget and Planning Division in the Ministry of Education, was sent to the Director of the Budget Division in the Ministry of Defence. Shmu'eli and Nativ, who corresponded on the topic three weeks earlier, were copied into the correspondence. In the letter, Marom disclosed that the IDF would pay half of the requested sum as follows:

> Based on the letter sent to us from the Commander of the Manpower Directorate of the IDF [Nativ] we would like you to transfer the sum of 12.5 million Israeli pounds to the Ministry of Education, according to budgetary clause 20-05-02-30 ... Attached is the Commander of the Manpower Directorate's letter. We would be grateful if you can copy your response to the [Ministry of] Finance, for the budgetary transfer.[40]

While Marom mentions that his letter includes a 'copy of the letter sent to us from the Commander of Manpower Directorate of the IDF', it was not attached to this letter nor was it found in the archival portfolio where the letter was located. It could be argued that this transfer, and the IDF's decision to allocate 12.5 million Israeli pounds to civilian rather than military issue, was deemed by someone to be inappropriate for the archive.

Later correspondence indicates that similar support was also granted in 1980–81, the third year of the five-year plan.[41] While little is known about this arrangement due to the scarcity of declassified documents, similar to previous years, it involved close cooperation between education and security bodies, reflected their shared interests and demonstrated that the military was a very dominant player. Moreover, this case study can serve as an example of the way in which the implications of the Israeli–Egyptian treaty, with its emphasis on peace, were subordinated with regards to Arabic studies to security considerations, financial exigencies and pressing Military Intelligence and IDF demands and perceptions. This shows the almost 'closed circuit' and automatic nature of the field of Arabic studies in Israel, and that it remained Military Intelligence-oriented even in times of peace.

Early in the second year of the five-year plan, Supervisor Gargir outlined anticipated progress during the 1980–81 academic year. According to Gargir:

> The next school year will be the second [year] of the five-year plan. This plan was approved by the Ministry of Education in order to double the number of pupils taking Arabic in the Hebrew school system, and in preparation for the age of peace [lit. *ṿe-liḳrat ʿidan ha-shalom*] ... Despite cutbacks in the budget of the Ministry of Education ... 50 new teachers will join the system, who will teach in 500 new classes, in which 15,000 new pupils will study ... Moreover, more than 450 pupils will study next year in the educational colleges and training institutions for [Arabic] teachers, which will include two Arabic seminars ... Furthermore, and with the help of the IDF, another course of Soldier-Teachers of 20 more young women will be launched soon ...[42]

This letter also includes the special formula of 'security and peace' seen earlier. While Gargir noted the decrease in the Ministry of Education budget, given the significant increase in Arabic pupils and teachers during 1979–80, it can be inferred that this was due to support provided by the IDF and Ministry of Defence. In fact, it is likely that the security establishment's contribution was substantial and may have even represented the majority of the financing necessary to achieve the improvements outlined by Gargir.

Financial support provided by the security establishment was also allocated to teacher training. A letter written by Professor Yoseph Ben-Shlomo, the head of the Pedagogic Secretariat at the Ministry of Education, to the five deans of the faculties of humanities in Israel's universities indicates this. In the letter, sent early in the second year of the five-year plan, Ben-Shlomo stated that:

> The Israeli Ministry of Education is currently preparing to increase Arabic studies in Jewish schools ... Our biggest difficulty is the lack

> of appropriate teachers. The IDF has allocated an amount of money to the Ministry of Education, for the next couple of years, which can be spent for the purpose of training Arabic teachers ... I contact you urgently so that your institution will be able to support us in this matter. Please forward to me plans that you think can help us [use this money for this cause] and include the budget that will be needed to cover them ...[43]

Unfortunately, also in this case, there were no files on record outlining responses from the deans and whether Ben-Shlomo's request received a positive response or not. One way or another, according to Supervisor Gargir, in 1978, prior to the launch of the five-year plan, 103,000 Jewish-Israeli pupils studied Arabic at all grade levels, and this number grew significantly in the following two years: in 1979, there were 121,000 pupils taking Arabic, and by 1980 their number had risen to 138,000.[44]

However, a year later, despite Supervisor Gargir's optimistic projections, there was a major setback. The State Comptroller's annual report, which included an audit of the finances for the year 1979–80, concluded that:

> the five-year plan aimed to double the number of pupils taking Arabic within five years ... but this rise is not as high as expected due to financial and bureaucratic limitations ... and especially since as soon as Arabic becomes an elective school subject in the intermediate school (where pupils can choose French instead) we experience a huge decline in the number of Arabic pupils (lit. *yored be-tsurah telulah mispar lomdei ha-safah ha-ʿAravit*) ...[45]

In response, the Ministry of Education acknowledged that the Comptroller's report was basically accurate. David Four, the newly appointed head of the Pedagogic Secretariat in the Ministry of Education, replied to the State Comptroller by noting that while it was true that the rise in the number of pupils was not as high as anticipated – 35 per cent in three years instead of the hoped for 60 per cent – the growth in numbers was still impressive. Four also noted that the Ministry of Education was determined to continue to try to meet the initial targets that it had set for itself.[46]

In light of this gap between expectations and reality, Supervisor Gargir conducted a survey of the field and, subsequently, established more realistic goals. In the new, modified version of the plan, Gargir predicted that by the end of the 1982 school year, 160,000 pupils from all age groups would be studying Arabic.[47] However, at the conclusion of that school year, he was yet again disappointed. The Ministry of Education, in facing its failure to reach its established targets, was forced to acknowledge a painful truth: it was being sabotaged over and over again by its own clients – pupils, parents and head teachers. In a letter sent by Supervisor Gargir to Four, from the Pedagogic Secretariat in the Ministry, Gagir complained that factors in the field were preventing Arabic studies from reaching its full potential. Gargir argued that due to cutbacks in the number of teaching hours allocated to all schools, and in light of the educational autonomy granted to elementary and intermediary schools, Arabic studies generally, and the five-year plan in particular, were experiencing major setbacks. According to Gargir, many schools decided to reduce the number of hours that they dedicated to Arabic and a significant number chose to cancel it entirely. He regarded this situation as severe and unacceptable (lit. *zehu matsav ḥamur she-ein le-hashlim ʾito*).[48]

The Minister of Education, Zeveulun Hammer, felt similarly pessimistic. This was made clear in a response to a parliamentary question posed by MK Dov Zakin (Labour). In his written response, Hammer mentioned that during the first four years of the five-year plan, there was a 50 per cent increase in the number of pupils taking Arabic, but 'unfortunately, and due to objective difficulties, the Arabic language has yet to become a compulsory school subject'.[49] Hammer then mentioned that despite attempts to introduce Arabic to all schools in Israel, 48 per cent of Jewish-Israeli 4th to 8th grade pupils did not study Arabic at all. While he stressed that his Ministry was doing its utmost to promote the study of Arabic 'for the fulfilment of the needs of the state in both security and peace', given the importance of the subject and the difficulties in creating substantial reforms, he recommended bringing the issue up for discussion with the Education Committee of the Knesset.[50]

The Ministry of Education's inability to implement its ambitious five-year programme is reflected in internal correspondence as well. In a letter that Four sent to Eliʿezer Shmuʾeli, the General Director of the Ministry in 1983, he theorised that the most acute problem concerning Arabic was the 'pyramidal structure of Arabic studies in Jewish-Israeli schools'.[51] Four was referring to the dramatic decrease in pupils continuing to study the language and, in particular, to the fact that pupil enrolment dropped precipitously during the transition period between elementary and intermediate school, and more significantly in the transition from intermediate to high school. While many pupils were willing to give Arabic a try, this did not lead to the long-term commitment envisioned by various stakeholders, with the Military Intelligence primary among them. In his letter, Four wrote that: 'In order to avoid these diminishing numbers, we need more money, so we can add hours to teach Arabic.'[52]

Due to the Ministry of Education's need to reduce their budget, Four sought additional support from the IDF. As with similar cases, the General Director of the Ministry of Education initiated contact with the Commander of the Manpower Directorate of the IDF in order to ascertain the nature of the assistance that the IDF was willing to provide. Following a meeting between the two, the IDF agreed to provide the Ministry of Education with new teachers and curricula. As a follow-up to the meeting, details of this agreement are outlined in a letter sent by Shmu'eli, the Director of the Ministry of Education, to Brig. ʿAmos Yaron, the newly appointed Commander of the Manpower Directorate of the IDF. In the letter, Shmu'eli thanked the senior officer for his readiness to help and then wrote that, 'The Ministry of Education would be grateful if the IDF was indeed able to provide personnel for the teaching of Arabic in elementary and intermediate schools [as discussed at the meeting].'[53] The next day, the IDF promised to offer the Ministry of Education further reinforcements (lit. *le-tagber*) by allocating more soldier-teachers to elementary schools in the context of that programme. The letter also referenced Yaron's acceptance of a Ministry of Education invitation to tour Israeli high schools (lit. *siyur be-vatey sefer*) in order to conduct a joint examination of Arabic studies in Jewish-Israeli schools.[54]

The joint tour reinforces the extent to which the education and military establishments were integrally connected one to the other in the context of Arabic language studies. It also corresponds – metaphorically and ideologically – to the 'joint journey' of military and civilian actors referenced before, in 1975, by the Chief of Intelligence.[55] Therefore, even in cases where pedagogic and civilian motivations drove the development of policy (for example, the five-year plan as a response to peace with Egypt), Arabic continued to be a joint educational–military project in which the military played a dominant role, and in which Palestinian citizens of Israel and actors who represent new and civilian thinking did not play a role at all. In all likelihood, as time passed, it became increasingly clear to the Ministry of Education that Arabic language studies would not advance without military cooperation and support. Therefore, it could be argued that the failure of the five-year plan demonstrated two points. First, that the rejection by the Israeli public was even more powerful than the combined work of educational and military forces. And, second, that Arabic could not even have been imagined as only 'standing' on its educational or civil virtues feet.

The 1986 meetings: changing the face of Arabic?

The 1984 elections had a significant influence on the relationship between the military and educational spheres in the field of Arabic studies and, as this section will show, the period following the elections brought them closer together than at any time prior to it. While Israeli archival law only allows for the declassification of files over 30 years old, there was sufficient documentation to allow for investigation of this period. Perhaps the full opening of the archives in the coming years will allow for more comprehensive research on the military–educational alliance during the time period in question.[56]

Yitzḥak Navon's appointment as Minister of Education in September 1984 significantly enhanced the cooperation between the military and educational establishments. Navon's biography epitomises the Jewish-Israeli attitude towards Arabic as a subject of study with equal importance given to war, education and peace. After all, Navon studied Arabic and spoke Arabic from an early age, was himself an Arabic teacher and in his past also held Arabic-oriented positions in Military Intelligence. This was a combination that positioned him at the heart of the debate on Arabic as a language for 'security and peace'.[57]

Navon's appointment as Minister of Education took place during a critical juncture. The five-year plan had just ended in relative failure and both the Military and the Ministry of Education were re-evaluating their priorities. Navon, the former President of Israel, with his wide-ranging expertise and years of experience, embodied a 'natural' connection between Israeli politics, Military Intelligence and education. One of Navon's earliest activities following his appointment was to make an examination of Arabic studies in all Jewish-Israeli schools with the aim of improving the way in which Arabic was studied and increasing the number of pupils who graduated with some proficiency in Arabic.

To this end, and this is the other side of Navon's coin, the Minister of Education had to find the most suitable person for this position, someone with the skills and experience needed to improve Arabic studies in the education system. Navon, with the support and encouragement of then Chief of Staff Moshe Levy did not have to hesitate a lot. The two well knew which expert was needed for this position and, not surprisingly, it was to be neither someone from the Hebrew University nor from the Ministry of Education. The decision was straightforward. The expert who was chosen to supervise the future Arabic programme and to assess and improve Arabic studies in Israeli school was the head of the IDF School of Arabic Studies: Col. Nissim ʿAtsmon.

Navon appointed ʿAtsmon following a very short period of consultations. He tasked him with both conducting comprehensive research into the way in which Arabic was taught in Jewish-Israeli schools and also with overseeing the implementation of his findings. The appointment of ʿAtsmon reflected the preference of military interests over educational interests in the realm of Arabic; ʿAtsmon was a senior Military Intelligence officer and the former Director of the IDF School of Arabic (also known as the 'Arabic Ulpan'). He was also one of the most prominent figures in the Ṭelem Unit: the Military Intelligence programme that aimed to promote Arabic studies in Jewish-Israeli schools and was an outcome of the 1973 War. In October 1985, ʿAtsmon submitted an initial report on his findings entitled, 'Arabic Studies in Hebrew Schools'. The report begins with a personal introduction by ʿAtsmon, where he notes his military background and his gratitude to the Ministry of Education and related stakeholders who assisted him in his research:

> I would like to express my great satisfaction with the special hospitality with which I was received by the Ministry of Education while conducting this research, including heads of departments, heads of districts, head teachers and Arabic teachers ... Moreover, it is obvious that without the support of the Minister of Defence, Chief of Staff, Military Intelligence and the IDF Spokesperson, all of my suggestions would not have been fruitful, since it has been proven that achievements cannot be reached through conventional acts. Arabic studies in Israel are in a critical situation and any paper written about this will only address part of the problem. I would therefore like to begin by asking all those who are going to work with me or above me, to show endless patience and support, since without these I will not be able to deal with the subject.[58]

In the report, which is over 40 pages in length, ʿAtsmon outlines a plan intended to promote the study of Arabic in schools. The short-term goal, as he envisioned it, was to improve the status of Arabic in Jewish-Israeli schools such that it would be on equal standing to that of English. He estimated that changing the negative attitude held by Jewish-Israeli pupils would require three to five years. ʿAtsmon's long-term goal, which he expected to be implemented over the course of eight years, was to change the formal status of Arabic from that of an elective to a compulsory subject in all school curricula. This second stage also included making Arabic an academic 'prioritised language', which meant that pupils would receive a bonus for taking Arabic in school when applying to academic studies.[59]

ʿAtsmon's report noted that 'Only 6 per cent of the pupils who begin studying Arabic in the 4th grade actually take their final exams in the 12th grade.'[60] According to him, this is related to negative attitudes towards the language held by head teachers and parents, a lack of continuity in the curricula at different grades, too few trained teachers and inadequate textbooks. ʿAtsmon recommended a new five-year plan in which Arabic would be studied from the 7th grade and the continuation of studies would be compulsory through the 12th grade. This reflected a change from the previous situation – established as a result of the Piamenta Committee – whereby Arabic studies began in the 4th grade, which was a decision that eventually dissatisfied the Military Intelligence officers, who wanted Arabic to be taught in high school.

ʿAtsmon recommended that pupils begin with Colloquial Arabic that used Arabic letters instead of Hebrew letters,[61] with a gradual shift to Literary Arabic taking place.[62] He believed that his recommendations would lead to improved attitudes towards the language and an increase in the number and quality of pupils studying the language. Accordingly, he added the following recommendations:

1. Pupils will receive recognition from the chancellors of universities regarding the importance of Arabic studies in high schools.
2. [The Ministry of Education will organise] conferences for intermediate schools and high schools, so that the new plan can be explained to them by the Ministry of Education, the IDF and scholars from academia.
3. [The Ministry of Education will organise] a conference with teachers of non-Arabic school subjects, in order to coordinate the study of Arabic culture through different school subjects.
4. [The IDF will] attach liaison officers from Military Intelligence to selected schools.
5. [The Ministry of Education and the IDF] will continue the initiative of the Oriental Youth Battalions and consider expanding it.
6. [The Ministry of Education] will explain [the new plan] to the public through the media.[63]

The goals were followed by schedules that were divided into responsibilities and themes such as 'Administrative Work', 'Pedagogic System', 'Textbooks', 'Surveys and Censuses', 'Meetings and Conferences' and 'Contact with the Public'. When reading through the document in

Hebrew, it brings to mind military language and framing more than anything else. The language is straightforward; the document is divided into points and sub-points, the schedules are strict and the document outlines what needs to be done at exactly what time during the school year. The terminology is also reminiscent of the military, for example the document phrases administrative work as the military-oriented, *ʿAvodat Maṭeh*. Lastly, the solutions proffered feature the active involvement of the military; for example, ʿAtsmon called for Military Intelligence liaison officers to be assigned to schools and for head teachers to be lectured by the IDF. Indeed, the report reads like something of an instruction guide for a military mission as opposed to an educational programme. However, since ʿAtsmon himself was *invited* by Navon to head this project and, since as ʿAtsmon emphasised, 'achievements cannot be reached through conventional acts', it can be argued that the new ambitious and military-oriented plan actually reflected the type of solution sought by the Israeli Ministry of Education.

The response to ʿAtsmon's plan was largely, although not entirely, positive. In November 1985, one month after the publication of the report, Col. Noʿam from the Military Intelligence Directorate published an article in the Military Intelligence bulletin *Ḥamanit* titled, 'Arabists in the Military Intelligence: It is Now or Never' (lit. *ʿArabisṭim be-Ḥaman: Lihyot ʾo Laḥdol*).[64] Noʿam's article echoed many of ʿAtsmon's recommendations. This suggests that the two corresponded regarding the report and may even have jointly come to the decision that Noʿam would highlight the subject in the Military Intelligence bulletin.

Irrespective of this, ʿAtsmon's dynamism helped to bring the debate regarding Arabic studies to new levels within Israeli society. One month later, in December 1985, the subject was again debated by Israeli lawmakers. MK Abba Eban, a former Israeli Minister of Foreign Affairs and Ambassador to the United States and the United Nations, initiated discussion of the topic following the renewed efforts to improve Arabic studies in the Ministry of Education. Interestingly, Eban – perhaps in response to the military tone of the report – asked ʿAtsmon to reconsider the nature of the military–educational alliance that was so fundamental to Arabic studies at the time. Strikingly, this alliance was pretty much unquestioned until this point, at least as much as the documents in the archive reveal.

Eban, a member of the Labour Party, was considered to be a relatively dovish parliamentarian and was part of the generation that had established the state. This gave him tremendous stature and perhaps also the leeway that he needed to sponsor a Knesset motion that, while noting the importance of Arabic, criticised the military-oriented solutions proposed by the report. His proposal, entitled 'Arabic Language Studies', was presented to the Knesset. Due to its importance, virtually the entire text of the speech is included here in Document 4.1.

Document 4.1 MK Abba Eban's Knesset motion, 'Arabic Language Studies'

Arabic Language Studies

MK Abba Eban

The lack of interest of Jewish-Israeli children in Arabic is part of a more comprehensive and severe problem, of associating the different streams of Zionism with separation ... But this [separatist approach] is the very opposite of Zionism. The Jewish liberation movement was yearning to breathe the air of the world... Zionism believed that the people of Israel would live as part of the world, while maintaining its uniqueness ...

We must admit that the Zionist movement and its pioneers did not excel in expressing our destiny to live as neighbours in this region with people whose language and culture are Arabic. Instead, a miserable slogan was widespread, proclaiming that the 'land with no people is waiting for the people with no land'. There was not a seed of truth in this slogan. And whoever builds his future on illusion, also buries his hope in sand.

Many in the past, and many among us today, live here without showing any curiosity about our neighbours on the other side of the wall. They are not asking: What is written on their [Arab neighbours] shops signs? What do the voices coming out of their houses say? What is their diction like? What is their culture? How do they understand their role in history? What are their sources of pride and honour? What are the assets that they have inherited from their fathers and what are the assets that they have endowed to humanity? And when there is no curiosity, questions are not asked; and when questions are not asked answers are not given. This is the story of our tendency to see the Arab only as an enemy in the battlefield.

In the many articles that I have read on Arabic studies in Israel there were comments from the Ministry of Defence regarding the need for Arabic-speakers. My intention is not to run away from this

(*continued*)

Document 4.1 Continued

reality, but I do not see it as the most meaningful reality. Our youngsters should not learn this language because 'it is the language of the enemy' but study it because it is a key to a magnificent culture, one of the most profound components of human civilisation.

Source: Quoted from MK Abba Eban's Knesset motion titled, 'Arabic Language Studies', presented to the Knesset, 18 December 1985, in Yosef Yunai (ed.), *Arabic in Hebrew Schools: A Collection of Documents* (Teʿudah: Israel Ministry of Education and Culture, 1992), pp. 175–6 (Hebrew).

In his speech, Eban challenged the widespread alienation from Arabic through an appeal to liberal Zionism. This stance, which stemmed from Eban's claim that separatism is the 'very opposite of Zionism', is debatable especially on examining the more popular and central streams of Zionism that emerged at the beginning of the twentieth century and remained prolific up until the present. Yet Eban's speech signalled a departure from the dominant discourse in two ways, he distanced himself from the prevalent 'peace-and-security' attitude that characterised Arabic studies and called to 'civilianise' the way in which Arabic was taught and learned in Jewish-Israeli schools.

While Minister of Education Navon responded to Eban, his answer did not address the latter's concerns regarding the militaristic orientation of the report released only two months prior. Instead, Navon noted that:

> [o]ur goal is that all Israeli pupils will study Arabic and will finish their studies in the 12th grade. This goal requires a reorganisation of the way in which Arabic is studied in school. We have therefore asked Mr Nissim ʿAtsmon to step in and help us with that.[65]

The decision to refer to Col. ʿAtsmon with the relatively benign title of 'Mr' was probably not an accident. As Navon strove to counter Eban's claims regarding the excessive involvement of Military Intelligence in Arabic, he may have decided to de-emphasise the military associations that stood at the heart of his current efforts by changing ʿAtsmon's title.

Eban's motion was forwarded to the Knesset's Education Committee, which subsequently dedicated two meetings to the issue. Held in January 1986, the Education Committee invited 29 'experts in Arabic studies' to attend these meetings and offer their advice, in the presence of the Committee members. The Education Committee, which, as an outside body, was tasked with examining a number of matters, consisted of both Jewish and – incredibly enough in the field of Arabic studies – Arab-Palestinian people. At the time, three of the MKs on the majority-Jewish Committee at the time were Palestinian citizens of Israel: Mr Tawfīq Ṭūbī (Democratic Front for Peace and Equality), MK ʿAbd al-Wahab Darawsheh (Labour Party) and MK Zeidan ʿAtashi (Shinuy Party). Their participation in these meetings was significant because, in all likelihood, for the first time since the founding of the state, Palestinian citizens of Israel whose mother tongue was Arabic were privy to the decision-making surrounding Arabic studies.

Likewise, an examination of the 29 'experts' invited to participate presents an important profile of the dominant voices and interests underlying Arabic studies. This profile was Jewish, Zionist, male and strongly political and security in nature. The list included four senior officers from Military Intelligence and 20 Jewish-Israeli experts who came from the Ministry of Education, Israeli academia, the Prime Minister's Office and the Ministry of Foreign Affairs. Over half of them had some connection – past or present – to Military Intelligence and 90 per cent of them were male. Interestingly, as well as the Arab MKs, another invitee was a Palestinian citizen of Israel, ʿAli Yaḥya. At the time, Yaḥya was a prolific Arabic teacher who taught at Ulpan ʿAḳiva, as well as at the Israeli Ministry of Foreign Affairs, the Israeli Police and in the Command and Staff College of the IDF. Yaḥya also served as Israel's first ever Arab ambassador. This should be highlighted as in all likelihood, Yaḥya's participation in the meeting and in the field of Arabic studies did not challenge the Jewish, Zionist and military hegemony over Arabic; in fact, he may have even been selected for this reason.[66]

The agenda of the first meeting, held on January 6 1986, was driven by a dominance of speakers from Military Intelligence. It opened with the Chairman of the Committee, MK Naḥman Raz, inviting ʿAtsmon to speak. ʿAtsmon presented the report's main findings and conclusions while also noting a specific problem: teachers who 'can either speak Colloquial Arabic but not read and write in Literary Arabic or can read and write in Literary Arabic but have no Colloquial skills'.[67] Ṭūbī, the Arab-Palestinian member of the Education Committee, suggested that hiring Palestinian citizens of Israel could represent a possible solution, as they both speak local Colloquial Arabic as their mother tongue and read and write Literary Arabic. Ṭūbī then asked how many Arab teachers teach Arabic in Jewish-Israeli schools. ʿAtsmon, who probably did not want to admit to the insignificant number of Arab teachers of Arabic in the Jewish-Israeli education system, responsed without going into details; he bluntly just said, 'I did not check this matter ... I currently do not have figures on it.'[68]

There was widespread support for expanding Arabic studies at the meeting. Following Ṭūbī's comments above, another of the Palestinian

Committee members, Darawsheh, pointed out that he had formerly been an Arabic teacher. He noted the importance of Arabic as a means for promoting dialogue and then stated that 'as long as Arabic is not a compulsory school subject for [Jewish-Israeli] children from 3rd grade, as Hebrew is compulsory for Arab children [in Israel], there is no point to this discussion'.[69] Interestingly, support for this proposal came from Col. Sha'ul Shoḥat of Military Intelligence. While the motives of the two – the Military Intelligence officer and the Palestinian citizen of Israel MK – indeed differed, their goal was the same; Shoḥat stated that Military Intelligence strongly supported making Arabic a compulsory school subject, noting that 'Military Intelligence views Arabic studies from a national perspective, not only in the context of military needs'.[70] Arabic philologist Professor Aryeh Levin also mentioned the need to make Arabic compulsory.[71] Further support came from Col. Benny Gilʿad from Military Intelligence, who headed the IDF School of Arabic. As the next speaker, he framed the debate in terms of the role of the army in the matter:

> The IDF finds this subject interesting because we [Military Intelligence] receive the [Jewish-Israeli] pupils who study Arabic ... Therefore, the IDF can help in diagnosing the problem. We are the first to receive high school graduates of Arabic studies, so we can accurately judge their level, capabilities and skills. Moreover, as we have considerable experience in teaching Arabic, we are happy to share this experience with the civil sphere... [72]

Gilʿad was followed by David Four, the head of the Pedagogic Secretariat. Four noted some of the practical difficulties involved in making Arabic compulsory, such as additional costs and the challenge of adding another subject to the already 'overloaded curriculum in Jewish-Israeli schools'.[73] However, his most interesting comment concerned the pupils themselves. He said: 'If we make Arabic a compulsory subject, we would be imposing on them three languages [Hebrew, English and Arabic]. There is not a single education system in the whole world that does this.'[74] Levin interjected, reminding Four that actually, 'I think that all the Arabs in Israel are studying three languages.'[75] A presumably embarrassed Four replied: 'I did not say it is impossible, I just meant that it is very difficult.'[76]

Four's comment was telling as it demonstrates a commonly held notion: Palestinian citizens of Israel simply did not exist in the mind of many Jewish experts discussing the teaching of Arabic. Indeed, the discourse was dominated by Jewish-Israelis and Jewish-Israeli concerns.

This incident triggered strong criticism from the only MK at the meeting who did not represent a Zionist party – Ṭūbī.[77] He said:

> The principal question is what do you want? Do you want Israeli children to study Arabic as mentioned by Abba Eban in order 'to get to know the neighbours on the other side of the wall'? I don't want them to look beyond a wall. I don't want walls. Neither inside nor outside ... If you want to teach Israelis Arabic as the language of the region in which they live, and I am well aware of the presence of Military Intelligence officers here, you should not focus on language teaching only but on the whole national policy. How can you expect your children to love Arabic if their textbooks still show the Arab as a thief and a cheat? You may not agree with me, but the problem is how to teach Arabic as the language of a people who need to be respected and with whom you will have to live for many generations. To live with them peacefully, both from outside and from inside.[78]

Rather courageously, not only did Ṭūbī criticise the topic of discussion but he also lashed out at the entire discourse surrounding it, including Eban's relatively nuanced stance. Ṭūbī's viewpoint was unheard of from within the field of Arabic studies. Unlike Eban, who stood for liberal Zionism, Ṭūbī spoke from outside of the Zionist discourse. He rejected the assumed and unquestioned separation between Jewish-Israelis and Arab-Palestinians and instead stressed the important role of Arabic in facilitating peaceful relations between Israel and its neighbours. Arguably, for others in the room, this position was completely irrelevant because it bore no relationship to the 'peace-and-security' formulation that dominated the discourse at the time. Perhaps feeling that Ṭūbī had crossed the boundaries of 'permissible debate', Chairman Naḥman Raz (Labour Party) said the following:

> I would like to express my deepest reservation about what was said here regarding an alleged alienation from the Jewish side towards Arabic ... This is just not correct ... Our problem is not related to negative attitudes [towards Arabic and Arab people] but to various professional-educational questions.[79]

In his comments, Raz strove to reframe the discussion as 'professional-educational'. Like others, he refused to address the loaded political and security implications of the matter or openly acknowledge the main actors and activities shaping it. It can be argued that due to Raz's response, Ṭūbī felt discouraged from continuing his participation in the debate. Whether this was the case or not, he did not attend the Knesset Education Committee's second discussion dedicated to Arabic studies in Jewish-Israeli schools.

The second meeting was held on 22 January 1986. ʿAtsmon again opened the meeting. However, his title at this meeting had changed to become 'Col. Nissim ʿAtsmon, the Ministry of Education', whilst only two weeks prior he had been referred to as 'Colonel ʿAtsmon, Representative of the IDF'. It is possible that this change was merely administrative, however, it may also reflect the fact that his various identities ('Mr', 'Colonel', 'IDF' or 'Ministry of Education') were viewed as being interchangeable. This overlap was consistent with the symbiotic relationship between the Ministry of Education and Military Intelligence, at least regarding Arabic studies.

Following ʿAtsmon's opening, Brig. Ephraim Lapid, who at the time served as the Spokesperson for the IDF, and previously served in Military Intelligence, was asked to speak. Inviting Lapid to speak as the first expert presenter is also indicative of the IDF's general dominance and the involvement of the Military Intelligence specifically, in the debate about Arabic studies. Lapid gave an overview of the importance of Arabic for Jewish-Israeli society while also noting the need to 'have a better understanding of our surroundings'.[80] In relation to the IDF, Lapid mentioned that the army suffered from a shortage of pupils studying Arabic. As a result, he spoke about Arabic courses prepared by the IDF (and given by Military Intelligence) for new recruits who may have not had previous experience in Arabic studies at school. According to Lapid, this created a problem:

> Because these students [who join Military Intelligence with no background in Arabic studies] are not coming from Oriental Studies in school, and therefore they also leave the field as soon as they leave the army. And then the academic system, the Ministry of Foreign Affairs, other political ministries and the Israeli Arabic-media, all suffer, as they all rely on the thin layer of graduates from Oriental Studies in schools.[81]

Lapid also reiterated the IDF's position that Arabic should be compulsory. He concluded his speech by saying that 'on behalf of the IDF, and the Chief of Staff, I would like to recommend the teaching of Arabic as a compulsory school subject, from intermediate schools and up to 12th grade'.[82]

Colonel No'am Shapira, Commander of the Information Collection Unit (*'Isuf*) of Military Intelligence,[83] was the next speaker. Similar to others, Shapira highlighted the importance of making Arabic a compulsory school subject in the service of both peace and security:

> As the commander of a unit that is totally reliant on Arabists, I need to say that Arabic must become a compulsory subject. If this does not happen, it will be just terrible. Terrible to us [Military Intelligence], but also terrible [for Israel] with regards to the windows of opportunity that we wish to open to the Arab world.[84]

Lt Col. Shlomo Katan, the Commander of the Ṭelem Unit, echoed Shapira's thoughts. Katan remarked that: 'Arabic is not an elective school subject, but a non-elected school subject ... for example, yesterday I went to a school in which only one boy chose Arabic for his final exams.'[85] Katan, demonstrating that he, as a Military Intelligence officer, was closely acquainted with the study of Arabic in schools and that he made visits to schools, mentioned the decline 'both in quality and quantity' of students taking Arabic. He then shared with those present the dismal number of 'less than 1000 students [studying Arabic] every year'.[86]

Avraham Yinon, the Supervisor of Arabic Studies, spoke at this point. The fact that Yinon's presentation followed that of three senior Military Intelligence officers was probably indicative of the centrality of the IDF in the debate in comparison to the relatively inferior status of Ministry of Education officials. Yinon emphasised the financial difficulties faced by his department and his great despair of trying to improve Arabic studies in Israel:

> I started working in the system in 1955, when Professor Kister was in charge of the Oriental Classes initiated by the Prime Minister's Office. At the time we had a lot of motivation as we knew we are doing it [teaching Arabic] for the security of Israel (lit. *yada 'nu she- 'anu 'ovdim le-ma'an biṭḥon medinat Yisrael*). Since then I have been involved in Arabic teaching, including in high schools, the Arabic intensive classes of the IDF, Arabic intensive classes of the Ministry of Defence, and the [Hebrew] University. For 30 years we have discussed the same things, and I feel that the Israeli establishment has an allergy to the topic.[87]

Yinon's remarks are significant as they represent the Ministry of Education's perspective on Arabic studies. Like others before him, rather than emphasising the civilian nature of Arabic, he mentioned teaching experiences in the IDF and the Ministry of Defence and 'the security of Israel'. Therefore, in all likelihood, the Ministry of Education perceived their work on this subject as being complementary to that of the security establishment. It also reveals the relative power of the two bodies. In other words, Yinon understood that regardless of his personal feelings, in order to be heard, he needed to present a viewpoint whose message was consistent with that of the military officers who preceded him. Another explanation can be that, for Yinon, the two were just naturally combined together.

Participants at the meeting – including philologists, teachers and military experts – were then invited to comment on the matter. Apparently all of the participants shared a basic assumption that Arabic was important for national security and that the military should have a role in the matter, and no one – especially not members from the Ministry of Education – challenged these assumptions. Rather, those at the meeting discussed the technical aspects of the issue, including the preferable age to begin studies and requisite teacher qualifications. In discussing a lack of suitable teachers, there was general agreement that Arabic teachers in Jewish-Israeli schools should be Jewish-Israelis. MK Shulamit Aloni from the left-wing Meretz Party (then Ratz) presented a dissenting voice when she asked, 'Why don't you consider having Arab teachers who can teach Arabic?'[88] In response, Kister ignored the substance of Aloni's comment and instead said that, 'the main question that we are trying to answer is not how to teach, but what do we want to teach'.[89] In all likelihood, the idea of hiring Arabs to teach Arabic was not raised again at that meeting. Irrespective of this, the anecdote illustrates the ongoing marginalisation of any idea that fell outside of the accepted and mainstream discourse regarding Arabic.

A week later, the Education Committee submitted its recommendations to the Minister of Education. In a pattern similar to when many other public statements were made on the subject, the recommendations did not include any reference to military considerations, yet can still be seen as being as politically loaded:

> Following two meetings in which various subjects were discussed, the Committee would like to state that one hundred years of Jewish life in Eretz Yisrael did not instil in the Israeli [Jewish] society the awareness of the supreme importance of knowing the region and its culture ... Lack of knowledge about the culture and the region is the reason for prejudice, alienation and hostility between people. These things have been discussed since the creation of Israel but the

> Committee has found that not enough has been done to change this situation ...[90]

This statement, in my view, reflects a dilemma lying at the heart of Jewish-Israeli society. Jewish-Israelis are conflicted; they do not want to be *of* the Middle East, in spite of the fact that they are *in* the Middle East. While the Committee's statement hints at this, a careful reading of the statement highlights limitations to this approach. The reference to 'one hundred years of Jewish life in *Eretz Yisrael*' ignores the presence of Jews in Palestine for generations prior to the founding of political Zionism at the end of the nineteenth century. Reading this statement in isolation, one gets the impression that the Jews only came to the region in the modern era and their arrival was due to Zionism and Zionist movements. This not only delegitimises the non-Zionist Jewish presence but also Palestinian-Jews who spoke Arabic as a first or second language, as well as Arab-Jews who immigrated to the country throughout, before and after the creation of the State of Israel, and knew Arabic well.

Furthermore, the Committee recognised that the '[l]ack of knowledge about the culture of the region is the reason for prejudice, alienation and hostility'. However, this seemingly ignores the dominant role played by the military in framing the issue at both meetings and their perception of their work as knowing 'the language of the enemy'. Indeed, their presence only helped to guarantee the preservation of the 'peace-and-security' formulation. Thus, the statement issued was, in fact, a continuation of the dominant line of thinking at the time. As a matter of fact, those formulating the statement were unable to conceive of the matter as falling outside of a Jewish, Zionist or military-oriented perspective.

The Education Committee advocated for making Arabic a compulsory school subject from the 7th to the 12th grade, which was the recommendation made by ʿAtsmon and by Lapid, and so can shed light on their dominance.[91] In the closing remarks, the statement emphasised the perilous state of Arabic language teaching at the time:

> Our report is a warning call to the Prime Minister, Minister of Education and Minister of Finance to help change the situation now, since if this does not happen, in a few years time [Jewish] Israeli society will find itself dangerously behind [the needs of the state], and it will be very hard to catch up, if at all.[92]

In light of the Committee's recommendations and the momentum generated by them, Minister of Education Navon asked ʿAtsmon to convene a follow-up meeting. Hosted by Navon's office and held on 28 January 1986, the meeting aimed to clarify strategies for promoting Arabic studies in Jewish-Israeli schools. Some 18 people attended the meeting – all of them Jewish-Israelis and the majority having a background in security issues.[93] Moreover, 16 of the 18 participants were men. This gender-biased atmosphere once again points to the extent to which Arabic studies in the more gender-neutral educational-civic sphere may have been hijacked by the military that is dominated by men.[94]

Navon opened the meeting by introducing two subjects for discussion: whether to teach Colloquial Arabic or Literary Arabic and at what age pupils should first be introduced to Arabic. This information was meant to assist ʿAtsmon and 'the small team that he will create' in implementing the decisions.[95] Navon prefaced this request by reiterating the importance of Arabic for 'peace and security'.[96]

Following expressions of gratitude to Navon, ʿAtsmon then shared his views on the matter. He noted that the meeting was taking place at a 'historical moment' that facilitated a 'serious practical discussion' about Arabic. ʿAtsmon continued:

> I look at the [Arabic studies] question from a national-strategic perspective and would like to echo the words of Minister Navon regarding the [importance of] Arabic not only for war, but also for peace. I call it 'the Naḥal'[(Hebrew acronym for 'Fighting Pioneer Youth'],[97] and I believe that Arabic studies are the sickle and the sword [the symbol of Naḥal]. Our goal is to create an 'Arabic Naḥal' [an Arabic fighting pioneer youth] that will be used also for peace.[98]

The coining of the term 'Arabic Naḥal' conjures up thoughts about the naming of a similar programme – the Oriental Youth Battalion (Gadnaʿ Mizraḥanim) of 1976. The selection of both of these names reflected the influence of the Military Intelligence and its involvement in Arabic studies in Jewish-Israeli schools and the obvious Jewish-Zionist and not inclusive and all-civilian nature of Arabic studies. The Gadnaʿ (the Hebrew acronym of Youth Battalions), for example, prepared Israeli pupils for military service. The Naḥal (a Hebrew acronym for Fighting Pioneer Youth) programme combined military service with the establishment of agricultural settlements.[99] Through the use of the names 'Arabic Naḥal' and 'Gadnaʿ Mizraḥanim,' military officers connected familiar and accepted Israeli notions with nationalistic connotations to Arabic. These terms brought together and conflated military, civilian and educational concepts. To these, they appended the words 'Arabic' or 'Oriental

Studies'. This use of language strengthened and created an authoritative connection between Arabic studies in schools and the military.

Next was IDF Spokesperson Lapid. Lapid also talked about the 'historic opportunity' at hand. He viewed this meeting as a chance to actually execute decisions and also mentioned the IDF's role in assessing the state of Arabic. Lapid said:

> We in the army can feel the changes [in the quality of Arabic studies] better than others, as we are not only the consumers of the Ministry of Education but we are the first 'station' on the journey of these pupils [who take Arabic] on their way to governmental positions, the media, academia and to all those organisations that need Arabists. Military Intelligence used to be the melting pot of future Israeli Oriental experts. Arabic experts from the Department of Arab Affairs [in the Prime Minister's Office], the Ministry of Foreign Affairs, the media and academia, all received their training in the [Jewish-Israeli] education system and Military Intelligence ... Today the status of Arabic studies is so low that it cannot produce the numbers required for the needs of the country.[100]

This important statement highlights the army's perception of itself as a 'national assessor' and producer of Arabic studies. Lapid emphasised that the army, as opposed to the school system, was better suited to evaluate if and in what ways Arabic was being properly taught ('We in the army can feel the changes better'). He also indicated that the military provided pupils with the training that they needed in order to continue along the 'journey' in roles requiring 'Orientalists' ('we are the first "station" on the journey of these pupils').

Lapid ended his presentation by reinforcing the importance of Arabic in peace-and-security:

> We [the IDF] believe that the main goal of Arabic studies is to get to know our neighbours in the region ... Acquiring skills in Arabic is a condition for better understanding of the people with whom we are neighbours. And this must be through a perception of peace and security, which are two concepts between which I do not differentiate.[101]

Lapid's perception of 'peace and security' is similar to that of others, including ʿAtsmon's reference to the 'sickle and sword' along with Navon's to the same idea during this same meeting. This points to the centrality of this notion among individuals who played a key role in framing and conceptualising the field of Arabic studies. It was understood, then, that the most 'balanced' Arabic expert was one who viewed Israeli security and peace in ways that, as phrased by Lapid, are inseparable one from the other, and Military Intelligence officers were mostly 'equipped' for this.

Despite the dominance of this discourse, Yoseph Moran, Supervisor of Arabic Studies in the Haifa District, presented a challenge. He began his statement by noting that his thoughts may be controversial. He then continued as follows:

> I do not think that the Arabic that I teach should be solely for the consumption of the army. I am saying this despite being a Military Intelligence man, and since I know this matter well ... Unlike most of the speakers here, I think that Arabic should be taught from an earlier age, during elementary school ... As argued by psycholinguists and other researchers, a pupil has a greater ability [to learn languages] at a young age. The sooner we teach a pupil a language, the closer this language will be to a mother tongue.[102]

Moran well knew that the majority of participants at the meeting supported Arabic education due to its important role in promoting national security. He therefore did not entirely reject the militaristic tone of the conversation; and he even clarified that point by saying that he was commenting as 'a Military Intelligence man', thus emphasising that he spoke as an insider and from a position of knowledge. What seemed to bother the participants about Moran's comments the most was his reference to Arabic as a 'mother tongue'. Responding to this point, Col. Benny Gil'ad, the head of the IDF School of Arabic commented: 'I strongly disagree with Mr Moran, who has tried to create here some new kind of mother tongue [Arabic for Jewish-Israelis]. We cannot agree with his statement. The people of Israel [Jewish-Israelis] cannot do such a thing.'[103]

Gil'ad's comment belies the space many Jewish-Israelis tried to place between themselves and Arabic. According to this line of thought, Arabic cannot attain a *mother tongue* status among Jewish-Israelis. Nor should Arabic be compared to Hebrew, even rhetorically. In other words, Arabic is Arabic and Hebrew is Hebrew and never the twain shall meet.

After thoroughly repudiating Arabic as a mother tongue for Jewish-Israelis, Gil'ad commented on the way in which Arabic should be taught in schools. He believed that teaching Colloquial Arabic prior to Literary Arabic was preferable 'for pedagogical reasons'. Nevertheless, he supported primarily emphasising Literary Arabic. Gilʿad gave his reasoning as follows:

> Our [military] experience teaches us that in order to bring our apprentices to the necessary level of fluency and skills in Colloquial Arabic or a certain dialect, which are required for our [Military Intelligence] needs, the best way to teach it is via Literary Arabic, and even via Classical Arabic, and via grammar, syntax and newspapers written in Literary Arabic. Following all this, it is easy to manoeuvre into one dialect or another, according to the needs of the army.[104]

What is most striking here is not the difference of opinion between Gilʿad and Moran but, rather, the ways in which the Military Intelligence officer views military-Arabic and Arabic studies within Jewish-Israeli schools. Gilʿad's preference for Literary Arabic was derived from its utility in the work of Military Intelligence as basic knowledge of Literary Arabic facilitates the mastery of many different Arabic dialects. Gilʿad, therefore, sought to ease the transition from compulsory education to Military Intelligence, and saw Arabic studies in school as nothing but a preparation for Arabic in Military Intelligence.

Katan, the Commander of the Ṭelem Unit, also spoke at the meeting and referred to the needs of Military Intelligence. He raised the issue of more females than males electing to study Arabic and its impact on Military Intelligence. Katan defined the problem as such:

> women cannot replace men in many of our units, such as front bases, outposts and missile ships [lit. *basis ḥoni ḳidmi, Ḥermon, Saṭilim*] and they cannot reach the same level of Arabic in [their] two years [of] service, as males can in their three years [of service]. For us in Military Intelligence, recruiting enough men who graduate with Arabic [skills] is an existential issue.[105]

Katan then addressed the diminishing numbers of Arabic graduates and its effect on Military Intelligence:

> Last year, due to insufficient numbers of [Arabic] graduates, we needed to train students ourselves ... In order to do so we recruited for military reserve service some of the people sitting here, from their universities and places of work, including Mr [Shlomo] Alon ... They helped us train 100 men in Arabic, in a project that cost millions of shekels.[106]

Katan's statement is indicative of the dominant role played by Military Intelligence officers in Arabic studies during the period in question. Furthermore, regarding the gender imbalance mentioned by him, the fact that his comments were left uncontested, indicates that others present there probably shared his concerns, or did not find this kind of rationalisation to be odd. Similarly, Supervisor Alon's service in the military reserves as an Arabic teacher in Military Intelligence was, in all likelihood, self-explanatory to all the participants at the meeting.

The last subject on Katan's agenda was the low status of Arabic among pupils. Katan noted that Military Intelligence had succeeded in increasing the number of pupils participating in Oriental Youth Battalions since its founding 1976. In his view, however, the project only highlighted pupil apathy in relation to Arabic. He said: 'I see 1200 pupils every year in the Youth Battalions and I speak to them, and I can tell you that Arabic for them is nothing but a meaningless combination of sounds' [lit. *gibuv ḥasar mashma'ut*].[107] Katan's contribution to this discussion not only highlights the nature of the military–educational relationship regarding Arabic at the time, but also the extent to which the military was directly involved in the educational arena. From his statements and figures supplied, it is clear that the majority of Jewish-Israeli pupil choosing to study Arabic in their later years at school also participated in Military Intelligence programmes.

Navon concluded the meeting by noting that a small team of experts, headed by 'Atsmon, would consider the comments brought up at the meeting and prepare a plan of action for the Ministry of Education. Following some friendly remarks that he made towards 'Atsmon ('can I call you Nissimiko, my friend?'),[108] Navon said:

> Finally, I would like to thank the IDF, for allowing us to borrow Nissim ['Atsmon]. I know that he is very enthusiastic about this matter, and I am sorry that the system cannot respond better to his passion ...[109]

These remarks are significant for two reasons: they highlight the friendly cooperation that had developed between Navon and 'Atsmon and, even more importantly, the partnership and shared values that characterised the relationship between Arabic experts from the Ministry of Education and the Military Intelligence. Given the gratitude that the Ministry of Education seemingly expressed towards the Military Intelligence and its affiliated experts, there is a sense that from the perspective of expertise the IDF was in charge, or at least seen as a top adviser on the matter, and definitely as an equal partner.

This process eventually led to the establishment of the *Shifʿat* Unit in 1986. This unit probably reflected the role of the Military Intelligence and its support of Arabic, as well as its confidence in its ability to improve Arabic language studies in Jewish-Israeli schools. Shifʿat's programme design – which reflected the heavy role of ʿAtsmon in the matter, as well as his military-educational philosophy – was a Military Intelligence unit inside the Ministry of Education whose goal was to promote the study of Arabic by Jewish-Israeli pupils and to improve the quality of instruction in the language. It was similar to, and worked closely with the Ṭelem Unit as both operated on the seam line between the military and civilian worlds. However, there was one minor difference between the two: while Ṭelem's perspective was primarily military, Shifʿat operated from a civilian perspective. As the next section will argue, the work of Shifʿat further blurs the boundaries between the military and the educational spheres such that it is hard to distinguish where the Ministry of Education ends and the Military Intelligence begins, and where Ṭelem ends and Shifʿat begins.

Mission accomplished: the creation of Shifʿat

Col. ʿAtsmon was subsequently given the authority to create an action plan, which he submitted to the Education Minister Navon in June 1986. ʿAtsmon's long-term recommendation was to make Arabic compulsory from the 7th to the 12th grade. He envisioned this taking place gradually, and wrote that it would require additional schools joining the programme, the training of new teachers, academic reinforcement for experienced teachers and a reassessment of the Arabic language curriculum in use at the time.[110] In relation to the poor status of Arabic among pupils and a general lack of respect afforded to Arabic teachers, ʿAtsmon recommended experimenting with a number of new initiatives aimed at encouraging the study of the language and then assessing their effectiveness. He also advocated the establishment of a 'Bulletin for Arabic Teachers', intended to improve teacher self-esteem and strengthen connections and relationships and the sense of community among teachers. Following this, during the same year, the *Journal of the Teachers of Arabic and Islam* was established, and it still exists to the present day.[111]

Arguably, ʿAtsmon's most far-reaching decision was to establish a new unit, military at its core that operated within the civilian sphere, which aimed to support Arabic studies in Jewish-Israeli schools. Overseen by Military Intelligence soldiers, it was a distinct unit within the Ministry of

Education whose aim was to increase the number of Jewish-Israeli pupils studying Arabic and their level of proficiency in the language. Initially, they decided to locate the unit at Beit Berl College, but it was subsequently transferred to the Israeli Center for Educational Technology in Tel Aviv.[112] A branch of the unit was also based at Ha-Kirya, the IDF headquarters in Tel Aviv.[113]

The unit was named Shifʿat, a Hebrew acronym that stands for the 'Unit for the Improvement of the Arabic Language and Culture' [lit. *Ha-Yeḥidah le-Ḳidum ha-Safah ha-ʿAravit ṿe-Tarbutah*]. Headed by ʿAtsmon, initially 20 soldiers were assigned to Shifʿat, but eventually it grew to consist of about 40 Military Intelligence-oriented personnel, the vast majority of them being active duty personnel. In addition to developing a new Arabic language curricula and textbooks, Shifʿat also launched a variety of different initiatives, including the creation of promotional materials regarding Arabic language studies. It also organised activities for pupils and teachers such as Arabic teacher training courses and provided support and teaching aids for teachers.[114] According to ʿAtsmon, to facilitate this, the budget for Shifʿat during its first year of operations was roughly $US150,000. This financial allocation steadily increased, reaching around $US4 million in 2000.[115]

Shifʿat, established in order to implement ʿAtsmon's recommendations, worked in close coordination with the Ministry of Education and particularly its department of Arabic studies. While most of its focus was on the teaching of Arabic and providing support to teachers, it also developed a number of programmes of a cultural nature. For example, Shifʿat organised (and the Ministry of Education subsidised) annual visits to Arab countries. Initially, pupils visited Egypt, while in later years there were also visits to Morocco and Jordan.[116] Interestingly, visits to the 'Arab world' did not include Palestinian areas within Israel, such as Nazareth, Al-Ṭayyiba or Umm al-Faḥm,which in the past were made only in connection with the Oriental Classes and the Military Government (officially ended in 1968). 'Visits to the Arab world' did not include towns and cities in the Occupied Palestinian Territories as well, such as Ramallah, Bethlehem, Jericho or Nablus. Perhaps, for the teachers, pupils, decision-makers and staff at Shifʿat, focusing on Egypt was better as the Palestinian areas, despite being so close, were locations that fell outside of the realm of 'the Arab world' or were considered unattractive or too sensitive for them to deal with.

In an interview with Col. Ret. ʿAtsmon that was conducted for the purpose of this research, ʿAtsmon agreed that Shifʿat's cultural aims were equal to its military aims. According to him, the decision to establish Shifʿat primarily stemmed from military considerations. He said:

> We established Shifʿat in order to resolve a serious problem ... Military Intelligence soldiers could not properly understand Arabic and it cost us lives ... We understood that we must have more and better people who chose Arabic at school.[117]

ʿAtsmon also commented on how his role as a colonel was perceived by personnel at the Ministry of Education. He said: 'I knew that people were sometimes concerned about me being an officer and interfering in educational matters ... therefore I minimised my military appearance, and did not attended meetings in uniform.'[118] ʿAtsmon said that he maintained regular contact with the Chief of Staff and the Chief of Intelligence, who 'helped me a great deal in my attempts to strengthen Arabic studies in schools'.[119] ʿAtsmon also said that the strategy to improve the status of Arabic by associating it with Military Intelligence was ultimately successful. In a similar interview that he gave to the newspaper *Davar*, he commented that, 'Arabic teachers have told me that the support of the army in Arabic studies has improved the prestige of Arabic as a school subject.'[120]

During the same years (1986–2000), Professor Aryeh Levin served as the Head of the Arabic Language Subject Committee in the Ministry of Education. Thus, he was familiar with Shifʿat and its activities but, interestingly, he was not disturbed by Military Intelligence involvement in educational matters, and believes that the analysis of this subject should be different. In a personal interview, Levin downplayed Shifʿat's military connection, saying that:

> Nissim [ʿAtsmon] did not come from the army in order to train soldiers, but in order to establish Arabic studies. All military projects [within the Ministry of Education] aimed at encouraging Arabic studies, and every project that does so, is positive. There was no pressure from the military to change the curriculum against the will of the Ministry of Education. I would say that Nissim gave his good services and was very dedicated to the cause, and if there was any kind of pressure on us I would not have agreed to this cooperation. Nissim did not advise [us on] what we [the Ministry of Education] should do, but only supported efforts already in existence.[121]

In contrast, Ran Lustigman, in his writings on the subject, believes that Shifʿat's main goal was to increase the 'production of Arabists for

Military Intelligence'.[122] Moreover, he writes that the army's extensive involvement in promoting Arabic language studies served to strengthen the notion that Arabic is the 'language of the enemy' rather than the 'language of the neighbour'.[123]

What is beyond any doubt is that Shifʿat was not created in a vacuum, rather its establishment represented the culmination of competing interests, historical processes, perceived necessity and power struggles. It also reflects, in my view, how the the Ministry of Education was at a complete loss as to how to improve and encourage the study of Arabic in Jewish-Israeli schools. Therefore, Shifʿat's creation should be viewed as the outcome of a strong cooperation between the IDF and the Ministry of Education in relation to Arabic studies, instead of a programme imposed on the Ministry from the outside.

Arabic in the 1990s and beyond: Shifʿat and its aftermath

Despite a dearth of archival material for the post-1986 period, a number of documents demonstrate that during this period the military continued to wield tremendous influence over Arabic studies in the education system. While, unfortunately, it is not possible to conduct serious and comprehensive research on the subject in the last decade of the twentith century until the present time, some brief examples demonstrate that the military–educational alliance continued to be central to Arabic language education. While cooperation and methodologies may have varied somewhat over the last two or three decades, the military–civil alliance remains central to the way in which Arabic is taught and learned by Jewish-Israelis.

An article written by a Military Intelligence officer and distributed to Arabic teachers in Jewish-Israeli schools in 1991 demonstrates the overlap between the military and the civil society also during this period. At the time, Meʾir Amots, a Military Intelligence officer, published the same article in *Ḥamanit* (*The Israeli Military Intelligence Journal*) and in the *Journal for the Teachers of Arabic* (a project initiated by Shifʿat) entitled, 'Translation from Arabic to Hebrew in the Military Intelligence Directorate'.[124] Amots begins his article by stating that: 'Military Intelligence is crying out for a new and improved recruitment of students of Arabic.'[125] He then argues that Jewish-Israeli schools apply three different methodologies when teaching pupils how to translate from Arabic into Hebrew: 'verbal', 'free' and 'practical'. According to Amots – and this is his main argument – schools should promote the 'practical method ... along the lines used in Military Intelligence' whose aim is accuracy and fluency.[126] Thus, the article encourages teachers to apply a specific military-recommended methodology in order to facilitate continuity between the education system and Military Intelligence.

This seemingly minor example elucidates the flow of information between the military and educational spheres and the complementary nature of the roles of Arabic teachers and military officials. The article, which was probably widely read by Jewish-Israeli Arabic teachers, focuses on Military Intelligence needs – in this case, 'practical translation' – and aims to promote the ease of transition between Arabic studies in the education system and military Arabic. Its publication in the civilian-educational journal of Arabic studies suggests that it was intended to help teachers to adapt their teaching methodologies such that it would increase the likelihood of their pupils being accepted by the Military Intelligence. This was most likely a mutual goal for both.

Another example from the same period is that of the establishment of the *Mekhinah* (religious pre-army school) in Rosh Pinna in the Upper Galilee in the 1990s. Its establishment elucidates the continuing involvement of the IDF in Arabic education. Intended for graduates of Yeshiva high schools, the Mekhinah in Rosh Pinna is probably the only educational institution in Israel that combines religious studies with Arabic. Not surprisingly, their purpose for teaching Arabic is to prepare graduates for work in Military Intelligence. Following a year of intensive Arabic language studies, and on graduation, the students are assigned to various units within Military Intelligence. In Military Intelligence, in the words of the head of the yeshiva, Rabbi Davidovich, students will 'deal with research and assessment of intelligence documents'.[127] The course is subsidised by the IDF, and includes visits to Military Intelligence bases.[128]

Research conducted by Alon Fragman in 2005 also sheds light on the subject of 'militarised-Arabic' in Israel. Fragman investigated Arabic textbooks used by Israeli universities during summer language courses. His study, which specifically investigates books in use during the 1980s, 1990s and 2000s, brings different examples that highlight Arabic studies in relation to security considerations and orientations. Fragman found that, overall, the books are characterised by a hostile and patronising attitude towards the Arabic language and culture. For example, in demonstrating the use of passive linguistic structures such as the *infaʿala* tense, the books included the following examples: 'it was reported from Beirut that a bomb had exploded' and 'the forces of the enemies were defeated and then withdrew'. Negation was demonstrated through sentences like, 'do not arrest that woman' and 'the police do not know what the three kidnappers demand'. The Arabic grammar topic titled

'The Five Names' included the following example of grammatical structures: 'we arrested his father-in-law'. While Fragman's research did not specifically investigate high school textbooks, he writes that 'it is still important to note that this method of study is used in both Military Intelligence and in Israeli university summer Arabic courses',[129] which I find telling. According to him, this method has contributed to the dislike that high school pupils show towards their Arabic studies.[130]

Dana Elazar-Halevy, however, analysed Arabic textbooks in use in Jewish-Israeli public schools. She found that newer textbooks – for example, those published in the 1990s and 2000s – were more focused on integration and the cultural aspects of Arabic-speakers than the politically oriented textbooks of the 1960s–1980s. She claims that this change in approach did not signal a change in Ministry of Education policy, rather it reflected the efforts of independent scholars. Elazar-Halevy was not able to assess the extent to which schools selected the newer texts as opposed to the more traditional and politically loaded ones.[131]

An examination of statements made by senior IDF officers in media outlets also sheds light on the nature of Arabic studies in the recent period. For example, in an interview with the popular daily *Maʿariv* in 2005, the then Chief of Staff Moshe Yaʿalon criticised the Ministry of Education for not providing the army with pupils who had sufficient knowledge of Arabic. Yaʿalon said:

> I am not sure that the education system provides the IDF with graduates with optimal skills ... Military Intelligence has a real shortage of new recruits who know Arabic ... The schools do not produce enough Arabic-speakers for the IDF, and Military Intelligence then needs to train its soldiers from the beginning.[132]

While Yaʿalon's position is not surprising, more interesting is the fact that his open criticism of the Ministry of Education did not stimulate any sort of debate – either educational or otherwise. This is just a mere anecdote that indicates that the Israeli public takes for granted and accepts the connection between Military Intelligence and Arabic studies in Jewish-Israeli schools, and does not see this relationship as problematic whatsoever.

Coming back to the work of Shifʿat Unit, it is noteworthy that in 2001, with no advance warning, the then General Director of the Ministry of Education, Ronit Tirosh shut down this unit. ʿAtsmon believes that the decision stemmed from internal political debates and political interests. This was despite the fact that Shifʿat was well established and, at the time, had about 40 soldiers on its staff.[133] The then new Minister of Education, Limor Livnat, and her General Director, Ronit Tirosh, were less sympathetic to Arabic and its teaching than Minister Navon and this might explain the decision to shut down Shifʿat. Tirosh actually went on record, saying that: '[the] Arabic language is identified in Israel with people who make our lives hard and damage our security ... This is a problem and therefore we suggest not forcing Arabic studies on pupils in schools as this would just not be beneficial.'[134] Views such as these and subsequent cuts to the 2001 Ministry of Education annual budget probably contributed to the decision to close Shifʿat.

Shifʿat's establishment, however, was significant not only because of the specific projects that it initiated but also because of the attitude regarding peace and security that it helped to perpetuate. In this respect, Shifʿat's mission was essentially the same as Ṭelem's, and Ṭelem can indeed be viewed as the military equivalent of Shifʿat. Although Shifʿat has been closed down, this definitely did not signal the end of the ongoing campaign for Arabic studies, as a joint project of the Ministry of Education and Military Intelligence. Also today, military and educational bodies in Israel continue to bring security-oriented interests to bear in the field of Arabic studies.

Indeed, the *Oriental Youth Battalion,* founded in 1976, is active to this day. Consistent with the original intention of the programme, pupils who participate in this week-long Military Intelligence-funded initiative are provided with a crash course in intelligence-related matters. The course, which is hosted by Givʿat Ḥavivah, provides an overview of the importance of Arabic for Military Intelligence. The participating 10th grade pupils explore subjects such as the Middle East, terror organisations, Arabic positions in Military Intelligence, current affairs, Arab culture and more. They also hear an intelligence lecture given by a senior Military Intelligence officer. The teachers of the Pupils are only allowed to participate on a limited basis; and they may join their pupils and attend 'classes given in the company commander forum' [lit. *forum plugati ṿe-shiʿurey Mem Pey*] and 'an Oriental folklore evening' [lit. *ʿerev folḳlor Mizraḥi*].[135] The programme, accordingly, educates pupils about the security implications of Arabic, encourages them to take their final exams in Arabic and then promotes their draft into Military Intelligence.

Two new programmes have been established in the more recent period, which indicates the ongoing context of military–edcuational Arabic projects. They are *Modiʿin ba-ʾOfeḳ* (Military Intelligence on the Horizon) and *Maḳne Daʿat* (Bestower of Knowledge). Both were founded by the Ṭelem Unit in the late 1990s. The first, Modiʿin ba-ʾOfeḳ, targets 11th grade pupils and is also hosted by Givʿat Ḥavivah. Fully funded by

Military Intelligence, pupils participate in this two-day programme under conditions that replicate those in the military. The seminar aims to 'maintain the motivation of the pupils to continue and study Arabic for the final exam, and to strengthen the relationship between the pupils and Military Intelligence in preparation for the upcoming stage of examinations and checks'. Similar to the Oriental Youth Battalion, Arabic pupils attend lectures on topics such as Military Intelligence, Arabic studies, global terrorism, the Middle East and Military Intelligence battle heritage. Here again, the programme includes an 'intelligential lecture by a senior Military Intelligence officer'.[136]

The second project, Maḳne Daʿat, is overseen by the Information Collection Unit (*'Isuf*) of Military Intelligence. Maḳne Daʿat works with Hebrew-speaking schools throughout the country to encourage 9th to 12th grade pupils to study Arabic. Accordingly, Military Intelligence councillors provide enrichment lessons (lit. *shiʿurey haʿasharah*) on a variety of topics, including Military Intelligence's heritage in battle, the Middle East, Islam and Arabic and more. To raise the profile of this initiative, Maḳne Daʿat's central annual activity is a national quiz. Following an intensive process, the approximately 5000 pupils who participate in the programme each year are narrowed down to 12 finalists, who then compete to win a prize. Quiz topics include Islam, Middle Eastern countries and their leaders, Military Intelligence heritage and Arabic vocabulary. The yearly quiz is hosted by the Faculty of Humanities at Tel Aviv University. In attendance are representatives of from the pupils' schools and the Ministry of Education, along with soldiers and officers from Military Intelligence.[137]

In contemporary Israel, Ṭelem is a consistent aspect of the military–educational landscape. Currently, the Ṭelem Unit either directly oversees or cooperates with the abovementioned programmes. Ṭelem's official website states that the unit aims to 'promote, encourage, nourish and market the study of Arabic all over Israel, in order to increase the potential number of pupils who will join Military Intelligence'.[138] Ṭelem's characterisation of itself includes both national security and peaceful elements, which signifies its continuation of the Arabic for 'peace and security' format. As its website states: 'We see great and crucial importance in teaching pupils Arabic and Islamic culture as a national existential component, and as a component that links us to the people in the region of the Middle East.' The Head of the Ṭelem Unit, Maj. Keren (her full name is not given in the original), states that the unit develops and renews its activities, and they currently include:

> The Oriental Youth Battalions, the seminars of Military Intelligence on the Horizon, activities hosted by the Israel Intelligence Heritage and

> Commemoration Centre (IICC), conferences for pupils on different positions in Military Intelligence, enrichment activities dedicated to Arabic and Military Intelligence, dissemination of teaching aides for the study of Arabic, the national Arabic quiz and more ...'[139]

Furthermore, and interestingly, just as in the earlier decades of statehood, Ṭelem asks high school Arabic teachers to send Military Intelligence information about 11th grade pupils of Arabic. Ṭelem provides teachers with two methods for submitting this information: by post or fax. Where teachers fail to submit this information on time, Ṭelem insinuates that this might negatively affect the pupils' chances of being accepted into Military Intelligence. Teachers are required to fill out a document that includes the pupil's full name and home address, their ID number and both their home and mobile phone numbers. The teacher is also asked to provide the phone number of the person in charge of Arabic studies in the pupil's school, in a process that all in all leaves no place for questions on the involvmenet and role of Military Intelligence in the Arabic class in school.[140]

Based on the publicly accessible material that characterises this short section of the research, it seems that Ṭelem's activities, and the Israeli field of Arabic language studies in general, are still shaped by similar networks, motivations and logic as that which was prevalent in previous decades. This is likely given that, even today, the primary motivation for pupils to study Arabic is that of being drafted into Military Intelligence.[141] Similarly, in the public education system, from the 7th to 12th grades, the vast majority of Arabic teachers are Jewish-Israelis.

The interesting phenomenon, therefore, is that over the past six decades – in a continuous and consistent way – the primary motivation to study Arabic in Israel has been tied to security considerations. This motivation is not restricted to the security establishment but has become part and parcel of the field of Arabic studies in Israeli society as a whole. A more contemporary example can demonstrate this. In January 2014, when Minister of Education Shai Piron, announced that he was going to reduce the number of obligatory years of Arabic studies from four (7th to 10th grades) to three (7th to 9th grades), the Arabic Language Subject Committee in the Ministry of Education responded with anger. In a letter sent to the Minister of Education and published in the Israeli media, the members of the educational committee, headed by Professor Eliezer Schlossberg, explained why Arabic is important to Israeli pupils and why the Minister of Education should avoid the cut. Of the five reasons mentioned, the *first* one was about the damage that this would bring to 'the national security of Israel' (lit. *pegiʿah be-biṭḥon ha-medinah*).

Committee members claimed that cutting the budget for Arabic language studies would 'dramatically reduce the number of pupils who could be assigned to Military Intelligence ... and this will certainly damage the state's national security'.[142]

Only after giving this *first* reason for the study of Arabic in Israel did they mention other reasons for this, including 'Arabic studies as a bridge for peace between Jews and Arabs', the official status of Arabic in Israel and so on. This is just one recent example of the ongoing dominance of security in the field of Arabic studies in Israel and of the centrality of the 'security and peace' mantra.

While much is the same, at least one significant integrative development has taken place. In 2006, the Abraham Fund – a non-profit Jerusalem-based organisation dedicated to the promotion of coexistence and equality between Jewish and Palestinian citizens of Israel – developed a unique and promising educational programme for Arabic studies. Its uniqueness lies in its focus on conversational Arabic, its welcoming civilian tone ('Yā Salām: Arabic as a Cultural Bridge'), the fact that it is geared towards primary school children, the culturally aware pedagogic team behind its development and because it is being taught by Palestinian citizens of Israel. As of 2013, there were some 100 teachers in the programme and it was being implemented in approximately 200 schools throughout Israel.[143] Nevertheless, the programme is limited to primary schools and does not directly influence the Arabic language curriculum and instruction at the intermediary and high schools levels. Furthermore, because the Abraham Fund is external to the Ministry of Education, its impact is limited. Beyond the primary level, it is unlikely that the programme will have a meaningful influence on the curriculum for the final exams, on the study of Arabic in high schools or on the dominance of military interests in Arabic education at higher grades.

In light of decades of close cooperation, the Military Intelligence's influence over Arabic studies and the relationship between the education system and Military Intelligence is firmly implanted. This link, as framed by Re'uven Snir, is actually a 'Gordian knot between Military Intelligence and Arabic studies'.[144] According to him, this knot 'was an element that, to put it mildly, did not improve the way Arabic was taught in the education system'.[145] Arabic, according to this line of argument, is not considered to be legitimate in the Jewish-Israeli identity, and is disqualified as a legitimate and positive element in the Jewish-Israeli identity. This is particularly true at the higher grade levels, where the tone is established by Military Intelligence. Its Jewish stakeholders – including Arabic teachers and Military Intelligence officers – put 'Arabic for security' before 'Arabic for peace'. As Snir puts it:

> There is no better proof of this [connection between Arabic studies and Military Intelligence] than the gap between the resources given to 'know your enemy' and those given to genuinely get to know Arab culture [in Jewish-Israeli society]. Only those who know both systems also know how huge this gap is.[146]

In light of Snir's comments, the subsequent chapter will investigate two Arabic language instruction academies in Israel: Givʿat Ḥavivah and Ulpan ʿAḳiva. Independent of the Ministry of Education, both are considered to be leading Arabic language programmes. Similarly, both have developed reputations as institutions that promote peace and Arabic studies from a 'coexistence perspective'. The comparative study that follows will indicate the extent to which military involvement, and the peace and security formulation, is the norm throughout Israel and whether it is possible to untie the 'Gordian knot' between fluency in Arabic and Military Intelligence.

5

Givʿat Ḥavivah and Ulpan ʿAḳiva

Arabic Studies Independent of the Ministry of Education

'Peace, peace,' they say, when there is no peace.
Shalom, shalom, ṿe-ein shalom.

Jeremiah 6:14

The securitised side of Peace

While the education system in Israel is the largest provider of Arabic language education, it is not the only sphere in which Jewish-Israelis can learn Arabic. Obviously, there is the military establishment (including the IDF, the Ministry of Defence, the General Security System known by its Hebrew acronym, *Shabak*, and the Mossad) where language study is intended directly to serve strategic and security interests. These frameworks of study are not examined by this research, as it is expected that in situations of political tension (and even among 'friendly' countries), learning languages widely used in the 'other's' country for the purpose of gleaning intelligence is part and parcel of every country's security apparatus. Examples that come to mind can include the Egyptian Military Intelligence studying Hebrew or American's need for Russian-speakers during the Cold War and so on. Therefore, what is of interest here is not Arabic studies in the military establishment – soldiers teaching soldiers or security personnel learning from security personnel – rather, the influence of the military establishment on Arabic studies in the civil sphere, as well as the military's needs and the discourse perpetuated in civilian bodies. As such, this study focuses on the military influence on traditionally civilian realms such as educational bodies, the school system and civil society organisations.

In order to enable a comparative look at the civilian realm, this chapter focuses on two Israeli institutions – Givʿat Ḥavivah and Ulpan

ʿAkiva – both espouse goals related to the strengthening of peace and civil society. Both institutions have well-known and established Arabic language programmes and each have received the UNESCO Prize for Peace Education, in 1998 and 2001, respectively. Founded in the 1960s, their point of departure was different from the Arabic in the education system that was shaped by the war of 1948.

An examination of these two institutions is instructive in that it facilitates a wider look at possibilities for Arabic language studies that are, for the most part, outside of the military establishment. Indeed, an analysis of their work helps to unravel the 'Gordian knot' between Arabic and security, referred to by Snir in the previous chapter. Therefore, this chapter will examine whether the growing influence of the military on Arabic in the education system, as analysed previously, holds true for two independent institutions – both of which have a mandate for promoting peace and coexistence. This comparative study will also shed additional light on the characteristics, power relations and motivating factors influencing the field of Arabic studies in Israel.[1]

Recruiting ʿAbd al-ʿAzīz al-Zuʿbī: Arabic studies at Givʿat Ḥavivah

Givʿat Ḥavivah, a lovely and inviting conference and seminar centre located in the Wādī ʿĀra region, east of the city of Ḥadera (in Arabic, al-Khuḍeira, meaning 'the green'), was established in 1949. It was founded by members of the socialist Zionist movement *Ha-Shomer ha-Tsaʿir* (The Youth Guard) in order to serve as an education centre for the kibbutzim movement on a national basis. Givʿat Ḥavivah was named in honour of Ḥaviva Reik, a Zionist activist who joined a British parachuting unit during the Second World War. Involved in several missions behind enemy lines, she was eventually captured and executed by the Nazis in 1944.

Givʿat Ḥavivah's stated aim is 'to build an inclusive, socially cohesive society in Israel by engaging divided communities in collective action towards the advancement of a sustainable, thriving Israeli democracy based on mutual responsibility, civic equality and a shared vision of the future'.[2] Of tremendous relevance to this research, in 1963, the Jewish–Arab Center for Peace at Givʿat Ḥavivah was established. The Center defined its mission as 'creating better relations between Arabs and Jews, better understanding of the essence of democracy and civil rights in Israel and building bridges with our Arab neighbours'.[3] During the same year, the Institute for Arabic Studies (lit. *Ha-Makhon le-Limudei ʿAravit*) was established under the auspices of the Center. Its activities include courses in Arabic language and Arab culture, including a wide variety of courses in Colloquial Arabic and Literary Arabic targeting youths and adults. In 1980, the Institute for Arabic Studies changed its name to the ʿAbd al-ʿAzīz al-Zuʿbī Institute for Arabic Studies, in honour of ʿAbd al-ʿAzīz al-Zuʿbī, a former Mayor of Nazareth and MK, who was one of the first founders and supporters of the Institute for Arabic Studies back in 1963.[4]

It is clear that, unlike the Jewish-Israeli education system, from the very beginning Givʿat Ḥavivah emphasised dialogue and integration over separation. Encounters between Arab-Palestinians and Jewish-Israelis were central to the work of the Jewish–Arab Center for Peace and the Institute for Arabic Studies. Unlike activities at the Ministry of Education, the Institute also included a substantial number of Palestinian citizens of Israel in their activities as teachers and participants in committees. Nevertheless, Givʿat Ḥavivah was, and still is, a Jewish-Israeli endeavour established by a Zionist party and located in the heart of the Palestinian region of Wādī ʿĀra. As such, it framed its work within the established boundaries of Zionist discourse, even if on its more 'liberal' edges. Accordingly, the familiar 'security and peace' formulation was evident here as well and set the tone for its work and its activities firmly within the Israeli body politic.

Already in the early days of the Institute for Arabic Studies, in 1966, there were indications of the security implications of its Arabic language instruction. A correspondence involving Yoseph Vashitz – one of Israel's pioneering Orientalists who was involved in researching the Palestinian society in Israel – is a good demonstration of this.[5] At the time, Vashitz oversaw the Institute's flagship Arabic programme – an intensive seven-month programme of Arabic language and Oriental studies ('The Oriental Class'). A student who was issued a call-up order to serve in the army reserves was worried that this would negatively impact on his successful completion of the course. In the hopes of getting his reserve service rescheduled, Vashitz wrote to the student's unit commander as follows:

> Your subordinate [name in original] is participating in an Oriental studies course at Givʿat Ḥavivah. Since Arabic language studies is the main part of the course, over 30 hours per week, his absence for a few days may mean that he will not graduate successfully. I wanted to highlight this to you, so that you can show consideration and reschedule his military reserve duty ... I hope that you consider his studies here important, and acknowledge the security value of the

> subject for which he dedicates his time (lit. *ein le-hitʿalem me-ʿerko ha-biṭḥoni shel ha-nose she-ʿalav hu maḳdish et limudav*) ...[6]

While the letter does not conclusively indicate a formal relationship between Givʿat Ḥavivah and the security establishment, nevertheless, in order to facilitate the students' completion of the course, Vashitz's appeal to the army was 'in its own language', making security considerations foremost to his argument. This initial, relatively trivial act, may have been an omen for the strengthening of relations between Arabic at Givʿat Ḥavivah and Military Intelligence in subsequent years, as will be demonstrated here, but can also hint at the emerging discourse in which Givʿat Ḥavivah participated.

The course referred to in the letter was Givʿat Ḥavivah's flagship programme. Entitled 'Arabic Language and Oriental Studies', it was also known as *Ha-Kitah ha-Mizraḥanit* [the Oriental Class] of Givʿat Ḥavivah. The course shared the same name as the Oriental Classes in the Jewish-Israeli school system, established in 1954 and discussed extensively in previous chapters. This selection of the programme's name hints at similarities between the courses, or at least the adoption of a similar discourse and understanding of boundaries in relation to the subjects studied. This, arguably, provides a context for the relatively 'natural' entrance of security interests into Givʿat Ḥavivah's Arabic language courses, as will be expanded on later.

While available documentation is not sufficient to establish the motivations underlying the initiation and development of Givʿat Ḥavivah's 'Oriental Class', it is possible to comment on the changes that took place in the Oriental Classes and its relation to student recruitment. A letter sent to the Kibbutzim Committee for Continuing Education by Vashitz in 1972 discusses considerations in recruiting students and sheds new light on the Oriental Classes:

> In the upcoming school year (1973) the Oriental Class at Givʿat Ḥavivah will enter its 10th year. During the first few years, the Class consisted of students who had finished their army service, but lately there are more students who join this class prior to their military service ... The Oriental Class aims to create a young reserve for activities that require knowledge of Arabic ... either as an initial stage before becoming Arabic teachers, or in order to train these youngsters for activity in the [Arabic] field: explaining [lit. *hasbara*] Arab society [to Jewish-Israelis], different activities [lit. *peʿiluyot*] among the Arabs and translation and [media] coverage operations [lit. *peʿulot*] ... We

> already have a few applications for the next year, and we prefer that the majority of students will be those after military service ...[7]

It is not clear whether pupils who chose to study in this programme prior to military service were motivated by serving in Military Intelligence and Arabic-oriented positions, however, given the difficulties facing the Oriental Classes in the education system and the generally low ranking of Arabic, in all likelihood this was the case. I believe that Vashitz's use of 'coded language' such as 'activity in the field' (lit. *peʿilut ba-sheṭaḥ)* 'operations' and 'explaining Arab society' further strengthens this perception. Militaristic sounding, his choice of words may represent an attempt to avoid reference to the security or political nature of most positions 'in the Arabic field' in Israel.

By 1973, the picture was much clearer. As discussed previously, the 1973 War crystallised the importance of knowledge of Arabic in Israel's political and security establishments and the public at large. While Givʿat Ḥavivah's mandate was more peace-oriented, given their positioning inside the centre of the Israeli establishment, they were not immune to these larger trends. This is supported by the documentation, including a letter written by Zvi Atkin, a former senior Military Intelligence officer[8] and the new Director of the Institute (at the time called the 'Institute for Arabic and Afro-Asian Studies') to Shmuʾel Toledano, the former head of the Mossad, who, at the time, served as the Adviser on Arab Affairs in the Prime Minister's Office. Atkin wrote as follows: 'it is only now, as the war is over, and as we reconvene the [Jewish–Arab] Center that I find time to thank you for the funding given by the Department of Arab Affairs [in the Prime Minister's Office] to our Arab–Jewish summer camp'.[9] Atkin was obviously advocating for the camps and their importance, and he added that '[t]he restrained behaviour of Israeli-Arabs [lit. *ʿamidatam shel ʿArviyey-Yisrael*] during the war has proved that these efforts to create understanding between the two people were not for nothing'.[10]

This interesting correspondence is worth examining from two different angles. First, it is important to point out the strong security and Military Intelligence credentials of both figures involved in this correspondence between allegedly two different spheres. This suggests that they did not see a contradiction between Arabic studies serving as a conduit both for peace and as a tool for Israeli security. Second, I argue that the justification used to support the continuation of the Arab–Jewish summer camps is reminiscent of projects that took place in the pre-state period, including the 'Courses for Jewish *Mukhtārs*' or the 'Good Neighbour Committees' managed by the SHAI of the Haganah; their main aim was to ensure the success of the Zionist project with minimal difficulties from the Arab side. Atkin's praise of the Arab–Jewish summer camps can be seen in the same light, as reflecting a politico-security concern, and activities that will maintain the continuation of Israeli control.

November 1973 ushered in the first record of official correspondence between Military Intelligence and Givʿat Ḥavivah regarding Arabic studies. As demonstrated previously, the post-1973 period was characterised by Military Intelligence's intense interest in Arabic language instruction in schools. This need for Arabic-speakers was most likely the context for a letter sent from the Military Intelligence's Selection Unit (lit. *ʾItur*) to the Director of the Institute of Arabic studies at Givʿat Ḥavivah. The letter notes that Givʿat Ḥavivah had yet to respond to a previous request for a list of students in the intensive Arabic course who were nearing graduation. As a reminder of the first letter, Military Intelligence attached a missive to this second letter. It noted that the previous letter sent by the IDF to Givʿat Ḥavivah had requested full lists of students graduating from the Arabic course, along with a written evaluation prepared by their teachers.[11]

The reason underlying Givʿat Ḥavivah's lack of response to the first request is not clear. Perhaps, the request by the Military Intelligence was seen as controversial within the institution and led to disagreements regarding the appropriate response. It may have been that there was a difference of opinion regarding cooperation with the Adviser on Arab Affairs (which did happen), as opposed to Military Intelligence. The former might have had more legitimacy in relation to Givʿat Ḥavivah's work as he was a figure from the Prime Minister's Office (and connected to the Labour Party government) and not a military figure writing from Military Intelligence, and was seen as an integral part of the national debate on Arabic studies, while Military Intelligence represented the army and a more straightforward connection to its needs and activities. In all likelihood, Givʿat Ḥavivah staff members were probably required to make principled decisions regarding cooperation with the security establishment at this point, thus explaining the reason for the delayed response.

While no response is on record, by 1976, and similar to the nature of the partnership between the military and the education system, open cooperation between the sides was already evident, includig the sharing of information on pupils that became a routine. For example, by November 1976, an agreement with the IDF stipulated that Military Intelligence's OSINT Unit (Open Sources Intelligence) *Ḥatsav* would send its publications to the Institute for Arabic Studies at Givʿat

Ḥavivah.[12] Givʿat Ḥavivah's Director, Yoseph Vashitz wrote the following to the IDF Spokesperson, with a copy of the letter also being sent to the Financial Department of the Ministry of Defence:

> I would like to thank you for renewing the arrangement between the Institute of Arabic Studies and Ḥatsav ... Would it be possible for our representative to visit you in order to clarify a few issues? Thank you very much again for your kind and supportive attitude.[13]

Vashitz's gratitude, as well as the reference to 'renewing' an existing agreement, is indicative of the ever closer relations between Givʿat Ḥavivah and Military Intelligence and the increasing institutionalisation of this relationship. Given that the letter was copied to the Financial Department of the Ministry of Defence, it also suggests a confluence of interests, including the possibility that Givʿat Ḥavivah would receive additional financial support from the security establishment.

Therefore, it is somewhat surprising that, during that same year, there was a rupture in relations between Givʿat Ḥavivah and the IDF. Givʿat Ḥavivah's senior staff were surprised when the IDF demanded that their 18-year-old pupils who had registered for the course – and who had already been given permission to postpone their army service for a year in order to participate – were instead required to join the army immediately. In light of the fact that the post-1973 War period was characterised by the IDF's increasing awareness of the need for Arabic on entrance to the military service, it is somewhat surprising that they then seemed to prefer recruits who had not yet studied Arabic. Indeed, Givʿat Ḥavivah's staff found this a bit odd and, consequently, decided to raise the matter with Gen. Rafael Ṿardi, the Commander of the IDF's Manpower Directorate. In correspondence relevant to this matter, Givʿat Ḥavivah asked the IDF to reconsider this decision. The IDF flatly refused; instead, it repeated its demand regarding the recruitment of 18-year-olds. This time, however, the demand from Givʿat Ḥavivah was sent via former MK Nathan Peled (who was associated with the kibbutz movement), to then Minister of Defence Shimon Peres.[14]

Yet Givʿat Ḥavivah was not successful in changing the IDF's decision. David Bar-Matsra, from the Security Department of the National Kibbutz Movement, sent out two separate letters updating the Secretariat of the Movement and prospective students about the unsuccessful attempts by Givʿat Ḥavivah – even that of Peled and the Security Department of the National Kibbutz Movement – to postpone student recruitment to the IDF. The letters also note the numbers of pupils in the course who had not yet entered military service and highlighted Giv'at Ḥavivah and Military Intelligence's relationship on the issue of Arabic:

> As our great efforts to convince the army to postpone the recruitment of the pupils to the IDF failed, we have to cancel this year's Oriental Class ... Over the last 13 years our courses were proven to be a great success, and most of our pupils were members of the kibbutzim, who finished 12th grade and were required to be immediately recruited to the IDF ... Out of 150 pupils who have finished this course [in the past 13 years], 100 have served in Military Intelligence and were praised for their achievements, as the IDF officer in charge of the encouragement of Arabic studies usually tells us ... It is therefore just absurd that exactly when the media is full of calls to our youth to study Arabic in order to fulfil the different needs of society, state and army, this project comes to an end.[15]

Bar-Matsra's letter clarifies that by 1976, most of the pupils in the Oriental Classes were 18 years old and that their intention of taking courses at the Institute for Arabic Studies was pre-Military Intelligence rather than for civilian or post-military purposes. It is also clear that Giv'at Ḥavivah's senior staff, despite working for the Jewish–Arab Center for Peace, found their role in training pupils to use Arabic for intelligence purposes to be completely acceptable or at least not publically debated. Therefore, it is not clear why the IDF decided to recruit pupils immediately, especially given that course graduates were seemingly viewed as an asset to the military. The numbers may offer a clue: only 100 soldiers from the course had been recruited into Military Intelligence in the span of thirteen years, less than 10 individuals per year on average. As this number was negligible, perhaps Military Intelligence decided that these individuals were not indispensible. Another possible explanation relates to the tremendous shortage of Arabic-speakers following the 1973 War; to overcome this problem, Military Intelligence officers may have decided to recruit as many soldiers as possible with the intention of training them themselves. The IDF may also have felt the need to increase their overall manpower and, thus, were determined to recruit anyone they could.

This incident aside, apparently the post-1976 years were characterised by improved relations between the two sides. And in fact, by 1978, Giv'at Ḥavivah and Military Intelligence had reached an agreement whereby pupils who were accepted by Giv'at Ḥavivah's Oriental Class were automatically entitled to a one-year postponement of their military service. This process was jointly administered by both bodies.[16]

Also in 1978, perhaps as an outcome of this development, Givʿat Ḥavivah became more public regarding their military connection. In a letter sent to the Security Department of the National Kibbutz Movement, Yoseph Vashitz, Director of the Institute for Arabic Studies, summarised the programme's progress. He wrote:

> Since 1963, we have held at Givʿat Ḥavivah an Oriental class, in which a big section of the pupils are boys and girls about to join the IDF. Besides the general importance of Arabic studies, for which we dedicate 85 per cent of our time, the graduates of the Oriental Class [use their Arabic] and play an important role in the IDF in positions that require knowledge of the language ... Due to the importance of this project, therefore, we urge you to recommend to young members of the kibbutzmin to join the [Oriental] Class ... Is not it a goal that we can perceive as one of a *national service* importance?[17]

To support his argument regarding the military and national importance of the course, Vahistz attached an article to the letter praising graduates of Givʿat Ḥavivah's Oriental Classes. The article featured an interview with the Chief of Intelligence, Gen. Shlomo Gazit, who spoke about the importance of the Oriental Classes generally, and specifically mentioned the programme at Givʿat Ḥavivah.[18] Furthermore, the fact that Arabic studies were a subject of discussion within the National Kibbutz Movement's Security Department and not its Education Department, provides another indication as to Givʿat Ḥavivah's steady drift towards the sphere of national security in a similar way to the processes that occurred in the education system, even before the creation of the state. This process is reminiscent of the pre-state period, when Arabic studies were discussed by the Political Department of the Jewish Agency as well as by its Education Department.

There are indications that, by the late 1970s, budgeting concerns were behind the growing closeness between the Oriental Classes and the political establishment. A letter sent in 1980 by the newly appointed Director of the Institute for Arabic Studies, Moshe Gabay, to Deputy Prime Minister Simḥa Erlikh sought financial support for the programme. Gabay wrote that even though the Oriental Classes was in its seventeenth year, due to the expense of providing Arabic language instruction at Givʿat Ḥavivah, the Institute required urgent assistance (lit. *ha-peʿilut ha-ʿanefah shelanu ʿomedet hayom be-sakanat tsimtsum drasṭit im lo ḥisul*).[19] Specifically, assistance was sought for activities relating to the Arabic language and culture and also to joint Jewish–Arab projects.

In response, Yitzḥak Reiter from the Bureau of the Adviser on Arab Affairs in the Prime Minister's Office wrote that: 'following the recommendation of the Adviser on Arab Affairs, we have decided to increase our support to your institution in a significant way. I will be able to provide you with accurate details in a few weeks' time and as soon as we receive a financial confirmation from the Ministry of Finance.'[20] During the subsequent budgetary year, Reiter indicated that the Adviser on Arab Affairs had decided to double the support provided to the Institute of Arabic Studies in Givʿat Ḥavivah.[21] This, I believe, was a complementary process; in exchange for governmental support, Givʿat Ḥavivah was more evidently expected to perform a 'national service'.

The ease with which Givʿat Ḥavivah seemingly accepted the interplay between peace and security reached new levels in 1980. At that time, and in light of his death the previous year, it was decided to name the Institute for Arabic Studies after ʿAbd al-ʿAzīz al-Zuʿbī. Accordingly, the Institute's name was changed to the ʿAbd al-ʿAzīz al-Zuʿbī Institute for Arabic Studies (Al-Zuʿbī, a Palestinian citizen of Israel, a Labour Party MK, the former Mayor of Nazareth and a founder of the Jewish–Arab Center in 1963). There is evidence of this dissonance in a number of letters between the Center and the IDF in January 1981 – a centre named after a Palestinian person that is dedicated to the peaceful study of Arabic and co-exitense on the one hand, and a direct connection with Military Intelligence and Arabic studies for the army on the other hand. For example, a letter from the Director of the Institute, Moshe Gabay, to Colonel Neḥemiah from the Ṭelem Unit in Military Intelligence, notes:

> I am writing to you again after I succeeded in recruiting 15 students who just graduated from high school to our Oriental Class. And all in all, we are going to have in the Oriental Class this year 21 students (15 before military service, and 6 after military service) ... In the last conversation that we had with Lt Col. Nissim ʿAtsmon [the IDF coordinator for the encouragement of Oriental and Arabic studies in Jewish-Israeli schools], we were promised that if we reached 15 students we would be given an instructor for the course, one of the soldier-teachers who has finished the [Military Intelligence Arabic] Ulpan, so that she can help us with our Arabic teaching. I would be grateful if this can be arranged by the beginning of the next school year in our Institute.[22]

This agreement, which specified that the Ṭelem Unit of Military Intelligence would 'donate' a soldier-teacher of Arabic to Givʿat Ḥavivah if at least 15 students were registered to take the Oriental Class, speaks for itself. It conclusively clarifies the nature of relations between the two sides, along with Givʿat Ḥavivah's dependence on financial and human support from political and military sources. The annual report of the Institute for Arabic Study's published in late 1981 indicates that this agreement was implemented. It states: 'the soldier's name is … and she is a teacher in the army. She will be in the [Oriental] Class as required.'[23]

The provision of staff was only one way in which Givʿat Ḥavivah and the military establishment, including Military Intelligence, worked together during this period. Archival documents indicate that from 1979 onwards, similar to the situation in high schools during the period, Givʿat Ḥavivah supplied Military Intelligence with the names of graduating pupils and teacher assessments of their ability to write in Arabic.[24] Givʿat-Ḥavivah also provided Military Intelligence with details regarding pupils who had registered for the course prior to military service and then subsequently discontinued their studies. A letter from the Institute to ʿAtsmon informed him that 'the pupil … was taken out of the Oriental Class due to low achievements. This was our last resort, and it followed various attempts made to encourage him to improve and finish the course successfully. I cannot remember when a similar case like this happened, and this is indeed very unfortunate.'[25] This letter indicates and reinforces the point that Military Intelligence was giving support to Givʿat Ḥavivah and, in return, the latter was required to teach Arabic and provide reports. Indeed, it seems that at this point, similar to the education system, Arabic studies at Givʿat Ḥavivah had lost much of its independence to the military and was now enmeshed in a complicated relationship of dependency.

Further evidence of the close relations between Givʿat Ḥavivah and the Military Intelligence comes from an examination of a commemorative event held in 1978. At that time, the Institute for Arabic Studies decided to celebrate the fifteenth anniversary of its flagship programme: the Oriental Class. All Oriental Class graduates were invited. The event was opened by the guest of honour, Shlomo Gazit, who had served at the time as the Chief of Intelligence.[26] The choice of speaker indicates how instrumental Military Intelligence was perceived to be in ensuring the long-term sustainability of this initiative and the Jewish-Israeli orientation of the ʿAbd al-ʿAzīz al-Zuʿbī Institute for Arabic Studies.

Close collaboration between Givʿat-Ḥavivah and Military Intelligence continued throughout the 1980s and even increased with the passage of time. A letter written in 1982 and drafted by Gabay, the new Director of the ʿAbd al-ʿAzīz al-Zuʿbī Institute for Arabic Studies, is indicative of these developments. Sent to the Security Department of the United Kibbutz Movement, Gabay requested permission to convene a meeting with Military Intelligence representatives in order to discuss a plan to open two additional Oriental Classes.[27] ʿAtsmon was copied into the letter thus indicating that, in fact, this was now a joint initiative with Military Intelligence. In response, ʿAtsmon wrote to Gabay as follows:

> For a long time I planned to write to you to express my deep gratitude for your magnificent project ... It is hard to express in this letter the great value of the graduates [of Givʿat Ḥavivah's Institute for Arabic Studies] in the IDF. I wish we had more like them in Military Intelligence [lit. *Halṿay ye-yirbu kmotam be-Ḥaman*] ... I hope that your work, which has lasted for 19 years, will become more and more successful, and *inshalla* in the next year you will open two [Oriental] Classes. We, from our side in the Ṭelem Unit, will give any help we can ... I am hopeful that the institute you are heading [the ʿAbd al-ʿAzīz al-Zuʿbī Institute for Arabic Studies] will receive a special recognition as a centre that trains Arabists [Israeli Orientalist experts] with high level of Arabic.
>
> With great respect and with friendship,
> Lt Col. Nissim ʿAtsmon.[28]

Significantly, Moshe Gargir, the General Supervisor of Arabic Studies in the Jewish-Israeli education system was copied into ʿAtsmon's letter. The culture of copying, I believe, is noteworthy and can be understood as political. For example, in copying ʿAtsmon into his letter to the Security Department of the Kibbutz Movement, Gabay wanted to ensure that Military Intelligence was aware of his efforts. In copying in Gabay at the Ministry of Education, ʿAtsmon was demonstrating that military involvement was appreciated by the Ministry that is in charge of Arabic studies. This 'linked' correspondence nurtured and strengthened an emerging network of key stakeholders involved in Arabic language education while also sharpening their shared vision of Arabic as an issue that touched on security and peace. Importantly, developments related to Arabic studies at Givʿat Ḥavivah continued to reflect changes taking place in the school system with a strong unifying factor: the involvement of the military – and even the leading role taken by the military, within both frameworks.[29]

Indeed, a decision to create two Oriental Classes was approved and, with it, an upgrading of relations between Givʿat Ḥavivah and Military Intelligence. Everyone involved with this initiative understood that these classes were the first step in subsequent recruitment into Military Intelligence. Accordingly, two classes opened in 1984 with a total of 40 pupils,[30] while two more classes opened in 1985 with a total of 41 pupils.[31] Givʿat Ḥavivah's newsletter explains that the pupils who participated in the eight intensive months of instruction offered in this programme,invested some 1040 hours in class time. Studies were broken down as follows: Literary Arabic (630 hours), Colloquial Arabic (160 hours), Oriental Studies (110 hours), Arabic in the media (46 hours), Arabic manuscripts (20 hours), enrichment (42 hours) and tours (32 hours).[32]

In addition, Jewish-Israeli pupils were also given the opportunity to meet Palestinian citizens of Israel. Givʿat Ḥavivah's bulletin includes a picture of one such meeting featuring two girls: one a Jewish-Israeli and the other a Palestinian citizen of Israel. More interesting than the picture itself is its subtitle, which reads: 'Tradition and modernity: a Jewish and Arab girl at a meeting in Givʿat Ḥavivah'.[33] The portrayal of the Palestinian in the picture as traditional is consistent with an orientalist view of the Arab-Palestinian 'East' as frozen in time in comparison with the modern Jewish-Israeli 'West'. Indeed, this supports the notion that the dominant discourse at the time had an Orientalist 'scent' and that this was evident in the Oriental Classes offered by Givʿat Ḥavivah specifically, and in Arabic studies offered by the Israeli Ministry of Education more generally. It also suggests that despite Givʿat Ḥavivah's stated emphasis on coexistence, in actuality – with regard to Arabic – the Institute adopted the predominant discourse about Arabic language and Arab culture in Israel and may have even had a role in shaping its border.

It seems that with the passing of time, practical considerations – and specifically the need to identify funding to continue operations – were driving the agenda and activities at the Jewish–Arab Peace Center at Givʿat Ḥavivah. Otherwise, it is hard to understand the letter from Gabay at Givʿat Ḥavivah to an officer at Military Post 2404, whereby he described the ʿAbd al-ʿAzīz al-Zuʿbī Institute for Arabic Studies as: 'the Israeli higher education institute for school graduates before they go to Military Intelligence' (lit. *zehu beit ha-sefer ha-gavoha ba-Arets ʿavur bogrey kitot yud-bet lifnei halikhatam le-ḥeil ha-modiʿin*).[34] Despite ʿAbd al-ʿAzīz al-Zuʿbī's fairly liberal inclinations, it probably would have made him spin in in his grave had he seen this. Indeed, what Gabay describes is a far cry from the statement of principles set out by the Institute in 1963, according to which it will serve 'as a house for the implementation of brotherhood between Jews and Arabs in Israel and in the whole region'.[35]

As the Institute gradually became a central address for Arabic studies, the nature and scope of their collaboration with Military Intelligence also continued to expand. For example, the IDF School of Arabic brought soldiers on field trips to Givʿat Ḥavivah a number of times where they visited its Arabic classes and library. Following one such outing, 1st Lt Eyal Zisser, a Commander at the Arabic Ulpan, wrote to Gabay, saying: 'it was an interesting visit and programme, which gave us a different angle regarding issues that we are all interested in'. Zisser signed off as follows: 'with hope for fruitful cooperation in the future'.[36]

While both sides were happy with this arrangement, there was a sense at Givʿat Ḥavivah that projects involving Military Intelligence were not sufficiently organised and that there was a need for more and better coordination between the two bodies. Using the regular official ʿAbd al-ʿAzīz al-Zuʿbī Institute letterheaded paper, Gabay sent Brig. Giyora Zoreʿa, the Chief Intelligence Officer a letter saying:

> During the last two decades the relationship between Givʿat Ḥavivah's Institute for Arabic Studies and Military Intelligence regarding the Oriental Classes have materialised and become close [lit. *halkhu ṿe-notsḳu bo ḳesharim haduḳim ʿim ḥeil ha-modiʿin*]. Year after year the graduates of the Institute are integrated into different positions in Military Intelligence and fulfil the necessary missions. The relations [between Givʿat Ḥavivah and Military Intelligence] have developed through different stages, but without proper planning. This is perhaps the reason for some of the difficulties and misunderstandings between us. Therefore, I would be grateful if we could arrange a meeting, in which we would present a work plan that will take our projects with Military Intelligence under consideration and will require the military unit attached to the Institute to operate in accordance with agreed regulations [lit. *tokhnit ha-meshalevet et ḳeshareinu ʿim ha-ḥayil, u-meḥayevet et ha-yeḥidah ha-tsevaʾit*] …
>
> With friendship, Moshe Gabay.[37]

Gabay's letter points to the strong collaboration that had developed between Givʿat Ḥavivah and Military Intelligence and their mutual desire to institutionalise these relations. It also hints at complementary interests between the two sides, with the Oriental Classes as a starting point and successful Military Intelligence service as the end goal. Moreover, the reference to a 'military unit attached to the Institute' and the request for a 'work plan' implies that Givʿat Ḥavivah had become dependent on the support of Military Intelligence and this was their rationale for institutionalising and better defining the relationship.

In 1986, Yoram Meron took over the directorship of the ʿAbd al-ʿAzīz al-Zuʿbī Institute for Arabic Studies. Meron had been active in joint Jewish–Arab endeavours, had dedicated his life to Arabic studies and published a number of books of traditional Arabic stories.[38] Himself a graduate of Givʿat Ḥavivah's Oriental Class (in 1964), he was a natural candidate for the position. He was also a committed Zionist liberal 'kibbutznik', who further encouraged the military–educational alliance that had been created. Meron, I believe, was also a pragmatist; he was fully aware of the tremendous interest of the Military Intelligence in Arabic studies and the negative repercussions of refusing to accept the financial incentives offered by it.

Therefore, soon after taking up the position, Meron contacted Lt Col. Herbert Zeʾev from Military Intelligence to explore new opportunities for cooperation. Meron's letter referenced a previous meeting where they had jointly considered the establishment of a course for soldier-teachers at Givʿat Ḥavivah. In the letter, Meron mentioned that he was aware that such a course was taking place at a different Israeli institution called Ulpan ʿAḳiva. He then noted that in case the current arrangement encounters difficulties, 'and only if this is the case ... I would like to suggest shifting the programme to the Institute of Arabic Studies at Givʿat Ḥavivah.'[39]

The contents of the letter help locate Givʿat-Ḥavivah in the field of Arabic studies in Israel. First, Meron starts his letter by referring to Zeʾev by his nickname, 'To: Lt Col. Velvalé'.[40] This hints at a degree of closeness between the men and, most probably, previous acquaintance. Second, in attempting to convince Zeʾev to move the Soldier-Teachers Course to Givʿat Ḥavivah, Meron mentions that 'holding it at the Institute of Arabic Studies ... will allow [the soldier-teachers] to exploit the Institute's contacts with the Arab population in order to practice Colloquial Arabic' [lit. *nitsul ha-magaʿim ʿim ha-ʾukhlusiya ha-ʿAravit ba-makhon le-shem tirgul ha-ʿAravit ha-meduberet*].[41] Meron also notes that ongoing coordination with the Supervisor of Arabic Studies at the Ministry of Education and the Department of Teacher Training would take place. Further on in the letter he mentions financial matters. According to Meron, '[w]e assume that the eight-month course will cost about $US5000 per pupil, and therefore for twenty apprentices the cost would be about $US100,000, including full dormitory costs, classes, language lab [lit. *maʿbadah leshonit*], textbooks, teachers and kosher food'.[42] Undoubtedly, this financial explanation was an important detail to mention, as the need for funding was a strong motivating factor for Meron as a director at Givʿat Ḥavivah.

Meron's letter is of interest on a number of other levels as well. First, it reveals that Givʿat Ḥavivah and Ulpan ʿAḳiva, Israel's most prolific peace-oriented centres for Arabic studies, were competing with each other for the favour of Military Intelligence. Although what they were competing for is not entirely clear, the competition may have been driven by ideological or financial factors. Regarding the Soldiers-Teachers project, it is important to remember that it was established by Military Intelligence in the aftermath of the 1973 War in order to increase the number of pupils studying Arabic in schools and subsequently to increase the number of students who could be recruited to Arabic-oriented positions in the IDF. Pupils who studied with teachers doing their active service, and while in uniform, most likely strengthened the association of Arabic with the military. Arguably, the Soldier-Teachers project promoted and strengthened this association, an outcome that the army favoured. Second, Meron's willingness to 'exploit the Institute's contacts with the Arab population' demonstrates that the Palestinian presence at Givʿat Ḥavivah was used, among other things, for marketing purposes and because their linguistic skills were valued. Undoubtedly, this 'exploitation' undermined Givʿat Ḥavivah's stated mission to bring Jewish and Palestinian Israelis closer together. Givʿat Ḥavivah's reliance on Military Intelligence and soldiers in active duty calls into question the extent to which Givʿat Ḥavivah was able to remain true to its mission.

The merging of missions between the Ministry of Education, Givʿat Ḥavivah and Military Intelligence was also in evidence in a subsequent letter. Sent by Meron to Rani Treinin, Givʿat Ḥavivah's General Director, the letter advocated for implementing the Soldier-Teachers course at Givʿat Ḥavivah. Meron wrote:

> Our Institute is currently examining an IDF request to establish a course for Soldier-Teachers at Givʿat Ḥavivah. This course is both prestigious and important, and may serve as a lever for the development of the activities of the Institute and for the advancement of relations between Givʿat Ḥavivah, the Ministry of Education and the IDF [lit. *ʿasuy le-shamesh manof le-ḳidum peʿilut ha-makhon ʿim Misrad ha-Ḥinukh ṿe-Tsahal*].[43]

Following this letter, and definitely by 1986, it was clear that both the Jewish–Arab Peace Center at Givʿat Ḥavivah (represented by the ʿAbd al-ʿAzīz al-Zuʿbī Institute for Arabic Studies) and the IDF had a mutual interest in promoting their relationship. Simultaneously, Givʿat Ḥavivah's relations with Military Intelligence and the Ministry of Education were stronger than at any other time subsequently. A number of factors contributed to this: first, Givʿat Ḥavivah implemented intensive Arabic courses and, uniquely, its programme of study provided pupils with the opportunity to speak directly to Palestinians. Second, and driven by the need to secure and increase revenue sources and the desire to achieve legitimacy within Jewish-Israeli society, Givʿat Ḥavivah was very open and even enthusiastically welcomed cooperation with Military Intelligence.

The nature of public events implemented by Givʿat Ḥavivah attest to the warm relations that they had cultivated with both Military Intelligence and the education system at this point. Every year Givʿat Ḥavivah hosted an Annual Meeting of Arabic Teachers for teachers in the Jewish-Israeli education system. Many of the invited speakers, including keynote presenters, were military figures; in 1987, this role was filled by Brig. Ephraim Lapid,[44] while Lt Yaʿacov Ṭal spoke in 1988.[45] These presentations dealt with various aspects of Arabic language education while also making a connection to the military. These events, and the selection of speakers, reflect the same web of relations and dependency noted earlier concerning the Ministry of Education. At this point, Givʿat Ḥavivah was now included in this network. Indeed, by planning events for teachers and including the military in the programme, it appears that the goals and directions of the three institutions in relation to Arabic had converged.

This converging of interests was also evident in a meeting that was held in 1986 between the Security Department of the Kibbutz Movement and Gen. Matan Ṿilnai, the Commander of the IDF Manpower Directorate.[46] The summary of the meeting notes that on the agenda was the creation of a pre-military course at Givʿat Ḥavivah. The course, referred to as '*Roshmei Bet*' [lit. 'Writers B'], was to be supervised by Military Intelligence. Unlike other programmes at Givʿat Ḥavivah such as the Oriental Class, this course aimed to train individuals to serve very specific Arabic-related roles in the military. Accordingly, in order to get accepted to the course, students were required to undergo testing and evaluation by Military Intelligence and, following successful completion of the course, would be placed in a specific unit in Military Intelligence. The summary of the meeting indicates that this project was one of many initiated during this period in order to deal with 'the problem of Arabic studies in the national education system'.[47]

This joint 'Roshmei Bet' initiative was launched by Military Intelligence and Givʿat Ḥavivah in 1987. The 25 young men, all of whom came from kibbutzim and who were selected to participate, were jointly recruited by Giv'at Ḥavivah and Military Intelligence.[48] The agreement between the parties stipulated that Giv'at Ḥavivah had the right to approve the curriculum prior to its launch while Military Intelligence had the prerogative to have additional study units at a later time. It even indicated that these units may be 'specifically in the Syrian colloquial dialect' and that Military Intelligence would provide appropriate instructors for this.[49] A letter outlining this agreement and written by Lt Col. Ze'ev also mentioned that the Chief of Intelligence had authorised the programme.[50] At the conclusion of the first year of this year-long course, Meron updated Ze'ev regarding its progress. In the correspondence, Meron uses Ze'ev's official title and full name but also refers to him by his nickname 'Ṿelvalé'. He notes that 21 of the 54 pupils who had participated in the two Oriental Classes that year also graduated from the pre-military Roshmei Bet course. The vast majority of those graduates were recruited by Military Intelligence. Meron also requested an increased financial allocation 'from $US1000 per pupil to $US2000'.[51]

The involvement of the Ministry of Education is also mentioned in the letter. Meron explained that the Ministry had reduced its financial allocation to the project and requested that Ze'ev use his 'connections in the Ministry of Education to change this decision'.[52] This anecdote yet again highlights the influential role of the Military Intelligence in the field of Arabic studies at the time and, specifically, its relative power in comparison to civil and educational figures, specifically in the Ministry of Education. This incident is reminiscent of other cases where professionals in education asked military colleagues to intervene on their behalf in order to convince their own superiors regarding specific issues. As such, they demonstrate the military's superior power and credibility in comparison with educators in nearly every issue relating to Arabic.[53]

Lastly, Meron's letter noted that in the subsequent year, 1988, they had contracted with a new tutor who would be responsible for instructing students in Arabic media, vocabulary and listening comprehension (lit. *ha'azanah*).[54] While Meron used the feminine version of the word 'tutor', it is unclear whether the individual was a solider or a civilian. The letter made one additional reference to women as Meron asked Ze'ev whether the 'army would consider supporting young women studying Arabic, because so far they have not received any help from you'.[55] Meron closed the correspondence with the words: 'with the expectation of continuing the fruitful cooperation with you'.[56]

The IDF did not immediately give Meron an answer regarding participation of young women in the course. Eventually, when an official response was finally issued by the Manpower Directorate, it said: 'We [the IDF] are not going to financially support young women studying Arabic ... The Military Intelligence has no quantitative or qualitative shortage in young women.'[57]

Meron's letter indicates the strength and importance of Givʿat Ḥavivah's relations with Military Intelligence. Furthermore, it seems that Givʿat Ḥavivah had begun to perceive itself as a kind of preparatory academy for Military Intelligence, whereby the goal if its flagship programme was to provide Military Intelligence with new recruits. Meron makes this clear in a letter that he sent to the Commander of the Manpower Directorate of the IDF, where he sought to have an increase in the IDF's financial support of the Arabic course. Meron wrote: 'the importance of our Arabic course for the new recruits [to Military Intelligence] goes without saying'.[58]

These relations were of tremendous help in another initiative, in 1987. Following a number of meetings between Meron and Zeʾev, the ʿAbd al-ʿAzīz al-Zuʿbī Institute for Arabic Studies created an Arabic course targeting the IDF South Lebanon Liaison Unit [lit., Hebrew acronym, *YAḲAL*]. This course 'would focus on the Lebanese dialect ... and include a visit to [Israeli-occupied] Southern Lebanon'.[59] The implementation of the course suggests that cooperation between Givʿat Ḥavivah and Military Intelligence strengthened, either for purely financial reasons, but perhaps also because of some ideological affinities with the IDF and Military Intelligence that altogether seemed to undermine its original vision and mission.

In 1987, Military Intelligence played a key role in Arabic language studies at Givʿat Ḥavivah. In November of that year, 12th grade pupils in Jewish-Israeli schools received information about Givʿat Ḥavivah's Oriental Classes on letterheaded paper with the logos of the IDF, the Ṭelem Unit and Givʿat Ḥavivah printed at the top of the page. Significantly, not only did this reflect the state of the partnership between the two institutions but was also virtually analogous to relations between the military and the education system a decade earlier. In 1977, for example, a flyer was sent to Jewish-Israeli high school head teachers bearing the logos of the Ministry of Education and the Ṭelem Unit.

By November 1987, the army had reapproved allowing students who are participating in the Oriental Classes to postpone military service. The brochure verifies this; it notes that 'the military service of all pupils accepted on the course will be postponed for one year ... and most of the graduates will undergo interesting and significant service in Military Intelligence'.[60] Similar letters, including invitations for open houses in which prospective pupils experience 'a sample lesson in Arabic', opportunities to meet with current Oriental Class pupils and participation in a lecture given by Military Intelligence officers 'on special programmes and the future military service in the IDF', were mentioned in the letters sent to 12th grade pupils beginning in 1987.[61]

In 1988 Givʿat Ḥavivah's Institute for Arabic Studies celebrated its twenty-fifth anniversary. Givʿat Ḥavivah's official bulletin was devoted to this occasion. The primary article highlighting this occasion provided the reader with some information on the Institute and its history:

> The Institute was named after ʿAbd al-ʿAzīz al-Zuʿbī because his public career symbolised the ideas by which it was established ... In the 1950s, al-Zuʿbī reached the conclusion that the right way to promote the interests of his people, and to promote peace, was through cooperation between Arabs and Jews ... in order to create understanding and respect between the two people ... Al-Zuʿbī was active in the Arab–Jewish Union for Peace and Equality, and was also among the editorial staff of the journal *New Outlook*, which strived to open a peaceful Arab–Israeli dialogue ... Al-Zuʿbī accompanied the Institute from its early days, and travelled to the US and Europe in order to do his utmost to secure moral and material help for the Institute. After he died, it was decided to name the Institute for Arabic Studies after him, as a sign of the cooperation between Jews and Arabs who are loyal to their people and strive to understand each other.[62]

Interestingly, at this most public forum, Givʿat Ḥavivah emphasised the Institute's peaceful goals over its security connections. Simultaneously, however, military connections continued to be well established. On Zeʾev's retirement from Military Intelligence, he sent a farewell letter to Meron and the staff at Givʿat Ḥavivah. In the letter, Zeʾev emphasised that he was grateful 'for the great cooperation we had over the years with the ʿAbd al-ʿAzīz al-Zuʿbī Institute for Arabic Studies'.[63]

Collaboration between Givʿat Ḥavivah and Military Intelligence continued in a similar fashion in subsequent years with the Oriental Class at the centre of this relationship. By 1992, some 90 pupils were participating in the Oriental Class annually,[64] and the presence of Military Intelligence personnel and soldier-teachers on campus was taken for granted.

Interestingly, the combination of peace, on the one hand, and work with Military Intelligence, on the other, began to attract media attention. A local newspaper found the situation to be somewhat perplexing; the article questioned how the Jewish–Arab Center for Peace had become so intricately associated with the IDF and Military Intelligence. The article notes that the Institute's flagship programme was an eight-month Oriental Class that was 'subsidised by the Ministry of Defence and from which most of the graduates continued on to Military Intelligence'.[65] It also notes that relations between Military Intelligence and Givʿat Ḥavivah became much closer in the 1980s, following a financial crisis within Kibbutz Movement. According to the writer, this factor – more than anything else – explained the nature of relations between the institutions and Givʿat Ḥavivah's dependence on the IDF. Meron, who was interviewed by the journalist, argued that 'the physical presence of the army here is minimal. I know that this is our weak point, since anyone who wants to attack us says that we are a branch of the Shabak [the General Security System].'[66] In his view, however, offering courses for Military Intelligence in an Institute that defined itself as promoting peace was not a contradiction. He stated that: 'I see in the army a positive element ... And I ask myself what kind of army and soldiers do we want? Don't you want our soldiers to know the Arabic language and culture [when they serve] during the Intifada?'[67]

Meron's views are mirrored by those of two additional interviewees. The first, a teacher at the Institute, believed that the military connection advanced the mutual interests of both sides. In his view, there was no conflict of interests, or as he put it: 'the army does not dictate anything to us'.[68] The second interviewee, the General Secretary of one of the nearby kibbutzim, supported the teacher's view. He characterised the importance of IDF support for the Institute as follows: 'The army helps us grow and its scholarships bring more people to Givʿat Ḥavivah.'[69]

Sarah Ozacky-Lazar, who directed the Jewish–Arab Center for Peace at Givʿat Ḥavivah from 1997 to 2004, affirmed that cooperation between the Institute and Military Intelligence began in the 1970s, and that over time it became stronger and more pronounced. In her view, this was due to a general lack of interest and demand for Arabic by the general public of all age groups for civilian purposes and specifically for the type of expensive and intensive courses offered by Givʿat Ḥavivah. The logic underlying the cooperation that developed, in her opinion, did not stem from a confluence of interests or similar ideological views, rather it was simply based on the principle of 'if you can't beat them, join them'.[70] Ozacky-Lazar further stated that:

> When we discussed this issue [Military Intelligence projects in Givʿat Ḥavivah] we thought that, at the end of the day, we were doing the right thing. We thought that perhaps it was better that soldiers who will

> be serving in Military Intelligence, whether we want that or not, will at least study at Givʿat Ḥavivah with its added values of education for peace and personal meetings with native Arabic-speakers.[71]

Justifications for Givʿat Ḥavivah's alliance with the military mentioned by Meron, Ozacky-Lazar, the unnamed teacher and the General Secretary of the neighbouring kibbutz reflect similar variations on the same theme. They carefully avoided praising the military or speaking of the military's influence on their programme, rather they highlighted the relationship in consumerist terms. According to them, the military was a (very powerful) customer of their high-level and professional services and, as such, it was willing to lend financial and other forms of support. Liberal values such as peace were not viewed as being in conflict with the first justification.

An examination of the views of Givʿat Ḥavivah's Palestinian staff regarding cooperation with the military provides another interesting angle on this issue. In general, Palestinian staff referenced increasing military presence and the infiltration of military imperatives in Givʿat Ḥavivah's work and unstated policy decisions. On the personal level, they also noted their own internal processes of justification and self-denial whilst teaching Israeli pre-Military Intelligence cadets at Givʿat Ḥavivah.[72]

Ḥasan ʿIraqī, who taught Arabic at the Institute for Arabic Studies in the 1980s and 1990s, shared his views on the Institute's growing 'securitisation'. He said, 'I never asked my pupils what they wanted to do with their Arabic when the course finished.'[73] Kamāl Rayyān, at one point the Institute's most senior Palestinian teacher, rationalised his involvement in the programme by saying that, 'I decided that as long as I did not teach people in uniform, I didn't mind.'[74] However, as time passed, Rayyān, in charge of Colloquial Palestinian Arabic and Arab Culture classes, became alarmed at the extent of the influence of the Military Intelligence on the Institute. Following a period of deep ambivalence, in 1997, he decided to resign. In an interview with a local newspaper, he argued that:

> I started to ask myself questions ... I started to look around me more and more. It then struck me that the only Arabic course that still existed in Givʿat Ḥavivah was the one preparing Jewish pupils to go to Military Intelligence. It was a course that contradicted all of my principles.[75]

In a personal interview given for this research, Rayyān noted that there was a strong financial incentive to continue working with Givʿat

Ḥavivah and this was an important consideration for him. According to him, 'working at Givʿat-Ḥavivah was much more profitable than working in an Arab school'.[76] Rayyān also mentioned that the Institute did not consult with him regarding the relationship with Military Intelligence. However, as this became more pervasive in the Institute with the passage of time, he became more aware of the extent of this relationship. He states that:

> I taught the 13th grade [the Oriental Class] and had 30 pupils ... and after a few years I realised that I was teaching almost 100 pupils annually, most of them boys, and that this was a more militaristic project than I had imagined.[77]

Rayyān specifically mentioned that in the late 1980s, the physical presence of officers from Military Intelligence was more pronounced and that he became more concerned. 'I remember asking the Director of the ʿAbd al-ʿAzīz al-Zuʿbī Institute for Arabic Studies whether Givʿat Ḥavivah was becoming a military camp, and he told me that 'this is not the case and that I should not be worried about it'.[78] Rayyān was not convinced. He said:

> There were gradually more and more educational meetings, in which the Jewish instructors participated, and in which I was not invited ... at the end of the courses I kept hearing that the pupils were having a party in a place called Glilot[79] but even though I was teaching them throughout the whole year, I was never invited.[80]

Rayyān was told that he was not invited to participate in these activities since they were 'sensitive', but was not given any further information. Eventually, Rayyān decided to leave. He stated that he did not regret the decision and, in fact, believes that maybe he should have left earlier. As he said:

> It took me a while to realise, but eventually I got it. Jewish[-Israeli] educators, who have taught Arabic within this context, were like inexperienced horse riders who were trying to ride a noble horse. And Arabic is a very noble horse, indeed. In contrast to what Arabic culture really is, the [Israeli] Jewish teachers who have written Arabic textbooks, be it [Dan] Becker or [Moshe] Piamenta or [Shlomo] Alon, have written them as former Military Intelligence soldiers writing for future Military Intelligence soldiers. This was and still is the problem of Arabic studies in Israel.[81]

Rayyān's experiences further elucidate the work of the Institute for Arabic Studies and, in particular, the nature of its flagship programme: the Oriental Class. Rayyān's position as an Arab and reactions to him – for example, when he was told not to worry about Military Intelligence or the decision to exclude him from events due to 'sensitive' issues – demonstrates that Givʿat Ḥavivah's decision to align itself with the military was detrimental to the cause of coexistence. Indeed, the incidents described here generated discomfort and resulted in exclusion and, thus, in accepting this alliance, Givʿat Ḥavivah prioritised security over peaceful coexistence and integration.

While Givʿat Ḥavivah's strong connection to Military Intelligence was perhaps de-emphasised by its directors, it has been publicly extolled by Military Intelligence – up until and including the current period. For example, according to the official IDF website, the Military Intelligence on the Horizon programme that targets 11th grade pupils is hosted by Givʿat Ḥavivah. The IDF informs the public that 'the seminar aims to strengthen the connection of the pupils with Military Intelligence ... and takes place at Givʿat Ḥavivah where the pupils also sleep and is conducted under military discipline'.[82] Another project mentioned by the IDF website is the Oriental Youth Battalions. The IDF describes the project as follows:

> this project is aimed at 10th grade pupils who study Arabic. It is a four-day seminar that takes place at Givʿat Ḥavivah under military discipline, and by the instructors and officers of Ṭelem: the Military Intelligence's Unit for the encouragement of Oriental studies.[83]

Givʿat Ḥavivah, for its part, de-emphasises its connection to Military Intelligence in public forums. Rather, the Institute prefers to emphasise the civilian and coexistence functions of the Jewish–Arab Center for Peace and the Institute for Arabic Studies. For example, a 1997 bulletin published by Givʿat Ḥavivah discusses the Oriental Class and states that: 'this year we had 52 students, of whom 9 were adults ... The year was a successful one, and the results of the examinations indicate the commitment of both teachers and students.'[84] There is no indication of military involvement as references to the military and student descriptions are absent. Even the fact that the vast majority of students would soon be joining Military Intelligence, and that they chose the course of Givʿat Ḥavivah because of this, are left unmentioned. Similarly, in 2006, when commenting on the 43rd cohort of the Oriental Classes, Givʿat Ḥavivah's website also neglects to mention a Military Intelligence connection. Rather, it simply states that 'the 43rd session of the annual Arabic course has finished. The graduates were examined in Arabic ... Their achievements were higher than average, which indicates the success of the course, in both Colloquial Arabic and Literary Arabic.'[85] One way to examine the validity of the argument that Givʿat Ḥavivah intentionally de-emphasises its connection to Military Intelligence is to investigate appearances of the words 'peace' [lit. *shalom*] and 'Military Intelligence' [lit. *Modiʿin*] on their website. Apparantely, and after I conducted this simple check, I was surprised to find out that the Givʿat Ḥavivah's website's search turned up 244 results for 'shalom' but not a single reference to 'Modiʿin'.[86]

As will be demonstrated below, Givʿat Ḥavivah has reaped substantial rewards for its work promoting integration and peace, thus indicating that attempts to downplay security involvement in its programme has been successful. Indeed, Givʿat Ḥavivah has successfully cultivated a public image as a civilian organisation that promotes peace and coexistence. In 1982, Suleimān Maṣalḥa, the head of the Kufr Qaraʿ Local Council, recommended the Institute for Arabic Studies for the Sylvia Schein Prize, an academic award in memory of the Haifa University professor of history. In a letter to the editor published in *New Outlook*, he did not reference collaboration between Givʿat Ḥavivah and Military Intelligence as, in all likelihood, he was unaware of this relationship. Maṣalḥa wrote:

> The Institute for Arabic Studies is doing its work quietly in order to bring Jews and Arabs closer. The people of the Institute work day and night to create work plans and projects ... not in order to get a raise in their salaries, but to create a new reality in Israel in which Arabs and Jews live together ... I therefore see it as my duty to recommend the Institute for Arabic Studies for the prize.[87]

In 1990, the Institute nominated itself for the Speaker of the Knesset Prize for Quality of Life. This prize is usually awarded to individuals and organisations that work to promote tolerance, integration and peace between different communities in Israel. Understandably, their application did not reference their cooperation with Military Intelligence:

> We would like to propose the ʿAbd al-ʿAzīz al-Zuʿbī Institute for Arabic Studies as a nominee for the Speaker of the Knesset Prize for Quality of Life for its encouragement and promotion of patience, tolerance and mutual respect and understanding, as well as good neighbourly

> relations ... The Institute was established in 1963 in order to bring Jews and Arabs closer together, study subjects related to the Middle East and the Arab community in Israel, and to introduce Jews and Arabs to each other, in a spirit of understanding and partnership. Since that day, the Institute has worked diligently to nourish these values ... Jews and Arabs are working together in complete equality, mutual appreciation and cooperation.[88]

In 1993, Giv'at Ḥavivah was awarded this prize. On bestowing the prize, then Minister of Education Amnon Rubinstein, who presented the award, noted that the decision to select Giv'at Ḥavivah was based on a recognition of its work in

> promoting humanist Zionism, and for strengthening the brotherhood between Jews and Arabs ... for a variety of activities that brought together Jewish and Arab students, and for its Arabic language teaching as a foundation for getting to know the Arab world and especially Israeli-Arabs.[89]

In 2001, Giv'at Ḥavivah was presented with the prestigious UNESCO Prize for Peace Education. The National Kibbutz Movement, in celebrating this achievement, wrote on its website:

> Giv'at Ḥavivah is the largest and oldest Israeli Institute for encouraging Jewish–Arab understanding and promoting peace. Since 1964 [*sic*], it has acted in order to achieve understanding and equality between Jews and Arabs, as well as to bring about peace and reconciliation. Due to its tireless activities on the theme of education, Giv'at Ḥavivah has become renowned for encouraging peace, human rights and democracy, all over the world, and it won the UNESCO Peace Prize for the year 2001.[90]

It is important to note that, throughout the years, Giv'at Ḥavivah has been involved in a high number of initiatives that have genuinely aimed at increasing understanding between Jews and Arabs, and had no military involvement whatsoever. However, it has elected to emphasise these activities over those that involve the IDF, the Ministry of Defence and Military Intelligence. Another point that is notewhorthy is that while in coexistence meetings, in which Jewish-Israeli and Palestinian citizens of Israel came together, there was no military element at all – neither hidden nor revealed – but when

Arabic was taught, it was difficult, even for Giv'at-Ḥavivah, to avoid processes of militarisation.

As this section has demonstrated – primarily through archival research conducted at Giv'at Ḥavivah itself – Giv'at Ḥavivah's connections with the Military, which began in 1963, developed and deepened considerably in the subsequent decades. Giv'at Ḥavivah has served and continues to serve as a willing host to many security-oriented projects, including Soldier-Teachers, Military Intelligence on the Horizon, the Oriental Youth Battalion and the Oriental Classes. These programmes and others initiated by Military Intelligence over the years have been partially or fully subsidised by Military Intelligence. Such projects are an integral aspect the landscape at Giv'at Ḥavivah and, as such, military views, policies and interests have influenced the nature of the organisation.

Simultaneously, Arab educational staff and others in the Palestinian community are not informed regarding the full extent of military involvement in Giv'at Ḥavivah's programmes, which makes Giv'at Ḥavivah's 'peace-and-security' mantra to be rather sophisticated. The Giv'at Ḥavivah decision-makers have managed to maintain close relations with the IDF and specifically with important commanders in Military Intelligence and prepare young Israeli adults for service in Military Intelligence, while simultaneously organising activities aimed at promoting peace without connecting them to the IDF or Military Intelligence whatsoever.

It seems that Giv'at Ḥavivah has been neither able nor willing to break out of the defined and accepted discourse surrounding Arabic studies in Israel. At the end of the day, perhaps despite its best intentions, it could not challenge the framers of Arabic in Israel, including the powerful voices of 'Atsmon, Lapid, Navon and Alon. Accordingly, it is unlikely that Giv'at Ḥavivah has been able to create a genuine revolution in the way in which Arabic is taught and studied in Israel. Furthermore, this comparative analysis highlights the extent to which the discourse around Arabic studies is dominated by security and the strength of this paradigm.

The following section will examine the evolution of Arabic studies at Ulpan 'Aḳiva while illuminating the ways in which, in comparison to Giv'at Ḥavivah, Ulpan 'Aḳiva navigated and gave expression to notions of peace and security. It will seek to understand whether and to what extent Ulpan 'Aḳiva was able to forge a different path and what the implications of this are for Arabic studies, the Arabic language and Jewish–Arab relations in Israel.

'Arabic as a bridgehead': Ulpan ʿAḳiva and Arabic studies

Ulpan ʿAḳiva is one of Israel's most renowned institutions of Hebrew language study. Established in 1951 in Nahariya on Israel's north coast, it was one of the country's first *ulpanim* (meaning, Hebrew language schools for adults). In part, its name is derived from its mission; Ulpan ʿAḳiva is named after Rabbi ʿAḳiva, one of Judaism's central and most essential contributors to the Mishnah, the Jewish oral law. According to Jewish folklore, Rabbi ʿAḳiva, who was a shepherd in his youth, only began studying at 40 years of age.

Ulpan ʿAḳiva's core mission was always to make Hebrew accessible to the masses. Accordingly, it marketed its programmes to Jewish and non-Jewish people along with Palestinian citizens of Israel. Founded by Shulamit Katznelson, an ardent Zionist and a former member of the paramilitary Zionist organisation Irgun, Katznelson was Ulpan ʿAḳiva's Director for 45 years until she retired in 1996. A few years after its establishment, Ulpan ʿAḳiva left its location in Nahariya and moved to the vicinity of Netanya on Israel's central coast. Ulpan ʿAḳiva's website describes the institution as a non-profit educational centre that teaches Modern Hebrew in the shadows of Biblical landscapes in the Land of Israel.[91]

In light of this openly Zionistic orientation and the focus on Hebrew, the decision also to offer classes in Arabic may be somewhat surprising. Ulpan ʿAḳiva was the only ulpan in Israel to offer Arabic language studies, and this course of studies was first introduced to the ulpan in the 1960s on a limited scale. However, the programme gained steam following the 1967 War. At that time, Ulpan ʿAḳiva expanded the scope of the courses that it offered and began to actively market their courses in Colloquial Arabic to Jewish-Israeli civilians, soldiers and civil servants. Ulpan ʿAḳiva gained notoriety for its unique course of study and particularly for its strong emphasis on Arabic that was useful for conversational and practical purposes. A combination of factors contributed to this emphasis, including an emerging need to communicate with Palestinians (particularly those residing in territories occupied by Israel in 1967 – the West Bank and the Gaza Strip) and also in order to address the growing domestic need for Arabic-speakers in response to national, political and security developments.

The first indication of the connection between Arabic language studies and security appears in November 1967. At that time, Col. Mordekhai [Mota] Gur, who was serving as the IDF Commander of the Gaza Strip, sent a letter to Ulpan ʿAḳiva. He wrote, 'the Gaza Military Regime Unit wants its officers to undergo accelerated Arabic courses according to the Ulpan ʿAḳiva special programme.'[92] Gur continued by stating that the courses are 'essential for the work of the officers, and I would therefore like to receive the dates of future courses. We would like to have at least 10 of our officers on each course.'[93]

Lt Col. Yitzḥaḳ Yitzḥaḳ, Commander of the Education Department of the IDF, made a similar request in December 1967, as follows:

1. We have been told by officers who took your [Arabic] course that you have developed an efficient and successful way to teach Colloquial Arabic.
2. We would like you to include a few of our officers on your next course.
3. We would like to urge you to bring forward the date for the start of the next course to enable us to send a few groups of officers.[94]

Both correspondences indicate an increased demand for courses that would enable Israeli soldiers to communicate with Arab people under Israeli military occupation. Meeting this demand required that Katznelson secures a competent Arabic teaching staff. In pursuit of this, she sent an urgent letter to Sha'ul Levin, the Head of the Education Department at the Municipality of Tel Aviv to try to convince him to 'lend' her Avraham Lavi, the Head of the Israeli Arabic Teaching Committee and one of Israel's most prolific Arabic instructors. She hoped that he would be able to join her staff. Katznelson wrote:

> Lately, great pressure has been put on us [at Ulpan ʿAḳiva] to teach Arabic. This week we were contacted by Col. Mota Gur, the military ruler of the Gaza Strip, asking us to bring forward the start of the Arabic courses ... we were also contacted by the Navy, which asked to send their officers to our courses on a regular basis ... We were also contacted by the IDF Chief Education Officer and by others ... I was happy to hear that also the Minister of Defence Moshe Dayan, Head of the Arab Department in the *Histadrut* [the General Federation of Labourers in the Land of Israel] Yaʿacov Cohen, and the Adviser on Arab Affairs in the Prime Minister's Office Shmu'el Toledano, have all contacted you and asked to release Lavi [for Ulpan ʿAḳiva] ... It is worth mentioning that already in the last few months we have had 85 students in Ulpan ʿAḳiva, including public figures, senior IDF officers, Ministry of Defence personnel, and civil servants ...[95]

Katznelson sent a similar letter to Yoseph Sarid, General Director of the Ministry of Education; she requested that he do his utmost to convince the Tel Aviv Municipality to answer her request favourably. In this letter, Katznelson noted that over 150 pupils had registered for upcoming courses in Colloquial Arabic.[96]

Consistent with the national mood outlined earlier in this book, both letters point to the tremendous demand and urgency for Arabic-speakers, at least within the security apparatus, in accordance with Israel's occupation of the Palestinian territories in 1967. Furthermore, the involvement of staff at the highest levels of the military – in this case, Gur and Dayan – indicates the perceived security implications of Arabic. The letters also shed light on Ulpan ʿAḳiva's position and reputation in Israel at the time and the way in which it strove to present or market itself to external bodies as part of the national and partriotic discourse surrounding the 1967 War.

Eventually, the pressure to release Lavi from the Oriental Classes in Tel Aviv and transfer him to Ulpan ʿAḳiva's was effective. In subsequent years, Lavi was instrumental in helping Katznelson to establish and develop an intensive course in Colloquial Arabic. This course was popular with various military figures and civil servants as it focused on proficiency in basic communication, thus facilitating interactions with Palestinian populations who did not speak Hebrew.[97]

Similar to what happened with the education system, in the post-1973 War period, demand for Arabic again increased. And, as with developments taking place in the realm of Jewish-Israeli education, Ulpan ʿAḳiva created a partnership with Military Intelligence. According to Ephraim Lapid, who at the time was a lieutenant colonel in Military Intelligence, the war and its aftermath was the impetus for the decision to initiate comprehensive cooperation with Ulpan ʿAḳiva. Lapid mentioned this in an article published in *Ḥamanit: The Israeli Military Intelligence Journal*. The article states that the 'relationship between Military Intelligence and the language centre in Ulpan ʿAḳiva started before the war', during the period of Chief of Intelligence Gen. Aharon Yariv, but became fully functioning and institutionalised only following the war:

> In 1974, senior officers in Military Intelligence, including Chief of Intelligence Gen. Shlomo Gazit, Brig. Ephraim Lapid and Col. Nissim ʿAtsmon, all expressed their concern about the shortage of Arabist personnel [lit. *miʿuṭ koʾaḥ ha-ʾadam ha-ʿArabisṭi*]. At that time, the Oriental Classes in the school system were experiencing shortages of pupils as well, to the extent that the army's needs could not be fulfilled. Military Intelligence officers scoured the whole country looking for institutions that would teach Arabic, as well as for

> ways in which to change the image of Arabic as a school subject ... Eventually, they found Ulpan ʿAḳiva, which since 1967 had been teaching Colloquial Arabic.[98]

The first point to of interest is *Ḥamanit*'s decision to publish an article highlighting Ulpan ʿAḳiva's cooperation with the military. Second, the article, while entitled 'Peace Starts at Home', brings to mind the 'peace' and 'security' formulation in Jewish-Israeli society and military discourse; indeed, this is the rationale used for teaching and learning Arabic. The article also mentions that cooperation between Military Intelligence and Ulpan ʿAḳiva began in the years 1967–73 under the tenure of the Chief of Intelligence, Yariv. And, finally, in this case as well, civilian figures involved in Arabic language studies had direct access to some of the military's most senior personnel.

By 1975, Ulpan ʿAḳiva was caught up in the same set of circumstances affecting the education system. Military Intelligence was pressuring both to promote Arabic studies among Jewish-Israeli pupils. An examination of projects initiated during this period – and particularly in the years following 1975 and 1976 – indicate that Ulpan ʿAḳiva took on an important role in this endeavour. The reorganisation of Military Intelligence in light of the Agranat Commission's recommendations strengthened military–educational alliances and Ulpan ʿAḳiva was soon caught up in this trend. In 1975, for example, Lapid sent a letter to the Youth Department at the Ministry of Education, requesting that they arrange a meeting between head teachers and five officers from Military Intelligence. In the letter, Lapid 'suggest[ed] inviting the following directors of education ... as well as Shulamit Katznelson, the Director of Ulpan ʿAḳiva'.[99]

Ulpan ʿAḳiva enthusiastically responded to the opportunity to be included in the 'establishment' (in this case the Ministry of Education and the IDF). These discussions culminated in the 1975 launch of an initiative entitled 'Arabic as a Bridgehead' [lit. *ʿAravit ke-Rosh Gesher*].[100] This project brought Jewish-Israeli and Palestinian pupils from Israel and the Occupied Territories together for a specified period of time (usually a week) and, during this period, Jewish-Israelis learned Colloquial Arabic and Palestinians pupils learned Hebrew. The project was backed by four organisations: the Military Intelligence, the Bureau of the Adviser on Arab Affairs in the Prime Minister's Office, Ulpan ʿAḳiva and the Ministry of Education. Undoubtedly, the nature of its backers, which included two military/political agencies, give clear indications as to some of the interests underlying its establishment. It was jointly funded by the Prime Minister's Office and the Youth Department in the Ministry of Education.[101]

Arabic as a Bridgehead was launched during the 1975 Passover holiday and targeted 10th grade pupils. At that time, Chief of Intelligence Shlomo Gazit sent a letter to Minister of Education Aharon Yadlin, where he noted that this programme represented one of the 'steps already implemented since we last met and decided to start a joint process of improving Arabic studies in Israel [lit. *me-'az hitḥalnu itkhem be-masa' le-'idud limud ha-safah ha-'Aravit ba-medinah*]'.[102] Gazit wrote that the programme was intended for Jewish-Israeli high school pupils of Arabic and was aimed at giving them 'a special status' (lit. *yetsirat 'status' meyuḥad le-lomdei ha-'Aravit be-vatey ha-sefer ha-tikhoniyyim*).[103] What was meant by 'special "status"', and why the word 'status' was written in inverted commas is unclear. In all likelihood, he was referring to the opportunity for Jewish-Israeli pupils to meet with Palestinian pupils to practice Colloquial Arabic with them. This was similar to the Oriental Classes courses offered by Giv'at Ḥavivah at the time. He may also have been alluding to a Military Intelligence connection or the special opportunity that pupils had to study Arabic in this unique format. Gazit's letter did not mention what the benefits were for Palestinian pupils participating in the project.

By the mid 1970s, the project started to attract the attention of external donors. In early 1976, Toledano, the Adviser on Arab Affairs at the Prime Minister's Office, asked Lapid to draft a note that could be attached to correspondence with the potential donor. This foreign donor, referred to as 'the philanthropist of the Bridgehead Project', was willing to provide Ulpan 'Aḳiva with a considerable sum of money in support of the project.[104] Lapid's involvement was meant to demonstrate the project's importance for Israeli security. According to Lapid, the text below was the version that the Military Intelligence hoped would be included:

> The IDF has a great interest in as large a number as possible of Israeli [Jewish] youth studying and knowing Arabic. It is the language of our neighbours beyond the border, and the language of the minority who resides among us. The IDF today needs a growing number of soldiers with knowledge of Arabic, especially for positions in Military Intelligence and the Military Regime [in the Occupied Territories]. We believe that knowing Arabic is a condition and a key to get to know, understand and speak with the Arab rival [lit. *ha-yariv ha-'Aravi*].[105]

While the letter makes some reference to peaceful purposes, it is tilted in favour of security; by use of the term 'rival', the letter suggests that the primary rationale for knowing, understanding and speaking Arabic is due to its security implications. References to Arabs in Israel's midst – whether Palestinians within Israel or those 'beyond the border' – and the references to the IDF, Military Intelligence and Military Rule in the Occupied Territories, further make the writer's intent obvious.

Importantly, the name of the project, 'Bridgehead', also has clear military connotations. According to the US Department of Defense, a '[B]ridgehead is an area of ground held or to be gained on the enemy's side of an obstacle.'[106] The Hebrew term for bridgehead is *rosh gesher*. Usage of this term became more common in Israeli society in the post-1973 period. In the Israeli lexicon for the Yom Kippur War, this term was intrinsically linked to critical military events:

> During the Yom Kippur War, each one of the Egyptian divisions and two of its corps established a bridgehead on the east side of the Suez Canal as part of the Crossing Battle. Later, Gen. Ariel Sharon's division created a bridgehead on the west side of the Canal.[107]

Uri Dan, Sharon's biographer, believed that this military event was so significant that he wrote a book named after it titled *Bridgehead*.[108] Given the relatively fresh memories of the war in Jewish-Israeli society at the time when the Bridgehead programme was established, in all likelihood, programme initiators hoped to directly link the two.

Despite the fact that encounters between Jews and Arabs were a fundamental element of the course, Israel's Arabic language press was not convinced that it was intended to bring the two sides closer together. The Communist Party's newspaper *Al-Ittiḥād* wrote an article focusing on the first Arabic as a Bridgehead course. Following a general description of the content of the course, the author of the article labelled the course a sham, 'since the Israeli authorities do not care about peace and brotherhood ... and they stick their political nose in these courses'.[109] The article went on to mock the course:

> When the pupils opened the gifts given to them by the organisers, the attempts at Zionisation and sterile political education were revealed ... it included the book *My Father's House* by Golda Meir, translated into Arabic by the writer Maḥmūd ʿAbbāsī ... as well as a pamphlet about Arabs in Israel, sorry – about 'Israeli Arabs' ... and from the field of literature, the organisers did not find anything but the journal *Liqāʾ* published by the Histadrut.[110]

The author concluded the article by informing its readers that only Jewish Members of Knesset attended the course's opening ceremony. MKs in attendance even made a point of mentioning that 'this land was promised to the people of Israel ... but even [King] David had assistants from different peoples'.[111] The author's meaning could not have been lost on Palestinian readers as the *Al-Ittiḥād* article was peppered with exclamation marks to signal their pervasive sense of dismay regarding the course organisers' attitude and the ideas that they were trying to convey.[112]

The Bridgehead project and its link to political Zionism was, in all likelihood, connected to the ideological underpinnings of the supporting organisations as well as to Katznelson's own political background. During those years, Katznelson was probably Israel's most dominant female figure in the field of Arabic studies. However, this did not lead her to challenge the rather masculine and military-oriented associations of Arabic language instruction. Furthermore, Katznelson and her brother Shmuʾel Tamir were both active members of the Irgun,[113] which was the main Revisionist Zionist paramilitary organisation. They were tenacious believers in the right of the Jewish people to 'Greater Israel', meaning all parts of historical Palestine.[114]

In all likelihood, this ideology also influenced the establishment of another project, started in 1979 and called 'Common Language: A Path to Understanding'. The target group for this course was settlers affiliated with the Gush Emunim movement, a nationalist-religious Zionist group that advocates Jewish settlement in the Occupied Palestinian Territories. Elkana – located in the north-western part of the West Bank – was the first settlement to participate in the programme, and was followed by three additional settlements that joined the project at a later time. The Director of the Department of Education of the Judea and Samaria Region at the Ministry of Education noted that: 'most of the villages [settlements] in Judea and Samaria [the West Bank] asked to participate in the programme ... This programme strives to encourage dialogue with the Arab villages ... and to help us [Jewish settlers] integrate into the region.'[115] While use of the word 'dialogue' seems to indicate peaceful intentions, it will be argued here that in reality 'peace' was actually another word for normalising the Israeli occupation. Interestingly, this project is reminiscent of other projects run during the pre-state period, when Arabic was taught in newly established Jewish colonies (lit. *moshavot*) located next to Palestinian villages. Politics and the expansion of territories, rather than integration, motivated the initiation of these projects.

Therefore, while on the micro-level projects of this nature were framed as ways to ease tension and resolve disputes, on the macro-level they facilitated the expansion of settlement within historical Palestine/Eretz Yisrael.

Both the Arabic as a Bridgehead and the Common Language: a Path for Understanding projects, along with others, facilitated the study of Arabic by Jewish-Israelis. In 1975, at the conclusion of the first Arabic as a Bridgehead programme, Katznelson, Lapid from Military Intelligence and Toledano, the Adviser on Arab Affairs in the Prime Minister's Office, met at Ulpan ʿAḳiva. Katznelson used this opportunity to request financial support for the Bridgehead programme and other Colloquial Arabic courses held by the institute. She justified the need accordingly: 'We had 17 courses at Ulpan ʿAḳiva in which civil servants, IDF personnel and students took part ... On top of this, we would like to receive your financial help in order to secure two Colloquial Arabic summer courses.'[116]

As a follow up to the meeting, Katznelson sent a letter to Toledano where she expressed her gratitude for his support in the Bridgehead project.[117] She asked the Adviser on Arab Affairs to remember 'that whatever decision [he makes] regarding future funding [to Ulpan ʿAḳiva] I pray that it will be for the benefit of the people who reside in Zion'.[118] Such a decision, she added, would be 'a real blessing'.[119] The letter was signed as follows: 'with most faithful greetings and friendship'.

This means that Ulpan ʿAḳiva's target audience was the Jewish people 'who reside in Zion'. It is clear that educational goals, security concerns and political considerations, as opposed to promoting integration nationally, were the forces driving the institution and its activities. Because Ulpan ʿAḳiva along with official governmental bodies shared a similar 'peace and security' vision for Arabic and each could assist the other, this proably facilitated cooperation between them. The initiation of the Soldier-Teachers project at Ulpan ʿAḳiva reflects a similar confluence of interests and shared perspectives. Brig. Ret. Lapid spoke about the origins of the course as such:

> The first time I met Shulamit [Katznelson] was in the first grade where she was my teacher ... and the next time was around 1976 when I was a lieutenant colonel in Military Intelligence, the Commander of Ḥatsav [Open Sources Intelligence Unit] ... It was after the Yom Kippur War and we had a shortage of Arabists. We tried to think about ways to train Arabic-speaking manpower. The two actions that we took were the creation of the course for Soldier-Teachers [at Ulpan ʿAḳiva] and the Youth Battalions [at Givʿat Ḥavivah].[120]

Lapid, of course, did not reference needing courses to serve peaceful aims, rather he focused on the need for Arabists and the willingness of both Ulpan ʿAḳiva and Givʿat Ḥavivah to contribute to the country's national-security needs in the aftermath of the 1973 War. Lapid also commented on Ulpan ʿAḳiva's Soldier-Teachers (*Morot-Ḥayalot*) project, noting that it first started in 1977 and that, following a break of a few years, resumed in the early 1980s. Eventually, this became one of Ulpan ʿAḳiva's most important Arabic projects.[121]

Further correspondence provides an indication of the nature of the cooperation that there was in the context of the Soldier-Teachers course. In 1980, Toledano sent a letter to Ulpan ʿAḳiva. Toledano's office had previously covered most of the expenses associated with the course and, in the letter, he asked his office's accountant to transfer 16,686 shekels to Ulpan ʿAḳiva 'for the Soldier-Teachers course'. He explained that the sum was being paid 'as part of our support in the blessed activities of Ulpan ʿAḳiva to bring Jews and Arabs closer together'.[122] Given the security and military orientation of the course, it is not clear why he also seemed to believe that it contributed to coexistence.

In 1981, Levinsky College also became a partner in the Soldier-Teachers project. Established in Tel Aviv in 1912 by the Ḥovevei Tzion [the Lovers of Zion] movement, Levinsky developed a strong reputation for itself and eventually became one of Israel's primary teacher training colleges. Levinsky College's pedagogic experience complemented and supported Ulpan ʿAḳiva's expertise in Arabic. This is demonstrated by a letter co-written by Avraham Rokheli, the President of Levinsky College, and Katznelson. Sent to Eliʿezer Shmuʾeli, the General Director of the Ministry of Education, the two presented their plans for cooperation and their shared security–educational vision for the project that they characterised as follows:

> Three elements have come together, Military Intelligence in the IDF that is very concerned with the diminishing numbers of pupils who took Oriental Studies in schools and in the universities; Ulpan ʿAḳiva that has greatly succeeded in promoting Arabic among varied populations and in ground-breaking ways; and Levinsky College to create a joint enterprise with a special and unique value: the Arabic course for Soldier-Teachers. This course, shared by Ulpan ʿAḳiva and Levinsky College, aims to train soldiers to become authorised Arabic teachers in elementary and intermediate [Jewish-Israeli] schools. According to the educational programme developed by these two institutions, Ulpan ʿAḳiva will be in charge of providing Colloquial

> Arabic and Literary Arabic training and Levinsky College will be in charge of pedagogic training. The soldier-teachers will stay at Ulpan ʿAḳiva and spend two days each week at Levinsky College. The Teaching Diploma will be signed by both institutions ... Prior to being accepted to the course, the Soldier-Teachers will need to be accepted by a joint committee of the IDF and Ulpan ʿAḳiva, and following this by a committee at Levinsky College.[123]

The course, most likely delayed by bureaucracy and management issues, was started two years later, in 1983. At this point, it had also received authorisation from the Supervisor of Arabic Studies in the Ministry of Education. All the parties involved agreed that 'part of the Arabic studies programme at Ulpan ʿAḳiva will be maintained by the IDF' (lit. *yetuḥzak ʿal-yedey shilṭonot ha-Tsava*).[124] Indeed, the course maximised the strengths and capabilities of all the partners: the Ministry of Education and Military Intelligence served as the providers and consumers of Arabic-speaking student-soldiers while Ulpan ʿAḳiva and Levinksy College were professional and educational consultants and service providers. The Commander of the Military Intelligence's Manpower Department commented on the importance of the programme for Military Intelligence as follows:

> Soldier-Teachers who teach in civilian schools are not only Arabic teachers. They are the ambassadors of Military Intelligence and represent it in schools.[125]

As Ulpan ʿAḳiva became more deeply associated with and involved in military-related projects, its notoriety grew accordingly. While in the beginning they might have been known for providing Colloquial Arabic courses, facilitating Jewish–Arab activities and running the Soldier-Teachers project, as these activities grew and developed, their standing nationally grew and they began to compete with Givʿat Ḥavivah. The two institutions found themselves in direct competition; both sought the favour of the military and strove to be selected for the implementation of projects initiated and funded by Military Intelligence. Likewise, both institutions hosted annual seminars and professional gatherings of Arabic teachers from Jewish-Israeli schools, events that frequently involved active participation by military and educational figures under the umbrella of the Ministry of Education. For example, in 1981, Ulpan ʿAḳiva held a seminar titled, 'The Training of Arabic Teachers', and the Chief of Intelligence, Yehoshuʿa Sagi, was invited to give the closing presentation.[126] This was a logical decision; Giv'at Ḥavivah behaved similarly in inviting, among others, Lapid and Lt Ya'acov Ṭal to gatherings of Arabic teachers.

Evidence for Ulpan 'Aḳiva's central role in Arabic studies for Jews in Israel comes from Katznelson's participation in the three crucial meetings on the matter in 1986.[127] These meetings presented Katznelson with the opportunity to reinforce her institution's commitment to Arabic studies and to express gratitude to partners that had supported those same programmes. During the first meeting, which was held by the Knesset's Education Committee, Katznelson said that 'sitting with us today are representatives of IDF and Military Intelligence ... who have always been very sensitive to what is happening [in the field of Arabic studies] and its importance for peace and security'.[128] She then mentioned Ulpan 'Aḳiva's Soldier-Teachers project, noting that it would not have succeeded without the help of Military Intelligence. Furthermore, Katznelson told the Committee members:

> I must say that without the Ministry of Defence this [Arabic project at Ulpan 'Aḳiva] would not have materialised and the whole model [of Ulpan 'Aḳiva] would not have been established if Military Intelligence and Ulpan 'Aḳiva did not share a similar 'madness' [lit. '*shiga'on*'] for Arabic.[129]

Indeed, Katznelson used this meeting as an opportunity to emphasise the mutual interests guiding the various parties teaching Arabic, the important role of the Ministry of Defence in the field and Ulpan 'Aḳiva's accrued expertise in this realm. Katznelson also said:

> We have teachers from Gaza and from Jenin who help us teach the Soldier-Teachers, and they do not find any contradiction in that ... Similarly, we have people from Gaza, from Jenin and from the Golan, and also military personnel. [Col.] Nissim 'Atsmon sits [in Ulpan 'Aḳiva] and creates a syllabus with an Arab from Nablus. And there is no contradiction in that.[130]

Katznelson clearly hoped to convey to her listeners the message that Ulpan 'Aḳiva was an inclusive institution that valued cooperation and common purpose with Palestinians. Her words are belied by the fact that she compared 'Atsmon with a nameless 'Arab from Nabulus'. This seems to indicate a fundamental imbalance in relations between the sides; indeed, Palestinian Arabs seem to be props whose purpose is to improve the Arabic of Jewish-Israeli pupils for their future work in the political echelon and in security-related fields. Moreover, the Palestinian contribution is characterised as 'help us teach the Soldier-Teachers'. Thus, it is reasonable to assume that Palestinian teachers had roles that were similar to those at Givʿat Ḥavivah, functional rather than as a means of promoting coexistence.

Katznelson stepped down from her position as Director of Ulpan ʿAḳiva in 1997. At that point she was 78 years old and was suffering from a number of health problems. The search for her replacement, which culminated in the appointment of Brig. Ret. Ephraim Lapid to the position, further points to the military dominance in the field. Lapid, who had spent many years in Military Intelligence, was thoroughly acquainted with Ulpan ʿAḳiva due to previous military–educational partnerships involving both institutions. He was also experienced in working with the media as he had served as IDF Spokesperson and Commander of the IDF Radio station. Following his appointment, Lapid mentioned his military background and the orientation of the projects in the civil sphere in an interview describing his qualifications. He said that working at 'Ulpan ʿAḳiva is very challenging ... Arabic is taught to Jews and Hebrew to Arabs in the context of mutual coexistence and recognition of the two cultures.'[131]

Lapid, arguably, is the physical embodiment of the dominant national discourse surrounding Arabic studies in Israel. For this reason, his appointment to the position is symbolic of trends in the field. Arabic was dominated by military figures and by men and he was a candidate with a rich military background. Lapid could speak simultaneously to the need for military–educational Arabic projects to promote national security while also noting the importance of Arabic 'in the context of mutual coexistence'. Thus, Lapid personified the double-talk regarding peace and security or, at the very least, the ability to frame the two as complementary. His appointment made perfectly clear who was a part of the conversation and who was being left out.

Lapid retired in 2000 to serve as Spokesperson for the Jewish Agency for Israel. Nevertheless, he continued to be committed both to Ulpan ʿAḳiva and Military Intelligence, as well as to the promotion of Arabic studies in Jewish schools. His successor, Esther Perron, continued the same ideological line of her predecessors, maintaining the 'peace and security' formula. During her tenure, for example, Military Intelligence implemented the Oriental Youth Battalions at Ulpan ʿAḳiva. As a reminder, this programme aimed to 'create contact between Military Intelligence and pupils who take Arabic as well as to encourage these pupils to continue studying Arabic with a view to serving in Military Intelligence'.[132] At the same time, Perron argued that 'only by getting to know each other will coexistence arise; only from understanding will peace come'.[133]

Interestingly, Ulpan ʿAḳiva, like Givʿat Ḥavivah, also showed a significant discrepancy between the extent of their cooperation with Military Intelligence and their public statements. In public, Israelis and those familiar with Israel associate both institutes – Ulpan ʿAḳiva and Givʿat Ḥavivah — with Jewish–Arab coexistence and peace. Military connections are downplayed, de-emphasised or ignored. The fruits of this strategy were reaped in the respectable number of civilian and peace prizes awarded to Ulpan ʿAḳiva. In 1982, Katznelson received a prize from the Israeli Inter-Religious Committee; in 1983, she received the Speaker of the Knesset Award for Quality of Life; and, in 1984, she was given a personal prize, Eshet Ḥayil [A Woman of Valour], by the Association for Nurturing Society and Culture. In 1986, Katznelson and Ulpan ʿAḳiva won the Israeli Education Award for Life Achievement. In granting this award, the committee emphasised that 'Ulpan ʿAḳiva was a centre of Hebrew humanism and human brotherhood.'[134]

In 1987, in light of financial difficulties faced by Ulpan ʿAḳiva, Katznelson wrote a letter to the Public Trustee to convince him to support her institute. Her letter emphasised harmonious coexistence and 'peace and security' as embodied by Ulpan ʿAḳiva:

> The Soldier-Teachers project, for example, is a unique course that has been running for eight years at Ulpan ʿAḳiva ... This project has promoted Arabic studies in Israel, and has become an educational model that harmoniously combines Arabic as a language of encounter, and a language of security [lit. *ha-meshalev be-harmonya et horaʾat ha-ʿAravit ke-sfat mifgash ṿe-ke-sfat biṭaḥon*] and in which the IDF has a keen interest.[135]

To support her case with the Public Trustee, Katznelson lobbied the Minister of Education and the Minister of Religious Affairs, asking both of them to communicate their support to the Public Trustee. Both obliged, as the Minister of Religious Affairs Zevulun Hammer phrased it: 'support should be given because Ulpan ʿAḳiva works to remove barriers and walls of separation from the lives of Jews and Muslims, Druze and Christians, inhabitants of the land who study there'.[136]

Ulpan ʿAḳiva's campaign was successful and the institution continued to play a central role in the field of Arabic studies in Jewish-Israeli society. In 1988, Yitzhak Rabin, who was then Minister of Defence, visited

Ulpan ʿAḳiva and spoke about its importance to Israeli society. During his visit, Rabin did not to mention Ulpan ʿAḳiva's military-oriented projects and collaborations; a rather odd decision, given his obvious role as Minister of Defence and in light of the fact that he felt it necessary to visit the institute while serving in this role.[137] Instead, in a public letter to Katznelson, Rabin wrote as follows:

> My visit to Ulpan ʿAḳiva was like sailing to a distant world. In these days, when we are all concerned about current problems, it felt like a cool breeze to see you and your teachers planting the seeds of future peace. Ulpan ʿAḳiva is an island of learning, achievements and brotherhood within the boiling world outside ... I wish all of you further successful years, and believe that thanks to you a better understanding between people will develop.[138]

In honour of Israel's fortieth anniversary in 1988, Ulpan ʿAḳiva hosted Israeli President Chaim Herzog. During his visit, Herzog met with various individuals involved with Ulpan ʿAḳiva and learned about their activities. Among those whom he met were the IDF Coordinator of Government Activities in the Occupied Territories and representatives of Military Intelligence. However, his speech focused exclusively on projects promoting coexistence.[139] Herzog, himself a founding father of Israeli Military Intelligence who served as Chief of Intelligence for five years,[140] commented:

> Ulpan ʿAḳiva is like a bridge over troubled water. It rises over the murky streams of hatred and violence, of national polarisation, of barriers and prejudices, of cultural gaps and differences of values, of distorted images, of lack of trust and intolerance. Ulpan ʿAḳiva is a meeting point for human beings. It is a meeting point of different religions and nationalities, and it creates understanding and mutual respect instead of alienation and revulsion.[141]

Herzog's speech – as with Rabin's letter – did not mention Ulpan ʿAḳiva's important role in promoting Israel's security. It seems, in fact, that there was a kind of 'silent agreement' by the partners to leave mention of security out of the picture. The majority of Jewish-Israelis were well aware of Arabic and its security implications, along with the extensive involvement of the security apparatuses in Arabic studies. However, they were not critical of this in general and, in particular, in relation to Arabic. Even so, talk of the securitisation of Arabic was not for public consumption and those involved desisted from mentioning 'security' and 'Military Intelligence'.

In 1988, Katznelson was awarded yet another prize, the Kavod la-Zulat [Respecting the Other] Prize by the Association for a 'Fine Eretz Yisrael'.[142] In 1992 and 1993, Katznelson came close to receiving the globe's highest honour for the promotion of peace when she was recommended for the Noble Peace Prize by 24 Members of Parliament in Europe and of the the US Congress.[143] Instead, the prize went to others who were better able to convince the Nobel Committee of their contribution to world peace. In 1992, the prize was given to Rigoberta Menchú Tum from Guatemala in recognition of her work for social justice and ethnocultural reconciliation based on respect for the rights of indigenous peoples. In 1993, Nelson Mandela and Frederik Willem de Klerk received the prize for facilitating a peaceful end to the apartheid regime and for laying the foundations for a democratic and more just regime in South Africa.

In light of her failure to win the Nobel Peace Prize and her attendant disappointment, President Herzog wrote the following to Katznelson:

> I was sorry to hear that you did not win the Nobel Peace Prize, but I hope that next year will be a year of good news for you, for Ulpan ʿAḳiva, and for all those who cherish peace and brotherhood.[144]

Katznelson did not pursue nomination again perhaps because the winners of the Nobel Peace Prize in 1994 were from the region: Yitzhak Rabin, Shimon Peres and Yassir Arafat were awarded the prize following the signing of the Oslo Accords and for their efforts to create peace in the Middle East.

Ulpan ʿAḳiva, however, had further accolades in the offing when, in 1998, it was awarded the UNESCO Prize for Peace Education. This preceded Givʿat Ḥavivah's receipt of the same prize by three years. Excited by the good news, Lapid, then Director of Ulpan ʿAḳiva, immediately faxed Motti Zaken, an Israeli 'Arab affairs' expert who was at the time the Adviser on Arab Affairs in the Prime Minister's Office. Lapid wrote: 'We are very happy to tell you that Ulpan ʿAḳiva has won the UNESCO Prize for Peace Education for the year 1998 ... I am sure that this is a great honour for Israel.'[145] Lapid attached the French and Hebrew versions of the official announcement to the fax:

> The prize is given to four educational institutions, from Ukraine, Norway, New Zealand and Israel ... Ulpan ʿAḳiva was found deserving of the prize for its continuous efforts and projects of coexistence

> between Jews and Arabs, Israelis and Palestinians, and teaching Arabic and Hebrew, and their cultures, to both peoples ... The prize will be given at the UNESCO headquarters in Paris on 15.12.1998, and the Israeli Ambassador to UNESCO and Ephraim Lapid, the Director of Ulpan ʿAḳiva, will receive it on the behalf of Israel.[146]

Similarly to Givʿat Ḥavivah, Ulpan ʿAḳiva convincingly presented itself as a civil organisation on the national and international stages. Its success at downplaying its military connections was either due to a good communications strategy or because the boundaries between civilian and military life in Israel have been so severely eroded that it is second nature for the institute's directors, on the one hand to promote peace to the public, and on the other to keep the military associations 'inside' as a 'responsible' behaviour of those who identify Israel's national security needs. Another explanation could be that Israel as a militarised society, did not know how to create genuine 'coexistence', and just what this word really means. Instead, the 'peace and security' formulation has been so effective that it has blurred the distinction between the civilian and military spheres in Israel and has taken as a given the overlap and integration of civilian and military organisations and interests.

It seems, however, that ulpan ʿAḳiva's real concerns were financial. Once again running into financial difficulties, Ulpan ʿAḳiva decided in 2007 to sell some land that it owned in a deal that *Haaretz* newspaper characterised as 'shady'.[147] However, this did not provide a permanent solution for Ulpan ʿAḳiva's financial woes. These were caused by a number of factors, including increased competition from newly established *ulpanim* and a drop in the number of new immigrants to the country. Sensing Ulpan ʿAḳiva's precarious position, the Ministry of Defence discontinued its support and stopped placing students on its courses. As an institute that selected a camel as its logo, the decision of the Ministry of Defences seems to have broken the proverbial camel's back and Ulpan ʿAḳiva was forced to shut down.[148]

During Ulpan ʿAḳiva's final decade of existence, and not unconnected to the death of its founder Shulamit Katznelson in 1999, it carried on a continuous struggle to retain its place in Israel's language education landscape. One can argue that there is a direct connection between the Ministry of Defence's decision to withdraw its financial support and Ulpan ʿAḳiva's closure. This highlights the dependency of Arabic studies on the security establishment. In other words, in all likelihood, support from the Ministry of Defence and the implementation of projects involving Military Intelligence were able – until that moment – to keep the institute afloat. Yet, Arabic studies without the military was perhaps just not sufficient to keep Ulpan ʿAḳiva alive.

Conclusion

At a conference in 2001 organised by the Citizens' Accord Forum between Jews and Arabs in Israel, various scholars were asked to discuss the subject, 'Loaded Words and Offensive Language in the Hebrew and Arabic Media'. Mordechai Kedar, a lecturer at the Department of Arabic at Bar-Ilan University and a former lieutenant colonel in Israeli Military Intelligence who is known as an Israeli expert in Arabic, was one of the main speakers. Drawing on his research on the Arab mass media, Kedar 'highlighted, in a rather one-sided way, a series of malicious words used by the Arabic press'.[1] He was followed by Salem Jubran, a Palestinian citizen of Israel, a poet and the former editor of the Literary Arabic journal *Al-Jadīd*. Jubran began his lecture with a personal comment. He said: 'It is a pity that you [the majority of Israelis] do not know Arabic. And, as for you, Professor, it is pity that you did study this language.'[2]

While allegedly a marginal anecdote, I believe that it captures in a poetic yet tragic way the distancing of Jews from Arabic over the last 100 years in Palestine/Israel. I see this incident as a metaphor, the tip of a very frozen iceberg described in this book. This anecdote unearths the competing values that Israeli and Palestinian communities attach to the Arabic language. On the one hand, the humane, rich and positive connotations that the language has in the Arab-Palestinian community and, on the other hand, the negative intimidating and security-based associations that the language conjures up in a considerable portion of the Jewish-Israeli public.

These competing tales of Arabic are personified by the two individuals mentioned above: first, Jubran, a leading Palestinian writer and educator who was the editor of several Arabic journals and the author of a number of books of poetry in Arabic. And, second, Kedar, an Israeli lecturer at the Department of Arabic at Bar-Ilan University and a scholar who served for 25 years in Military Intelligence and in academia, specialising in a very wide range of subjects including, 'Syria, Arab Political Discourse, Arab Mass Media, Islamic Groups, Israeli Arabs, Muslim Brotherhood and Other Islamist Groups'.[3]

This allegedly minor anecdote vividly reflects far more widely held views about the development of Arabic language studies for Jewish-Israelis, as this book has uncovered. Arabic emerges as a language that is *spoken* by Arab people but is *controlled* by Jewish-Israeli experts. In other words, Arabic as a language that, for one specific community in historical Palestine, has ceased to serve as a vehicle for communication and has turned into a weapon in the battlefield of domination and control.

The military–education partnership

As demonstrated in the book – and in contrast to other periods in history in which Arabic among Jewish people was not a cause for pity – the last 100 years in Palestine/Israel have witnessed the securitisation of Arabic studies among the Jewish people. The roots of this process are found in the rise of Zionism in Palestine, the encounter with the local Arab-Palestinians as well as with the Zionist decision to push for Hebrew unilingualism. The more obvious processes of politicisation and securitisation gained pace following the heated conflict in Palestine, and evidently following the years 1936–39 and the clashes between Jews and Arab-Palestinians. This created a shift in the way in which Arabic was studied and perceived by the Zionist administration. It was a crucial historical moment in Palestine that saw a rise in tensions between Jews and Arabs. Parallel to this, and in the same spirit, this period also witnessed a dramatic rise in Arabic studies projects that were created by the Zionist leadership and that tied together political, security-oriented and educational motivations and needs. During this period, and more evidently following the creation of the State of Israel in 1948, it became clear that the evolving field of Arabic studies in Jewish educational institutions was heavily influenced by the political conflict and by security-oriented considerations, and policies were shaped by a closed network of Jewish-Israeli experts who had the 'license' to teach Arabic and to study and explain 'the Arab world'.

A combination of social, political and security-oriented processes led to this situation. These are critical for our understanding of the ultimate direction that Arabic language studies would take within the Israeli school system. Following the 1948 War, and in light of the Arab–Israeli conflict and the alleged lack of 'practicality' of Arabic studies in the newborn state, Arabic suffered from a serious image problem in the Jewish-Israeli school system. Consequently, very few pupils elected to study the language. Similarly, the Ministry of Education paid little attention and allocated meagre funding to Arabic language studies. However, the need for Arabic-speakers grew stronger in two 'areas' related to the IDF. The first was the Military Government, which was in charge of controlling, administering and supervising the life of the Palestinians living inside of Israel. The second was the Military Intelligence, which was responsible for collecting and gathering information, analysing data and observing from afar the Arab people living outside the borders of Israel. These two 'areas' in which the need for Arabic-speakers was actually felt in Israel epitomise the ongoing dissimilation project of the Zionist movement concerning the Arab world and its culture, and can explain the securitisation of Arabic studies in Israel.

The above mentioned 'gap' between the unattractiveness of Arabic studies in the civil education system on the one hand, and its importance for Israel's security establishment on the other, resulted in the cooperation between the two spheres and in the 'birth' of the 'Arabic for peace and security' mantra. The complementary interests of the two spheres provided the basis for collaboration between the institutions. The Ministry of Education benefited from the national-security connotations of Arabic and from the IDF's ability to convince pupils of the 'practicality' of and the crucial need for Arabic studies. The security establishment benefited by increasing its influence on the national level, bringing together 'peace and security' and gaining a direct say in the numbers and skills of pupils who could later be trained as soldiers in Military Intelligence. Following this, and more evidently following the 1967 and 1973 wars, civilian scholars who had no past or present connection to security and who did not see themselves as part of the 'peace and security' mantra were not invited to play a meaningful role in the debate and their voice did not seem to be missed.

The 'peace and security' mantra was mentioned over and over again by different actors in the Israeli network of Arabic studies and, as this book has shown, it was indeed a core value of the field of Arabic studies in Israel. Following Shlaim in *The Iron Wall*, who showed how 'seeking peace' proved to be an Israeli myth that only helped to justify the ongoing conflict, this book uncovered how the 'peace and security' mantra saw the latter setting the tone at all significant crossroads. At the end of the day, the study of Arabic for security purposes has been rationalised in the name of peace. In this way, the field of Arabic studies has been one more victim of this Israeli ideological construction. In this case, however, Arabic studies were responsible not only for a reproduction of knowledge but for the reproduction of 'victims' – of the Israeli 'Military Intelligence fodder'.[4]

An important element that contributed to this reproduction of knowledge and students was made up of the actors collaborating in the 'peace and security' Arabic networks. It might seem striking to someone not familiar with Israeli society, but despite being from the 'military sphere' or from the 'educational sphere' the actors who collaborated in the field of Arabic studies seemed to be very similar to one another and were actually working as one. Their ongoing need for each other continued to push the two parties together and even strengthened their relationship over time. The Ministry of Education and related educational institutions, in their attempts to promote the study of Arabic and to this end in light of their dire need for funding, found in the military a partner that provided the matter legitimacy and offered the educational institutions both funding and expertise. All in all, while different instrumental interests were indeed the impetus for initial cooperation, these institutions were also bound by shared ideology and personal backgrounds, the power relations in the field and the simple equation of 'supply and demand' in the field of Arabic studies. Perhaps this explains why the Ministry of Education and civil institutions that taught Arabic were so quick to acquiesce to military pressure and why the military, ultimately, became such a dominant actor in the field.

These partnerships between military and educational actors have been successful and enduring because the linked network of Arabic experts enabled them to glide easily between the civilian and military spheres. On top of this, the security experts came to be seen as 'objective', 'balanced' and definitely highly respected voices in the field. This reality, in which the security and civil expertise blended into one discourse, can explain the fact that over the course of some six decades these bodies have produced virtually no genuine new thinking regarding Arabic teaching, and they have created no meaningful change in the way that Arabic is taught nor in the achievements and proficiency of the students in the language.

Participation in these networks bolstered the stakeholders' perceptions that they were 'on the same page' or, using Shulamit Katznelson's words: 'share a similar "madness"' for Arabic. The holding of widely shared values and assumptions also explains the extensive use of 'coded language', as explained in the book. Such group-talk was instantly recognised and understood by the actors who belonged to the network. 'The army of Arabists', as I titled them, all of whom were members of the same 'old boys club', supported and validated each others' positions and worked in an interconnected environment characterised by open and fluid borders – open, that is to anyone who fit a certain profile.

The notion that key players operated in an environment characterised by open borders and interchangeable roles can be demonstrated by the biographies of four individuals profiled extensively in this study. Brig. Ret. Ephraim Lapid, for example, started in the Oriental Classes (*Ha-Megamah ha-Mizraḥanit*) the intensive Arabic programme in schools that was established by the Prime Minister's Office. He later served in Military Intelligence, was subsequently appointed to serve as IDF Spokesperson and eventually served as the Director of Ulpan ʿAḳiva. Col. Ret. Nissim ʿAtsmon started his career in Military Intelligence and was then recruited by the Ministry of Education to head a military-education unit called Shifʿat, established for the promotion of Arabic studies. Professor Meʾir Kister, a distinguished scholar at the Hebrew University's Institute of Oriental Studies, served in the pre-state period at the Haganah Arabic Broadcasting Service, and later headed the Oriental Classes funded by the Prime Minister's Office. Former Israeli president, Yitzḥak Navon, who was appointed Minister of Education in 1984, had previously held security duties as he headed the Arab Bureau, the Military Intelligence wing of the Haganah in Jerusalem over the years 1946–49 and had also worked as an Arabic teacher in Jewish-Israeli schools. As Minister of Education, he appointed Col. Nissim ʿAtsmon, the former head of the Arabic School of the IDF, to serve as the director of Shifʿat.

The career histories of these individuals illustrate the boundaries of the field of Arabic studies in Israel, the extent to which various networked parties moved back and forth between relevant positions and the fluid nature of the field. The IDF, Ministry of Education, Ministry of Defence, Ministry of Foreign Affairs and Prime Minister's Office created a well-defined territory in which central actors were united in the context of a nation-in-arms under the themes of 'security and peace'. Similar phenomena were at work in semi-military, semi-educational bodies analysed in the book, such as Ṭelem in Military Intelligence and Shifʿat in the Ministry of Education. These units demonstrate the extent to which there was a symbiosis between the military and educational spheres.

This symbiosis also determined the identity of the 'perfect' Arabic expert. The 'Gordian knot', to use Snir's words, that links Arabic studies and security considerations and that enabled movement within the field, meant that accepted expertise in Arabic and Arab affairs was exclusively produced by Jewish-Israelis. These individuals were by and large connected to the security apparatus at some point and were obviously also influenced by mainstream Zionist thought. These elements lie behind the exclusion – and almost complete absence – of Palestinian citizens of Israel in this realm. As this book demonstrates, their voices have not been heard in any meaningful way, in spite of the fact that Arabic is their native tongue and that they are the consumers of Arabic culture, literature, music and art. They have not been seen as desired – and many times not even legitimate – candidates to teach Arabic, nor as experts who can participate in, let alone lead, educational discussions about Arabic studies. They were also not seen as legitimate partners in various campaigns to strengthen the status of Arabic in Israel – especially those conducted by the Ministry of Education. In other words, since the Palestinian citizens of Israel did not 'speak' the language of 'peace and security' and were not part of the 'secret sharing' and the 'coded language' used by different Jewish-Israeli actors, they were simply not invited to the Jewish-Israeli Arabic 'club' and, strikingly, the Jewish-Israeli members of the club did not miss them.

This exclusion was of course related to the securitisation of Arabic studies in Israel. As Arabic increasingly became associated with security needs and bodies in Jewish-Israeli society, no genuine involvement on the part of the Palestinian citizens of Israel was regarded as necessary or even desired. For example, Military Intelligence requires pupil evaluations from their Arabic teachers in high school and also initiates Arabic activities that bring together Military Intelligence soldiers and high school Arabic pupils. This direct connection between Arabic and security in the Israeli school system necessarily excluded Arabs because, as Palestinian citizens, they were subjects of suspicion and objects of state-induced alienation who could not be trusted in matters regarding security. Therefore, the process of the securitisation of Arabic in Israel also implied its de-Arabisation.

Lastly, and in addition to this, the research uncovers some significant outcomes of the *securitisation of school subjects*, most interestingly the acquiescence, even active involvement, of educational figures in responding to the needs of the security apparatus. It shows that in order to prove their continuing relevance to a society, especially in the midst of a political and military conflict, educational figures such as language teachers, supervisors and directors of civil language centres internalised the security terminology, vision and discourse, almost totally dismissed the Arab-Palestinian expertise and presented their successes and financial demands in relation to their contribution to the military establishment, and they sometimes even did so without reference to philological, pedagogical, academic or educational debates and considerations. This was done in order to fit into the dominant and sweeping national security discourse – a process characterised either by active cooperation with the security establishment or by waving the 'peace and security' card and proving the relevance of Arabic studies in schools to the country's security interests.

The banality of military involvement in Arabic studies enabled Jewish-Israeli society at large and Jewish-Israeli pupils of Arabic in particular to overlook the depth, complexity and problematic educational repercussions of this reality. The special political situation in Israel, the blurring of borders between the civilian and military sectors, together with the 'peace and security' mantra, helped to blind pupils of the language to the security dominance of Arabic studies. They did not necessarily notice that their curriculum, or the field of Arabic studies at large, were being manipulated for ideological goals, that the programme of study did not include intellectual and cultural aspects of the language, that fluent Arabic-speakers were lacking and, more importantly, that their views about the language and its native speakers were shaped by security considerations.

From language policy and back to Israeli Arabic

One of the main findings of this research is that language – a seemingly benign and innocuous field – can, in fact, be thoroughly harnessed for security ends. Such a situation results in narrow understandings and biased worldviews among its learners. In this regard, this research provides a glimpse into the general influence that security considerations can have on a country's language policy, as well as on how security justifications are used to manipulate language studies in highly charged political conflicts. This book also adds an internal look at how language policies are created and at the roles that various bodies play in such situations. It demonstrates how an ongoing conflict can distort the relations between educational, political and security figures and how, in these situations, the centrality of the military in shaping a country's language policy is evident. In such situations, figures like the Minister of Defence, Chief of Staff, Chief of Intelligence, senior officers from Military Intelligence and military units that specialise in training and teaching, as well as political units such as the Prime Minister's Office or the Ministry of Foreign Affairs, all take part in the debate about language studies in school, each playing a central and decisive role in shaping a country's language policy.

This book therefore provides an opportunity to understand how language policy is crafted and implemented, while focusing on the security considerations and actors. In other words, this research shows how times of conflict create an ongoing imbalance between the educational sector and the security-political ones, pushing the educational authorities to follow policies beyond their pedagogical purposes and values. Following on from this, I argue that a language policy that is placed – even partially – in the hands of military figures is a recipe for a distorted version of language studies that, on the whole, seems unable to serve visionary and peaceful needs.

It has been shown that when a language is transformed from a living, breathing entity to a mere object or tool for security purposes, it becomes distorted or 'loses its soul'. Similar analysis of connections between foreign language studies and the involvement of military and state actors and interests in educational systems can, of course, be applied to other case studies. For example, it applies to the study of German in the USA following World War I, the study of English in the USSR during the Cold War and the study of Arabic in the USA following 9/11, including the American Title VI foreign language education programmes and the work of the National Security Language Initiative (NSLI).

The sociopolitical situation, however, as well as other factors, make the Israeli case qualitatively different. These factors include Israel's geographical location in an Arabic-speaking region and the constitution of its own population. The Mizraḥi community in Israel, most of which arrived from Arabic-speaking countries, makes up a considerable part of the Jewish population of the country[5] and 20 per cent of Israeli citizens are Arab-Palestinians whose first language is Arabic. Israel's demographics, the close relation between Hebrew and Arabic as two Semitic languages, the official status of Arabic in Israel, the place of the military in the Jewish-Israeli ethos and the way in which the military permeates broader aspects of society have significant repercussions on Jewish-Israeli society, making this a rather unique case study. In other words, the securitisation of Arabic studies in Israel has crucial repercussions on the Jewish-Israeli perception of its region – the Middle East, on relationship between Israel and its Arab neighbours and on the relationship between Jewish-Israelis and their Palestinian fellow citizens.

One of the results of the unique circumstances of the Israeli case study, of the closed network of Jewish-Israeli experts and of the ongoing securitisation of the field, was that it set the stage for a new 'type' of Arabic. This 'type' of the language, which I called 'Israeli Arabic', resulted from the dominance of security and political considerations to the detriment or even complete denial of cultural engagement, coexistence and integration into the region. This 'Israeli Arabic' was an outgrowth of relationships between Jewish-Israeli actors in a field of Arabic studies – relationships that were nationalistically oriented, security-aware and Zionist in nature. Therefore, this 'type' of Arabic is not found in Arab countries, of course, nor does it resemble in any way Arabic that is taught in Europe or North America. Arabic language instruction in those regions includes its native speakers in the framing of curricula and being a fluent Arabic-speaker there gives one an advantage in the field, not a disadvantage as this book shows. Therefore, in the Jewish-Israeli case, instead of being a subject with inherent cultural, educational and human value, 'Israeli Arabic' has become a means to achieve a strategic aim.

This book contends that the security orientation of Arabic studies has become a fundamental part of how the language is studied and understood by Jewish-Israelis. This has rendered the study of the language as a Jewish-Israeli, Zionist and military endeavour that is Arab-free and intended to achieve a very specific aim. In this context, it is interesting to recall the way in which Kamāl Rayyān, one of the few Arab-Palestinian teachers in the field, saw the situation: as Arabic textbooks that were written by 'former Military Intelligence soldiers writing for future Military Intelligence soldiers'. As such, rather than contributing to a better understanding of the language and culture, Arabic studies in Israel has ultimately achieved almost the opposite: 'Israeli Arabic' distanced Jewish-Israeli pupils from the Arab world and from Arab people, and did this while also more clearly demarcating the 'borders' between 'us' and 'them'.

As such, the Arabic language in Israel, as studied in Jewish institutions, rather than serving as a bridge to understanding, connections and communication has, in fact, come to be a point of division. This is one important characteristic of 'Israeli Arabic'. Unlike Arabic elsewhere, 'Israeli Arabic' instils in its Jewish speakers a fear of Arabic-speaking people, while making the Arab people afraid of those Jewish people who study or who know 'Israeli Arabic'. It is a security-associated language and an Arab-free one, and as such is suspicious until proven innocent.

Furthermore, 'Israeli Arabic' is a language that provides its pupils with unique language skills. It puts the passive skills of reading and listening at the top, far beyond the active skills of the learner, characterised mostly by speaking and writing. Besides the fact that these passive skills represent the vast majority of the missions of Military Intelligence units in Israel – where the translation of texts and especially intelligence listening capabilities are at the top[6] – which is probably not coincidental, it seems that this language has even deeper layers of rationalisation. Instead of aiming for an active interaction between Jews and Arabs, for a letter that can be sent or a dialogue that can be created, 'Israeli Arabic' is a silent language that listens from afar, that 'decodes' texts, mostly from newspapers, as if Arabic was simply a frozen language of an enemy. 'Israeli Arabic', in a similar way to a military post or a Military Intelligence antenna, enables its pupils to reconnoitre the Arab world through binoculars, to look at it quietly from the outside, but not to interrelate with Arab people generally and with the Palestinian citizens of Israel more particularly. 'Israeli Arabic' perpetuates the worldview of the main actors who shaped the field of Arabic studies, including their fears and their security-oriented backgrounds.

With Arabs excluded from this process, the circle is thus closed. This creates a very limited 'horizon of expectations' as the pupils' knowledge and beliefs about Arabic are constrained by their teachers' experiences. Thus, pupils are unlikely to consider using Arabic for purposes that fall outside the boundaries of this closed circle. This view of Arabic – as a new liberal example of 'gated communities' – is consistent with the way in which Jewish-Israelis view their country: '*in* the Middle East, but not *of* the Middle East'.

The way in which language can so thoroughly become a part of the security discourse, context and establishment is one of the most tragic conclusions of this book, as it demonstrates how language study can be manipulated for the denial of social relationships, the denial of history and sometimes even the denial of the self. It shows that the study of a 'security-oriented' language can bring about narrow understandings and flat and binaric worldviews, but also that language itself can be easily manipulated to serve the aspirations of the security establishment until it 'loses its soul'. In other words, it is not only the roots and outcomes of studying languages in a security environment that have been uncovered through this research, but the distortion of language itself, the relationships between its speakers, and the creation of a new, politicised, one-dimensional, history.

The consequences of this situation are crucial. History demonstrates that an Israel that is stronger militarily is not necessarily safer and certainly has not promoted peaceful well-being. In the six decades since its establishment, Israel has not achieved relations of true peace or warmth with any country in the Middle East – all of which are Arabic-speaking. It is likely that the Israeli tendency to understand the region through the lens of security or, at the very least, through security-educational Jewish endeavours, has resulted in a narrow and distorted understanding of the Middle East. The nature of Arabic language studies and the 'type' of Arabic that it has produced in Israel has laid the groundwork and supported the continuation of a limited discourse framed by the Jewish, Zionist and security-oriented concerns of its creators. This book shows that situations of conflict open up a space that allows issues of security to frame and shape language policy. For better or for worse, languages and their study can create and promulgate a specific political or military vision of the 'enemy' or, 'them' in opposition to 'us'.

The time has come for Israel to acknowledge openly the central role of security in shaping Arabic language studies in Jewish-Israeli society. Denial and disregard of this unspoken yet clearly known phenomenon stands in the way of serious and honest discussion regarding the role of Arabic in the shaping of contemporary Jewish-Israeli society and perception. All in all, in order to transform Arabic study among Jewish-Israelis into a tool for entering and embracing the intellectual and civilian life of the majority of the people in the Middle East, nothing less than a revolution in the field of Arabic studies is required.

Appendices

Appendix 1 A photograph of three Jewish boys dressed in Ha-Shomer clothes [1935–45]
Source: The Rehovot Archive.

25/6

مُقْتَطَفَاتٌ مِنَ الصُّحُفِ العَرَبِيَّةِ

לקט מתוך העתונות הערבית

מחברת ב

לוקט וסודר ע״י

קבוצת מורים לערבית

בהוצאת ראובן מס ירושלים, תש״א

בחוברת הזאת יש קצת שנויים לעומת החוברת הקודמת הצריכים באור:
העירו מורים ומוסדות שנוח להם יותר לקבל חוברות בעלות הקף מצומצם ולעתים
ונות. משום כך העמדה חוברת זאת על שמונה עמודים.
ועוד העירו מורים שתלמידיהם מבקשים ידיעות על דבר המלחמה ואינם רוצים
תפק בחומר מן המזרח הקרוב בהוה. בקשה זו נתמלאה כאן. חלק הידיעות ממין
יוכל להמסר לקריאה בבית.
לים וניבים מסוימים שניתן להם באור בחוברת הקודמת לא נתבארו שנית בחוברת הזאת.
מורים ומתלמדים מתבקשים להביע דעתם אם הם מסכימים לשיטה זו או אם הם
צים שכל חוברת תחשב כעומדת ברשות עצמה.
הצעות לשכלולים ותקונים נא לשלח אל מחלקת החנוך של הועד הלאומי ירושלם.
ת. ד. 7061.

התכן

גרמות ١—٤. ידיעות מקומיות ٤—٥. ידיעות מן הארצות השכנות ٦—٧
קטע מנאומו של עבאס מחמוד אלעקאד ٧—٨.

رَسَائِلُ خَطِيرَةٌ ١) يَحْمِلُهَا السَّفِيرُ الأَمِيرِكِيُّ لِرُومَا

ـدن – نشرت جريدة الديلي
سكتش ٢) أَنْبَاءً هَامَّةً بِقَلَمِ رئيس
تحريرها ٣) جاء فيها ان المستر
فليبس السفير الاميركي في روما قد
غادَرَ وشنطن عائداً الى ايطاليا
ومعه رسالتان من الرئيس
روزفلت. في الأُولَى تَشْجِيعٌ ٤)
للأُسْرَةِ المَالِكَةِ ٥) الايطالية وفي
الثانية تَحْذِيرٌ ٦) للسنيور
موسوليني. وقال المحرر ان الرئيس
روزفلت يقوم الآن بعمل
دِبْلُومَاسِيٍ ٧) وهو على اِتِّصَالٍ ٨)
بالحكومة البريطانية وان هذا
العمل ستكون له فائدة كبيرة
لبريطانيا في البحر المتوسط.

الصراط المستقيم

١) חשובים, בעלי ערך ٢) Daily Sketch ٣) ראש המערכת, עורך ٤) דברי עדוד
٥) משפחת המלוכה ٦) התראה ٧) פעולה דיפלומטית ٨) בא בקשרים, בא במגע.

Appendix 2 The pamphlet *Selection from the Arabic Press* (Hebrew, *Leḳeṭ min ha-Ītonut ha-ʿAravit*)
Source: Dated 23 January 1940, CZA/J17/6734.

ל א ל פ ר ס ו ם

יחידה ד.צ. 1030

צ ה ל

כ"ב אייר תשכ"ד
4 במאי 64

לכבוד

הועד הארצי של המורים לערבית

בבתי הספר התיכוניים העבריים

הנדון: מכתבכם בקשר לשינויים בתקנון בחינות בגרות

1. לצה"ל דרושים חיילי חובה, בוגרי תיכון, יודעי השפה הערבית למילוי תפקידים שונים.

2. צה"ל קבל עד השנה שעברה חיילים אלה מבין בוגרי המגמה המזרחית ומבין הנבחנים בבחינות בגרות בשפה הערבית, כאשר המגמה המזרחית מהווה כ-35% והנבחנים בשפה הערבית הוו 65%.

3. לאור דרישות מוגברות של צה"ל בסוג הנ"ל של בוגרים, יזם ראש אמ"ן פגישה עם משרד החינוך ועם היועץ לעניני ערבים במשרד ראש הממשלה, במגמה לעודד לימוד הערבית בבתי הספר התיכוניים, וכן במטרה להגברי את המגמה המזרחית, וזה עוד לפני פרסום התקנות החדשות. כתוצאה מפגישה זו סוכם למנות ועדה בהשתתפות הגורמים הנ"ל.

4. ב-26.2.64 שלח ראש אמ"ן מכתב למנהל הכללי של משרד החינוך, בו הוא מציע הקמת הועדה הנ"ל, ומפרט את תפקידיה. בין היתר כלל ראש אמ"ן "מתן אפשרות לנבחנים בבחינות בגרות לבחור במקצוע הערבית כאלטרנטיבה למקצוע אחר (הסטוריה) במגמה ההומנית והחברתית". וזאת כתוצאה מפירסום התקנות החדשות.

5. מכל האמור לעיל ברור לכם שצה"ל מעוניין בהגברת לימוד השפה הערבית בבתי־הספר התיכוניים, ולא לצמצומה.

6. בקשר לרמת החיילים בוגרי תיכון שנבחנו בבחינות בגרות בשפה הערבית הנני לציין שרמתם טובה, והם מבצעים את תפקידיהם המיועדים בהצלחה. רמתם זו בשפה אינה נופלת מחבריהם בוגרי המגמה המזרחית. אך למרות האמור הייתי מקדם בברכה כל עליה ברמת הידיעות במקצוע זה.

א. שרוני, סגן אלוף

בשם מפקד היחידה

Appendix 3 Letter titled 'Not for Publication' sent by Lt Col. Avraham Sharoni, Military Intelligence Officer, to Avraham Lavi, Head of the National Committee of Israeli Arabic Teachers

Source: Dated 4 May 1964, ISA/K-484/24.

סודי

מדינת ישראל

אל אל"מ י. הרכבי - ראש אמ"ן - מטכ"ל

מאת היועץ לעניני ערבים - משרד ראש הממשלה

ירושלים, תאריך כ"ד בטבת תשי"ז
28 בדצמבר 1956

מס 1250/4/ 439

הנדון: גיוס מסיימי המגמה המזרחית
בבתי הספר התיכוניים

המחסור החמור בכוח אדם בעל הכשרה מתאימה לעבודה בענינים ערביים, גורם לקשיים רבים בכל פעולה בשטח המדיני והאדמיניסטרטיבי. אין ספק כי צה"ל, ובמיוחד אגף המודיעין מרגיש בחסרון זה במדה לא פחותה מאתנו. יש לדאוג, איפוא, לפיתוח קאדרים שיוכלו למלא תפקידים בשטחים אלה. זוהי פעולה לטוח ארוך, שדורשת השקעת מאמצים רבים, התאמת המנגנון החינוכי לצרכים מיוחדים אלה, ועקיבה מתמדת אחר התפתחותם של האנשים שעתידים להיות מועמדים לעבודה.

עובדת הכניה שלפיה יעברו מועמדים לשרות בשטח הערבי הכשרה בת 7 שנים ומעלה. בשלב ראשון על הצעירים להתמסר ללימודי מזרח מוגברים בשתי שנות הלימוד האחרונות של בית הספר התיכון.

במשך שרותם הצבאי נועדו האנשים לעבוד בשטח הערבי, לנצל בו את ההכשרה שרכשו בבית הספר ויחד עם זה להתמסות בתפקידים, להשתלם ולהתפתח. הלימודים באוניברסיטה, במשך שלוש השנים יכוונו למקצועות המזרחיים, ויחד עם זאת יתמחה כל מועמד באופן אינדיבידואלי לקראת התפקיד שייראה כמתאים לתכונותיו ונטיותיו.

2./.

Appendix 4 Letter sent by Shmu'el Divon, Adviser on Arab Affairs in the Prime Minister's Office, to Col. Yehoshafat Harkabi, Chief of Intelligence
Source: Dated 28 December 1956, IDFA/2004/1308-192.

מדינת ישראל

אל

מאת

תאריך

מס

.2.

צעדים ראשונים לבצוע התכנית כבר נעשו. כיום לומדים 66 תלמידים בארבעה בתי ספר תיכוניים במסגרת המגמה המזרחית, ובה רוכשים הם ידיעה טובה בערבית, בהסטוריה ובגיאוגרפיה של המזרח התיכון, ונפגשים להיכרות ראשונה עם ההווי הערבי בארץ תוך כדי שהייה של חודש ימים באזורי המיעוטים. כזכור בוצעה יציאת התלמידים בקיץ זה במסגרת הצבא, וספק הוא אם היתה זוכה לאותה הצלחה ללא עזרתו.

בין שני שלבים אלה מהווה השרות הצבאי חוליה מקשרת בעלת חשיבות חיונית, כי כאן בלבד יכול איש לרכוש נסיון מגוון בעבודה מעשית ורק במסגרת זו ניתן לעמוד על אופיו. יש ליחס חשיבות רבה לכך שלא יאבד הקשר עם האיש המשרת בצבא ואף תוך כדי שרותו אין להזניח את השתלמותו התיאורטית.

בשיחתנו מיום 22.10.56 עמדנו על כך שהיה רצוי מכל הבחינות, הן של צרכי אמ'ן והן מבחינת הדאגה לקאדרים בעתיד, שאלה מיוצאי הצבא מבין מסיימי המגמה המזרחית אשר במיון יימצאו מתאימים לשרות בח'מן, יוצבו לחיל אף אם דרגת בריאותם גבוהה. המדובר כאן על מכסימום של 26 אנשים לשנה. מאחר שבנות עד כה גם נתקבלו לחמ'ן ומאחר שיש לצפות לכך שחלק מן הנערים לא יהיו בעלי סוג בריאות מתאים לחי'ר, יש להניח שמספר כה מועט של אנשים לא ישפיע לרעה על מכסות הגיוס השונות, בעוד התועלת שאפשר להפיק מהם בזמן שרותם הסדיר היא ניכרת.

אודה לך מאד אם תביא ענין זה להכרעת הפיקוד העליון של צה"ל.

ב ב ר כ ה,

ש. דיבון

Appendix 4 Continued

לשכת היועץ לענייני ערבים

ירושלים, כ' באלול תשכ"ג
8 בספטמבר 1963

1/2

לכבוד
סא"ל אברהם שרוני,
ד.צ. 2408,
<u>צ ה " ל</u>

הנדון: <u>בוגרי המגמה המזרחית בחמ"ן</u>

בעקבות שיחתנו בענין זה מבקש הייתי לדעת
מהו היקף המחזור של בוגרי המגמה המזרחית המצטרף
לשדרות חמ"ן מידי שנה ומהי מידת קליטתם
בתפקידים השונים.

האם מספר הבוגרים מספיק ובאיזו מידה רצוי
להרחיב את מסגרת המגמה המזרחית בבתי הספר
התיכוניים בארץ בהתאם לצרכיו של חיל המודיעין
על כל שלוחותיו.

בברכה,

אורי שטנדל

Appendix 5 Letter sent by Ori Stendel, Office of the Adviser on Arab Affairs, to Lt Col. Avraham Sharoni, Military Intelligence officer
Source: Dated 8 September 1963, ISA/GL-13927/19).

כ ל ל י   ה ת נ ה ג ו ת

1. בצרת הנה עיר ערבית, מנהגי תושביה ואורח מחשבתם אינם חופפים לאלה שבערים עבריות בישראל.
זכור שלא כל המקובל בחברתך מקובל גם כאן.

2. הערבים בכלל והנצרתי בפרט הנו רגיש לתגובותיך, גם אם לא יביע זאת.
שקול איפוא דבריך.

3. אין להמצא בתחום נצרת בהופעה חיצונית מרושלת. הקפד על כן על נקיונך ועל לבושך.

4. בעברך ברחובות העיר שים דגש על התנהגות מאופקת ותרבותית (המנע מצעקות ושיחה קולנית). בשיחה עם תושב שמעהר בסבלנות, ענה בנימוס ולענין.

5. קבל כל דעה המושמעת באזניך ברוח דמוקרטית, ותהיה זו הדעה הבלתי מקובלת עליך ביותר.

6. הנך מצווה שלא להכנס לכל ויכוח מדיני ולא לנקוט כל עמדה בכל הנוגע ליחסי ישראל-ערב ובעית המעוטים במדינה. בנושאים אלה שמע ואל תכנס בויכוח.

7. בכל פניה מתושב אליך לסייע בידיו בכתב או בעל-פה אצל איזה גורם צבורי או פרטי שהוא, עליך לסרב באדיבות.
זכור! אינך צבור מתווך לבקשות או תלונות שהן.

8. בסיורך בעיר עם חבריך אל תגיב לגבי התגרויות, באם תקרינה.

9. מעמדה של האשה בחברה הערבית שונה מאשר בחברה העברית, לפיכך המנע מהלצות בנושא זה או יחס חפשי שהיית מרשה לעצמך בחברתך.

10. הדגש בהופעתך שהנך תלמיד, ואין זה מתפקידך לעסוק בחנוך הצבור או הפרט לפי הרוח המקובלת בחברתך.
הדגש יחסך לשפה והתרבות הערבית כגשר לקשירת יחסים.

11. אינך רשאי לבקר אצל תושבים בלי נטילת רשות מוקדמת ממדריכך. כמו־כן אינך רשאי להזמין אורחים מהחוץ בתקופת השתלמותך אלא באישור מדריכך.

12. אין לקבל כל טובת הנאה מהתושבים בין בצורת מתנות או בכל צורה אחרת שהיא.
אין בשום פנים להכביד על האורח ולסעוד על שולחנו.

13. יש להזהר מכל פגיעה בערכי הדת המוסלמית או הנוצרית ובמקומות קדושים.

Appendix 6 'Rules of Behaviour'
Source: Dated 1960, ISA/GL-13919/10.

ט"ז אדר א' תשל"ו
16 פברואר 76

מטה הכללי
ראש אגף המודיעין

נתקבל בלשכת השר
בתאריך
20. II. 1976

שר החינוך והתרבות

הנדון: תכנית למורי הערבית במערכת החנוך

אדוני השר,

מצ"ב מכתב סא"ל לפיד, המשמש במרכז הפעילות באגף המודיעין לעידוד למורי הערבית והמזרחנות.

על מנת שלא לאחר את ההכנות לקראת שנת הלמודים תשל"ז, אודה לך אם נקבע פגישת תיאום לגיבוש תכנית העבודה לשנה הבאה.

הנני ממליץ כי לפגישה זו יוזמנו גם:
ד"ר דן רונן, עוזר השר.
מר עמנואל יפה, ראש המזכירות הפדגוגית.
ד"ר כרמי יוגב, יו"ר המזכירות לחינוך העל יסודי.
מר י. אייל, המפקח על מורי הערבית.

בברכה,

שלמה גזית - אלוף
ראש אגף המודיעין

Appendix 7 Letter sent by Shlomo Gazit, Chief of Intelligence, to Aharon Yadlin, Minister of Education
Source: Dated 16 February 1976, ISAGL-13133/8.

לשכת ראמ"ג

ה נ ד ו ן: מצב לימוד הערבית במערכת החינוך

מנקודת מבט של חמ"ן - הצעה במ"ט לשר החינוך

מב-כם: ל/4981/581.11 (סע' 3) מ-2.2.76

כללי

1. מצב לימוד הערבית במדינה נמצא בירידה:

א. כמותית - בעיקר ביחס לגברים.

ב. איכותית - לצרכי צה"ל אין מספיק בוגרי מגמה מזרחנית, והבוגרים שלמדו ערבית כשפה זרה שניה אינם עונים לדרישות של חמ"ן.

2. מסמך זה יפרט את:

א. הסיבות העיקריות לירידה בלימוד הערבית.

ב. הפעולות שננקטו ע"י חמ"ן לעודד לימוד הערבית.

ג. הצעות לשיפור.

הסיבות העיקריות לירידה (לפי הבנתנו)

3. לפי תכנית הלימודים החדשה בחטיבה העליונה מקצוע הערבית הינו מקצוע בחירה ומעצם הגדרתו הופך המקצוע למשני אפילו ביחס למקצועות בחירה אחרים הקוסמים יותר (כגון: לימודי מחשב, צרפתית ועוד) עקב זאת ישנה ירידה מהותית בעיקר במספר הבנים לומדי הערבית. להלן נתונים שנאספו ממגעינו עם בתי הספר:-

שנים	מספר בנים בכתה י"א	מספר בנים בכתה י"ב	מהם במגמה מזרחנית כתה י"א	מהם במגמה מזרחנית כתה י"ב
תשל"ה	716	613	109	89
תשל"ו	562	469	98	96

4. המקצוע אינו מבורך במורים אפקטיביים היכולים להניע תלמידים המתלבטים בבחירת כיוון ללמוד את השפה הערבית, וזו נחשבת כמקצוע חסר-יוקרה בבתי הספר.

Appendix 8 The Lapid Report
Source: Dated 1976, p. 1, ISA/GL-13133/8.

משרד החינוך והתרבות
אגף הנוער
הפקוח על פעולות של"ח
2.2.77

(מ " ט מ)
(טיפוח לימודי המזרחנות)

בבא הגבה לישראל
ד.צ 1090

לשכת היועץ לעניני ערבים
נתקבל ביום
10.II.1977.

לכ'

הנדון : כנס מנהלים

רקע

1. במסגרת פעולות חיל המודיעין ומשרד החינוך והתרבות בטיפוח תודעת המזרחנות במערכת החינוך יערך גם השנה כנס של מנהלים מבתי ספר על יסודיים כדי ללבן בצורתא את הנושא.

2. הדיון ישולב בסיור באזור הגדר הטובה והרצאת ראש אמ"ן.

תכנית הסיור

3. הסיור יתקיים ביום ש לישי 8 מרץ 1977 לפי התכנית הבאה : –

א. 08.30 – איסוף מתחנה המרכזית ת"א ליד קולנוע מרכז –מנהלים מאזור י–ם והדרום.
ב. 08.40– איסוף תחנת רכבת ארלוזורוב –מורים מאזור ת"א והמרכז.
ג. 09.00 – איסוף בצומת נתניה בכביש החוף(ליד צריף הוועד למען החייל)
ד. 09.15 – איסוף בצומת חדרה,כביש החוף ליד ביתן איסוף חיילים.
ה. 10.00 – תחנה מרכזית חיפה ליד התחנה להסעות מיוחדות.
ו. 11.30 – בירנית–פגישה עם מח"ט 300 הסבר על הגזרה.
ז. 13.30 – מעבר דובב –הסבר על הגדר הטובה מפי המפקד במקום.
ח. 14.30 – ארוחת צהריים באכסניית תל–חי.
ט. 15.30 – סקירת קמ"ן פיקוד צפון.
י. 16.00 – סקירת ראש אמ"ן.
יא. 17.00 – חזרה לת"א דרך :1) טבריה–חיפה
2) טבריה–צומת גולני–חדרה–נתניה–ת"א.
יב. 20.30– פיזור משוער :ת"א–ארלוזורוב ותחנה מרכזית ת"א.

מנהלה

4. הסיור יתבצע באוטובוסים.
5. דמי השתתפות סמליים בסך 20 ל״י (יגבו ביום הכנוס)
6. נבקשכם למלא את הטופס הרצ"ב ולשלוח אליגו בהקדם האפשרי ל–ד.צ 1090 צ.ה.ל

בברכת למד עברית
סא"ל עצמון נסים

עב/חצ

Appendix 9 Invitation sent by Col. Nissim ʿAtsmon, Military Intelligence officer, to Israeli principals
Source: Dated 2 February 1977, ISA/G-13969/2.

Appendix 10 Symbol of the Haganah: a sword encompassed by an olive branch
Source: Wikimedia, 'Haganah'.

Appendix 11 Symbol of the IDF: a sword encompassed by an olive branch
Source: Wikimedia, 'IDF'.

ndix No. 1

שר הבטחון

הקריה, ט"ו באייר תשל"ח
22 במאי 1978

נתקבל בלשכת השר
22. V. 1978

ק/ 4781

שר החינוך והתרבות

הנדון: הנהגת למוד ערבית חובה בחטיבה העליונה במערכת החינוך בישראל

זה שנים נעשית בארץ פעולה צבורית מצד ועדות הכנסת, אנשי צבור, מחנכים ובעיקר מטעם צה"ל/חיל המודיעין, ביחד עם משרד החינוך והתרבות, במגמה להרחיב את למודי הערבית במערכת.

לדאבוני פעולות אלה לא נחלו הצלחה. על אף ההתעוררות הצבורית והעליה במודעות לחשיבות הנושא, נמצא מספר התלמידים הלומדים ערבית בירידה. נערים ונערות שוקלים את השיקול הפרקטי של ההשקעה שעליהם להשקיע בלמודים שאינם תורמים במישרין למטרה הסופית - עמידה במבחני הבגרות. וכל אמצעי השכנוע והפתוי שיביאו ללמוד ב"התנדבות" - מעלים חרס.

הגענו לאחרונה למצב בו מספר הבוגרים בערבית אינו מספק יותר אפילו את הכמות הדרושה לצה"ל, במסגרת שרות חובה, וזאת בנוסף לרמה הירודה של הערבית השגורה בפיהם של הבוגרים היום.

במצב ענינים זה נראה לנו רק פתרון חד-משמעי לקידום מקצוע לימוד זה: קביעת הערבית כמקצוע לימוד חובה (שפה זרה שניה, כמו אנגלית) וזאת כולל בחטיבה העליונה (כתות י - יב).

ברורים לנו הקשיים בישום תוכנית זו באשר להכשרת מורים, חבור ספרי לימוד וכו'. אך ללא קביעת המקצוע כחובה לא יזוז הטפול בנושא, אם נשפוט גם לפי נסיון העבר.

הנני מציע, איפוא, כי תתקבל החלטה ברורה בכוון זה, וכי משרד החינוך והתרבות יגבש תכנית 5 שנתית לצורך ההערכות המעשית עד להחלת החלטה זו על פני כלל מערכת החינוך.

מערך חיל המודיעין וצה"ל ישמחו, כמובן, להמשיך בשתוף הפעולה המעשי עם משרד לקידום נושא הוראת הערבית, ובמידת האפשר נשתדל אולי אף להרחיב את פעולתנו בשטח זה.

ב ב ר כ ה ,

עזר ויצמן

Appendix 12 Letter sent by Ezer Weizman, Minister of Defence, to Zevulun Hammer, Minister of Education

Source: Dated 22 May 1978, ISA/GL-17938/14.

מרכז ללימודים ערביים ואפרו־אסיניים בגבעת חביבה

مركز للدراسات العربية - والافروسيوية - غبعات حبيبه

CENTRE FOR ARAB AFRICAN AND ASIAN STUDIES – GIVAT HAVIVA

GIVAT HAVIVA
P. O. Menashe
PHONE 063-78944

غبعات حبيبه
البريد المتجول منشه

גבעת חביבה
דאר נע מנשה
טל. 063-78944

30.11.80

לכבוד
אלוף (מילואים) שלמה גזית
לשכת ראש אמן
הקריה
תל - אביב

שלום וברכה,

מזה חמש עשרה שנה, שהמכון ללימודים ערביים מטפח את לימוד השפה הערבית ומגביר את התודעה המזרחנית בקרב תלמידיו. בוגריו שמספרם מגיע ל- 350 מפוזרים בעשרות ערים וישובים.

מזכירות המכון, החליטה ליזום כינוס של כל הבוגרים, ביום חמישי 15 בינואר 1981.

אהיה אסיר תודה, באם תאות, לתת את הרצאת הפתיחה משעה 13.00 עד השעה 14.30 על הנושא: "תמורות ושינויים בעולם הערבי".

בכבוד רב

משה גבאי
מנהל המכון

Appendix 13 Letter sent by Moshe Gabay, Director of the Institute for Arabic Studies at Giv'at Ḥavivah, to Gen. Ret. Shlomo Gazit
Source: Dated 30 November 1980, YYA/40-9.2-10.

הַמכון ללימודים ערביים
معهد الدراسات العربية
Institute for Arabic Studies

18 בפברואר 1986
קש - 1

לכבוד
לשכת קצין מודיעין ראשי
תת אלוף גיורא זורע
ד.צ. 02090
<u>צה"ל</u>

שלום וברכה ,

לאחר שני עשורים; לפעילותו של המכון ללימודים ערביים, הלכו ונוצקו קשרים הדוקים, עם חיל המודיעין, במסגרת הכיתות המזרחנות.
שנה בשנה, השתלבו בוגרי המכון במסגרות החיל, ומילאו בו תפקידים בהתאם למשימות שהוטלו עליהם.

הקשרים נתפתחו שלבים שלבים, מבלי שנטבע בהם חותם התכנון ואולי זו הסיבה, שהתעוררו לאחרונה לא מעט קשיים ואי-הבנות, המחלישים את יכולתנו להמשיך וללמד את השפה הערבית, לבוגרי כיתות י"ב.

אודך, אם נוזמן לשיחה, כדי להציג תוכנית עבודה המשלבת ביתר-שאת את קשרינו עם החייל ומחייבת את היחידה הצבאית הקשורה עם המכון לפעול בהתאם להנחיות שתיקבענה.

בברכה ובידידות,

משה גבאי

ע"ש עבד אל-עזיז זועבי • גבעת-חביבה סמינריון הקבוץ הארצי השומר הצעיר, ד.נ. מנשה, מיקוד 37850, טלפון: 063-78944
على اسم عبد العزيز الزعبي ، جبعات حبيبه – بريد مهتجول منشه ، ٣٧٨٥٠، تلفون: ٧٨٩٤٤–٠٦٣
GIVAT-HAVIVA HAKIBBUTZ HA'ARTZI HASHOMER HATZAIR M.P. MENASHE 37850, TEL: 063-78944

Appendix 14 Letter sent by Moshe Gabay, Director of the ʿAbd al-ʿAzīz al-Zuʿbī Institute for Arabic Studies at Givʿat Ḥavivah, to Brig. Giora Zoreʿa, Military Intelligence officer
Source: Dated 18 February 1986, YYA/6-20.2.40.

22.4.75

الاتحاد ٢٢-٤-٧٥

عربية ـ عبرية كرأس جسر للسلام ـ نعم
ولكن تحت حراب الاحتلال والعدمية القومية ـ لا !!

نتانيا ـ لمراسل خاص ـ انتهت يوم السبت ٥ـ٤ـ٧٥ فى (أولبان عقيبا) بالقرب من نتانيا دورة لطلاب من الصفوف العاشرة اليهودية والعربية بهدف تعليم اللغة العبرية للطلاب العرب والعربية للطلاب اليهود ، كل هذا بهدف جعل معرفة اللغة لكلا الطرفين حافزا للتعارف والاخوة والسلام .

كل هذا حسن وجيد من حيث الفكرة العامة . ولكن الحقيقة الواضحة هو ان سلطات المعارف (المعراخية) لا تدفع شيئا لله من اجل السلام والاخوة هكذا !! فلا بد أن تحشر انف سياستها حتى فى مثل هذه الدورات ، ولكن يبدو ان العتمة لم تعد على قد الحرامى . فعندما جاء وزير المعارف ليحاضر او ليناقش هب فى وجهه الطلاب اكثر من مرة واحرج فى اكثر من موضوع . وهذه المرة احرجه الطلاب اليهود أيضا .

والمفتش للمدارس الدرزية (!!) احرج هو ايضا عندما ساله الطلاب عن قضايا معلميهم ولماذا يطردونهم احيانا؟! وكانت عينتهم هذه المرة المعلمة تفريد أبو رحمة !! التى طردت من عملها لاسباب سياسية محضة ، ولكن حضرة المفتش لم يعترف بهذا بل عزاه لقصورات المعلمة (كذا!) .

وطيلة ايام الدورة السبعة كانوا يحاولون اقناع الطلبة بان هذه الدورة ليست سياسية . ولكن عندما فتحت المحافظ التى قدمت لهم كهدية انكشفت محاولات الصهينة والتثقيف السياسى العقيم ! فقد أهدى المشرفون على الدورة الطلاب كتاب « بيت أبى » لغولده مئير وترجمة الاديب محمود عباسى !! ـ طبعا ـ ودوسية عن الاقليات !! فى اسرائيل وكراسة عن العرب فى اسرائيل عفوا (عرب اسرائيل ١٩٧٣) وفى المجال الادبى لم يجدوا سوى مجلة « لقاء » التى تصدرها الهستدروت !!

ولاثبات ان الدورة غير سياسية !! ابدا ضللوا بعض ابناء وبنات الجولان المحتل لحضور الدورة التى ركزها السيد اهرون زبيدة وهو أيضا مركز التربية والتعليم فى الجولان المحتلة .

وفى نهاية الاحتفال تكلم عضو الكنيست مودعين وعضو الكنيست ورئيس لجنة الثقافة فى الكنيست شخطرمان ورئيس بلدية نتانيا !! كل هذا والمسالة غير سياسية ابدا وحتى عندما يبررون وجود العرب « بأن هذه الارض مؤكدة وموعودة لشعب اسرائيل .. وقد كان لداوود مساعدون من الشعوب الاخرى ..!! » يا سلام . هل رأيتم ايها الآباء هذه الدورات الدراسية !! لماذا ؟!!

تعزيــــة

الى الاخ مسرور قطان
تعازينا القلبية بوفاة
أخيكم

نعيمة ومنشى خليفة

Appendix 15 Article published in *Al-Ittiḥād* about the initial course called 'Arabic as a Bridgehead' at Ulpan ʿAḳiva
Source: *Al-Ittiḥād*, 22 April 1975, ISA/GL-17080/6.

משרד החינוך והתרבות   המחלקה להכשרת עובדי הוראה

המכללה לחינוך ע"ש לוינסקי

כ"ח אדר ב' תשמ"ד
1 באפריל 1984

34/5

כבוד
ד"ר אליעזר שמואלי, מנכ"ל
משרד החנוך והתרבות
ירושלים

נכבדי,

שלושה גורמים חברו יחדיו - אגף המודיעין בצה"ל שמגלה דאגה מעובדת הירידה המתמדה במספר התלמידים הפונים למגמות המזרחנות בבתי הספר ובאוניברסיטאות;

אולפן עקיבא, שרשם דף מזהיר בקידום הוראת הערבית לאוכלוסיות מגוונות בדרכים בלתי שגרתיות ומכללת לוינסקי - להגשמת מפעל בעל ערך סגולי ואף ייחודי: קורס מורות חילות להוראת ערבית.

מטרת קורס מורות חיילות המשותף לאולפן עקיבא ולמכללת לוינסקי להכשיר מורה מוסמכת להוראת הערבית לביה"ס היסודי ולחטיבת הביניים.

על פי התכנית שהתגבשה ע"י שני המוסדות אולפן עקיבא מקבל על עצמו את הקניית השפה הספרותית והמדוברת לתלמידי הקורס ואילו מכללת לוינסקי תעסוק בהכשרה הפדגוגית.

התלמידים ישהו באולפן עקיבא בתנאי פנימיה. יומיים בשבוע יעמדו התלמידים לרשותה של מכללת לוינסקי.

התעודה שיקבלו בוגרי הקורס תהיה משותפת למכללת לוינסקי ולאולפן עקיבא.
התואר יהיה: מורה מוסמך. אם ישובו בוגרי הקורס ללמוד שנה נוספת במכללה, לאחר הוראה במסגרת השירות הצבאי, יוכלו לקבל תעודת מורה מוסמך בכיר.

אנו מניחים שנסיונו של כל אחד משני הגורמים שנותנים יד לקורס זה עשוי להביא לתוצאות מצויינות.

בברכה

ד"ר אברהם רוכלי
מנהל.

שולמית כצנלסון
מנהלת אולפן עקיבא

Appendix 16 Letter co-written by Avraham Rokheli, President of Levinsky College, and Shulamit Katznelson, Director of Ulpan ʿAḳiva, sent to Eliʿezer Shmuʾeli, General Director of the Ministry of Education

Source: Dated 1 April 1981, ISA/GL-18661/8.

הנשיא

ירושלים, י"ז בניסן התשנ"ג
8 באפריל 93
24-18053336

לכבוד
גב' שולמית כצנלסון
מנהלת אולפן עקיבא
החוף הירוק
ת"ד 6086
נתניה 42160

שולמית יקרה,

אני אסיר תודה לך על מכתבך, על תוכנו המאלף והמעודד ועל דברי הברכה אשר השפעת עלי.

את יודעת היטב שאני מודע לא רק לעבודת-הקודש שנעשית באולפן עקיבא על ידך ועל ידי צוות נפלא ומסור של עובדים - יהודים בעלי תחושת שליחות לאומית וערבים מהארץ ומהשטחים, המאמינים ומקדישים עצמם לדו-קיום של כולנו בארץ זו.

הצטערתי שלא זכית בשנה שעברה בפרס נובל לשלום ותקוותי היא שהשנה הבא שנת בשורה לך, לאולפן ולכל שוחרי השלום והאחוה.

כבוגר האולפן, שמורה לך ולאולפן פינה חמה בלבי - אותה אנצור לתמיד.

בברכה,

Appendix 17 Letter sent by President Chaim Herzog to Shulamit Katznelson, Director of Ulpan ʿAḳiva

Source: Dated 8 April 1993, from 'Photos: Ulpan ʿAḳiva', Heritage Section, Netanya, official website, 4 August 1993, available at: http://www.netanya-moreshet.org.il/Info/PicShow.aspx?src=../../View_files/HeapItem_pic/034651/HP_034651_28.jpg&titl (accessed 26 July 2010) (Hebrew)

Federico Mayor
Directeur général de l'Organisation des Nations Unies pour l'éducation, la science et la culture
vous prie de bien vouloir honorer de votre présence la cérémonie de remise du

Prix UNESCO 1998 de l'éducation pour la paix

à l'Organisation non gouvernementale

EDUCATORS FOR PEACE AND MUTUAL UNDERSTANDING (UKRAINE)

et de mentions d'honneur aux Organisations non gouvernementales suivantes :

Fridtjof Nansen Academy (Norvège)
World Court Project (Nouvelle-Zélande)
Ulpan Akiva Netanya (Israël)

le mardi 15 décembre 1998, à 18 h 30, dans la salle IV

Maison de l'UNESCO
125, avenue de Suffren, Paris 7e

La cérémonie sera suivie d'une réception

R.S.V.P. (regrets seuleme
Tél 01 45 68 38

Appendix 18 UNESCO Prize for Peace Education, letter sent to Ulpan ʻAḳiva
Source: In French, 10 December 1998, ISA/G-10391/13.

ULPAN AKIVA NETANYA أولبان عقيبا - نتانيا **אולפן עקיבא נתניה**
International Hebrew study center מרכז ללימוד השפה העברית, תרבות ישראל וידע הארץ
Founded - 1951 By Shulamith Katznelson *נוסד - תשי"א ע"י שולמית כצנלסון*

אולפן עקיבא נתניה

זוכה פרס הוקרה של אונסק"ו לחינוך לשלום ל-1998

פרס הוקרה של אונסק"ו לחינוך לשלום ל-1998 מוענק לארבעה מוסדות חינוך: מאוקראינה, מנורבגיה, מניו-זילנד ואולפן עקיבא מישראל.

פרס ההוקרה מוענק לאולפן עקיבא על פעולות מתמשכות לדו-קיום בין יהודים וערבים, ישראלים ופלסטינים והוראת השפות עברית וערבית ותרבותן לבני שני העמים.

אולפן עקיבא נוסד ב-1951 ע"י שולמית כצנלסון ומאז למדו בו כ-80 אלף בוגרים מישראל וגם מ-143 ארצות בעולם, באווירה של קירוב לבבות ואחווה אנושית.

הפרס יוענק בטקס חגיגי במרכז אונסק"ו בפריז, ביום שלישי, ג' חנוכה תשנ"ט, 15.12.98 ויקבלו אותו בשם ישראל, השגריר לאונסק"ו אבי שוקת ומנכ"ל אולפן עקיבא אפרים לפיד.

רח' זלמן שזר 3, ת"ד 6086 נתניה דרום, מיקוד: 42160 טלפון: 09-8352312/3 פקס: 09-8652919
3 ZALMAN SHAZAR ST. POB: 6086 NETANYA, 42160 TEL: 972-9-8352312/3 FAX: 972-9-8652919
E-mail: ulpanakv@netvision.net.il http://www.ulpan-akiva.org.il

אונסקו.doc

Appendix 19 Translation into Hebrew of the UNESCO Prize for Peace Education award letter sent to Ulpan ʻAḳiva
Source: Dated 10 December 1998, ISA/G-10391/13.

Notes

Introduction: Arabic and Security in Israel

1. See Joshua Fishman, *The Sociology of Language: An Interdisciplinary Social Science Approach to Language in Society* (Rowley, MA: Newbury House, 1972), p. 4.
2. I am using 'spoken by a considerable percentage of Mizraḥi Jews' and not 'the first language of Mizraḥi Jews' as the immigration was from Arabic-speaking countries that had been under colonial rule, and, as such, sections of the Jewish communities studied in schools and spoke the language of the coloniser as their first language and spoke Arabic as a second and even third language. A discussion on the relationships between the coloniser's language (mostly English or French) and Arabic among Jews in Arab countries in the Middle East is indeed fascinating, but beyond the scope of this work. It can be argued, though, that in the shadow of colonisation, Jews in Arab countries – especially families from upper classes – preferred to invest in French and English and not firstly in Arabic. On immigrating to Israel, therefore, there was a double estrangement from Arabic: from the lower classes in their places of origin and from Arab-Palestinians in light of the Arab–Zionist conflict.
3. This notion draws, of course, on the work of Bourdieu and his definitions of a field as 'structured social space ... a field of forces, a force field ... which contains people who dominate and people who are dominated', in Pierre Bourdieu, *On Television* (New York: New Press, 1998), pp. 40–1. In accordance with his framework, the field of Arabic studies is scrutinised in the book as a space in which different actors try to preserve or transform the way in which the language is studied in the context of the power struggles and inequalities between the different actors and institutions involved.
4. In the book, I will use the concepts of 'Orientalism' and Orientalist perceptions following the Saidian concept of Orientalism as 'a style of thought based upon ontological and epistemological distinction made between "the Orient" and (usually) "the Occident"', in Edward Said, *Orientalism* (Harmondsworth: Penguin, 1995), p. 2.
5. See, for example, Henriette Dahan-Kalev, 'The "Other" in Zionism: The Case of the Mizrahim', *Palestine–Israel Journal of Politics, Economics and Culture* 8 (1) (2001), p. 94.
6. For further reading, see Yonatan Mendel, 'Re-Arabising the De-Arabised: The Mista'aravim Unit of the Palmach', in Ziad Elmarsafy et al. (eds), *Debating Orientalism* (London: Palgrave Macmillan, 2013), pp. 94–116. The Mista'aravim Unit of the Haganah (also known as *Ha-Maḥlaḳah ha-Surit* or the 'Syrian Platoon') operated during 1940–43 (ibid., p. 97). The Mista'aravim Unit of the Palmach (also known as *Ha-Maḥlaḳah ha-'Aravit*, the 'Arab Platoon', or *Ha-Shaḥar*, 'The Dawn') operated during 1943–50 (ibid., p. 99).
7. For further reading on Israeli militarism, see Baruch Kimmerling, 'Militarism in Israeli Society', *Theory and Criticism*, 4 (Autumn 1993), pp. 123–40

(Hebrew); Uri Ben-Eliezer, *The Making of Israeli Militarism* (Bloomington: Indiana University Press, 1998) (Hebrew); Uri Ben-Eliezer, 'The Military Society and the Civil Society in Israel: Signs of Anti-Militarism and Neo-Militarism in a Post-Modern Period', in Majid al-Haj and Uri Ben-Eliezer (eds), *In the Name of Security: The Sociology of Peace and War in Israel in Changing Times* (Haifa: University of Haifa, 2003), pp. 29–76 (Hebrew).

8. In order to understand the way in which *military*-oriented values were adopted by society in general, I make use in the book of the notion of 'common sense' as highlighted by Antonio Gramsci, the Italian political theorist and thinker. For further reading about his notion of 'common sense' and his analysis of the education system, see Diana C. Coben, 'Metaphors for an Educative Politics: "Common Sense", "Good Sense", and Educating Adults,' in Carmel Borg et al. (eds), *Gramsci and Education* (Lanham, MD: Rowman & Littlefield, 2002), pp. 263–90; Joseph Francese, *Perspectives on Gramsci: Politics, Culture and Social Theory* (New York: Routledge, 2009).
9. Applying Ben-Eliezer's analysis of Israel as a 'nation-in-arms', helped me to understand better the nationalist perception that dominates Jewish-Israeli society's understanding of the army. The concept of Israel as a 'nation-in-arms' includes the central place of the army in Jewish-Israeli society, and the social, cultural and political importance of the IDF in Israel. See Uri Ben-Eliezer, 'A Nation-in-Arms: State, Nation, and Militarism in Israel's First Years', *Comparative Studies in Society and History*, 37 (2) (1995), pp. 264–85.
10. *Policy networks*, following Peterson and Bomberg refers to 'clusters of actors, each of which has an interest, or stake in a given policy sector and the capacity to help determine policy success or failure'. See John Peterson and Elizabeth Bomberg, *Decision-Making in the European Union* (Basingstoke: Macmillan Press, 1999), p. 8; see also John Peterson, 'Policy Networks', *Political Science Series 90*, Vienna: Institute for Advanced Studies, July 2003, p. 1, available at available at: http://www.ihs.ac.at/publications/pol/pw_90.pdf (accessed 14 November 2012). 'Social networks', following Hedin, helped me to focus on the 'relations between individual persons, for the actions of the individual, for social movements and organisations' (Astrid Hedin, *The Politics of Social Networks: Interpersonal Trust and Institutional Change in Post-Communist East Germany*, Lund: Lund University Press, 2001, p. 55). See also Milroy's emphasis on the informal nature of relationships in social networks and the fact that they can act 'as a mechanism both for exchanging goods and services, and for imposing obligations and conferring corresponding rights upon its members', in Lesley Milroy, *Language and Social Networks* (Oxford: Basil Blackwell, 1980), pp. 46–7.
11. Compare this with the pioneering research on Israel of Barak and Sheffer in which they looked into Israel's security network and described it as a particular type of 'policy network'. According to them: 'The Israeli security network is a complex and fluid type of relationship between acting and retired individuals and groups of security officials and civilian actors, one that is ultimately capable of shaping policymaking in general and determining concrete policies and their implementation.' See Oren Barak and Gabriel Sheffer, 'Israel's "Security Network" and its Impact: An Exploration of a New Approach', *International Journal of Middle East Studies*, 38 (2) (2006), p. 238.
12. Throughout the book I mention the concept of *securitisation*. This term, as developed by the Copenhagen School, and in the context of this book,

helped me to analyse the process of making Arabic studies a *security-important* issue. I make use in this notion – as well as in the idea that it is not a frozen concept but a move, which takes political considerations or educational considerations – and make them part of the world of security. See Barry Buzan et al., *Security: A New Framework for Analysis* (London: Lynne Rienner Publishers, 1998), p. 24. See also the way in which Williams adds to this definition the importance of 'securitising' through speech-acts as well as the question of security representation. See Michael C. Williams, 'Words, Images, Enemies: Securitization and International Politics', *International Studies Quarterly*, 47 (4) (2003), p. 513.

13. According to Jane, 'a hidden curriculum consists of some of the outcomes or by-products of schools or of non-school settings, particularly those states which are learned yet are not openly intended'. See Martin Jane, 'What Should we Do with a Hidden Curriculum When we Find One?,' in Henry A. Giroux and David Purpel (eds), *The Hidden Curriculum and Moral Education: Deception or Discovery?*, (Berkeley, CA: McCutchan Publishing Corporation, 1983), p. 144. Compare this with Haralambos, who argues that the hidden curriculum 'consists of those things pupils learn through the experience of attending school rather than the stated educational objectives', in Michael Haralambos, *Sociology: Themes and Perspectives* (London: Collins Educational, 1991), p. 1.

1 Rooting Security in Arabic Soil: When Zionism Met Arabic

1. Yehuda Amichai, from the poem, 'Huleikat: The Third Poem about Dicky', in ibid., *Yehuda Amichai: A Life of Poetry 1948–1994*, trans. by Benjamin and Barbara Harshav, 1st edn (New York: Harper Perennial, a Division of Harper Collins Publishers, 1995), p. 410; originally published in Hebrew in ibid., *Even a Fist was once an Open Palm with Fingers* (Jerusalem: Schocken, 1989).
2. I borrow this term from Uhlmann, who referred to the connection between Arabic and security in Israel as a 'public secret'. See Allon J. Uhlmann, 'The Field of Arabic Instruction in the Zionist State', in James Albright and Allan Luke (eds), *Pierre Bourdieu and Literacy Education* (New York: Routledge, 2008), p. 107.
3. Quoted in a report titled, 'Arabic Studies in Hebrew Schools in Israel', conducted by Shmu'el Shay, Tamar Tsemah and Haviva Bar and submitted to the Ministry of Education in August 1988. Found in, Israel State Archive, Jerusalem (ISA), PR-10/4461.
4. See Adva Him Younes and Shira Malka, *Developing a Curriculum in Arabic for Intermediate and High Schools in the Jewish Sector* (Jerusalem: Henrietta Szold Institute, National Institute for Research in the Behavioral Sciences and the Pedagogic Secretariat in the Ministry of Education, 2006), pp. 11, 78, 159 and 185, available at: http://meyda.education.gov.il/files/Tochniyot_Limudim/DochotMechkarim/Aravit.pdf (accessed 14 November 2012) (Hebrew).
5. Most famously is the research of Kraemer who argued that because of the ongoing conflict, only the *instrumental* and *national security* orientations provide the motivation to study the language in schools. See Roberta Kraemer, 'Social Psychological Factors Related to the Study of Arabic among Israeli Jewish High School Students' (PhD thesis, School of Education, Tel

Aviv University, 1990), pp. 173–4. See also Amara who similarly identified the supremacy of the military in Arabic studies in Israel. Amara noted that Arabic in Jewish-Israeli schools is taught as a security language and calls for it to be 'civilianised'. See Muḥammad Amara, *Teaching Arabic as a Foreign Language in Jewish Schools in Israel* (Haifa: Jewish–Arab Center, University of Haifa, 2008) (Hebrew).

6. See *The Or Committee Report: The Commission of Inquiry into the Clashes between the Security Forces and Israeli Citizens in October 2000* (Jerusalem: Judicial Authority, State of Israel, August 2003), chapter 1, article 19 (Hebrew). The Or Committee, made up of Theodor Or, Hashem Khatib and Shimon Shamir, investigated the clashes between the Israel Police and Palestinian citizens of Israel during demonstrations at the beginning of the Second Intifada in October 2000. The clashes resulted in 13 Palestinian citizens of Israel being shot dead by police forces. The report is available at: http://elyon1.court.gov.il/heb/veadot/or/inside_index.htm (accessed 4 June 2014).
7. Yoav Stern, 'Poll: 50% of Israeli Jews Support State-Backed Arab Emigration', *Haaretz*, 27 March 2007.
8. Ahiya Raved, 'Youth Believe Arabs Dirty', *Ynetnews*, 1 September 2007, available at: http://www.ynetnews.com/articles/0,7340,L-3350467,00.html (accessed 4 June 2014).
9. Yossi Klein, 'Look! An Arab Speaking Hebrew', *Haaretz*, 12 July 2013 (my emphasis). Unit 8200 is the Israeli Central Collection Unit of the Intelligence Corps and the biggest unit in the IDF. See Daniel Byman, *A High Price: The Triumphs and Failures of Israeli Counterterrorism* (Oxford: Oxford University Press, 2011), p. 339.
10. There are, though, quite a few examples of 'medieval' Jewish compositions from Byzantion and the Middle East written in Hebrew and there is a substantial corpus of medieval 'Eastern' correspondence in Hebrew preserved in the Genizah. See, for example, Ben Outhwaite, 'Lines of communication: Medieval Hebrew letters of the 11th century', in Esther-Miriam Wagner et al. (eds), *Scribes as Agents of Language Change* (Berlin: De Gruyter Mouton, forthcoming).
11. Bernard Lewis, *The Jews of Islam* (Princeton, NJ: Princeton University Press, 1987), p. 62.
12. See: Tony Maalouf, *Arabs in the Shadow of Israel: The Unfolding of God's Prophetic Plan for Ishmael's Line* (Grand Rapids, MI: Kregel Publications, 2003), pp. 30–1.
13. Ibid., quoted from Paul Johnson, *History of the Jews* (New York: Harper and Row, 1987), pp. 177–8.
14. S. D. Goitein, *Jews and Arabs: Their Contacts through the Ages* (New York: Schocken Books, 1955), p. 130.
15. Lewis, *The Jews of Islam*, p. 77.
16. For further reading about this period and the history of the Jewish people in the Middle East, see Mark R. Cohen, *Under Crescent and Cross: The Jews in the Middle Ages* (Princeton, NJ: Princeton University Press, 1994); Goitein, *Jews and Arabs*; Daniel Frank (ed.), *The Jews of Medieval Islam: Community, Society, and Identity* (Leiden: E. J. Brill, 1995); and Lewis, *The Jews of Islam*.
17. For further reading, see Zion Zohar, *Sephardic and Mizrahi Jewry: From the Golden Age of Spain to Modern Times* (New York: New York University Press, 2005), p. 44;

Joshua Blau, *The Emergence and Linguistic Background of Judaeo-Arabic: A Study of the Origins of Middle Arabic* (Jerusalem: Ben-Zvi Institute, 1981).

18. Hebrew remained the dominant language in Jewish liturgical poetry. Nevertheless, Arabic was also used for this, as a second language. It is also important to distinguish between the situation of the Jews in Europe and the Jews in the Middle East. For the Jews in Europe, Arabic texts were translated en masse into Hebrew from the middle of the twelfth century onwards, while Eastern Jews continue to read and write in Arabic. For further reading, see Moritz Steinschneider, *Jewish Arabic Literature: An Introduction* (Piscataway, NJ: Gorgias Press, 2008).
19. For further reading, see Gregor Schwarb, 'Vestiges of Qaraite Translations in the Arabic Translation(s) of the Samaritan Pentateuch', *Intellectual History of the Islamic World,* 1 (1–2) (2013), pp. 115–57; Sidney H. Griffith, *The Bible in Arabic: The Scriptures of the 'People of the Book' in the Language of Islam* (Princeton, NJ: Princeton University Press, 2013); and Michael of Albany and Walid Amine Salhab, *The Knights Templar of the Middle East* (San Francisco, CA: Weiser Books, 2006), p. 53.
20. See Gad Freudenthal, 'Arabic and Latin Cultures as Resources for the Hebrew Translation Movement: Comparative Considerations, Both Quantitative and Qualitative', in Gad Freudenthal (ed.), *Science in Medieval Jewish Cultures* (New York: Cambridge University Press, 2011), p. 75.
21. Lewis, *The Jews of Islam,* p. 67.
22. In a striking contrast, the way in which modern Israel relates to Arabic today would have been neither possible nor fathomable during these earlier periods. While today there is a clear distinction between 'Arabic' and 'Jewish communities', between 'Arabic' and 'Jewish intellectual creation' and between 'Jewish communities' and 'Arab communities', back then Arab-Jewish identity, and the hyphen between them, represented the completion of one identity, not a contrast between two. Arabic was associated with daily life along with literary, scientific and philosophical masterpieces.
23. Quoted in Goitein, *Jews and Arabs,* p. 10.
24. I used this figure following the estimation of Moses ben Mordecai Bassola regarding the number of Jews in Palestine/Eretz Yisrael at the beginning of the sixteenth century, in Yitzhak Ben-Zvi, *Eretz Yisrael and its Settlement during the Ottoman Era* (Jerusalem: Yad Yitzhak Ben-Zvi Institute, 1975), p. 150.
25. This was also the case from 1516, when the Ottoman era in the region began. Despite the fact that the official empire language was then Ottoman Turkish (which was written in Arabic and contained significant vocabulary from this language as well as morphological structures) the regional lingua franca remained Arabic. See, for example, Cornelis Versteegh, *The Arabic Language* (Edinburgh: Edinburgh University Press, 2001), pp. 226–41.
26. For further reading on the *Musta'ribūn,* see Jonathan Gribetz, 'Musta'ribūn', Norman A. Stillman (executive ed.), *Encyclopedia of Jews in the Islamic World,* Brill Online, 2013, available at: http://referenceworks.brillonline.com/entries/encyclopedia-of-jews-in-the-islamic-world/mustaribun-SIM_000669 (accessed 4 June 2014).
27. For further reading, see Minna Rozen, 'The Position of the *Musta'rabs* in the Inter-Community Relationships in Eretz Israel from the End of the 15th Century to the End of the 17th Century', *Cathedra,* 17 (October 1980), pp. 73–101 (Hebrew).

28. The exact percentage of Jews in Palestine prior to the rise of Zionism is unknown. However, it probably ranged from 2 to 5 per cent. According to Ottoman records, a total population of 462,465 resided in 1878 in what is today Israel/Palestine. Of this number, 403,795 (87 per cent) were Muslim, 43,659 (10 per cent) were Christian and 15,011 (3 per cent) were Jewish (quoted in Alan Dowty, *Israel/Palestine*, Cambridge: Polity, 2008, p. 13). See also Mark Tessler, *A History of the Israeli–Palestinian Conflict* (Bloomington, IN: Indiana University Press, 1994), pp. 43 and 124.
29. These donations are known in Hebrew as *kaspei ha-ḥaluka*. See Menachem Friedman, *Society and Religion: The Non-Zionist Orthodoxy in the Land of Israel* (Jerusalem: Yad Yitzḥak Ben-Zvi Institute, 1988), p. 7 (Hebrew).
30. See, for example: Naphtali Kinberg and Rafael Talmon, 'Learning of Arabic by Jews and the use of Hebrew among Arabs in Israel', *Indian Journal of Applied Linguistics*, 20 (1–2) (1994), pp. 37–54.
31. See Netanel Katzburg, 'The Education Debate in the Old Yishuv', *Shana be-Shana* (1966), pp. 299–312 (Hebrew). See also Bernard Spolsky and Elana Shohamy, *The Languages of Israel: Policy, Ideology and Practice* (Clevedon: Multilingual Matters, 1999), p. 138.
32. Spolsky and Shohamy, *The Languages of Israel*. See also Reuven Snir, *Arabness, Jewishness, Zionism: A Struggle of Identities in the Literature of Iraqi Jews* (Jerusalem: Yad Yitzḥak Ben-Zvi Institute, 2005), p. 520 (Hebrew); ibid., '"Ana min al-Yahud": The Demise of Arab-Jewish Culture in the Twentieth Century', *Archiv Orientální*, 74 (2006), pp. 387–424.
33. On the familiarity of the Sephardim with the Arabic language and their general integration into the local Arab culture, see, Eliezer Ben-Rafael and Stephen Sharot, *Ethnicity, Religion and Class in Israeli Society* (Cambridge: Cambridge University Press, 1991), p. 26; Andrew Forbes and David Henley, *People of Palestine* (Chiang Mai: Cognoscenti Books, 2012); Israel T. Naamani, *The State of Israel* (New York: Praeger, 1980), p. 36; and Amos Daniely, *A Queen without a Crown* (Tel Aviv: Keter, 2006), p. 167.
34. Bernard Spolsky, 'Language in Israel: Policy, Practice and Ideology', in James E. Alatis and Tan Ai-Hui (eds), *Georgetown University Round Table on Language and Linguistics* (Washington, DC: Georgetown University Press, 1999), p. 165.
35. Max Weinreich, *History of the Yiddish Language* (New Haven, CT: Yale University Press, 2008).
36. See, for example, Gene Bluestein, *Anglish/Yinglish: Yiddish in American Life and Literature* (Athens, GA: University of Georgia Press, 1989).
37. See, for example, Yitzhak Korn, *Jews at the Crossroads* (East Brunswick, NJ: Cornwall Books, 1983), p. 159.
38. Mordecai Kosover, *Arabic Elements in Palestinian Yiddish: The Old Ashkenazic Jewish Community in Palestine, its History and its Language* (Jerusalem: R. Mass, 1966), p. 100.
39. Ibid., p. 99.
40. Ibid., pp. 105–10.
41. Ibid, p. 114.
42. Ibid.
43. Ibid., p. 253.
44. Ibid., p. 246.
45. Ibid., p. 122.

46. Ibid., p. 144.
47. For further reading, see Avi Shlaim, *The Iron Wall: Israel and the Arab World* (New York: W. W. Norton, 2001); Benny Morris, *The Birth of the Palestinian Refugee Problem Revisited* (Cambridge: Cambridge University Press, 2004); and Ilan Pappé, *The Ethnic Cleansing of Palestine* (Oxford: Oneworld, 2006).
48. Anita Shapira, *Land and Power: The Zionist Resort to Force, 1881–1948* (Stanford, CA: Stanford University Press, 1992), p. 56.
49. On the importance of Arabic as a symbol of Zionist nativism, see Oz Almog, *The Sabra: The Creation of the New Jew* (Berkley, CA: University of California Press, 2000).
50. Quoted in Rachel Elboim-Dror, *The Hebrew Education in Eretz Israel* (Jerusalem: Yad Yitzhak Ben-Zvi Institute, 1990), p. 129 (Hebrew).
51. Some of the Zionist immigrants actually regarded the Palestinian *fallāḥs* as Jews who had remained on the land after the destruction of the Jewish Temple in Jerusalem in 70 AD, and who later converted to Islam. This view was expressed by Israel's first prime minister David Ben-Gurion, who argued that the Palestinian *fallāḥs* were Jewish farmers who in the hardest times preferred changing their religion to leaving their land. See Gil Eyal, *The Disenchantment of the Orient: Expertise in Arab Affairs and the Israeli State* (Stanford, CA: Stanford University Press, 2006), p. 53.
52. According to Herzl's vision, the future Jewish inhabitants of Eretz Yisrael would speak European languages (mainly German). For further reading on the denigrating attitude of Herzl towards Hebrew and Yiddish, see Shlomo Avineri, 'Theodor Herzl's Diaries as a Bildungsroman', *Jewish Social Studies*, 5 (3) 1999, p. 22.
53. Theodor Herzl, *Altneuland:The Old-New Land* (Tel Aviv: Babel Publishers, 1997), pp. 98–9 (Hebrew).
54. On the connection between subsidisation and the Zionist aim of the exclusion of Arab workers, see Gershon Shafir, *Land, Labor and the Origins of the Israeli–Palestinian Conflict, 1882–1914* (Berkeley, CA: University of California Press, 1996), p. 61.
55. Gershon Gera, *The Ha-Shomer Book* (Tel Aviv: Israel Ministry of Defence, 1985), p. 20 (Hebrew).
56. Quoted in Baruch Kimmerling, *Immigrants, Settlers, Natives: The Israeli State and Society between Cultural Pluralism and Cultural Wars* (Tel Aviv: 'Am 'Oved, 2004), p. 127 (Hebrew).
57. For a photograph of three Ha-Shomer members, see Appendix 1.
58. This corresponds with Hever's literary analysis of Zionist literature. Hever points out that in the literary sphere there was no denial of the Palestinian 'other' but an attempt to situate him in an inferior position. Through what Hever depicted as a 'masking mechanism', Zionist literature strives to depict a Palestinian 'other' who is similar to the Zionist 'self' but is less ominous, and also to focus on the powerfulness of the 'self' and so ensure the subordination of the 'other'. See Hannan Hever, 'Territoriality and Otherness in Hebrew Literature of the War of Independence', in Laurence Jay Silberstein and Robert L. Cohn (eds), *The Other in Jewish Thought and History: Constructions of Jewish Culture and Identity* (New York: New York University Press, 1994), pp. 242–3.
59. Avraham Yaari, 'Hashomer Learns Sheepherding', in Levi Soshuk and Azriel Eisenberg (eds), *Momentous Century: Personal and Eyewitness Accounts of the*

Rise of the Jewish Homeland and State 1875–1978 (Cranbury, NJ: Cornwall Books, 1984), pp. 75–9.

60. Ibid.; and Kimmerling *Immigrants, Settlers, Natives*, p. 29.
61. For further reading about the concept of Jewish labour in Zionism, see Zachary Lockman, *Comrades and Enemies: Arab and Jewish Workers in Palestine, 1906–1948* (Berkeley, CA: University of California Press, 1996), pp. 50–3; and ibid., 'Railway Workers and Relational History: Arabs and Jews in British-Ruled Palestine', *Society for Comparative Study of Society and History*, 35 (3) (1993), pp. 608–9.
62. Spolsky and Shohamy, *The Languages of Israel*, p. 71.
63. According to the Semitic linguistic system, the root of each verb consists of two to four letters, and can be conjugated according to different forms called *binyanim* in Hebrew or *awzān* in Arabic.
64. Eli'ezer Ben-Yehuda, 'Sources for Filling in the Missing Parts in our Language', *Proceedings of the Hebrew Language Council*, Vol. 4 (Jerusalem: Hebrew Language Council, 1912), p. 9 (Hebrew).
65. See, for example, the Names Committee of the Jewish National Fund (JNF) that ruled in 1949 that if an Arab village had a name that was probably a 'corruption of the original Jewish name' but that helped to keep the 'original Jewish name', then its name needed to be changed 'to the historical Hebrew *original* one.' In Noga Kadman, *On the Side of the Road and in the Margins of Consciousness: The Depopulated Palestinian Villages of 1948 in the Israeli Discourse* (Jerusalem: November Books, 2008), p. 58 (Hebrew).
66. Snir, '"Ana min al-Yahud"', p. 389.
67. Quoted in Elboim-Dror, *The Hebrew Education in Eretz Israel*, p. 360. See also Alan Dowty, '"A Question that Outweighs all Others": Yitzhak Epstein and Zionist Recognition of the Arab Issue', *Israel Studies* 6 (1) (Spring 2001), pp. 34–54.
68. Quoted in Yosef Gorni, *Zionism and the Arabs, 1882–1948: A Study of Ideology* (Oxford: Oxford University Press, 1987), p. 48.
69. Quoted in Spolsky and Shohamy, *The Languages of Israel*, p. 139.
70. Herzl, for example, believed that the very Zionist existence in Palestine was in order to serve 'as an outpost of European culture against oriental barbarism'. See: G. N. Giladi, *Discord in Zion: Conflict between Ashkenazi and Sephardi Jews in Israel* (London: Scorpion, 1990), p. 208.
71. Robert C. Gardner and Wallace E. Lambert, *Attitudes and Motivation in Second Language Learning* (Rowley, MA: Newbury House, 1972).
72. In Shmuel Moreh, 'The Study of Arabic Literature in Israel,' *Ariel: The Israel Review of Arts and Letters*, Cultural and Scientific Relations Division, Ministry of Foreign Affairs, December 2001, available at: http://www.mfa.gov.il/MFA/MFAArchive/2000_2009/2001/12/The%20Study%20of%20Arabic%20Literature%20in%20Israel (accessed 14 November 2012).
73. Liora R. Halperin, 'Orienting Language: Reflections on the Study of Arabic in the Yishuv', *Jewish Quarterly Review*, 96 (4) (2006), p. 481.
74. Avino'am Yellin,'About Teaching Arabic in the Hebrew High Schools – 1939', in Jacob M. Landau (ed.), *Teaching Arabic as a Foreign Language* (Jerusalem: School of Education of the Hebrew University and the Ministry of Education, 1961), p. 75 (Hebrew) (original emphasis).
75. Ibid.

76. Proceedings of the Arabic Teachers Committee, 10 April 1938, Central Zionist Archives, Jerusalem (CZA), J17/319.
77. Ibid.
78. Proceedings of the Arabic Teachers Committee, 14 June 1939, CZA/J17/7236.
79. Ibid.
80. Quoted in Yisrael Ben-Ze'ev, 'Report on Arabic Studies' (1946), in Yosef Yunai (ed.), *Arabic in Hebrew Schools: A Collection of Documents* (Jerusalem: Israel Ministry of Education, 1992), p. 37.
81. However, neither Goitein in 1936 nor Ben-Ze'ev in 1937 mentioned an explicit security-oriented problem in hiring Palestinian teachers or in using Palestinian textbooks.
82. Eyal, *The Disenchantment of the Orient*, p. 60.
83. Barak and Sheffer, 'Israel's "Security Network"', p. 243.
84. Moshe Brill, 'The Basic Vocabulary of Arabic Daily Press – 1940', in Landau (ed.), *Teaching Arabic as a Foreign Language*, p. 145.
85. A copy of the *Selection from the Arabic Press* newsletter can be seen in Appendix 2.
86. The letter was signed by 'Ovadia Lalu, Me'ir Plessner, Aviva Turovcky and Eliyahu Ḥabuba and dated 23 January 1941, CZA/J17/6734.
87. Ben-Ze'ev letter to Avraham Arnon, head of the General Stream of Education, 3 June 1943, CZA/J17/322.
88. According to Moshe Sharett, the head of the Political Department of the Jewish Agency, the *Arabic Palcor* was 'a daily bulletin [in Arabic] published by the Political Department ... and aiming to highlight our strength and successes in the country', and *Agence D'Orient* was 'a similar instrument operating from Egypt ... and striving to emphasise our growing strength in Eretz Yisrael'. Mentioned in Sharett's lecture entitled 'An Introduction to the Arab Question', 6 May 1940, CZA/S25/22201.
89. An explanation is given in a document entitled 'Summary of the Political Department Activities in the Field of Arabic', 6 June 1945, CZA/S25/22170.
90. See 'Odeda Ya'ari, *Contour Lines: The Story of Deni Agmon, the Commander of the Mista'aravim Unit* (Tel Aviv: Beit ha-Palmach, 2006) (Hebrew).
91. Gil Eyal, 'Between East and West: The Discourse on the "Arab Village" in Israel', *Theory and Criticism*, 3 (Winter 1993), p. 49 (Hebrew).
92. Mendel, 'Re-Arabising the De-Arabised, pp. 94–116.
93. In 'Proceedings: Arabic Teaching in the Jewish School System', 13 July 1944, CZA/J17/6734.
94. 'The Proceedings of the Summit of Arabic Teachers of the Jewish Agency', 14–15 August 1945, ISA/GL-18945/10.
95. Memorandum entitled, 'Teaching Arabic in the Jewish National Council's Institutions in 1945–1946', signed by Ben-Ze'ev, CZA/J1/5853.
96. Goitein was a member of the 'Professional Advising Committee' for the 'Courses for Jewish *Mukhtars*'. One recorded meeting of the committee took place on 17 June 1944, see the letter sent by Eliyahu Sasson, the head of the Arab Bureau, to his deputy, Miriam Glickson, 12 November 1944, CZA/S25/22167.
97. S. D. Goitein, 'On the Teaching of Arabic – 1946', in Landau (ed.), *Teaching Arabic as a Foreign Language*, p. 13.
98. Ben-Ze'ev letter to Arnon, 21 December 1942, CZA/J17/322.
99. The memorandum, signed by Yitzḥak Shamoush, 30 September 1942, CZA/S25/22165.

100. Quoted in Israel Ministry of Education, *The Book of Education and Culture: Annual Report 1951* (Jerusalem: Israel Ministry of Education, 1951), p. 100 (Hebrew).
101. Sarah Ozacky-Lazar and Mustafa Kabaha, 'The Haganah by Arab and Palestinian Historiography and Media', *Israel Studies*, 7 (3) (2002), p. 49.
102. 'Proceedings of the Committee', 19 June 1944, CZA/S25/22167.
103. 'Proceedings of the Meeting', 13 July 1944, CZA/J17/6734.
104. Ibid., 21 August 1944, CZA/S25/3020.
105. Ibid., 26 November 1945, CZA/J17/5853.
106. Ibid.
107. Correspondence between Gymnasia High School and the Political Department, September and October 1947, CZA/S25/3020.

2 Whose Language is it, Anyway? Arabic in Jewish-Israeli Schools, 1948–67

1. Quoted in Uri Ben-Eliezer, 'A Nation in Uniform and War: Israel's First Years', *Zmanim*, 49 (1994), p. 57 (Hebrew).
2. This number does not include the internal refugees who became citizens of Israel, yet were displaces of their villages, towns and cities during 1947–49.
3. Avi Shlaim, *The Iron wall: Israel and the Arab World* (London: Allen Lane, 2000), 54.
4. Benny Morris, 'Revisiting the Palestinian Exodus of 1948', in Eugene L. Rogan and Avi Shlaim (eds), *The War for Palestine: Rewriting the History of 1948* (Cambridge: Cambridge University Press, 2007), p. 40.
5. Quoted in Kimmerling, *Immigrants, Settlers, Natives*, p. 141.
6. Ilan Saban, 'Deeply Divided Societies: A Framework for Analysis and the Case of the Arab-Palestinian Minority in Israel', *New York University Journal of International Law and Politics*, 36 (2004), p. 925; see also Ilan Saban and Muhammad Amara, 'The Status of Arabic in Israel: Reflections on the Power of Law to Produce Social Change', *Israel Law Review*, 36 (2) (2002), pp. 5–39.
7. In Robert Cooper, *Language Planning and Social Change* (Cambridge: Cambridge University Press, 1989), p. 100.
8. Saban, 'Deeply Divided Societies', pp. 926–8.
9. Alexander Yakobson, 'A National Minority in a Democratic Nation-State', in Elie Rekhess and Sarah Ozacky-Lazar (eds), *The Arabs in Israel: The Status of the Arab Minority in the Jewish Nation-State* (Tel Aviv: Dayan Center, 2005), p. 21 (Hebrew); see also Alexander Yakobson and Amnon Rubinstein, *Israel and the Family of Nations: The Jewish Nation-State and Human Rights* (Milton Park: Routledge, 2008), pp. 150–1.
10. Muḥammad Amara and ʿAbd al-Raḥman Marʿi, *The Policy of Language Education towards the Arab Citizens in Israel* (Beit Berl: Markaz Dirāsāt al-Adab al-ʿArabī, 2004), p. 30 (Arabic).
11. Saban and Amara, 'The Status of Arabic in Israel', p. 18.
12. Ibid., p. 19 (my emphasis).
13. Saban, 'Deeply Divided Societies', p. 929.
14. See Meital Pinto, 'On the Intrinsic Value of Arabic in Israel: Challenging Kymlicka on Language Rights', *Canadian Journal of Law and Jurisprudence*,

20 (2007), pp. 143–72; Spolsky and Shohamy, *The Languages of Israel*, p. 118; and Uhlmann, 'The Field of Arabic Instruction'.

15. See, for example, Aviad Bakshi, 'Is Arabic an Official Language of Israel?', Institute for Zionist Strategies, November 2011, available at: http://izsvideo.org/papers/bakshi2011.pdf (accessed 15 December 2013) (Hebrew).
16. See, for example, Ilan Saban 'A Lost Bilingual Voice in the Dark?', *'Iyunei Mishpaṭ: Tel Aviv University Law Review*, 27 (1) (2003), pp. 109–38 (Hebrew); Pinto, 'On the Intrinsic Value of Arabic in Israel'.
17. See, for example, Ro'i Nahmias, 'Arabic at the Airport?', *Ynetnews – Yediʿot Aḥaronot Website*, 28 May 2005, available at: http://www.ynetnews.com/articles/0,7340,L-3091528,00.html (accessed 26 September 2013).
18. The word *Nakba* here refers to the uprooting and displacement of Palestinians in the years 1947–49.
19. For an example of the ongoing centrality of this view in Israel, see the article, 'Former IDF Chief Says Israeli Arabs Remain fifth Column', *Israel Today*, 23 November 2008, available at: http://www.israeltoday.co.il/NewsItem/tabid/178/nid/17600/Default.aspx (accessed 15 December 2013).
20. Shlomo Morag, 'Teaching Arabic: In Light of Reality – 1948', in Landau (ed.), *Teaching Arabic as a Foreign Language*, p. 50.
21. Emmanuel Kolewitz, 'Teaching the Language through the Study of Documents', *Journal for the Teachers of Arabic and Islamic History*, 14 (April 1991), p. 18 (Hebrew).
22. Ibid.
23. Ibid.
24. Ben-Ze'ev letter to Dr Ben-Yehuda, General Director of the Ministry of Education, 4 September 1949, CZA/J17/7827 (my emphasis).
25. Ben-Ze'ev letter to Ben-Yehuda, 15 March 1950, CZA/J17/7956 (my emphasis).
26. For further reading on Bourdieu's work on cultural reproduction and the way in which his writing influenced the 'new sociology of education', see Pierre Bourdieu and Jean-Claude Passeron, *Reproduction in Education, Society and Culture* (London: Sage Publications, 1990); Kathleen Bennett de Marrais and Margaret D. LeCompte, *The Way Schools Work: A Sociological Analysis of Education* (New York: Addison Wesley Longman, 1998), pp. 17–30; Michael Dale, 'Stalking a Conceptual Chameleon: Ideology in Marxist Studies of Education', *Educational Theory*, 36 (3) (1986), pp. 241–57; and Henry Giroux, 'Theories of Reproduction and Resistance in the New Sociology of Education: A Critical Analysis', *Harvard Educational Review*, 53 (3) (1983), pp. 257–93.
27. Quoted in Eliyahu Bourak, 'Report on the Teaching of Arabic', (1947), in Yunai (ed.), *Arabic in Hebrew Schools*, p. 65 (Hebrew).
28. Ibid.
29. Mendel, 'Re-Arabising the De-Arabised', p. 94.
30. Eyal, *The Disenchantment of the Orient*, p. 71.
31. Mendel, 'Re-Arabising the De-Arabised', p. 67.
32. The difference between 'liberation' and 'independence' is in the original. Both refer to the 1948 War; see Israel Ben-Ze'ev, 'About Teaching Arabic in High Schools – 1948', in Landau (ed.), *Teaching Arabic as a Foreign Language*, pp. 52–3.
33. Many researchers have stressed the lack of motivation of Jewish-Israeli pupils to study Arabic. See, for example, Spolsky and Shohamy, *The Languages of Israel*, pp. 139–40; Ḥezi Brosh, 'The Influence of Language Status on

Language Acquisition: Arabic in the Israeli Setting,' *Foreign Language Annals*, 26 (3) (1993), pp. 347–58; Roberta Kraemer, 'Social Psychological Factors Related to the Study of Arabic among Israeli High School Students: A Test of Gardner's Socioeducational Model', *Studies in Second Language Acquisition*, 15 (1) (1993), pp. 83–106.

34. Ziv, letter to Professor Rieger, 23 December 1953, ISA/GL-18945/10 (my emphasis).
35. Ziv letter to Rieger, undated, in ibid.
36. Ben-Ze᾽ev's letter to Shoḥat, 4 September 1956, ISAGL-1305/1.
37. Y. Ophir, 'The Youth in Israel Do Not Want to Study Arabic', *Ḥerut*, 25 April 1957 (Hebrew), found in ISA/GL-1846/11.
38. From an internal letter sent by Yisrael Ben-Ze᾽ev to the Pedagogic Secretariat, undated, in Yunai (ed.), *Arabic in Hebrew Schools*, p. 77.
39. Thomas Albert Sebeok, *Current Trends in Linguistics: Linguistics in South-West Asia and North Africa* (Paris: Mouton, 1970), p. 738.
40. See, for example, Ben-Ze᾽ev's letter to the Deputy Director of the Ministry of Education, in which he complains that the Ministry does not seem to embrace the idea of teaching Arabic on a national level15 May 1959, ISA/GL-1846/11.
41. Ben-Ze᾽ev's letter to Gavri᾽eli, 4 December 1960, ISA/GL-1846/11.
42. See, for example, Israel's current prime minister Benjamin Netanyahu's use of this term, which proves its centrality to Israeli discourse; Peter Beaumont, 'Netanyahu Turns to Nazi Language,' *The Guardian*, 10 July 2009, available at: http://www.guardian.co.uk/commentisfree/2009/jul/10/netanyahu-nazi-language-settlements (accessed 4 June 2014).
43. Ben-Ze᾽ev letter to Abba Eban, 28 June 1961, ISA/GL-1846/11.
44. Spolsky and Shohamy, *The Languages of Israel*, p. 142.
45. Ori Stendel letter to Reḥav῾am ῾Amir, 10 October 1963, ISA/GL-13927/19.
46. Ibid.
47. Ibid.
48. Arabic Teachers Committee letter, 13 February1964, ISA/GL-4780/19.
49. Avraham Lavi letter to Dr Ḥanokh Rinot, 24 May 1964, ISA/K-484/24.
50. Ibid. Lavi did attach a letter sent to him personally by Lt Col. Avraham Sharoni, titled 'Not to be Published', 4 May 1964. The letter can be seen in Appendix 3.
51. These joint recommendations were mentioned by the Minister of Education in a speech tot the Knesset in 1967. He was referring then to the previous committees' recommendation to strengthen Arabic studies in schools. See Minister Zalman Aran's speech to the Knesset, 13 November 1967, ISA/GL-13172/11.
52. In Gen. Aharon Yariv letter to the Director of the Ministry of Education, Prime Minister's Office and Manpower Directorate of the IDF, 26 April 1964, ISA/GL-4780/19.
53. The 'part-time' issue is mentioned in the Israeli Arabic Teachers' Union's letter of complaint to the Knesset Education Committee, 17 June 1964, ISA/K-484/24.
54. The Israeli Arabic Teachers' Union's letter to all MKs, 17 June 1964, ISA/K-484/24.
55. 'Proceedings of the Knesset Education Committee', 24 June 1964, ibid.

56. Ibid.
57. 'Conclusions' in 'Proceedings of the Knesset Education Committee, 24 June 1964, ibid.
58. Lavi letter to Rinot, 7 December 1964, ISA/GL-4768/16.
59. See Shoḥat letter to Rinot, in which he summarised the Ministry of Education's efforts in the field of Arabic, 20 April 1965, ibid.
60. Ibid.
61. Shoḥat letter to Supervisor Eyal, 17 October 1965, ISA/GL-1013/15.
62. Rinot letter to Shoḥat, 14 November 1965, ISA/GL-4780/19.
63. Lt Col. Ostrovsky letter to Shoḥat, 28 January 1966, ibid.
64. Lt Col. Ostrovsky letter to Shoḥat, 15 May 1966, ibid.
65. Ya'acov Eyal invitation letter to Lt Col. Sharoni, 18 April 1966, ISA/GL-1013/15.
66. Ibid.
67. Quoted in Moshe 'Azuz, 'The Training Unit of the Israeli Military Intelligence's SIGINT Unit: The First Days', *We Will Do and We Will Listen*, Journal for the Veterans of Israeli Central Collection Unit of the Intelligence Corps, 10 (June 2000), p. 10 (Hebrew).
68. The summary of the meeting is found in Lt Col. Sharoni letter to. Rinot, 6 January 1967, ISA/GL-13172/11.
69. Ibid.
70. Ibid.
71. Information taken from Supervisor Eyal letter to the Director of the Ministry of Education, 28 February 1967, ISA/GL-13133/5.
72. The Committee's Minutes, 28 February 1967, ibid. In 1967, 65,000 Israeli pounds (lira) were roughly equivalent to 463,000 New Israeli Shekels (NIS) or about GBP85,000 at current rates.
73. For further reading, see Yonatan Mendel, 'A Sentiment-Free Arabic: On the Creation of the Israeli Accelerated Arabic Language Studies Programme', *Middle Eastern Studies*, 49 (3) (2013), pp. 383–401.
74. Palmon's letter, 23 February 1950, Israel Defense Forces and Defense Establishment Archives, Tel ha-Shomer (IDFA), 854/52/1.
75. Gen. Laskov letter, 31 July 1950, ibid.
76. Ibid.
77. Mentioned in a letter sent on behalf of Laskov to the Chief of Intelligence, 25 July 1950, ibid.
78. Col. Gibli letter to Shabak head office, 20 August 1950, ibid.
79. Palmon's programme was attached to Laskov's letter to the head of the Intelligence Department in the IDF, 23 August 1950, ibid.
80. Ministry of Foreign Affair letter to Prime Minister's Office, 12 January 1951, ISA/GL-17111/17.
81. See Uri Brener, *For a Jewish Independent Army: The United Kibbutz Movement in the Haganah 1939–1945* (Ramat Ef'al: Yad Tabenkin – Research and Documentation of the Kibbutz Movement, 1985), p. 213 (Hebrew).
82. Arthur Biram was a Zionist educator and served as head teacher of the Hebrew Reali School in Haifa. His expertise was in Hebrew and Arabic philology. During the 1930s, he arranged for his pupils to be recruited to serve in the Haganah. David Ayalon, who studied at the Hebrew Reali School in Haifa, was a scholar and expert in Islamic studies. Ayalon was a professor at the Institute

of Oriental Studies at the Hebrew University, and before 1948 worked in the Political Department of the Jewish Agency. Post-1948, he worked in the Middle East Department of the Ministry of Foreign Affairs, which dealt with security issues as well as political concerns related to the Middle East. Yehoshu'a Palmon was Israel's first Adviser on Arab Affairs. Previously he served in the Haganah's intelligence service and as the commander of the first Jewish Mista'aravim Unit. Ya'acov Shim'oni was also among the founders of the intelligence service of the Haganah. He later headed the Arab Bureau of the Jewish Agency, the IDF Psychological Warfare Department and the Middle East Department of the Ministry of Foreign Affairs, and also served as the Adviser on Arab affairs for the Israeli Embassy in the USA. 'Ezra Danin was among the founders of the intelligence service of the Haganah. In 1948, he was appointed Adviser on Arab Affairs to the Ministry of Foreign Affairs. Avraham Ya'ari was a bibliographer and one of the most important researchers of the Jewish presence in Palestine. His most notable book is *The Goodly Heritage: Memories Describing the Life of the Jewish Community of Eretz Yisrael from the Seventeenth to the Twentieth Centuries* (Jerusalem: Youth and Hechalutz Department of the Zionist Organization, 1947).

83. Information is taken from the summary of the Oriental Classes project prepared by the Adviser on Arab Affairs, 17 September 1958, ISA/GL-13912/5. See also Uri Dromi, 'The End of the Kister Era', *Ha'aretz*, 27 August 2010 (Hebrew).
84. The words 'village' and 'surrounding' were both given in single form. This may indicate the one-dimensional way in which the Israeli establishment perceived the Palestinian population of Israel and their villages, towns and cities. In Laskov letter titled, 'Assistance of the IDF to the Oriental Class', 8 May 1956, IDFA/1960/86-18.
85. Gibli letter to the Northern Command, 3 June 1956, ibid.
86. Emmanuel Marx letter to Col. Shaḥam, 24 August 1956, IDFA/1960/86-18.
87. Marx's summary, 15 August 1956, ibid.
88. Ibid.
89. Walter Eitan letter to General Director of Ministry of Education, September 1956, ibid.
90. Ibid.
91. Ibid.
92. Shmu'el Divon letter to the Director of the Ministry of Education, 2 September 1956, ibid.
93. Ibid. The reference to a distinct 'Arab mentality' demonstrates the project's inter-ministerial nature, as well as its rather Orientalist attitude. See, for example, Said's critique of Harold W. Glidden, 'The Arab World', *American Journal of Psychiatry*, 128 (8) (1972), pp. 984–8. In the article, Glidden attempted to explain the behaviour of 'the Arabs' through an analysis of the 'Arab mentality and way of life'. Said, *Orientalism*, pp. 48–9.
94. Divon letter to the Director of the Ministry of Education, 2 September 1956, IDFA/1960/86-18.
95. Ibid.
96. Ibid.
97. Divon letter to Col. Harkabi, 28 December 1956, IDFA/2004/1308-192.
98. Ibid. The letter is reproduced in Appendix 4.

99. During 1956, the Gymnasia School in Jerusalem also established an Oriental Class.
100. Divon letter to Harkabi, 28 December 1956, IDFA/2004/1308-192.
101. This will be made clear later on in the book, when it will be shown how officials in charge of Arabic studies from the realms of education, politics and security expressed concerns about the increasing number of women studying Arabic compared with the decreasing number of men.
102. Marx letter to the Military Governor of the Northern Command, 14 April 1957, IDFA/1966/263-1070 (my emphasis).
103. Mentioned in K. Kadish letter, IDF Department for Civilian Affairs, to the Military Governor of the Northern Command, 30 May 1957, IDFA/1960/86-18.
104. Avraham Yinon, 'Summary of the Colloquial Arabic Course', 15 July–3 August 1957, ibid.
105. Ibid.
106. Ibid.
107. Ibid.
108. Ibid. By 'Arab problem' (lit. *ha-be'ayah ha-'Aravit*), Yinon meant the place of Palestinian citizens in Israel and their relationship with the state. This term was also prominent in pre-state Zionist jargon in the context of political challenges that the Zionist movement had to face in dealing with the Palestinian population. See, for example, Jacob Shavit, *Jabotinsky and the Revisionist Movement, 1925–1948* (New York: Routledge, 1988), pp. 244–71. The ongoing use of the term 'problem' during the pre-state period as well as in the period following the establishment of the state, and especially in relation to *citizens* of the same state is very telling as it indicates the unchanging attitude of the Zionist and Israeli bodies to the local Arab-Palestinians, defining them and speaking about them as a 'problem' rather than as equal rights citizens.
109. Letter from the Military Adjutant to the Adviser on Arab Affairs, 30 January 1958, IDFA/2004/1308-204.
110. See, for example, Stendel letter to the Oriental Classes, in 1964, in which he asked for the names and evaluations of the pupils needed for the IDF, 'as we ask every year', 15 March 1964, ISA/GL-13927/19.
111. The Adviser on Arab Affairs letter to Lt Col. Halperin, 22 May 1958, IDFA/2004/1308-204. The letter is marked: 'To be sent to Military Intelligence only.'
112. This can further explain the fact that teachers of Arabic in Jewish-Israeli schools had a Jewish, Zionist and security orientation. Palestinian teachers would have probably found it much harder to cooperate with the militaristic orientation of Arabic studies, let alone with sending evaluations for use by Military Intelligence.
113. Stendel letter to Sharoni, 8 September 1963, ISA/GL-13927/19. The letter is reproduced in Appendix 5.
114. Marx letter to the Oriental Classes, 3 November 1958, ISA/GL-13912/5.
115. Letter sent to Maj. Ṭal from the office of the Adviser on Arab Affairs, 8 November 1961, ISA, GL-17041/19.
116. Intelligence-5 letter to the IDF Adjutant, 18 June 1958, IDFA/2004/1308-204. For further reading on Intelligence-5, see Amos Gilboa and Ephraim Lapid,

Masterpiece: An Inside Look at Sixty Years of Israeli Intelligence (Tel Aviv: Yedi'ot Aḥaronoth, 2008), p. 36 (Hebrew).

117. See, for example, the letter sent from the office of the Chief of Intelligence to the Military Government, in which the former asked that units in the Military Intelligence send soldiers who graduated from Oriental Classes to the annual gathering: letter, 14 September 1958, IDFA/1960/86-18.
118. The summary of the meeting was sent from the Chief of Intelligence to the Military Intelligence Department of Planning, 13 October 1958, IDFA/2004/1308-204.
119. Ibid.
120. For example, in the 1960 gathering, which took place at the IDF headquarters in Tel Aviv, the Chief of Intelligence, many senior officers of the Military Intelligence and all the teachers of the Oriental Classes were invited. The Chief of Intelligence attended the gathering. This meeting included a lecture by Divon, the head of the Middle East Department at the Ministry of Foreign Affairs, entitled 'Contemporary Events in the Middle East': Information mentioned in an invitation sent by the Prime Minister's Office to all Arabic teachers in the Oriental Classes, 8 December 1960, ISA/GL-17041/19.
121. According to Israeli law, all Jewish-Israeli men, unless granted an exemption, must serve for a period of one month every year in the IDF Reserve Forces until the age of 45.
122. Letter from the office of the Chief of Intelligence to the office of the Adviser on Arab Affairs, 4 June 1958, IDFA/2004/1308-204.
123. Divon letter to Lt Col. Ḥefets, 20 March 1960, ISA/GL-13919/10.
124. For further reading about militaristic values and Jewish-Israeli schools, see Haggith Gor, *The Militarization of Education* (Tel Aviv: Babel Publishers, 2005) (Hebrew); ibid., 'Education for War in Israel: Preparing Children to Accept War as a Natural Factor of Life', in Kenneth J. Saltman and David A. Gabbard (eds), *Education as Enforcement: The Militarization and Corporatization of Schools* (New York: Routledge, 2010), pp. 209–17; and Henriette Dahan-Kalev, 'Officers as Educators: The Ex-Military in the Israeli School System', *Israel Affairs*, 12 (2) (2006), pp. 268–83.
125. Mentioned in Marx letter to Ziv, 18 August 1958, ISA/GL-13912/5. These schools included two in Haifa, the Hebrew Reali School and Beit Ḥinukh; two in Tel Aviv, 'Ironi Alef and 'Ironi Dalet; and two in Jerusalem, the Hebrew Gymnasia and Beit ha-Kerem School. Further information about the schools participating in the Oriental Classes is found in, 'Summary of the Oriental Classes Project', developed by the Adviser on Arab Affairs, 17 September 1958, ibid.
126. Letter from the office of the Adviser on Arab Affairs to all pupils participating in the 'Triangle' visit, 23 June 1958, ibid.
127. These were some of the points of agreements between the Military Government and Marx. Mentioned in a letter sent by the Military Government's Northern Command, 26 June 1958, IDFA/1960/86-18.
128. Mentioned in a letter sent by the Military Government's Northern Command to the Operations Department of the Military Government, 10 July 1958, ISA/GL-13912/5.
129. Gayatri Chakkravorty Spivak, 'Can the Subaltern Speak?', in Bill Ashcroft et al. (eds), *The Postcolonial Studies Reader* (New York: Routledge, 1995), pp. 24–8.

130. Mentioned in a letter sent by the Military Government's Northern Command to the Operations Department of the Military Government, 10 July 1958, ISA/GL-13912/5.
131. Ibid.
132. The teachers' summary sent to Me'ir Kister, 1 August 1958, ISA/GL-13912/5.
133. Ibid.
134. See Mustafa Kabha and Dan Caspi, 'From Holy Jerusalem to the Spring', *Panim: A Quarterly of Culture, Society and Education* 16 (March 2001), pp. 44–55, available at: http://www.itu.org.il/Index.asp?ArticleID=1205&CategoryID=502&Page=1 (accessed 4 June 2014) (Hebrew); Mustafa Kabha, 'Arabic Journalism in Israel as a Tool for the Creation of a New Identity 1948–2006', *The Sectorial Media in Israel*, 5 (Tel Aviv: Chaim Herzog Institute for Media Politics and Society, Tel Aviv University, December 2006), pp. 6–37 (Hebrew).
135. See, for example, Ilana Kaufman, *Arab National Communism in the Jewish State* (Gainesville, FL: University Press of Florida, 1997), pp. 54–6; Amal Jamal, *The Arab Public Sphere in Israel* (Bloomington, IN: Indiana University Press, 2009), pp. 48–9.
136. Jamal, *The Arab Public Sphere in Israel*, p. 53.
137. Mentioned in a letter from Na'im Sofer, the office of the Adviser on Arab Affairs, to the Ministry of Defence's Department of Construction and Housing, 15 May 1960, IDFA/2009/22/27.
138. The Hasbara programme is mentioned in a letter sent by Me'ir Jarraḥ from the Hasbara Department to Dr Melkman, head of the Hasbara Department, 4 July 1960, ibid.
139. Barukh Mazor, 'Summary of the Oriental Classes' Experience in the Arab Area – 1960', in Landau (ed.), *Teaching Arabic as a Foreign Language*, p. 69.
140. Ibid.
141. Ibid.
142. Gil Eyal has shown how the concept of the *ḥamūla* and its importance in Arab-Palestinian communities not only reflected an Orientalist orientation regarding the Arab 'other' and an attitude of superiority, but was also, to a certain extent, an outcome of Israeli policies. For example, the Military Government encouraged division by *ḥamūla*s as a strategy for divide and rule. This was later reflected in Israeli academic research about the 'distinctiveness' of the *ḥamūla*. See Eyal, 'Between East and West', pp. 41–3.
143. Also see Appendix 6.
144. Dani Rabinowitz, 'Oriental Nostalgia: The Transformation of the Palestinians into "Israeli Arabs"', *Theory and Criticism*, 4 (Autumn 1993), pp. 141–51 (Hebrew); Elie Podeh, *The Arab–Israeli Conflict in Israeli History Textbooks, 1948–2000* (Westport, CT: Greenwood Press, 2002), p. 48.
145. Mansour's article in *Ha'aretz*, date unspecified, found in, ISA/GL-13919/10.
146. Ibid.
147. Ibid.
148. Eyal, *The Disenchantment of the Orient*, p. 4. In discussing Mizraḥanut, Eyal is referring to Orientalism, which in this context means the Israeli field of Oriental studies.
149. Mentioned in Stendel letter to Financial Department of the Ministry of Defence, 10 June 1963, IDFA/2009/22/27.

150. Supervisor Eyal letters to Ziv and to the Adviser on Arab Affairs, 1 March 1963, ISA/GL-1013/15. See also ISA/GL-13927/19.
151. Stendel letter to Gen. ʿAmit, 29 October 1963, ISA/GL-13927/19.
152. The letter, 24 December 1963, ISA/GL-1013/15.
153. For further reading on Unit-515, see Gilboa and Lapid *Masterpiece*, p. 64.
154. Ibid.
155. The study of French in Israeli schools was strongly encouraged as a result of the Cultural Agreement between Israel and France in 1959. See Susan Hattis Rolef, *Political Dictionary of the State of Israel* (New York: Macmillan, 1987), p. 117.
156. Rehavʿam ʿAmir, the Adviser on Arab Affairs, could not participate in the meeting. See his letter of apology, 10 January 64, ISA/GL-13927/19.
157. 'Proceedings of the Meeting' (handwritten), signed by representative of the Ministry of Education, entitled 'The Oriental Classes', 7 January 63, ibid.
158. Ibid.
159. Ibid.
160. Ibid.
161. Ibid.
162. This probably meant that the whole programme (11th and 12th grades) included about 200 pupils. This figure (115 pupils) is mentioned in the response of Aharon Yadlin, Deputy Minister of Education, to Parliamentary Question 2535, Knesset, 16 May 1967, ISA/GL-13172/11.
163. Interview with Professor Re'uven Snir, conducted by the author, University of Haifa, 23 June 2008.
164. Eyal, *The Disenchantment of the Orient*, p. 283.
165. Interview with Professor Aryeh Levin, conducted by the author, Hebrew University of Jerusalem, 20 April 2009.
166. Ibid.

3 Recruiting Arabic for War: The Influence of the 1967 and 1973 Wars on Arabic Studies in Jewish-Israeli Schools

1. My translation. The quotation is taken from the critical political play *Shits* written by Israeli playwright Ḥanoch Levin in 1975, two years after the Yom Kippur War.
2. See, for example, Tom Segev, *1967: Israel, the War, and the Year that Transformed the Middle East* (New York: Picador, 2008); Avi Shlaim and William Roger, *The 1967 Arab–Israeli War: Origins and Consequences* (Cambridge: Cambridge University Press, 2012); Michael B. Oren, *Six Days of War: June 1967 and the Making of the Modern Middle East* (Oxford: Oxford University Press, 2002); Samir A. Mutawi, *Jordan in the 1967 War* (Cambridge: Cambridge University Press, 1987).
3. Ministry of Education, press release, 29 June 1967, ISA/GL-13172/11.
4. For further information about the financial aspects of the Israeli occupation, see Yusif A. Sayigh, 'Dispossession and Pauperisation: The Palestinian Economy under Occupation', in George Abed (ed.), *The Palestinian Economy: Studies in Development under Prolonged Occupation* (New York and London: Routledge, 1988), pp. 259–86; Tobias Kelly, *Law, Violence and Sovereignty among West Bank Palestinians* (Cambridge: Cambridge University Press, 2006), pp. 56–7.

5. Quoted in Shiri Lev-Ari, 'Know the Neighbour', *Ha'aretz*, 26 February 2003 (Hebrew).
6. Quoted in 'Push to Learn Hebrew and Arabic Delights Bi-Lingual Teacher', *The Jerusalem Post*, 17 May 1968.
7. Avi Raz showed how post-1967 Israel had the opportunity to reach peace with its Arab neighbours through land swaps. According to his findings, though, Israeli diplomacy was ineffective and in the final calculation, the Israeli leadership preferred land over peace. See Avi Raz, *The Bride and the Dowry: Israel, Jordan, and the Palestinians in the Aftermath of the June 1967 War* (New Haven, CT, and London: Yale University Press, 2012).
8. Parliamentary Question 2913, Knesset, 28 July 1967, ISA/GL-13133/5.
9. Shraga 'Adiel, letter to all head teachers of Jewish-Israeli schools, 31 July 1967, ISA/GL-13133/5.
10. Mentioned in 'Special Report on Arabic Studies', Ministry of Education, 13 October 1967, ibid.
11. Mentioned in Dr Dan Ronen, Minister's Assistant, letter to Shoḥat, Deputy Director of the Ministry of Education, 6 September 1967, ISA/GL-13172/11.
12. Special Announcement, Director of Ministry of Education, 21 September 1967, ibid.
13. Yonatan Mendel, 'Diary: How to Become an Israeli Journalist?', *London Review of Books*, 30 (5) (2008), p. 31.
14. Shoḥat letter to Minister of Education, 22 September 1967, ISA/GL-13172/11.
15. Ibid.
16. 'Special Announcement' (lit. 'Ḥozer Mankal Meyuḥad'), dated 9 October 1967, quoted in Yunai (ed.), *Arabic in Hebrew Schools*, p. 85–7. The announcement was composed by the General Director of the Ministry of Education and was widely disseminated in the different departments of the Ministry of Education.
17. Parliamentary Question 2492, Knesset, 13 November 1967, ISA/GL-13172/11.
18. Mentioned in a letter sent from Eliyahou Mansour, Supervisor of Arabic Studies in primary and intermediate schools, to the Pedagogical Secretariat, 20 March 1969, ISA/GL-13133/5.
19. Mentioned in a letter from Ya'acov Eyal to Ya'acov Sarid, 16 July 1968 (the meeting was held on 15 July 1968), ISA/GL-13172/11.
20. Ibid.
21. As a reminder, at a meeting held on 6 January 1967, Sarid, the then Vice Director of the Ministry of Education, and Gen. Aharon Yariv, the Chief of Intelligence, decided that it 'is not necessary to demand that Arabic be made obligatory in all high schools, and instead a joint effort of the Ministry of Education and the IDF will be made to focus on a few chosen high schools that will agree to teach the language', in ISA/GL-13172/11.
22. Shraga 'Adiel's article in *La-Merḥav*, 11 June 1969, ISA/GL-13133/10.
23. Mentioned in ibid.
24. Mentioned in Mansour's report for the Committee of the Ministry of Education, 25 November 1969, ISA/GL-13133/10.
25. Mentioned in 'Proceedings of the Committee of Arabic Teachers in Hebrew Schools', 25 October 1970, ibid.
26. Yariv letter to Director of Ministry of Education, 24 April 1972, ISA/GL-13173/1.
27. This document was found in the 1980 Israeli State Comptroller Report,No. 31 about the history of Arabic Studies in Jewish-Israeli schools, ISA/GL-17918/3.

28. Ibid.
29. Maj. Aharon Hadar letter to Shoḥat, 4 March 1973, ISA/GL-13133/7.
30. Ben-Eliezer, *The Making of Israeli Militarism*, p. 224.
31. See, for example, Horowitz Dan and Moshe Lissak, *Trouble in Utopia: The Overburdened Polity of Israel* (Albany, NY: State University of New York Press, 1989), p. 225; Gad Barzilai, *Wars, Internal Conflicts, and Political Order: A Jewish Democracy in the Middle East* (New York: State University of New York Press, 1996), p. 223; A. R. Luckham, 'A Comparative Typology of Civil–Military Relations', *Government and Opposition*, 6 (1) (1971), pp. 24–5; Yoram Peri, *Generals in the Cabinet Room: How the Military Shapes Israeli Policy* (Washington, DC: US Institute of Peace Press, 2006); Amir Bar-Or, 'The Making of Israel's Political-Security Culture', in Gabriel Sheffer and Oren Barak (eds), *Militarism and Israeli Society* (Bloomington, IN: Indiana University Press, 2010), pp. 259–79.
32. The evaluation of 'low probability' may have haunted the commanders of the Israeli Military Intelligence during the subsequent 18 days of battles, and most likely did so throughout the rest of their lives. For further reading on this specifically and the 1973 War generally, see Ronen Bergman and Gil Meltser, *The Yom Kippur War: A Moment of Truth* (Tel Aviv: Miskal, 2003), p. 36 (Hebrew); Walter Boyne, *The Two O'Clock War: The 1973 Yom Kippur Conflict and the Airlift that Saved Israel* (New York: Thomas Dunne Books, 2002); Simon Dunstan, *The Yom Kippur War: The Arab–Israeli War of 1973* (Oxford: Osprey Publishing, 2007); Chaim Herzog, *The War of Atonement: The Inside Story of the Yom Kippur War* (London: Greenhill Books, 2003); and Shlomo Nakdimon, *A Low Probability for War: The Background and Consequences of the Yom Kippur War* (Jerusalem: Revivim, 1982) (Hebrew).
33. See, for example, Oded Granot, 'Intelligence Corps', in *IDF and its Corps: Encyclopedia of Army and Security*, ed. by Ilan Kfir, Ya'akov Erez and Yehouda Schiff (ed.-in-chief) (Tel Aviv: Revivim, 1981), p. 143 (Hebrew); 'The Intelligence Corps of the IDF was Established: Its Chief is Dov Tamari' *Davar*, 15 November 1976, p. 2; and 'The Agranat Commission', The Knesset Online Lexicon, available at: http://main.knesset.gov.il/About/Lexicon/Pages/agranat.aspx (accessed 14 November 2012) (Hebrew).
34. Algom's testimony before the Agranat Commission, 4 December 1973, Ministry of Defence Online Archive, available at: http://www.archives.mod.gov.il/Pages/Exhibitions/Agranat2/YairAlgom/mywebalbum/index.html (accessed: 16 December 2012).
35. Prior to his position at the Ministry of Foreign Affairs, Divon was the Adviser on Arab Affairs at the Prime Minister's Office.
36. Divon's testimony before the Agranat Commission, 5 December1973, Ministry of Defence Online Archive, available at: http://www.archives.mod.gov.il/Pages/Exhibitions/Agranat2/ShmuelDibon/mywebalbum/index.html (accessed: 16 December 2012).
37. See, for example, a letter from Yeḥezkel Shemesh to Binyamin Gur-Aryeh, both officials at the Office of the Adviser on Arab affairs, in which they refer to Lapid as 'the person appointed by the Chief of Staff to head the activities to encourage Arabic and Oriental studies [in the school system]', 11 February 1977, ISA/G-10391/13.

38. Interview with Brig. Ret. Ephraim Lapid, conducted by the author at the Meir Amit Intelligence and Terrorism Information Center, Ramat Hasharon, 28 June 2008.
39. Ibid.
40. Ilan Naḥam, 'Cultural Mediation: Avraham Sharoni – From Military Intelligence to the Arabic–Hebrew Dictionary', *Pe'amim*, 122–3 (2010), pp. 193–211 (Hebrew). See also, 'Amir Rapaport, 'Eavesdropping Unit 8200: This is How it All Began', *NRG-Ma'ariv*, 14 October 2008, available at: http://www.nrg.co.il/online/1/ART1/798/764.html (accessed 15 December 2013) (Hebrew).
41. Ibid., pp. 207–8.
42. An interesting personal comment made by Snir is relevant to this phenomenon. When remembering his first Arabic–Hebrew dictionary, which was not the one that Sharoni had written, he mentioned that it was given to him and his fellow classmates by Military Intelligence officers. According to Snir, it was a dictionary written by David Ayalon and Pesaḥ Shen'ar that had the Military Intelligence symbol on it. Snir said: 'I didn't open the dictionary then for reasons opposite to those that make me not open it today,' in Snir, *Arabness, Jewishness, Zionism*, p. 1.
43. Supervisor Eyal letter to Minister of Education, 22 August 1974, ISA/GL-13133/9, (emphasis in original).
44. Supervisor Eyal letter to Minister of Education, 5 November 1974, ibid.
45. Ibid.
46. Ibid.
47. Gazit, Chief of Intelligence, letter to Yadlin, Minister of Education, 3 April 1975, ISA/GL-17918/4.
48. Yaffe letter to Lt Col. Lapid, 13 April 1975, ISA/GL-17938/14.
49. 'The Lapid Report' was attached to the letter sent by the Chief of Intelligence to the Minister of Education, 16 February 1976, ISA/GL-13133/8. Gazit's letter and the first page of the report can be seen in Appendix 7 and Appendix 8.
50. Chief of Intelligence letter to Minister of Education, 16 February 1976, ISA/GL-13133/8.
51. Minister of Education letter to Director of the Ministry, 25 February 1976, ibid.
52. The programme is attached to Maj. 'Atsmon's letter to the Ministry of Education, 30 April 1976, ISA/GL-17938/14.
53. Ibid.
54. 'Atsmon letter to Prime Minister's Office, 2 February 1977, ISA/G-13969/2.
55. The first record that I found of the existence of the Ṭelem Unit is from 27 February 1976. It is a letter sent by the Ministry of Education to 'Atsmon regarding the need to make the Arabic language a compulsory subject at school, ISA/GL-17938/14.
56. A copy of the invitation letter with the joint letterhead is provided in Appendix 9.
57. My emphasis. In 'Atsmon invitation to Prime Minster Office, 2 February 1977, ISA/G-10391/13.
58. Ibid.
59. Supervisor Gargir letter to head of Department of Teachers' Training, 25 April 76, ISA/GL-17918/3.
60. Ibid.

61. Ibid.
62. Quoted in Nuzhat Katsav's bill, titled 'Encouragement of the Study of the Arabic Language Due to its Importance for Security and Peace (1976)', in Yunai (ed.), *Arabic in Hebrew Schools*, pp. 107–8.
63. Ibid. Katsav worked as a presenter with the Arabic Radio of the Israel Broadcasting Authority (IBA). For further details, see Nuzhat Katzav, *Swallows of Peace: With Arab and Druze Women in Israel* (Tel Aviv: Sifriyat Maʿariv, 1998) (Hebrew). A much more political, less naive and more security-oriented analysis of Israeli broadcasts in Arabic can be found in Hillel Cohen and Yu Wang, 'Marketing Israel to the Arabs: The Rise and Fall of the *Al-Anbaa* Newspaper', *Israel Affairs*, 15 (2) (2009), pp. 190–210; Kabha and Caspi, 'From Holy Jerusalem to the Spring'; and Jamal, *The Arab Public Sphere in Israel*, p. 108.
64. Katsav's bill, 'Encouragement of the Study of the Arabic Language', in Yunai (ed.), *Arabic in Hebrew Schools*, pp. 107–8.
65. Ibid.
66. Mentioned in ibid., pp. 107–8. See also Supervisor Gargir letter to head of the Department of Teachers' Training, 25 April 1976, ISA/GL-17918/3.
67. Ben-Eliezer, 'The Military Society and the Civil Society in Israel', p. 50.
68. Yehouda Shenhav, *The Arab Jews: A Postcolonial Reading of Nationalism, Religion, and Ethnicity* (Stanford, CA: Stanford University Press, 2006), p. 3.
69. The biggest waves of Arab-Jewish immigration to Israel took place in close proximity to the time of the creation of Israel, in the early 1950s, mostly from Iraq, Syria, Yemen and Egypt. However, additional waves, mostly from Morocco, arrived in the early 1960s. In the early 1970s, the Mizraḥi community in Israel constituted the majority of the Jewish population in the country. See Uri Ram, *The Changing Agenda of Israeli Sociology: Theory, Ideology and Identity* (New York: State University of New York Press, 1995), p. 97; and Shlomo Swirsky, *Israel: The Oriental Majority* (London: Zed Press, 1989).
70. See Mendel, 'Re-Arabising the De-Arabised', pp. 94–116.
71. For further information about the Ashkenazi/Mizraḥi social divide in Israel, the demise of Arab-Jewish identity and for a social analysis of Arab-Jews, see Ella Shohat, 'Sephardim in Israel: Zionism from the Standpoint of its Jewish Victims', *Social Text*, 19 (Autumn 1988), pp. 1–35; ibid., 'The Invention of the Mizrahim', *Journal of Palestine Studies*, 29 (1) (1999), pp. 5–20; Sami Shalom Chetrit, 'Mizrahi Politics in Israel: Between Integration and Alternative', *Journal of Palestine Studies*, 29 (4) (2000), pp. 51–65; Snir, '"Ana min al-Yahud"', pp. 387–424; Shenhav, *The Arab Jews: A Postcolonial Reading*; Aziza Khazzoom, 'The Great Chain of Orientalism: Jewish Identity, Stigma Management, and Ethnic Exclusion in Israel', *American Sociological Review*, 68 (4) (2003), pp. 481–510; and Joseph Massad, 'Zionism's Internal Others: Israel and the Oriental Jews', *Journal of Palestine Studies*, 25 (4) (1996), pp. 53–68.
72. Amnon Raz Krakotzkin, 'Exile within Sovereignty: A Critique of the 'Negation of Exile' in Israeli Culture', *Theory and Criticism*, 4 (Autumn 1993), pp. 23–55 (Hebrew).
73. Yasir Suleiman, 'Charting the Nation: Arabic and the Politics of Identity', *Annual Review of Applied Linguistics*, 26 (2006), p. 135.
74. Yehoud Shenhav, *The Arab Jews: Nationalism, Religion, Ethnicity* (Tel Aviv: ʿAm ʿOved, 2003), p. 114. See also Shenhav's fascinating analysis of the subject in

the chapter titled 'How did the Arab Jews become Religious and Zionist?', in ibid., *The Arab Jews: A Postcolonial Reading*, pp. 77–109.

75. Shohat, 'Sephardim in Israel', pp. 1–35.
76. See, for example, Suleiman's critique of Spolsky and Cooper's *The Languages of Jerusalem*, in which the authors treat the Arabic language as part of the group of 'non-Jewish languages'. In Yasir Suleiman, *A War of Words: Language and Conflict in the Middle East* (Cambridge: Cambridge University Press, 2004), pp. 167–73. For comparison, see Bernard Spolsky and Robert Cooper, *The Languages of Jerusalem* (Oxford: Clarendon Press, 1991).
77. Eliachar's article titled, 'Education is Needed to Get to Know our Neighbours', was published on 1 April 1970, in the Sephardic Movement journal, *Ba-Maʿarakhah*. It is quoted in Elie Eliachar, *Living with Palestinians* (Jerusalem: Vaʿad ʿEdat ha-Sephardim bi-Yerushalayyim, 1975), p. 225 (Hebrew).
78. Eliezer Ben-Rafael and Ḥezi Brosh, 'A Sociological Study of Second Language Diffusion: The Obstacles to Arabic Teaching in the Israeli School', *Language Planning and Language Problems*, 15 (1) (1991), pp. 1–24; see also Suleiman, *A War of Words*, p. 157.
79. Henri Tajfel (ed.), *Differentiation between Social Groups: Studies in the Social Psychology of Intergroup Relations* (London: Academic Press, 1978).
80. Kraemer, 'Social Psychological Factors' (PhD thesis), p. 73.
81. Suleiman, *A War of Words*, p. 157.
82. Supervisor Eyal letter to Minister of Education, 5 November 1974, ISA/GL-13133/9.
83. Basoḳ letter to Minister of Education, 25 March 1976, ISA/GL-17918/4.
84. Minutes of the Knesset Education and Culture Committee, Discussion about Arabic Language Studies, 7 November 1976, ISA/K-504/13.
85. Ibid.
86. Interview with Professor Sasson Somekh, conducted by the author, Cambridge, 26 June 2009.

4 Israel's Army of Arabists: 1976 and Beyond

1. My translation. Taken from the song 'Ḥilik Portselina', performed by Habiluyim, an Israeli theatrical rock and polka band. The lyrics and melody are by Yami Visler and Noam Inbar.
2. As mentioned, the first evidence that I came across regarding Ṭelem was from 27 December 1976. It was in a letter that the Ministry of Education sent to ʿAtsmon about the need to make Arabic a compulsory subject, ISA/GL-17938/14. In the years following 1976, evidence of correspondence regarding the unit became much more common.
3. For further information, see Ṭelem's official page on the Military Intelligence website, available at: https://www.aman.idf.il/SIP_STORAGE/files/1/70981.pdf (accessed 14 November 2013).
4. See, for example the 'Lapid Report', which was attached to the letter sent by the Chief of Intelligence to the Minister of Education, 16 February 1976, ISA/GL-13133/8. For further information on the image of English and French studies in Jewish-Israeli society in comparison with Arabic, see Ben-Rafael and Brosh, 'A Sociological Study of Second Language Diffusion';

Eliezer Ben-Rafael, 'A Sociological Paradigm of Bilingualism: English, French, Yiddish and Arabic in Israel', in Hanna Herzog and Eliezer Ben-Rafael (eds), *Language and Communication in Israel* (New Brunswick, NJ: Transaction Publishers, 2001), pp. 289–310.

5. Mentioned in Avner Kligman, *The Israel Prize: 1996* (Jerusalem: Israeli Ministry of Culture, 1996), p. 37 (Hebrew).
6. Yaffe letter to Lapid, 30 November 1976, ISA/GL-17938/14.
7. Piamenta Committee Recommendations, June 1977, ISA/GL-13133/8. For further reading about the committee, see 'The Piamenta Report' (1977), in Yunai (ed.), *Arabic in Hebrew Schools*, pp. 135–7.
8. Ibid.
9. Ibid.
10. Ibid. Compare with Ran Lustigman, 'Teaching Arabic in Hebrew Schools in Israel' (Hagar: Jewish–Arab Education for Equality, 2008), available at: http://www.hajar.org.il/hajar/docs/publication/he-run%20lustigman.doc (accessed 14 November 2012) (Hebrew).
11. See Moshe Piamenta, *Speak Arabic: An Introduction to Eretz Yisraeli Arabic* (Tel Aviv: Ma'ariv, 1968) (Hebrew). The book was reprinted twice, in 1973 and 1975.
12. The book was first published by the Ministry of Defence and Ṭelem, and was only later reprinted by a civilian publishing house (Yedi'ot Aḥronot). This shows the extent to which 'security and peace' are intertwined in Israel. The same situation took place regarding Sharoni's Arabic–Hebrew dictionary. Ḥakim's decision to have the Chief of Intelligence as the author of the foreword, as well as the fact that the textbook was published by an Israeli scholar in a Ministry of Defence's publishing house, serve to demonstrate the central place of Military Intelligence in the field of Arabic studies in Israel.
13. The use of the singular form, 'way of thinking', is in the original.
14. The foreword, written by Gen. Shlomo Gazit, in Avraham Ḥakim, *Colloquial Eretz-Yisraeli Arabic* (Tel Aviv: Ma'arakhot, Israel Ministry of Defence, 1976), p. 1 (Hebrew).
15. See, for example, Eliyahu Agasi, *Colloquial Arabic* (Jerusalem: Arab Publishing House, 1968) (Hebrew); Binyamin Ḥakimi, *Colloquial Arabic for Beginners* (Tel Aviv: Mishlav, 1978) (Hebrew); and Yom-Ṭov Ophir, *Colloquial Arabic* (Jerusalem: Open University of Israel, 1977) (Hebrew).
16. Ḥakim, *Colloquial Eretz-Yisraeli Arabic*, p. 4.
17. Madeleine Korbel Albright and William Woodward, *Madam Secretary: A Memoir* (New York: Miramax Books, 2005), p. 369. One can argue that this quotation corresponds with some key elements of Zionist political history, such as Ben-Gurion's 1939 'We shall fight side by side with the British in our war against Hitler as if there were no White Paper, and we shall fight the White Paper as if there were no war.' In James L. Gelvin, *The Israel–Palestine Conflict: One Hundred Years of War* (Cambridge: Cambridge University Press, 2007), p. 119.
18. See Jonathan Rynhold, 'Peace and Security in the 2006 Israeli Elections', *Israel Affairs*, 13 (2) (2007), pp. 384–400.
19. The symbols of the Haganah and of the IDF can be seen in Appendix 10 and Appendix 11.
20. Suleiman, *A War of Words*, p. 213.
21. Rabinowitz, 'Oriental Nostalgia'.

22. Vardi letter to Minister of Education, 24 November 1977, ISA/GL-17938/14. The meeting was held on 6 November 1977.
23. The summary of the meeting is mentioned in Gargir's letter to the Deputy Director of the Ministry of Education, 27 January 1978. According to the letter, the meeting took place on 22 December 1977, ISA/GL-17918/4.
24. Letter from the Pedagogic Secretariat to the Assistant of the Deputy Director of the Ministry, 21 May 1978, ISA/GL-17918/4.
25. Minister of Defence Ezer Weizman letter to Minister of Education Zevulun Hammer, 22 May 1978, ISA/GL-17938/14 (my emphasis). The letter is reproduced in Appendix 12.
26. Hammer letter to Weizman, 6 June 1978, ISA/GL-17938/14.
27. The minutes of the meeting between Minister Hammer and the Chief of Staff were not found. However, the meeting was referred to in a letter sent from the office of the Minister of Education to the General Director of his Ministry, 18 February 1979, ISA/GL-17918/5.
28. Letter by Ben-Shlomo, 28 January 1979, ISA/GL-17918/5.
29. Letter by Supervisor Gargir, 6 February 1979, ISA/GL-17918/5.
30. My emphasis. See Uhlmann, 'The Field of Arabic Instruction', p. 105. Also see ibid., 'Arabic Instruction in Jewish Schools and in Universities in Israel: Contradictions, Subversion, and the Politics of Pedagogy', *International Journal of Middle East Studies*, 42 (2) (2010), p. 303; and ibid., 'Policy Implications of Arabic Instruction in Israeli Jewish Schools', *Human Organization*, 70 (1) (2001), p. 102.
31. Uhlmann, 'Policy Implications of Arabic Instruction'.
32. 'The State Comptroller's Report – 1980', in Yunai (ed.), *Arabic in Hebrew Schools*, p. 157.
33. In 'Proceedings of the Education Committee of Israeli Knesset', a meeting dedicated to Arabic studies in Jewish-Israeli schools, 7 November 1976, ISA/K-504/13.
34. Letter from Director of the Ministry of Education to Chief of Staff, 30 June 1983, ISA/GL-17918/3.
35. This was mentioned in an interview with Tikva Levy who participated in the first course of Soldier-Teachers. The interview was conducted by the author in Tel Aviv on 30 July 2010.
36. Ibid.
37. Shmu'eli's letter, 7 March 1979, is mentioned in ISA/GL-17938/14. The sum of 25 million Israeli pounds (lira) is equivalent to about GBP2.7 million at the exchange rate in 2013.
38. Information from IDF Commander of Manpower Directorate letter to General Director of the Ministry of Education, titled 'Summary of Personal Meeting', 2 July 1979, ISA/GL-17938/14.
39. Ibid.
40. Marom letter to Ministry of Defence, 24 July 1979, ISA/GL-17918/5.
41. The transfer took much longer than anticipated and the IDF demanded a full accounting of how the money was spent. When the money transfer was delayed, the Ministry of Education suggested receiving it by deducting the same amount from a debt that the Ministry of Education had accumulated with the IDF, however eventually the money was transferred as planned. The same amount was given in 1980–81. For further reading, including long

and detailed correspondence between the two sides, and for annual financial breakdowns, see ISA/GL-17939/1, ISA/GL-17918/3 and ISA/GL-17918/6.

42. Supervisor Gargir letter to Spokesperson of Ministry of Education, 8 August 1979, ISA/GL-17918/5. The 'Arabic Seminars' referenced by Gargir primarily trained Arabic teachers for the Arab sector in Israel, not for Jewish-Israeli schools. It is also worth mentioning that the Palestinian teachers who were approved for work in Jewish-Israeli classes were mostly from the Druze community. As noted, they were a very small minority of Arabic teachers in Jewish-Israeli schools. For further reading, see Alon Fragman, 'The Integration of Arab Native Teachers as Teachers of Arabic in Hebrew-Speaking Schools: Intended Policy or Arbitrary Strategy?', *Annual of Language and Politics of Identity*, 2 (2008), pp. 55–79.
43. Ben-Shlomo letter to the five deans, 2 September 1979, ISA/GL-17918/6.
44. Information taken from Gargir's summary on the discussion about Arabic Studies, held at the office of the Director General of the Ministry of Education, 15 January 1980, ibid.
45. The State Comptroller's report is quoted in a document sent from S. Grinbaum, the head of the Assessment Unit at the Ministry of Education, to the Head of the Pedagogic Secretariat, 19 February 1981, ibid.
46. David Four's letter to M. Gadish from the State Comptroller's Office, 22 January 1981, ISA/GL-17918/3.
47. Information taken from a letter sent by Supervisor Gargir to Y. Cohen, the Spokesperson of the Ministry of Education, 5 August 1981, ibid.
48. Supervisor Gargir letter to head of Pedagogic Secretariat, 31 May 1982, ibid.
49. Minister of Education's response to MK Dov Zakin's Parliamentary Question, 1983, ibid.
50. Ibid.
51. Four letter to General Director of Ministry of Education, 28 August 1983, ISA/GL-17918/3.
52. Ibid.
53. General Director of the Ministry of Education letter to Yaron, 25 December 1983, ibid.
54. This is mentioned in a letter sent from the Head of Office of the Manpower Directorate of the IDF to the General Director of the Ministry of Education, 26 December 1983, ISA/GL-17939/1.
55. Chief of Intelligence Shlomo Gazit letter to Minister of Education, 3 April 1975, ISA/GL-17918/4.
56. I wish to express my gratitude to the authorities at the Israeli State Archives and at the Israel Ministry of Education Archive who permitted the declassification of various files covering the period 1979–2009. This enabled me to conduct more updated research. Research on this time period was also made possible due to the kind help offered by Dr Shlomo Alon, the former General Supervisor of Arabic Studies at the Ministry of Education. He provided me with the minutes of three important discussions that took place in January 1986. My gratitude towards Dr Alon will be mentioned in every instance where the research was based on files he that made accessible to me. The proceedings of these meetings can also be found in the Knesset's records of meetings held by the Education Committee.
57. Yitzḥak Navon was born in 1921 to a Sephardic family and spoke Arabic from an early age. He studied Arabic literature and Islam at the Hebrew

University. During the years 1946–49, he headed the Arab Bureau, the Military Intelligence wing of the Haganah, in Jerusalem. Following the creation of the State of Israel, he served in various political positions including those of the: chief of the Office of Prime Minister Ben-Gurion and Prime Minister Moshe Sharett (1952–63); Director of the Cultural Department in the Ministry of Education (1963–65); head of the General Zionist Council (1972–78); and head of the Defence Committee of the Knesset (1975–77). He was appointed President of the State of Israel in 1978, and served in this position until 1983. In 1984, he returned to the Knesset as the Minister of Education and served in this position until 1990. Today, Navon serves as Honorary President of the Abraham Fund Initiative, an Israeli–American non-governmental organisation that strives to advance coexistence of Jews and Arabs living in Israel.

58. Col. Nissim ʿAtsmon, Military Intelligence, 'Arabic Studies in Hebrew Schools', submitted to the Minister of Education on 3 October 1985, p. 1 (Hebrew). The report was given to me, courtesy of Dr Shlomo Alon, former General Supervisor of Arabic Studies at the Ministry of Education.
59. This also meant that Israeli university students would be expected to reach an agreed level of Arabic as a condition for their acceptance to university. in ibid., p. 2
60. Ibid., p. 3.
61. The study of Colloquial Arabic using Hebrew letters was suggested by the 1976 Piamenta Committee.
62. ʿAtsmon, 'Arabic Studies in Hebrew Schools', 3 October 1985, p. 14.
63. Ibid., p. 15.
64. Col. Noʿam, 'Arabists in the Military Intelligence: It is Now or Never', *Ḥamanit: The Israeli Military Intelligence Journal*, 2 (November 1985), pp. 22–3 (Hebrew). The full name of the author is not given in the original, but it could be Colonel Noʿam Shapira, who will be mentioned later in this chapter.
65. Quoted from MK Abba Eban's Knesset motion titled, 'Arabic Language Studies', presented to the Knesset, 18 December 1985, in Yunai (ed.), *Arabic in Hebrew Schools*, pp. 175–6.
66. One can argue that inviting Yaḥya as a representative of the Israeli 'Arab sector' to speak only highlights the limitations of the debate. Yaḥya can be regarded as a 'hybrid' whose function was to establish the 'purity' of the discussion. The notions of 'purification' and 'hybridity' are taken from the work of Latour. While the hybrid is 'purified' according to his work, here we see a different process of an alleged 'hybridisation' of the purified Jewish-Israeli discourse, which only reassures the purity of the debate. For further reading, see Bruno Latour, *We Have Never Been Modern* (Cambridge, MA: Harvard University Press, 1993); Yehouda Shenhav, 'Nationalism was Never Modern – and Secular: On Purification and Hybridity in the Thought of Bruno Latour', *Theory and Criticism*, 26 (Spring 2005), pp. 75–88 (Hebrew).
67. Minutes of the Meeting, 6 January 1986, courtesy of Dr Shlomo Alon.
68. Ibid., p. 7. It is unclear whether ʿAtsmon did or did not know the answer to Toubi's question. However, according to the documentation, he did not seriously investigate this question either before or after the meeting.
69. Ibid., p. 9.
70. Ibid., pp. 12–13.

71. Ibid., p. 14.
72. Ibid., p. 16.
73. Ibid.
74. Ibid., p. 17.
75. Ibid.
76. Ibid.
77. MK Darawsheh was a member of the Labour Party. In 1988, he created the Arab Democratic Party. Zaidan ʿAtashi, who only participated in the second meeting, was a Druze MK affiliated with the Likud Party. During the years 1972–76, he served as the Israeli Consul in New York. In the 1980s, he served in various Zionist parties such as the Democratic Movement for Change (headed by former Chief of Staff Yigael Yadin) and the Movement for Change and Initiation, headed by Professor Amnon Rubinstein. Tawfīq Ṭūbī, himself a communist, was a member of the Democratic Front for Peace and Equality (known in Arabic as *al-Jabha*, and in Hebrew as *Ḥadash*).
78. Minutes of the Meeting, 6 January 1986, Education Committee of the Knesset. See n. 56 above. Given to me, courtesy of Dr Shlomo Alon. The proceedings of this meeting can be also found in the Knesset's records.
79. Ibid.
80. Minutes of the Meeting, 22 January 1986, courtesy of Dr Shlomo Alon.
81. Ibid., p. 3.
82. Ibid., p. 4.
83. For further reading on Col. Shapira as the 'Chief of Intelligence for Unit 848 [known today as 8200]', see Amir Oren, 'From Anwar Sadat to Ben Zygier: A Tale of Israeli Intelligence Failures', *Haaretz*, 7 July 2013, available at: http://www.haaretz.com/opinion/.premium-1.534208 (accessed 16 November 2013).
84. Minutes of the Meeting, 22 January 1986, p. 5, courtesy of Dr Shlomo Alon.
85. Ibid., p. 7.
86. Ibid.
87. Ibid.
88. Ibid., p. 11.
89. Ibid.
90. 'The Conclusions of the Education Committee of the Knesset Regarding MK Abba Eban's Knesset Motion', given on 29 January 1986, in Yunai (ed.), *Arabic in Hebrew Schools*, p. 178.
91. Ibid., p. 179. Interestingly, this seems to correspond perfectly with Brig. Lapid's concluding remarks to the committee, which were: 'On behalf of the IDF, and the Chief of Staff, I would like to recommend the teaching of Arabic as a compulsory school subject, from intermediate schools and up to the 12th grade.'
92. Ibid., p. 180.
93. The list of participants included: Minister Yitzḥak Navon, Col. Nissim ʿAtsmon, Brig. Ephraim Lapid, Lt Col. Shlomo Katan, Col. Benny Gilʿad, Lt Col. Yig'al Schwartz (former Arabic instructor in the IDF), Mr Yeḥezkel (Ḥezi) Brosh (Arabic teacher in the IDF and at Lewinsky College), Dr Shlomo Alon (Supervisor of Arabic Studies), Ms Aviva Landman (Director of Arabic Studies,Reali Hebrew School, Haifa), Mr Avraham Yinon (former Supervisor of Arabic Studies), Mr Yoseph Moran (Supervisor of Arabic Studies,

Haifa District), Mr Emmanuel Koplewitz (Director of the Arab Education Department, Ministry of Education), Mr David Four (Pedagogic Secretariat, Ministry of Education), Professor Yehoshuʿa Blau (Hebrew University), Professor Meʾir Kister (Hebrew University), Professor Moshe Piamenta (Hebrew University), Mr Asher Stern (Ulpan ʿAḳiva) and Ms Shulamit Katznelson (Ulpan ʿAḳiva).

94. See, for example, Baruch Kimmerling, 'Patterns of Militarism in Israel', *European Journal of Sociology*, 34 (1993), p. 216.
95. Minutes of the Meeting, 28 January 1986, courtesy of Dr Shlomo Alon.
96. Ibid., p. 1.
97. *Naḥal* is a Hebrew acronym for 'The Fighting Pioneering Youth'. It is an IDF Infantry Brigade.
98. Minutes of the Meeting, 28 January 1986, p. 5, courtesy of Dr Shlomo Alon.
99. For further reading about Naḥal and its role in the military culture in Jewish-Israeli society, see Ben-Eliezer, 'A Nation-in-Arms', p. 276.
100. Minutes of the Meeting, 28 January 1986, p. 7, courtesy of Dr Shlomo Alon.
101. Ibid.
102. Ibid., p. 22.
103. Ibid., p. 32.
104. Ibid.
105. Ibid.
106. Ibid., p. 27.
107. Ibid., p. 27.
108. Ibid., V-6.
109. Ibid., p. 7.
110. Col. ʿAtsmon's Action Plan, Submitted to the Education Minister Navon in June 1986, Yunai (ed.), *Arabic in Hebrew Schools*, pp. 181–4.
111. Ibid.
112. Ibid.
113. Interview with Col. Ret.Nissim ʿAtsmon, conducted by the author, Raʿanana, 1 August 2008.
114. See Aryeh Levy and Irit Miro, *The Arabic National Exam: Results and Discussion about the Teaching of Arabic* (Tel Aviv: School of Education, Tel Aviv University, 1995) (Hebrew); Lustigman, 'Teaching Arabic in Hebrew Schools in Israel'.
115. ʿAtsmon said that these sums are only estimates. Interview with ʿAtsmon, Raʿanana, 1 August 2008.
116. As a pupil in the mid-1990s, I participated in a trip to Egypt. For further reading about these trips, see *Givʿat Ḥavivah Bulletin*, 22 (1997), found in ISA/G-13969/2; and Ran Lustigman,'Teaching Arabic in Hebrew Schools: A Call for Rethinking the Place of Arabic Studies in the Ministry of Education's Programme for Shared Life', in Mandel Conference for Education: 60 Years of Education in Israel – Past, Present, Future, Kfar ha-Maccabiah, 18 December 2008, pp. 167–79, available at: http://my.mli.org.il/Mli_Pdf/Graduate/Mandel.LUSTIGMAN.pdf (accessed 18 December 2012) (Hebrew).
117. Interview with ʿAtsmon, Raʿanana, 1 August 2008.
118. Ibid.
119. Ibid.

120. In Yael Fishbain, '"We have Brought up a Generation of Deaf-Mutes": An interview with Colonel Nissim ʿAtsmon', *Davar*, 31 March 1989 (Hebrew).
121. Interview with Levin, Hebrew University of Jerusalem, 20 April 2009.
122. Lustigman, 'Teaching Arabic in Hebrew Schools: A Call', p. 173.
123. Ibid.
124. Me'ir Amots, 'Translation from Arabic to Hebrew in the Military Intelligence Directorate', *Ḥamanit: The Israeli Military Intelligence Journal*, 17 (April 1991), pp. 50–3 (Hebrew); and ibid., 'Translation from Arabic to Hebrew in the Military Intelligence Directorate', *Journal for the Teachers of Arabic and Islamic* History, 14 (April 1991), pp. 19–21.
125. Ibid.
126. Ibid.
127. The *Mekhinah* in Rosh Pina, official website, available at: http://www.mrp.org.il/ (accessed 28 December 2010).
128. 'Training the People of Intelligence: In Rosh Pina it was Decided – Your Mind is What is Important', *Mabat Malam: Journal of the Israeli Intelligence, Heritage and Commemoration Centre*, 50 (October 2007), p. 29 (Hebrew).
129. Alon Fragman, 'The Grammar Translation Method in Arabic Language Teaching 2005–2006', *E-mago: Israeli Online Magazine for Culture and Content*, 24 September 2006, available at: http://www.e-mago.co.il/Editor/edu-1260.htm (accessed 16 December 2012) (Hebrew).
130. Ibid.
131. See Dana Elazar-Halevy, 'Nationalistic Spirits and Militaristic Perceptions in Arabic Studies in Israel', *Dor le-Dor: Journal for the Studies in the History of Jewish Education in Israel*, 34 (2009), p. 31 (Hebrew); ibid., 'Language of Peace, Language of War: Nationalism and Militarism in the History of Arabic Teaching in Jewish Schools in Israel' (MA thesis, School of Education, Tel Aviv University, 2009) (Hebrew).
132. The article, written by Uri Binder and published in *Maʿariv* in 2005 was found in the Ministry of Education Archive, Jerusalem (MoEA), 722 (1 January 2004–31 December 2005).
133. Interview with ʿAtsmon, Raʿanana, 1 August 2008.
134. Quoted in Lev-Ari, 'Know the Neighbour'.
135. Mentioned in the 'Oriental Youth Battalion', webpage of the official Military Intelligence website, available at: https://www.aman.idf.il/modiin/general.aspx?catId=60611 (accessed 17 November 2013). Although it may be possible to examine this programme and its impact on pupils through a variety of mediums, due to the proximity of the events written about and this research (covering a period of only 10 to 15 years ago), the archival material is inaccessible until at least 30 years before it is declassified). The information presented here is solely derived from official Military Intelligence sources.
136. Mentioned in the *Modiʿin ba-'Ofeḳ* webpage of the official Military Intelligence website, available at: https://www.aman.idf.il/modiin/general.aspx?catId=60612 (accessed 17 November 2013).
137. Information is taken from the Special Announcements, Southern District, Israel Ministry of Education, August 2004, available at: http://www.edu-negev.gov.il/chozerm/ (accessed 17 November 2013); Amal Education Network, special explanation on *Maḥne Daʿat*, available at: http://tinyurl.

com/q9hu4yd (accessed 17 November 2013); and Elhanan Miller, 'Army in the Classroom: IDF Attempts to Encourage the Study of Arabic in Israeli High Schools', paper presented at the Conference on Language, Conflict and Security in the Middle East, Centre of Islamic Studies, University of Cambridge, 11 April 2010.

138. The official Ṭelem 2013 newsletter, available at: https://www.aman.idf.il/SIP_STORAGE/files/1/70981.pdf (accessed in 16 December 2012).
139. Ibid., p. 3.
140. Ibid., pp. 22, 32 and 33.
141. As mentioned earlier, in a survey conducted in 2006, it was found that 62.9 per cent of Jewish-Israeli pupils who chose Arabic in high school did so, among other reasons, out of a desire to serve in Military Intelligence (Him Younes and Malka, *Developing a Curriculum in Arabic*, p. 11).
142. The letter, dated 16 January 2014, was attached to the online article published on the website of the Israeli Army radio station, Galei Tzahal. In Yaʿarah Barak,'Minister of Education Piron Reduces Arabic Studies', *Galei Tzahal Online*, 23 January 2014, available at: http://glz.co.il/1064-34809-he/Galatz.aspx (accessed 15 February 2014) (Hebrew).
143. See Dadi Komem, 'Education Starts from Within', *NRG-Maʿariv*, 18 March 2013, available at: http://www.nrg.co.il/online/1/ART2/453/210.html#.UUeUmRgjyVc.facebook (accessed 17 November 2013); for further information on the *Yā Salām* Programme, see the programme's official website, available at: http://yasalam.galim.org.il/about.html (accessed 17 November 2013).
144. Snir, *Arabness, Jewishness, Zionism*, p. 1.
145. Ibid.
146. Reʾuven Snir, 'Jews as Arabs: The Status of Research', *Ruʾaḥ Mizraḥit: MEISAI Electronic Journal*, 2 (Summer 1995), p. 15 (Hebrew).

5 Givʿat Ḥavivah and Ulpan ʿAḳiva: Arabic Studies Independent of the Ministry of Education

1. The research of these two organisations was made possible due to assistance provided by the Director General of the Ministry of Education and the Director General of the Prime Minister's Office. They provided me with access to specific files under their responsibility that had been classified up until this point. I also want to note the kind help I received from employees at the Yad Yaʿari Archive in Givʿat Ḥavivah (YYA) who enabled my study of the history of this institution.
2. Givʿat Ḥavivah, official website: http://www.givathaviva.org.il/english/ (accessed 22 November 2013).
3. The Jewish–Arab Center for Peace, Givʿat Ḥavivah, official website, available at: http://www.givathaviva.org.il/english/peace/ (accessed 22 November 2013).
4. ʿAbd al-ʿAzīz al-Zuʿbī was an MK with the United Workers Party (a Zionist socialist movement) and also was an MK in the Labour Party. For information about the Institute for Arabic Studies, see its official page, available at: http://www.givathaviva.org.il/hebrew/arabic_studies/arabic-studies-odot1.htm (accessed 22 November 2013) (Hebrew).

5. One can argue that the rather Orientalist and, at times, Jewish-oriented perspective, of Vashitz's researches are in evidence in the titles of his two books, *The Arabs in Eretz Yisrael* (Tel Aviv: Sifriyat ha-Po'alim, 1947) (Hebrew) and *The World of the Bedouins* (Giv'at Ḥavivah: Institute for Arabic Studies, 1976) (Hebrew).
6. Vashitz letter to Commander of the Reserve Unit, 27 October 1966, YYA/40-1.2(13).
7. Quoted in a letter sent from Vashitz to the Kibbutzim Committee of Continuing Education Programmes, 6 March 1972, YYA/40-3.2(6).
8. In the 1948 War, Atkin served as the Chief of Intelligence of the Israeli Southern Command.
9. Atkin letter to Toledano, November 1973, ISA/GL-17080/5.
10. Ibid.
11. Letter from Selection Unit of the Military Intelligence to Giv'at Ḥavivah, 26 November 1973, YYA/40-3.2(6).
12. For further reading on this unit, see Ephraim Lapid, 'Collecting Information in Preparation for the Six-Day War (1967)', in Amos Gilboa and Ephraim Lapid (eds), *Israeli's Silent Defender: An Inside Look at Sixty Years of Israeli Intelligence* (Jerusalem: Gefen Publishing House and the Israel Intelligence Heritage and Commemoration Center, 2012), p. 66.
13. Vashitz letter to IDF Spokesperson, 26 November 1976, YYA/6-20.2.40.
14. Details are taken from three update letters sent from Giv'at Ḥavivah to prospective pupils, 19 and 29 August and 16 September 1976, YYA/(6)2.5-40.
15. David Bar-Matsra letter to Secretariat of the National Kibbutz Movement, 29 August 1976, ibid.
16. See Giv'at Ḥavivah's announcement regarding 'Arabic and Middle Eastern Studies' in 1978, where this is explicitly mentioned, n YYA/40-17.2(6).
17. My emphasis. Vashitz letter to Security Department of the National Kibbutz Movement, 25 July 1978, YYA/40-5.2(12).
18. Ibid.
19. Moshe Gabay letter to Simḥa Erlikh, 23 June 1980, YYA/G-13969/2.
20. Yitzḥak Reiter letter to Gabay, Director of the Institute for Arabic Studies, 14 July 1980, ibid.
21. See Reiter letter to Atkin, 19 May 1981, and Atkin letter to Gur-Aryeh from the office of the Adviser on Arab Affairs, 4 May 1981, ibid. A year later, the Adviser on Arab Affairs gave Giv'at Ḥavivah a stipend of 30,000 shekels. See Atkin letter to Reiter, 29 May 1983, ibid. In 1984, the Adviser on Arab Affairs increased its support to Giv'at Ḥavivah, granting it 100,000 shekels (this sum is estimated to be worth about NIS3 million today). See Reiter letter to Atkin, 8 November 1984, ibid.
22. Gabay letter to Neḥemiah, 5 November 1981, YYA/40-9.2(10).
23. The report from 1981 may be found in YYA/40-7.2(5).
24. See, for example, letters from the Ṭelem Unit in Military Intelligence to Giv'at Ḥavivah, 12 October 1980 and 11 January 1983, or a letter dated 19 November 1979 with names of pupils sent from Giv'at Ḥavivah to the Military Intelligence, YYA/40-9.2(10).
25. The letter was from the 'Abd al-'Azīz al-Zu'bī Institute for Arabic Studies (signed by Gabay) to 'Atsmon from the Ṭelem Unit, 22 January 1983, YYA/40-9.2(10).

26. Information about Gazit's lecture at Giv'at Ḥavivah is found in Gabay's invitation letter to Gazit, 30 November 1980, ibid. The invitation letter is reproduced in Appendix 13.
27. Gabay letter to Security Department of the United Kibbutz Movement, 23 November 1982, YYA/40-9.2(10).
28. ʿAtsmon letter to Gabay, 19 December 1982, ibid.
29. It is interesting to note the similarity in the way in which Arabic words and idioms were used to signify interest and connection between the different Jewish-Israeli actors of the network. Compare, for example, ʿAtsmon's expressions '*in shā ʾAllāh* in the next year' to Supervisor Eyal's 'welcoming you with *ahlan wa-sahlan*' that was mentioned in a letter sent to Lt Col. Sharoni two decades earlier.
30. Givʿat Ḥavivah newsletter, Vol. 6, ISA/G-13969/2.
31. Ibid., Vol. 7, ibid.
32. Ibid.
33. Ibid.p. 17.
34. Gabay letter to an officer at Military Post 2404, 7 November 1983, ISA/G-13969/2.
35. Quoted in Orly Shlomo-Na'or, 'The Army Helps them Grow Up', *Emtsaʿ Ḥadera* (the city of Ḥadera's local newspaper), 5 June 1992 (Hebrew).
36. 1st Lt Eyal Zisser letter to Gabay, 6 January 1984, YYA/40-9.2(10). Later in life, Zisser became a professor of Middle East Studies at Tel Aviv University and was appointed Director of the Moshe Dayan Center at the university. He also served as the Dean of Humanities.
37. Gabay letter to Zoreʿa, 18 February 1986, YYA/6-20.2.40. The letter is can shown in Appendix 14.
38. See, for example, Yoram Meron and Reyad Kabha, *The Tails of the Valley* (Givʿat Ḥavivah: Jewish–Arab Center for Peace, 1993) (Hebrew); Yoram Meron et al., *The Pomegranate's Aril* (Givʿat Ḥavivah: Jewish–Arab Center for Peace, 1997) (Hebrew); Yoram Meron et al., *A Legendary Village* (Givʿat-Ḥ avivah: Jewish–Arab Center for Peace, 2005).
39. Meron letter to Ze'ev, 16 June 1986, YYA/6-20.2.40.
40. Ibid.
41. Ibid.
42. Ibid.
43. Meron letter to Treinin, 18 December 1986, YYA/40-13.2(13).
44. In his speech, Lapid noted the importance of teaching Literary Arabic over Colloquial Arabic; in Ḥezi Brosh, 'The Effect of Learning Colloquial Arabic in Elementary School on Achievement in Literary Arabic in the Seventh Grade' (PhD thesis, School of Education, Tel Aviv University, 1988), pp. 56–7 (Hebrew).
45. Ṭal's presentation was to 450 teachers of Arabic. He spoke about an anticipated shortage of 'Arabists' in Military Intelligence; in: 'Israelis are not Fluent in the Arabic Language', *Jewish World*, 15 December 1988.
46. The significance of the IDF Commander of the Manpower Directorate in discussions about Arabic studies in Jewish-Israeli schools was highlighted earlier, including hisinvolvement in debates about Arabic in Jewish-Israeli high schools that took place in 1964 and 1977.
47. The summary, sent by Capt. David Maimon to the IDF Commander of the Planning Department, was entitled 'Arabic Studies – Givʿat Ḥavivah', 9 October 1986, YYA/6-20.2.40.

48. Ze'ev letter to Chief Intelligence Officer, Unit 8200, Training Base 15, and Unit 225, 23 February 1987, ibid.
49. Ibid.
50. Ibid.
51. Meron letter to Ze'ev, 13 September 1987, ibid.
52. Ibid.
53. This, for example, was the case with the request made by Supervisor Ben-Ze'ev in 1944 that Eliyahu Sasson, of the Arab Bureau of the Political Department of the Jewish Agency, contact the Head of the Education Department, as well as the request by Dr Ziv in 1964, who as Head of the Teaching Division at the Ministry of Education asked the Chief of Intelligence to send the summary of their meeting to the General Director of the Ministry.
54. Meron letter to Ze'ev, 13 September 1987, YYA/6-20.2.40. It is not clear whether Meron was referring to military eavesdropping or regular listening comprehension. The word used in Hebrew, *ha'azanah*, has a double meaning.
55. Ibid.
56. Ibid.
57. In Col. Moti Shapira, Commander of the Manpower Directorate, Military Intelligence, letter to Meron, 6 June 1988, ibid.
58. Meron letter to Commander of Manpower Directorate, 25 May 1988, ibid.
59. The course outline, as suggested by Meron to Ze'ev, is found in ibid.
60. Ibid.
61. See, for example, 'Invitation to Meet the Oriental Class', a letter that references a meeting scheduled for 15 February 1988, ibid. See also, letter from Meron to head teachers, 24 May 1988, ibid.
62. Written by Yoseph Vashitz, ed. by Sarah Ozacky-Lazar, *Giv'at-Ḥavivah Bulletin*, 13 (1988), found in ISA/G-13969/2.
63. Ze'ev letter to Meron, May 1988, YYA/6-20.2.40.
64. Shlomo-Na'or, 'The Army Helps them Grow Up'.
65. Ibid.
66. Ibid.
67. Ibid.
68. Ibid.
69. Ibid.
70. Interview with Dr Sarah Ozacky-Lazar, conducted by the author, Van Leer Jerusalem Institute, 22 December 2007.
71. Ibid.
72. Yedaya has demonstrated that the de-politicisation of Palestinians under Israeli rule has been enforced through the creation of economic dependency and the need to obtain clearance from Israeli security authorities to work in the Jewish-Israeli labour market. See Ella Yedaya, 'Building the Enemy: Palestinian Workers Constructing Israeli Settlements' (MA thesis, Department of Social Anthropology, Cambridge University, 2010).
73. Quoted in Shlomo-Na'or, 'The Army Helps them Grow Up'.
74. Ibid.
75. Ben Zilka and Dvir Bar, '"A Different Voice": Interview with Kamal Rayyan', *Zman Tel Aviv* (Tel Aviv Times), 24 May 2002 (Hebrew).
76. Interview with Mr Kamāl Rayyān, conducted by the author, Kafr Bara, 28 June 2008.

77. Ibid.
78. Ibid.
79. According to an article in *Ma'ariv*, Glilot refers to a major Military Intelligence base in Israel. See Doron Naḥum, 'Military Intelligence Base 8200: An Open Military Zone', *NRG-Ma'ariv*, 22 October 2006, available at: http://www.nrg.co.il/online/1/ART1/494/701.html (accessed 14 November 2014) (Hebrew).
80. Interview with Rayyān, Kafr Bara, 28 June 2008.
81. Ibid.
82. 'Military Intelligence in the Horizon Seminar', IDF, official website, available at: https://www.aman.idf.il/modiin/general.aspx?catId=60612 (accessed 12 August 2010).
83. Ibid.
84. Giv'at Ḥavivah *Bulletin*, 22 (1997), found in ISA/G-13969/2.
85. Giv'at Ḥavivah, official website, available at: http://www.givathaviva.org.il/hebrew/arabic_studies/arabic_studies.htm (accessed 19 July 7.2010).
86. In actuality, the word *modi'in* generated four results but none of them related to 'Military Intelligence'. Rather, they all referred to a high school in the city of Modi'in, located between Jerusalem and Tel Aviv. The search was made via the following website: http://www.givathaviva.org.il (accessed 23 November 2013).
87. Suleimān Maṣalḥa letter to editor of *New Outlook*, 21 March 1982, found in YYA/40-9.2(10).
88. Giv'at Ḥavivah letter to secretary of the Speaker of the Knesset Prize for Quality of Life, 25 June 1990, ISA/G-13969/2.
89. The education prize is mentioned in the *Giv'at Ḥavivah Bulletin*, 18 (1993), p. 3, found in ibid.
90. 'Giv'at Ḥavivah: The Kibbutzim Seminar Centre', Ḥavatselet: Cultural and Educational Institutions of the National Kibbutz Movement, available at: http://www.havatzelet.org.il/heb/mosdot/ghaviva.htm (accessed 19 July 2010).
91. Ulpan 'Aḳiva, official website (accessed 28 December 2010). As Ulpan 'Aḳiva was closed in 2010, its website no longer functions.
92. Gur letter to Ulpan 'Aḳiva, 30 November 1967, ISA/GL-13172/11.
93. Ibid.
94. Yitzḥaḳ, letter to Ulpan 'Aḳiva, 4 December 1967, ibid.
95. Katznelson letter to Levin, 14 December 1967, ibid.
96. Katznelson letter to Sarid, 14 December 1967, ibid.
97. Information is taken from a *Jerusalem Post* article entitled, 'Push to Learn Hebrew and Arabic Delights Bi-Lingual Teacher', which featured an interview with Avraham Lavi, published 17 May 1968, found in CZA/A453/10.
98. Ophir Ḥakham, 'Peace Starts at Home', *Ḥamanit: The Israeli Military Intelligence Journal*, 17 (April 1991), p. 46 (Hebrew). Similar insights were given in an interview with Brig. Ret. Ephraim Lapid, conducted by the author, Meir Amit Intelligence and Terrorism Information Center, Ramat Hasharon, 28 June 2008.
99. Mentioned in Lapid letter to Dr Dan Ronen, Youth Department, Ministry of Education, 22 April 1975, ISA/GL-17938/14. In fact, Katznelson was invited, as evidenced by internal handwritten correspondence within the Ministry of Education, 'To: Johnny, From: Ilana', 29 April 75, ibid.

100. 'Arabic as a Bridgehead' was the official name of the project, but it was also known as 'Colloquial Arabic as a Bridgehead' and 'Hebrew and Arabic as a Bridgehead'.
101. Information is taken from General Secretary, Ulpan ʿAḳiva, letter to Shmuʾel Toledano, Adviser on Arab Affairs, 16 March 1975, ISA/GL-17080/6. See also the official advertisement for the course, in ibid.
102. Chief of Intelligence Shlomo Gazit letter to Minister of Education, 3 April 1975, ISA/GL-17918/4.
103. Ibid.
104. Mentioned in Lapid letter to Toledano, entitled, 'Military Intelligence's Recommendation to Support the Bridgehead Project', copied to Katznelson, 9 January 1976, ISA/G-10391/13.
105. Ibid.
106. US Department of Defense, *The Dictionary of Military Terms* (New York: Skyhorse Publishing, 2009), p. 73. According to another US source, '[a Bridgehead is] an area of ground, in a territory occupied or threatened by the enemy, which must be held or at least controlled, so as to permit the continuous embarkation, landing or crossing of troops and material, and/or to provide maneuver space requisite for subsequent operations', in US Joint Military Terminology Group, *The Military Dictionary* (Darby, PA: Diane Publishing, 1987), p. 56.
107. Eitan Haber and Ze'ev Schiff, *Yom Kippur War Lexicon* (Or Yehuda: Zmora Bitan, 2003), pp. 376–7 (Hebrew).
108. See Uri Dan, *Bridgehead* (Tel Aviv: A. L. Publishing, 1975) (Hebrew).
109. 'Arabic-Hebrew as a Bridgehead for Peace – Yes, but Under the Spears of Occupation and National Nihilism – No!!', *Al-Ittiḥad*, 22 April 1975 (Arabic), found in ISA/GL-17080/6). The author of the article was not named.
110. Ibid.
111. Ibid. The *Al-Ittiḥad* article is provided in Appendix 15.
112. For further information about the *Al-Ittiḥad* newspaper and its political critique of the Zionist movement and Israel, see Jamal, *The Arab Public Sphere in Israel*, pp. 47–50.
113. During the British Mandate in Palestine, and due to Shmuʾel Tamir's membership in the Irgun, the British expelled him to Kenya. During the 1970s, he became Minister of Justice for Likud in Menachem Begin's government (1977–80).
114. In my interview with ʿAtsmon, he said that, 'my strongest memory of Katznelson is her political views. She was very much to the right. She was a real hardcore right-winger.' Interview with ʿAtsmon, conducted by the author, Raʿanana, 1 August 2008.
115. Quoted in Yoseph Aḥimeʾir, 'A Common Language: A Path for Dialogue', *Maʿariv*, 1 July 1979 (Hebrew).
116. Mentioned in Katznelson letter to Toledano (the letter was sent after the meeting), 9 May 1975, ISA/GL-17080/6.
117. Ibid.
118. Ibid.
119. Ibid.
120. Orit Reʾuveni, 'Ephraim Lapid will be the Director of UlpanʿAḳiva', *Emtsaʿ Netanya*, 1 August 1997 (Hebrew).

121. The Soldier-Teachers Course, which was established in 1977 at Ulpan ʿAḳiva, was somewhat reduced in scope between 1978 and 1983 because then Chief of Staff Refaʾel Eitan decided that an institution that brought Jews and Arabs together was not an appropriate venue for a military course such as Soldier-Teachers. However, following Eitan's retirement in April 1983, the course resumed at Ulpan ʿAḳiva. See Ḥakham, 'Peace Starts at Home'.
122. Gur-Aryeh letter on behalf of the Adviser on Arab Affairs, to accountant at Prime Minister's Office, 28 December 1980, ISA/G-10391/13.
123. The letter that Katznelson and Rokheli sent to Shmuʾeli, 1 April 81, ISA/GL-18661/8. The letter is shown in Appendix 16.
124. See a letter sent from the Department of Teacher Training at the Ministry of Education to the Financial Department at the Ministry of Education, 18 June 1984, in ibid. See also the summary of a meeting that took place at the Ministry of Education, 9 April1984, in ibid.
125. This is an excerpt from a speech given by the Commander of the Manpower Department of Military Intelligence at a ceremony at Ulpan ʿAḳiva. See 'Upon Finishing the 11th Session of the Soldier-Teachers Course', *Ḥamanit: The Israeli Military Intelligence Journal*, 15 (August 1990), p. 20 (Hebrew).
126. This information is found in Ulpan ʿAḳiva and the Ministry of Education's 'Invitation to a Day Seminar: The Training of Arabic Teachers', 30 January 1981, ISA/GL-17950/39.
127. Two of the meetings were held by the Knesset Education Committee and another in Minister Navon's office. I analysed these three meetings extensively in the previous chapter.
128. Minutes of the Meeting, 6 January 1986, given to me courtesy of Dr Shlomo Alon.
129. Ibid.
130. Ibid.
131. Mentioned in Reʾuveni, 'Ephraim Lapid'.
132. For information regarding Youth Battalion activities that took place at Ulpan ʿAḳiva, see, for example, 'Youth Battalion Activity in 2004', Dror Education and Cultural Institution, official website, 24 October 2004, available at: http://tinyurl.com/napwrm9 (accessed 28 December 2010) (Hebrew).
133. Esther Perron, 'In Memory of Shulamit Katznelson', *Hed ha-ʾUlpan ha-Ḥadash: An Educational Journal for Hebrew Studies*, 86 (Autumn 2004), p. 2 (Hebrew).
134. Information is taken from, 'Shulamit Katznelson 1919–1999', Heritage Section, Netanya, official website, available at: http://www.netanya-moreshet.org.il/Info/hi_show.aspx?id=29666 (accessed 28 December 2010) (Hebrew).
135. Katznelson letter to Public Trustees, 10 June 1987, ISA/GL-18686/17.
136. Letter from Minister of Religious Services to Public Trustee, 19 October 1987, ibid.
137. As Minister of Defence, Rabin's visit may also indicate a strengthening of relations between Ulpan ʿAḳiva and the Ministry of Defence.
138. The letter is found in the photo collections section of the city of Netanya's official website. See 'Photos: Ulpan ʿAḳiva', Heritage Section, Netanya, official website, available at: http://www.netanya-moreshet.org.il/Info/hi_show.aspx?id=34651&t=2 (accessed 28 December 2010) (Hebrew).
139. See Chayim Herzog's visit to Ulpan ʿAḳiva, 'Schedule of the Visit', 18 February 1988, ISA/GL-18686/17.

140. For further reading, see Stewart Steven, *The Spymasters of Israel* (New York: Ballantine Books, 1986), p. 30; and Amir Gil, 'With USD100,000 we Established MI: An Interview with the Israeli President Chayim Herzog', *Ḥamanit: The Israeli Military Intelligence Journal*, 1 (October 1984), pp. 6–9 (Hebrew).
141. Herzog speech at Ulpan ʿAḳiva, 18 February 1988, ISA/GL-18686/17.
142. In Hebrew, *Ha-Tnuʿah le-Maʿan Eretz Yisrael Tovah*.
143. Mentioned in 'Photos: Ulpan ʿAḳiva: Shulamit Katznelson's Nomination for the Nobel Peace Prize', Netanya, official website, available at: http://www.netanya-moreshet.org.il/Info/PicShow.aspx?src=../../View_files/HeapItem_pic/034651/HP_034651_31.jpg&title (accessed 28 July 2010) (Hebrew).
144. Herzog letter to Katznelson, 'Photos: Ulpan ʿAḳiva', Heritage Section, Netanya, official website, 4 August 1993, available at: http://www.netanya-moreshet.org.il/Info/PicShow.aspx?src=../../View_files/HeapItem_pic/034651/HP_034651_28.jpg&titl (accessed 26 July 2010) (Hebrew). The letter is shown in Appendix 17.
145. Lapid letter to Zaken, faxed, 10 December 1998, ISA/G-10391/13.
146. The UNESCO award letter was attached to Lapid's letter, 10 February 1998, ibid. The original UNESCO announcement, in French, can be seen in Appendix 18, and the translated announcement in Hebrew in Appendix 19.
147. Amir Zohar, 'How Do you Say "Shady Business Plan" in Hebrew?', *Haʾaretz*, 2 August 2008, available at: http://www.haaretz.co.il/hasite/objects/pages/PrintArticle.jhtml?itemNo=951785 (accessed 28 December 2010) (Hebrew).
148. For further reading about the closure of Ulpan ʿAḳiva, see Shiri Ostfeld, 'A New International Ulpan was Opened in Netanya: Will Replace the Mythological Ulpan ʿAḳiva,' *Kol ha-Sharon* (Voice of the Sharon), 1 February 2010, available at: http://www.local.co.il/netanya/65761/article.htm (accessed 14 November 2012) (Hebrew).

Conclusion

1. Quoted in Rubik Rosenthal, 'The Notables of Kfar Saba', *Maʿariv*, 8 March 2001 (Hebrew).
2. Ibid.
3. Information taken from the official website of Begin–Sadat Center for Strategic Studies, Bar-Ilan University, available at: http://besacenter.org/author/mkedar/ (accessed 25 August 2013).
4. I use 'Military Intelligence fodder' following Snir, who coined this term. Snir argued that the direct association between Arabic studies in Israeli schools and service in Military Intelligence had created pupils who are nothing less than 'Military Intelligence Fodder' (lit. *Basar Modiʿin*). Snir paraphrased 'cannon fodder' (lit. *basar totaḥim*). In the same article, Snir argued that the policy behind Arabic teaching in Jewish-Israeli schools is determined by 'Ashkenazi Orientalists who pretend to know the "Arab mentality".' In Reʾuven Snir, 'Military Intelligence Fodder', *Haʾaretz*, 20 August 1995 (Hebrew).

5. See Ram, *The Changing Agenda of Israeli Sociology*, p. 97; Yossi Yonah, 'War by Other Means', *New Statesman*, 31 October 2005, available at: http://www.newstatesman.com/node/151887 (accessed 28 December 2013); and Swirsky, *Israel*.
6. See, for example, Nicky Hager, 'Israel's Omniscient Ears', *Le Monde Diplomatique*, English Edition, September 2010, available at: http://mondediplo.com/2010/09/04israelbase (accessed 15 February 2014).

Bibliography

Theses

Brosh, Ḥezi, 'Hashpa'at Limud ha-'Aravit ha-Meduberet be-Vet ha-Sefer ha-Yesodi 'al ha-Heisegim be-'Aravit ha-Safrutit be-Khitah Zayin shel Ḥativat ha-Beinayim' (The Effect of Learning Colloquial Arabic in Elementary School on Achievement in Literary Arabic in the Seventh Grade), PhD thesis, School of Education, Tel Aviv University, 1988 (Hebrew)

Elazar-Halevy, Dana, 'Sfat Shalom, Sfat Milḥamah: Le'umiyut ve-Militarizm be-Toldot Hora'at ha-'Aravit be-Vatei ha-Sefer ha-'ivriyyim be-Yisrael' (Language of Peace, Language of War: Nationalism and Militarism in the History of Arabic Teaching in Jewish Schools in Israel), MA thesis, School of Education, Tel Aviv University, 2009 (Hebrew)

Kraemer, Roberta, 'Social Psychological Factors Related to the Study of Arabic among Israeli Jewish High School Students', PhD thesis, School of Education, Tel Aviv University, 1990

Yedaya, Ella, 'Building the Enemy: Palestinian Workers Constructing Israeli Settlements', MA thesis, Department of Social Anthropology, Cambridge University, 2010

Newspapers and other news media articles

'Abdel-Jawad, Saleh, 'War by Other Means', *Al-Ahram Weekly*, 16 May 2001, available at: http://weekly.ahram.org.eg/1998/1948/359_salh.htm (accessed 14 August 2013)

Aḥime'ir, Yoseph, 'Safah Meshutefet: Shvil le-Hidabrut' (A Common Language: A Path for a Dialogue), *Ma'ariv*, 1 July 1979 (Hebrew)

"Arabiyyā–'Ibriyyā ka-Ra's Jisr li-al-Salām – Na'am, wa-Lakin taḥt Hirāb al-Iḥtilāl wa-al-'Admiyyā al-Qawmiyyā – Lā!!' (Arabic-Hebrew as a Bridgehead for Peace: Yes, but Under the Spears of Occupation and National Nihilism – No!!), *Al-Ittiḥād*, 22 April 1975 (Arabic)

Barak, Ya'arah,'Minister of Education Piron Reduces Arabic Studies', *Galei Tzahal Online*, 23 January 2014, available at: http://glz.co.il/1064-34809-he/Galatz.aspx (accessed 15 February 2014) (Hebrew)

Beaumont, Peter, 'Netanyahu Turns to Nazi Language', *The Guardian*, 10 July 2009, available at: http://www.guardian.co.uk/commentisfree/2009/jul/10/netanyahu-nazi-language-settlements (accessed 4 June 2014)

Davar, 'The Intelligence Corps of the IDF was Established: Its Chief is Dov Tamari', 15 November 1976, p. 2

Dromi, Uri, 'Tam 'Idan Kister' (The End of the Kister Era), *Ha'aretz*, 27 August 2010 (Hebrew)

Fishbain, Yael, 'Gidalnu Dor shel Hershim-'Ilmim' ('We Have Brought up a Generation of Deaf-Mutes': An Interview with Nissim Atzmon', *Davar*, 31 March 1989 (Hebrew)

Hager, Nicky, 'Israel's Omniscient Ears', *Le Monde Diplomatique*, English Edition, September 2010, available at: http://mondediplo.com/2010/09/04israelbase (accessed 15 February 2014)

Israel Today, 'Former IDF Chief Says Israeli Arabs Remain fifth Column', 23 November 2008, available at: http://www.israeltoday.co.il/NewsItem/tabid/178/nid/17600/Default.aspx (accessed 15 December 2013)

The Jerusalem Post, 'Push to Learn Hebrew and Arabic Delights Bi-Lingual Teacher', 17 May 1968

Klein, Yossi, 'Look! An Arab Speaking Hebrew', *Haaretz*, 12 July 2013

Komem, Dadi, 'Education Starts from Within', *NRG-Ma'ariv*, 18 March 2013, available at: http://www.nrg.co.il/online/1/ART2/453/210.html#.UUeUmRgjyVc.facebook (accessed 17 November 2013) (Hebrew)

Lev-Ari, Shiri, 'Da' et ha-Shakhen' (Know the Neighbour), *Ha'aretz*, 26 February 2003 (Hebrew)

Mendel, Yonatan, 'Diary: How to Become an Israeli Journalist?', *London Review of Books*, 30 (5) (2008), p. 31

Nahmias, Ro'i, 'Arabic at the Airport?', *–Ynetnews – Yedi'ot Aḥaronot Website*, 28 May 2005, available at: http://www.ynetnews.com/articles/0,7340,L-3091528,00.html (accessed 26 September 2013)

Ophir, Y., 'Ha-No'ar be-Yisrael lo Rotse Lilmod 'Aravit' (The Youth in Israel Do Not Want to Study Arabic), *Ḥerut*, 25 April 1957 (Hebrew)

Oren, Amir, 'From Anwar Sadat to Ben Zygier: A Tale of Israeli Intelligence Failures', *Haaretz*, 7 July 2013, available at: http://www.haaretz.com/opinion/.premium-1.534208 (accessed 16 November 2013)

Ostfeld, Shiri, 'Neḥnakh 'Ulpan Bein-Le'umi le-'Ivrit: Yaḥlif et 'Ulpan 'Aḳiva ha-Mitologi she-Nisgar' (A New International Ulpan was Opened in Netanya: Will Replace the Mythological Ulpan 'Aḳiva), *Kol ha-Sharon* (Voice of the Sharon), 1 February 2010, available at: http://www.local.co.il/netanya/65761/article.htm (accessed 14 November 2012) (Hebrew)

Raved, Ahiya, 'Youth Believe Arabs Dirty', *Ynetnews*, 1 September 2007, available at: http://www.ynetnews.com/articles/0,7340,L-3350467,00.html (accessed 4 June 2014)

Re'uveni, Orit, 'Ephraim Lapid Yenahel et 'Ulpan 'Aḳiva' (Ephraim Lapid will be the Director of Ulpan 'Aḳiva), *Emtsa' Netanya* (Netanya's local newspaper), 1 August 1997 (Hebrew)

Rozenthal, Rubik, 'Nikhbadei Kfar Saba' ('The Notables of Kfar Saba), *Ma'ariv*, 8 March 2001 (Hebrew)

Shlomo-Na'or, Orly, 'Ha-Tsava 'ozer Lahem Ligdol' (The Army Helps them Grow Up), *Emtsa' Ḥaderah* (Ḥadera's local newspaper), 5 June 1992 (Hebrew)

Shohamy, Ilana, Ofra Inbar and Smadar Donitsa-Shmidt, 'Lilmod 'Aravit Kedei le-Dabér, Lo Rak Kedei le-Ragél' (Study Arabic in Order to Speak, Not Only in Order to Spy), Letters to the Editor, *Ha'aretz*, 12 April 2001 (Hebrew)

Snir, Reuven, 'Basar Modi'in' (Military Intelligence Fodder), *Ha'aretz*, 20 August 1995 (Hebrew)

Stern, Yoav, 'Poll: 50% of Israeli Jews Support State-Backed Arab Emigration', *Haaretz*, 27 March 2007

Ṭal, Ya'acov, 'Israelis are not Fluent in the Arabic Language', *Jewish World*, 15 December 1988

Yonah, Yossi, 'War by Other Means', *New Statesman*, 31 October 2005, available at: http://www.newstatesman.com/node/151887 (accessed 28 December 2013)

Zilka, Ben and Dvir Bar, 'Kol Aḥer' ('A Different Voice': Interview with Kamal Rayyan), *Zman Tel Aviv* (Tel Aviv Times), 24 May 2002 (Hebrew)

Zohar, Amir, 'Eikh Omrim be-'Ivrit "Kombinah"' (How Do you Say 'Shady Business Plan' in Hebrew?), *Ha'aretz*, 2 August 2008, available at: http://www.haaretz.co.il/hasite/objects/pages/PrintArticle.jhtml?itemNo=951785 (accessed 28 December 2010) (Hebrew)

Secondary sources

Agasi, Eliyahu, *'Aravit Meduberet* (Colloquial Arabic), Jerusalem: Arab Publishing House, 1968 (Hebrew)

Albany, Michael of and Walid Amine Salhab, *The Knights Templar of the Middle East*, San Francisco, CA: Weiser Books, 2006

Albright, Madeleine Korbel and William Woodward, *Madam Secretary: A Memoir*, New York: Miramax Books, 2005

Allen, Roger, 'Perspectives on Arabic Teaching and Learning', *Modern Language Journal*, 88 (2) (2004), pp. 275–8

Almog, Oz, *The Sabra: The Creation of the New Jew*, trans. by Haim Watzman, Berkeley, CA: University of California Press, 2000

Amara, Muḥammad, *Hora'at ha-'Aravit ke-Safah Zarah be-Vatei ha-Sefer ha-Yehudiyyim be-Yisrael* (Teaching Arabic as a Foreign Language in Jewish Schools in Israel), Haifa: Jewish-Arab Center, University of Haifa, 2008 (Hebrew)

Amara, Muḥammad and 'Abd al-Raḥman Mar'i, *Siyāsat al-Tarbiyā al-Laghawiyā Tujāh al-Muwātinīn al-'Arab fī Isrā'īl* (The Policy of Language Education towards the Arab Citizens in Israel), Beit Berl: Markaz Dirasāt al-Adab al-'Arabī, 2004 (Arabic)

Amichai, Yehuda, *Gam ha-Egrof hayah pa'am Yad Petuḥa ve-Etsba'ot* (Even a Fist was once an Open Palm with Fingers) (Jerusalem: Schoken, 1989) (Hebrew)

Amichai, Yehuda, *Yehuda Amichai: A Life of Poetry 1948–1994*, trans. by Benjamin and Barbara Harshav, 1st edn, New York: Harper Perennial, a Division of Harper Collins Publishers, 1995

Amots, Me'ir, 'Targum me-'Aravit le-'Ivrit be-Ḥaman' ('Translation from Arabic to Hebrew in the Military Intelligence Directorate), *Ḥamanit: Biṭa'on Ḥeil ha-Modi'in* (Ḥamanit: The Israeli Military Intelligence Journal), 17 (April 1991), pp. 50–3 (Hebrew)

Amots, Me'ir, 'Targum me-'Aravit le-'Ivrit be-Ḥaman' (Translation from Arabic to Hebrew in the Military Intelligence Directorate'), *Journal for the Teachers of Arabic and Islamic History*, 14 (April 1991), pp. 19–21 (Hebrew)

Avineri, Shlomo, 'Theodor Herzl's Diaries as a Bildungsroman', *Jewish Social Studies* 5 (3) 1999, pp. 1–46

'Azuz, Moshe, 'Ma'arakh ha-Hadrakha ba-Yehidah: Ha-Yamim ha-Rishonim' (The Training Unit of the Israeli Military Intelligence's SIGINT Unit: The First Days), *Na'aseh ve-Nishma'* (We Will Do and We Will Listen, Journal for the Veterans of Israeli Central Collection Unit of the Intelligence Corps), 10 (June 2000), pp. 9–12 (Hebrew)

Bakshi, Aviad, 'Is Arabic an Official Language of Israel?', Institute for Zionist Strategies, available at: http://izsvideo.org/papers/bakshi2011.pdf (accessed 15 December 2013) (Hebrew)

Bar-Or, Amir, 'The Making of Israel's Political-Security Culture', in Gabriel Sheffer and Oren Barak (eds), *Militarism and Israeli Society*, Bloomington, IN: Indiana University Press, 2010, pp. 259–79

Barak, Oren and Gabriel Sheffer, 'Israel's "Security Network" and its Impact: An Exploration of a New Approach', *International Journal of Middle East Studies*, 38 (2) (2006), pp. 235–61

Barak, Oren and Gabriel Sheffer, 'The Study of Civil–Military Relations in Israel: A New Perspective', *Israel Studies*, 12 (1) (2007), pp. 5–12

Barzilai, Gad, *Wars, Internal Conflicts, and Political Order: A Jewish Democracy in the Middle East*, New York: State University of New York Press, 1996

al-Batal, Mahmoud, 'Arabic and National Language Educational Policy', *Modern Language Journal*, 91 (2) (2007), pp. 268–71

al-Batal, Mahmoud and Kirk Belnap, 'The Teaching and Learning of Arabic in the United States: Realities, Needs, and Future Directions', in Kasem Wahba, Zeinab Taha and Liz England (eds), *The Handbook for Arabic Language Teaching Professionals in the 21st Century*, Mahwah, NJ: Erlbaum, 2006, pp. 389–99

Ben-Eliezer, Uri, '"'Uma be-Madim" ve-Milḥama: Yisrael bi-Shenoteha ha-Rishonot' (A Nation in Uniform and War: Israel's First Years), *Zmanim*, 49 (1994), pp. 50–65 (Hebrew)

Ben-Eliezer, Uri, 'A Nation-in-Arms: State, Nation, and Militarism in Israel's First Years', *Comparative Studies in Society and History*, 37 (2) (1995), pp. 264–85

Ben-Eliezer, Uri, *The Making of Israeli Militarism*, Bloomington, IN: Indiana University Press, 1998

Ben-Eliezer, Uri, 'Ha-Ḥevrah ha-Tsva'it ve-ha-Ḥevrah ha-Ezraḥit be-Yisrael: Giluyim shel Anti-Militarizm ve-Neo-Militarizm be-ʿidan Post-Moderni', (The Military Society and the Civil Society in Israel: Signs of Anti-Militarism and Neo-Militarism in a Post-Modern Period), in Majid al-Haj and Uri Ben-Eliezer (eds), *Be-Shem ha-Bitaḥon: Sociologiya shel Shalom ve-Bitaḥon be-Yisrael be-ʿidan Mishtané* (In the Name of Security: The Sociology of Peace and War in Israel in Changing Times), Haifa: University of Haifa, 2003, pp. 29–76 (Hebrew)

Ben-Rafael, Eliezer, *Language, Identity, and Social Division: The Case of Israel*, New York: Clarendon Press, 1994

Ben-Rafael, Eliezer, 'A Sociological Paradigm of Bilingualism: English, French, Yiddish and Arabic in Israel', in Hanna Herzog and Eliezer Ben-Rafael (eds), *Language and Communication in Israel*, New Brunswick, NJ: Transaction Publishers, 2001, pp. 289–310

Ben-Rafael, Eliezer and Ḥezi Brosh, 'A Sociological Study of Second Language Diffusion: The Obstacles to Arabic Teaching in the Israeli School', *Language Planning and Language Problems*, 15 (1) (1991), pp. 1–24

Ben-Rafael, Eliezer and Stephen Sharot, *Ethnicity, Religion and Class in Israeli Society*, Cambridge: Cambridge University Press, 1991

Ben-Rafael, Eliezer et al., 'Linguistic Landscape as Symbolic Construction of the Public Space: The Case of Israel', *International Journal of Multilingualism*, 3 (1) (2006), pp. 7–30

Ben-Yehuda, Eliezer, 'Mekorot le-Malé ha-Haser bi-Leshonenu' (Sources for Filling in the Missing Parts in our Language), *Zikhronot Vaʿad ha-Lashon ha-ʿIvrit*

(Proceedings of the Hebrew Language Council), Vol. 4, Jerusalem: Hebrew Language Council, 1912, pp. 3–16 (Hebrew)

Ben-Ze'ev, Yisrael, 'Le-Hora'at ha-'Aravit be-Vet ha-Sefer ha-Tikhon – 1948' (About Teaching Arabic in High Schools – 1948), in Jacob M. Landau (ed.), *Hora'at ha-'Aravit ke-Lashon Zarah* (Teaching Arabic as a Foreign Language), Jerusalem:School of Education of the Hebrew University and the Ministry of Education and Culture, 1961, pp. 52–3 (Hebrew)

Ben-Ze'ev, Yisrael, 'Report on Arabic Studies' (1946), in Yosef Yunai (ed.), *'Aravit be-Vatei Sefer 'Ivriyim: Osef Mismakhim* (Arabic in Hebrew Schools: A Collection of Documents), Te'udah: Israel Ministry of Education and Culture, 1992, pp. 37–41 (Hebrew)

Ben-Zvi, Yitzhak, *Eretz Yisrael and its Settlement during the Ottoman Era*, Jerusalem: Yad Yitzhak Ben-Zvi Institute, 1975

Bergman, Ronen and Gil Meltser, *Milḥemet Yom Kippur: Zeman Emet* (The Yom Kippur War: A Moment of Truth), Tel Aviv: Miskal, 2003 (Hebrew)

Blau, Joshua, *The Emergence and Linguistic Background of Judaeo-Arabic: A Study of the Origins of Middle Arabic*, Jerusalem: Yad Yitzhak Ben-Zvi Institute, 1981

Blommaert, Jan (ed.), *Language Ideological Debates*, New York: Mouton de Gruyter, 1999

Bluestein, Gene, *Anglish/Yinglish: Yiddish in American Life and Literature*, Athens, GA: University of Georgia Press, 1989

Bourak, Eliyahu, 'Report on the Teaching of Arabic', (1947), in Yosef Yunai (ed.), *'Aravit be-Vatei Sefer 'Ivriyim: Osef Mismakhim* (Arabic in Hebrew Schools: A Collection of Documents), Te'udah: Israel Ministry of Education and Culture, 1992, pp. 43–66 (Hebrew)

Bourdieu, Pierre, 'Symbolic Power', in Denis Gleeson (ed.), *Identity and Structure: Issues in the Sociology of Education*, Driffield: Nafferton Books, 1977, pp. 112–19

Bourdieu, Pierre, 'The Forms of Capital', in John G. Richardson (ed.), *Handbook of Theory and Research for the Sociology of Education*, New York: Greenwood, 1986, pp. 241–58

Bourdieu, Pierre, *On Television*, New York: New Press, 1998

Bourdieu, Pierre and Jean Claude Passeron, *Reproduction in Education, Society and Culture*, London: Sage Publications, 1990

Boyne, Walter, *The Two O'Clock War: The 1973 Yom Kippur Conflict and the Airlift that Saved Israel*, New York: Thomas Dunne Books, 2002

Brener, Uri, *Le-Tsava Yehudi 'Atsma'i: Ha-Kibbutz ha-Me'uḥad ba-Haganah 1939–1945* (For a Jewish Independent Army: The United Kibbutz Movement in the Haganah 1939–1945), Ramat Ef'al: Yad Tabenkin – Research and Documentation of the Kibbutz Movement, 1985 (Hebrew)

Brill, Moshe, ''Otsar Milot ha-Yesod ba-'Itonut ha-Yomit ha-'Aravit – 1940 (The Basic Vocabulary of Arabic Daily Press – 1940), in Jacob M. Landau (ed.), *Hora'at ha-'Aravit ke-Lashon Zarah* (Teaching Arabic as a Foreign Language), Jerusalem: School of Education of the Hebrew University and the Ministry of Education and Culture, 1961, pp. 141–54 (Hebrew)

Brosh, Ḥezi, 'The Influence of Language Status on Language Acquisition: Arabic in the Israeli Setting', *Foreign Language Annals*, 26 (3) (1993), pp. 347–58

Brosh, Ḥezi, 'The Sociocultural Message of Language Textbooks: Arabic in the Israeli Setting', *Foreign Language Annals*, 30 3 (1997), pp. 311–26

Burak, Eliyahou, 'Matarah Mugderet le-Limud 'Aravit' (A Defined Aim for the Teaching of Arabic), *Hed ha-Ḥinukh: The Echo of Education – The Journal of the Israeli Teachers' Association* (1947), pp. 50–8 (Hebrew)

Burak, Eliyahou, 'Limud ha-Safah ha-'Aravit be-Vet ha-Sefer ha-'Ivri – 1947' (Teaching Arabic in the Hebrew School), in Jacob M. Landau (ed.), *Hora'at ha-'Aravit ke-Lashon Zarah* (Teaching Arabic as a Foreign Language), Jerusalem: School of Education of the Hebrew University and the Ministry of Education and Culture, 1961, pp. 90–3 (Hebrew)

Buzan, Barry, Ole Waever and Jaap de Wilde, *Security: A New Framework for Analysis*, London: Lynne Rienner Publishers, 1998

Byman, Daniel, *A High Price: The Triumphs and Failures of Israeli Counterterrorism*, Oxford: Oxford University Press, 2011

Chetrit, Sami Shalom, 'Mizrahi Politics in Israel: Between Integration and Alternative', *Journal of Palestine Studies*, 29 4 (2000), pp. 51–65

Coben, Diana C., 'Metaphors for an Educative Politics: "Common Sense", "Good Sense", and Educating Adults', in Carmel Borg, Joseph A. Buttigieg, and Peter Mayo (eds), *Gramsci and Education*, Lanham, MD: Rowman & Littlefield, 2002, pp. 263–90

Cohen, Hillel, *Good Arabs: The Israeli Security Agencies and the Israeli Arabs, 1948–1967*, Berkeley, CA: University of California Press, 2010

Cohen, Hillel and Yu Wang, 'Marketing Israel to the Arabs: The Rise and Fall of the *Al-Anbaa* Newspaper', *Israel Affairs*, 15 2 (2009), pp. 190–210

Cooper, Robert L., *Language Planning and Social Change*, Cambridge: Cambridge University Press, 1989

Dabashi, Hamid, *Post-Orientalism: Knowledge and Power in Time of Terror*, New Brunswick, NJ: Transaction Publishers, 2009

Dahan-Kalev, Henriette, 'Officers as Educators: The Ex-Military in the Israeli School System', *Israel Affairs*, 12 2 (2006), pp. 268–83

Dahan-Kalev, Henriette and Udi Lebel, 'Generalim be-Vatei ha-Sefer' (Generals in Schools), *Politika* (Winter 2004), pp. 27–40 (Hebrew)

Dale, Michael, 'Stalking a Conceptual Chameleon: Ideology in Marxist Studies of Education', *Educational Theory*, 36 (3) (1986), pp. 241–57

Dan, Uri, *Rosh Gesher* (Bridgehead), Tel Aviv: A. L. Publishing, 1975 (Hebrew)

Daniely, Amos, *A Queen without a Crown*, Tel Aviv: Keter, 2006

Donitsa-Schmidt, Smadar, Ofra Inbar and Elana Shohamy, 'The Effects of Teaching Spoken Arabic on Students' Attitudes and Motivation in Israel', *Modern Language Journal*, 88 (2) (2004), pp. 217–28

Dowty, Alan, '"A Question that Outweighs all Others": Yitzhak Epstein and Zionist Recognition of the Arab Issue', *Israel Studies*, 6 (1) (2001), pp. 34–54

Dowty, Alan, *Israel/Palestine*, Cambridge: Polity Press, 2008

Dror Education and Cultural Institution, 'Youth Battalion Activity in 2004', official website, 24 October 2004, available at: http://tinyurl.com/napwrm9 (accessed 28 December 2010) (Hebrew)

Dumper, Michael, *The Politics of Jerusalem Since 1967*, New York: Columbia University Press, 1997

Dunstan, Simon, *The Yom Kippur War: The Arab–Israeli War of 1973*, Oxford: Osprey Publishing, 2007

Eagleton, Terry, *Literary Theory: An Introduction*, Minneapolis, MN: University of Minnesota Press, 2008

Elazar-Halevy, Dana, 'Ruḥot Le'umiyut ve-Tfisot Militaristiot be-Limudei ha-'Aravit be-Yisrael' (Nationalistic Spirits and Militaristic Perceptions in Arabic Studies in Israel), *Dor le-Dor: Journal for the Studies in the History of Jewish Education in Israel*, 34 (2009), pp. 7–32 (Hebrew)

Elboim-Dror, Rachel, *Ha-Ḥinukh ha-'Ivri be-Eretz Yisrael* (The Hebrew Education in Eretz Israel), Jerusalem: Yad Yitzḥak Ben-Zvi Institute, 1990 (Hebrew)

Eliachar, Elie, *Liḥyot 'im Falasṭinim* (Living with Palestinians), Jerusalem: Va'ad 'Edat ha-Sephardim bi-Yerushalayyim, 1975 (Hebrew)

Elisar, Eliyahou, *Liḥyot 'im Falastinim* (To Live among Palestinians), Jerusalem: Va'ad 'Adat ha-Sephardim bi-Yerushalayyim, 1975 (Hebrew)

Eyal, Gil, 'Bein Mizraḥ le-Ma'arav: Ha-Si'aḥ 'al "ha-Kfar ha-'Aravi" be-Yisrael' (Between East and West: The Discourse on the "Arab Village" in Israel), *Theory and Criticism*, 3 (Winter 1993), pp. 39–55 (Hebrew)

Eyal, Gil, 'The Discursive Origins of Israeli Separatism: The Case of the Arab Village', *Theory and Society*, 25 (3) (1996), pp. 389–429 (Hebrew)

Eyal, Gil, 'Dangerous Liaisons between Military Intelligence and Middle Eastern Studies in Israel', *Theory and Society*, 31 (5) (2002), pp. 653–93

Eyal Gil, *Hasarat ha-Kesem min ha-Mizraḥ: Toldot ha-Mizraaḥanut be-'Idan ha-Mizraḥiyyut* (The Disenchantment of the Orient: Expertise in Arab Affairs and the Israeli State), Jerusalem: Van Leer Institute, 2005 (Hebrew)

Eyal, Gil, *The Disenchantment of the Orient: Expertise in Arab Affairs and the Israeli State*, Stanford, CA: Stanford University Press, 2006

Fishman, Joshua, *The Sociology of Language: An Interdisciplinary Social Science Approach to Language in Society*, Rowley, MA: Newbury House, 1972

Forbes, Andrew and David Henley, *People of Palestine*, Chiang Mai: Cognoscenti Books, 2012

Foucault, Michel, *Discipline and Punishment*, London: Tavistock, 1977

Fragman, Alon, 'Shitat ha-Tirgum-Dikduk be-Hora'at ha-Safah ha-'Aravit 2005–2006' (The Grammar Translation Method in Arabic Language Teaching 2005–2006), *E-mago: Israeli Online Magazine for Culture and Content*, 24 September 2006), available at: http://www.e-mago.co.il/Editor/edu-1260.htm (accessed 16 December 2012) (Hebrew)

Fragman, Alon, 'The Integration of Arab Native Teachers as Teachers of Arabic in Hebrew-Speaking Schools: Intended Policy or Arbitrary Strategy?', *Annual of Language and Politics and Politics of Identity*, 2 (2008), pp. 55–79

Francese, Joseph, *Perspectives on Gramsci: Politics, Culture and Social Theory*, New York: Routledge, 2009

Frank, Daniel (ed.), *The Jews of Medieval Islam: Community, Society, and Identity*, Leiden: E. J. Brill, 1995

Freudenthal, Gad, 'Arabic and Latin Cultures as Resources for the Hebrew Translation Movement: Comparative Considerations, Both Quantitative and Qualitative', in Gad Freudenthal (ed.), *Science in Medieval Jewish Cultures*, New York: Cambridge University Press, 2011, pp. 74–105

Friedman, Menachem, *Society and Religion: The Non-Zionist Orthodoxy in the Land of Israel*, Jerusalem: Yad Yitzḥak Ben-Zvi Institute, 1988 (Hebrew)

Galaskiewicz, Joseph, 'Interorganizational Networks Mobilizing Actions at the Metropolitan Level', in Robert Perrucci and Harry R. Potter (eds), *Networks of Power: Organizational Actors at the National, Corporate, and Community Levels*, New York: Aldine de Gruyter, 1989, pp. 81–96

Gardner, Robert C. and Wallace E. Lambert, *Attitudes and Motivation in Second Language Learning*, Rowley, MA: Newbury House, 1972

Gazit, Shlomo, *The Carrot and the Stick: Israel's Policy in Judaea and Samaria, 1967–68*, Washington, DC: B'nai B'rith Books, 1995

Gelvin, James L., *The Israel–Palestine Conflict: One Hundred Years of War*, Cambridge: Cambridge University Press, 2007

Gera, Gershon, *Sefer Ha-Shomer* (The Ha-Shomer Book), Tel Aviv: Israel Ministry of Defense, 1985 (Hebrew)

Gil, Amir, 'Be-Me'ah Elef Dollar Hekamnu et Heil ha-Modi'in' (With USD100,000 we Established the Military Intelligence Force: An Interview with the Israeli President Chayim Herzog), *Ḥamanit: Biṭa'on Ḥeil ha-Modi'in* (Ḥamanit: The Israeli Military Intelligence Journal), 1 (October 1984), pp. 6–9 (Hebrew)

Giladi, G. N., *Discord in Zion: Conflict between Ashkenazi and Sephardi Jews in Israel*, London: Scorpion, 1990

Gilboa, Amos and Ephraim Lapid, *Masterpiece: An Inside Look at Sixty Years of Israeli Intelligence*, Tel Aviv: Yedi'ot Aḥaronoth, 2008

Giroux, Henry, A., 'Theories of Reproduction and Resistance in the New Sociology of Education: A Critical Analysis', *Harvard Educational Review*, 53 (3) (1983), pp. 257–93

Glidden, Harold W., 'The Arab World', *American Journal of Psychiatry*, 128 (8) (1972), pp. 984–8

Goitein, S. D., ''Al Hora'at ha-'Aravit – 1946' (On Teaching Arabic – 1946), in Jacob M. Landau (ed.), *Hora'at ha-'Aravit ke-Lashon Zarah* (Teaching Arabic as a Foreign Language), Jerusalem: School of Education of the Hebrew University and the Ministry of Education and Culture, 1961, pp. 11–34 (Hebrew)

Goitein, S. D., *Jews and Arabs: Their Contacts through the Ages*, New York: Schocken Books, 1974

Gor, Haggith, *Militarizm ba-Ḥinukh* (The Militarization of Education), Tel Aviv: Babel Publishers, 2005 (Hebrew)

Gor, Haggith, 'Education for War in Israel: Preparing Children to Accept War as a Natural Factor of Life', in Kenneth J. Saltman and David A. Gabbard (eds), *Education as Enforcement: The Militarization and Corporatization of Schools*, New York: Routledge, 2010, pp. 209–17

Gorni, Yosef, *Zionism and the Arabs, 1882–1948: A Study of Ideology*, Oxford: Oxford University Press, 1987

Granot, Oded, 'Intelligence Corps', in *IDF and its Corps: Encyclopedia of Army and Security*, ed. by Ilan Kfir, Ya'akov Erez and Yehouda Schiff (ed.-in-chief), Tel Aviv: Revivim, 1981, p. 143 (Hebrew)

Gribetz, Jonathan, 'Musta'ribūn', Norman A. Stillman (executive ed.), *Encyclopedia of Jews in the Islamic World*, Brill Online, 2013, available at: http://referenceworks.brillonline.com/entries/encyclopedia-of-jews-in-the-islamic-world/mustaribun-SIM_000669 (accessed 4 June 2014)

Griffith, Sidney H., *The Bible in Arabic: The Scriptures of the 'People of the Book' in the Language of Islam*, Princeton, NJ: Princeton University Press, 2013

Haber, Eitan and Ze'ev Schiff, *Lexicon Milḥemet Yom Kippur* (Yom Kippur War Lexicon), Or Yehuda: Zmora Bitan, 2003 (Hebrew)

Ḥakham, Ophir, 'Ha-Shalom Mathil ba-Bayit' (The Peace Starts at Home), *Ḥamanit: Biṭa'on Ḥeil ha-Modi'in* (Ḥamanit: The Israeli Military Intelligence Journal), 17 (April 1991), p. 46 (Hebrew)

Ḥakim, Avraham, *'Aravit Meduberet Eretz Yisraelit* (Colloquial Eretz-Yisraeli Arabic), Tel Aviv: Ma'arakhot, Israel Ministry of Defense, 1976 (Hebrew)

Ḥakimi, Binyamin, *'Aravit Meduberet le-Matḥilim* (Colloquial Arabic for Beginners), Tel Aviv: Mishlav, 1978 (Hebrew)

Halperin, Liora R., 'Orienting Language: Reflections on the Study of Arabic in the Yishuv', *Jewish Quarterly Review*, 96 4 (2006), pp. 481–9

Haralambos, Michael, *Sociology: Themes and Perspectives*, London: Collins Educational, 1991

Ḥavatselet: Cultural and Educational Institutions of the National Kibbutzim Movement, 'Giv'at Ḥavivah: The Kibbutzim Seminar Centre', available at: http://www.havatzelet.org.il/heb/mosdot/ghaviva.htm (accessed 19 July 2010)

Hedin, Astrid, *The Politics of Social Networks: Interpersonal Trust and Institutional Change in Post-Communist East Germany*, Lund: Lund University Press, 2001

Herzl, Theodor, *Altneuland: Eretz Yeshanah-Ḥadashah* (The Old-New Land'), Tel Aviv: Babel Publishers, 1997 (Hebrew)

Herzog, Chaim, *The War of Atonement: The Inside Story of the Yom Kippur War*, London: Greenhill Books, 2003

Hever, Hannan, 'Territoriality and Otherness in Hebrew Literature of the War of Independence', in Laurence Jay Silberstein and Robert L. Cohn (eds), *The Other in Jewish Thought and History: Constructions of Jewish Culture and Identity*, New York: New York University Press, 1994, pp. 236–52

Him Younes, Adva and Shira Malka, *Likrat Pitu'aḥ Tokhnit Limudim be-'Aravit le-Ḥativat ha-Beinayim ve-ha-Ḥativah ha-'Elyonah* (Developing a Curriculum in Arabic for Israeli-Jewish Intermediary and High Schools), Jerusalem: Henrietta Szold Institute, National Institute for Research in the Behavioral Sciences and the Pedagogic Secretariat in the Ministry of Education, 2006, available at: http://meyda.education.gov.il/files/Tochniyot_Limudim/DochotMechkarim/Aravit.pdf (accessed 14 November 2012) (Hebrew)

Horowitz, Dan, *Trouble in Utopia: The Overburdened Polity of Israel*, Albany, NY: State University of New York Press, 1989

Horowitz, Dan and Moshe Lissak, *Metsukot be-Otopiya: Ḥevrah be-'Omes-Yeter* (Troubles in Utopia: Israel, a Society Under Over-Pressure), Tel Aviv: 'Am 'Oved, 1990 (Hebrew)

Israel Defense Forces (IDF), 'Military Intelligence in the Horizon Seminar', official website, available at: https://www.aman.idf.il/modiin/general.aspx?catId=60612 (accessed 12 August 2010)

Israel Ministry of Education, *The Book of Education and Culture: Annual Report 1951*, Jerusalem: Israel Ministry of Education, 1951

Jamal, Amal, *The Arab Public Sphere in Israel*, Bloomington, IN: Indiana University Press, 2009

Jane, Martin, 'What Should we Do with a Hidden Curriculum When we Find One?', in Henry A. Giroux and David E. Purpel (eds), *The Hidden Curriculum and Moral Education: Deception or Discovery?*, Berkeley, CA: McCutchan Publishing Corporation, 1983, pp. 122–39

Jiryis, Sabri, *The Arabs in Israel, 1948–1966*, Beirut: Institute for Palestine Studies, 1968

Johnson, Paul, *History of the Jews*, New York: Harper and Row, 1987

Kabha, Mustafa, 'Ha-'itonut ha-'Aravit be-Yisrael ke-Makhshir le-'itsuv Zehut Ḥadashah 1948–2006' (Arabic Journalism in Israel as a Tool for the Creation of a New Identity 1948–2006), *Ha-Tikshoret ha-Migzarit be-Yisrael* (The Sectorial Media in Israel), 5 (Tel Aviv: Chaim Herzog Institute for Media Politics and Society, Tel Aviv University, December 2006), pp. 6–37 (Hebrew)

Kabha, Mustafa and Dan Caspi, 'Mi-Yerushalayyim ha-Qedosha ve-ʿad ha-Maʿayan' (From Holy Jerusalem to the Spring), *Panim: A Quarterly of Culture, Society and Education*, 16 (March 2001), pp. 4455, available at: http://www.itu.org.il/Index.asp?ArticleID=1205&CategoryID=502&Page=1 (accessed 4 June 2014) (Hebrew)

Kadman, Noga, *Be-Tsidei ha-Derekh u-ve-Shulei ha-Todaʿah* (On the Side of the Road and in the Margins of Consciousness: The Depopulated Palestinian Villages of 1948 in the Israeli Discourse), Jerusalem: November Books, 2008 (Hebrew)

Katzav, Nuzhat, *Snuniyot ha-Shalom: ʿIm ha-Nashim ha-ʿArviyot ve-ha-Druziyot be-Yisrael* (Swallows of Peace: With Arab and Druze Women in Israel), Tel Aviv: Sifriyat Maʿariv, 1998 (Hebrew)

Katzburg, Netanel, 'The Education Debate in the Old Yishuv', *Shana be-Shana* (1966), pp. 299–312 (Hebrew)

Kaufman, Ilana, *Arab National Communism in the Jewish State*, Gainesville, FL: University Press of Florida, 1997

Kelly, Tobias, *Law, Violence and Sovereignty among West Bank Palestinians*, Cambridge: Cambridge University Press, 2006

Khazzoom, Aziza, 'Tarbut Maʿaravit, Tiyug Etni, ve-Sgirut Ḥevratit: Meqorot le-ʿi ha-Shivyon ha-Etni be-Yisrael' (Western Culture, Stigma, and Social Closure: The Origins of Ethnic Inequality among Jews in Israel), *Israeli Sociology: A Journal for the Study of Society in Israel*, 1 (2) (1999), pp. 385–428 (Hebrew)

Khazzoom, Aziza, 'The Great Chain of Orientalism: Jewish Identity, Stigma Management, and Ethnic Exclusion in Israel', *American Sociological Review*, 68 (4) (2003), pp. 481–510

Kimmerling, Baruch, *The Israeli State and Society: Boundaries and Frontiers*. Albany, NY: State University of New York Press, 1989

Kimmerling, Baruch, 'Militarizm ba-Ḥevrah ha-Yisraelit' (Militarism in Israeli Society), *Teʾoria u-Vikoret* (Theory and Criticism), 4 (Autumn 1993), pp. 123–40 (Hebrew)

Kimmerling, Baruch, 'Patterns of Militarism in Israel', *European Journal of Sociology*, 34 (1993), pp. 196–223

Kimmerling, Baruch, *Meḥagrim, Mityashvim, Yelidim: Ha-Medinah ve-ha-Ḥevrah be-Yisrael: Bein Ribui Tarbuyot le-Milḥamot Tarbut* (Immigrants, Settlers, Natives: The Israeli State and Society between Cultural Pluralism and Cultural Wars), Tel Aviv: ʿAm ʿOved, 2004 (Hebrew)

Kinberg, Naphtali and Rafael Talmon, 'Learning of Arabic by Jews and the use of Hebrew among Arabs in Israel', *Indian Journal of Applied Linguistics*, 20 (1–2) (1994), pp. 37–54

Kligman, Avner, *The Israel Prize: 1996*, Jerusalem: Israeli Ministry of Culture, 1996, p. 37 (Hebrew)

Kolewitz, Emmanuel, 'Horaʾat ha-Safah be-Reʾi ha-Mismakhim' (Teaching the Language through the Study of Documents), *Journal for the Teachers of Arabic and Islamic History*, 14 (April 1991), pp. 9–18 (Hebrew)

Korn, Yitzhak, *Jews at the Crossroads*, East Brunswick, NJ: Cornwall Books, 1983

Kosover, Mordecai, *Arabic Elements in Palestinian Yiddish: The Old Ashkenazic Jewish Community in Palestine, its History and its Language*, Jerusalem: R. Mass, 1966

Kraemer, Roberta, 'Social Psychological Factors Related to the Study of Arabic among Israeli High School Students: A Test of Gardner's Socioeducational Model', *Studies in Second Language Acquisition*, 15 (1) (1993), pp. 83–106

Kraemer, Roberta and Elite Olshtain, 'Perceived Ethnolinguistic Vitality and Language Attitudes: The Israeli Setting', *Journal of Multilingual and Multicultural Development*^, 10 (1989), pp. 197–212

Landau, Jacob M., 'Hebrew and Arabic in the State of Israel: Political Aspects of the Language Issue', *International Journal of the Sociology of Language*, 67 (1987), pp. 117–33

Landau, Jacob M. (ed.), *Hora'at ha-'Aravit ke-Lashon Zarah* (Teaching Arabic as a Foreign Language), Jerusalem: School of Education of the Hebrew University and the Ministry of Education and Culture, 1961 (Hebrew)

Lapid, Ephraim, 'Collecting Information in Preparation for the Six-Day War (1967)', in Amos Gilboa and Ephraim Lapid (eds), *Israeli's Silent Defender: An Inside Look at Sixty Years of Israeli Intelligence*, Jerusalem: Gefen Publishing House and Israel Intelligence Heritage and Commemoration Center, 2012, pp. 65–70

Latour, Bruno, *We Have Never Been Modern*, Cambridge, MA: Harvard University Press, 1993

Lefkowitz, Daniel, *Words and Stones: The Politics of Language and Identity in Israel*, Oxford: Oxford University Press, 2004

Levy, Aryeh and Irit Miro, *Ha-Mivḥan ha-Artzi be-'Aravit: Heisegim ve-Heibetim be-Hora'at ha-Miktso'a* (The Arabic National Exam: Results and Discussion about the Teaching of Arabic), Tel Aviv: School of Education, Tel Aviv University, 1995 (Hebrew)

Levy, Aryeh and Shlomo Pasternak, *'Aravit Meduberet be-Vet ha-Sefer ha-'Ivri be-Yisrael* (Teaching Spoken Arabic in Hebrew Schools in Israel), Tel Aviv: Tel Aviv University School of Education, 1976 (Hebrew)

Lewis, Bernard, *The Jews of Islam*, Princeton, NJ: Princeton University Press, 1987

Lissak, Moshe, 'Boundaries and Institutional Linkages between Elites: Some Illustrations from Civil–Military Relations in Israel', *Politics and Society*, 1 (1985), pp. 129–48

Lockman, Zachary, 'Railway Workers and Relational History: Arabs and Jews in British-Ruled Palestine', *Society for Comparative Study of Society and History*, 35 (3) (1993), pp. 601–27

Lockman, Zachary, *Comrades and Enemies: Arab and Jewish Workers in Palestine, 1906–1948*, Berkeley, CA: University of California Press, 1996

Lockman, Zachary, *Contending Visions of the Middle East: The History and Politics of Orientalism*, Cambridge: Cambridge University Press, 2004

Luckham, A. R., 'A Comparative Typology of Civil–Military Relations', *Government and Opposition*, 6 (1) (1971), pp. 5–35

Lustigman, Ran, 'Hora'at ha-'Aravit be-Vatei Sefer 'Ivriyyim be-Yisrael' (Teaching Arabic in Hebrew Schools in Israel), (Hagar: Jewish–Arab Education for Equality, 2008), available at: http://www.hajar.org.il/hajar/docs/publication/he-run%20lustigman.doc (accessed 14 November 2012) (Hebrew)

Lustigman, Ran, 'Hora'at ha-Safah ha-'Aravit be-Vatei Sefer 'Ivriyyim: Shki'ah Nugah – Hashivah Meḥudeshet 'al Merkaziyutam shel Limudei ha-Safah ha-'Aravit be-Misgeret Mediniyut Misrad ha-Ḥinukh le-Ḥayyim Meshutafim' (Teaching Arabic in Hebrew Schools: A Call for Rethinking the Place of

Arabic Studies in the Ministry of Education's Programme for Coexistence), in *Kenes Mandel le-Ḥinukh: 60 Shnot Ḥinukh be-Yisrael – ʿAvar, Hoveh, ʿAtid* (Mandel Conference for Education: 60 Years of Education in Israel – Past, Present, Future), Kfar ha-Maccabiah, 18 December 2008, pp. 167–79, available at: http://my.mli.org.il/Mli_Pdf/Graduate/Mandel.LUSTIGMAN.pdf (accessed 14 November 2012) (Hebrew)

Maalouf, Tony, *Arabs in the Shadow of Israel: The Unfolding of God's Prophetic Plan for Ishmael's Line*, Grand Rapids, MI: Kregel Publications, 2003

de Marrais, Kathleen Bennett and Margaret D. LeCompte, *The Way Schools Work: A Sociological Analysis of Education*, New York: Addison Wesley Longman, 1998

Massad, Joseph, 'Zionism's Internal Others: Israel and the Oriental Jews', *Journal of Palestine Studies*, 25 (4) (1996), pp. 53–68

Mazor, Barukh, 'Sikumim min ha-Shehiyah ha-Limudit shel Talmidei ha-Megamah ha-Mizraḥit ba-Shetaḥ ha-ʿAravi – 1960' (Summary of the Oriental Classes' Experience in the Arab Area – 1960), in Jacob M. Landau (ed.), *Horaʾat ha-ʿAravit ke-Lashon Zarah* (Teaching Arabic as a Foreign Language), Jerusalem: School of Education of the Hebrew University and the Ministry of Education and Culture, 1961, pp. 67–75 (Hebrew)

Mekhinah, Rosh Pina, official website, available at: http://www.mrp.org.il/ (accessed 28 December 2010)

'Mekhinim et Anshei ha-Modiʿin: Be-Rosh Pinah Kovʿim – ha-Rosh Koveʿa' (Training the People of Intelligence: In Rosh Pina it was Decided – The Mind is What is Important), *Mabat Malam: Journal of the Israeli Intelligence, Heritage and Commemoration Centre*, 50 (October 2007), p. 29 (Hebrew)

Mendel, Yonatan, 'Re-Arabising the De-Arabised: The Mistaʿaravim Unit of the Palmach', in Ziad Elmarsafy, Anna Bernard and David Attwell (eds), *Debating Orientalism*, London: Palgrave Macmillan, 2013, pp. 94–116

Mendel, Yonatan, 'A Sentiment-Free Arabic: On the Creation of the Israeli Accelerated Arabic Language Studies Programme', *Middle Eastern Studies*, 49 (3) (2013), pp. 383–401

Meron, Yoram and Reyad Kabha, *Agadot ha-Vadi* (The Tails of the Valley), Givʿat-Ḥavivah: Jewish–Arab Center for Peace, 1993 (Hebrew)

Meron, Yoram, Reyad Kabha and Abu Rafiʿ Raya, *Agadah shel Kfar* (A Legendary Village), Givʿat-Ḥavivah: Jewish–Arab Center for Peace, 2005 (Hebrew)

Meron, Yoram et al., *Garger ha-Rimon* (The Pomegranate's Aril), Givʿat-Ḥavivah: Jewish–Arab Center for Peace, 1997 (Hebrew)

Miller, Elhanan, 'Army in the Classroom: IDF Attempts to Encourage the Study of Arabic in Israeli High Schools', paper presented at the Conference on Language, Conflict and Security in the Middle East, Centre of Islamic Studies, University of Cambridge, 11 April 2010

Milroy, Lesley, *Language and Social Networks*, Oxford: Basil Blackwell, 1980

Morag, Shlomo, 'Horaʾat ha-ʿAravit: le-ʾor ha-Metsiʾut – 1948' (Teaching Arabic: In Light of Reality – 1948), in Jacob M. Landau (ed.), *Horaʾat ha-ʿAravit ke-Lashon Zarah* (Teaching Arabic as a Foreign Language), Jerusalem: School of Education of the Hebrew University and the Ministry of Education and Culture, 1961, pp. 49–51 (Hebrew)

Moreh, Shmuel, 'The Study of Arabic Literature in Israel', *Ariel: The Israel Review of Arts and Letters*, Cultural and Scientific Relations Division, Ministry for Foreign Affairs, December 2001, available at: http://www.mfa.gov.il/

MFA/MFAArchive/2000_2009/2001/12/The%20Study%20of%20Arabic%20 Literature%20in%20Israel (accessed 14 November 2014)

Morris, Benny, *Righteous Victims: A History of the Zionist–Arab Conflict, 1881–2001*, New York: Vintage Books, 2001

Morris, Benny, *The Birth of the Palestinian Refugee Problem Revisited*, Cambridge: Cambridge University Press, 2004

Morris, Benny, 'Revisiting the Palestinian Exodus of 1948', in Eugene L. Rogan and Avi Shlaim (eds), *The War for Palestine: Rewriting the History of 1948*, Cambridge: Cambridge University Press, 2007, pp. 37–59

Mutawi, Samir A., *Jordan in the 1967 War*, Cambridge: Cambridge University Press, 1987

Naamani, Israel T., *The State of Israel*, New York: Praeger, 1980

Naḥam, Ilan, 'Cultural Mediation: Avraham Sharoni – From Military Intelligence to the Arabic–Hebrew Dictionary', *Pe'amim*, 122–3 (2010), pp. 193–211 (Hebrew)

Naḥum, Doron, 'Basis ha-Modi'in 8200: Shetaḥ Tzva'i Patu'aḥ' (Military Intelligence Base 8200: An Open Military Zone), *NRG-Ma'ariv*, 22 October 2006, available at: http://www.nrg.co.il/online/1/ART1/494/701.html (accessed 14 November 2014) (Hebrew)

Nakdimon, Shlomo, *Svirut Nemukhah* (A Low Probability for War: The Background and Consequences of the Yom Kippur War), Jerusalem: Revivim, 1982 (Hebrew)

(Col.) No'am, "Arabisṭim be-Ḥaman: Lihyot 'o Laḥdol (Arabists in the Military Intelligence: It is Now or Never), *Ḥamanit: Biṭa'on Ḥeil ha-Modi'in* (Ḥamanit: The Israeli Military Intelligence Journal), 2 (November 1985), pp. 22–3 (Hebrew)

Ophir, Yom-Ṭov, *'Aravit Meduberet* (Colloquial Arabic), Jerusalem: Open University of Israel, 1977 (Hebrew)

Oren, Michael B., *Six Days of War: June 1967 and the Making of the Modern Middle East*, Oxford: Oxford University Press, 2002

Outhwaite, Ben, 'Lines of Communication: Medieval Hebrew Letters of the 11th Century', in Esther-Miriam Wagner, Ben Outhwaite and Bettina Beinhoff (eds), *Scribes as Agents of Language Change*, Berlin: De Gruyter Mouton, forthcoming

Ozacky-Lazar, Sarah and Mustafa Kabaha, 'The Haganah by Arab and Palestinian Historiography and Media,' *Israel Studies*, 7 (3) (2002), pp. 45–60

Pappé, Ilan, "Al Gadna' Mizraḥanut: ha-Academyah ha-Yisraelit ve-ha-Mizraḥ ha-Tikhon ba-Me'ah ha-21' (On the Youth Arabic Battalion: Israeli Academy and the Middle East in the 21st Century), *Ru'aḥ Mizraḥit* (MEISAI Electronic Journal), 4 (Summer 2006), pp. 22–6 (Hebrew)

Pappé, Ilan, *The Ethnic Cleansing of Palestine*, Oxford: Oneworld, 2006

Pavlenko, Aneta, '"Language of the Enemy": Foreign Language Education and National Identity', *International Journal of Bilingual Education and Bilingualism*, 6 (5) (2003), pp. 313–31

Peri, Yoram, *Generals in the Cabinet Room: How the Military Shapes Israeli Policy*, Washington, DC: US Institute of Peace Press, 2006

Perron, Esther, 'Le-Zikhrah shel Shulamit Katznelson' (In Memory of Shulamit Katznelson), *Hed ha-ha-'Ulpan ha-Ḥadash* (The New Ulpan Echo: An Educational Journal for Hebrew Studies) 86 (Autumn 2004), p. 2 (Hebrew)

Peterson, John, 'Policy Networks', *Political Science Series 90*, Vienna: Institute for Advanced Studies, July 2003, p. 1, available at: http://www.ihs.ac.at/publications/pol/pw_90.pdf (accessed 14 November 2012)

Peterson, John and Elizabeth Bomberg, *Decision-Making in the European Union*, Basingstoke: Macmillan Press, 1999

Piamenta, Moshe, *Speak Arabic: An Introduction to Eretz Yisraeli Arabic*, Tel Aviv: Maʿariv, 1968 (Hebrew)

Pinto, Meital, 'On the Intrinsic Value of Arabic in Israel: Challenging Kymlicka on Language Rights', *Canadian Journal of Law and Jurisprudence*, 20 (2007), pp. 143–72

Podeh, Elie, *The Arab–Israeli Conflict in Israeli History Textbooks, 1948–2000*, Westport, CT: Greenwood Press, 2002

Rabinowitz, Dani, 'Nostalgyah Mizraḥit: Eikh Hafkhu ha-Falasṭinim le-"ʿArviyei Yisrael"?' (Oriental Nostalgia: The Transformation of the Palestinians into "Israeli Arabs"'), *Teʾoria u-Vikoret* (Theory and Criticism), 4 (Autumn 1993), pp. 141–51 (Hebrew)

Ram, Uri, *The Changing Agenda of Israeli Sociology: Theory, Ideology and Identity*, New York: State University of New York Press, 1995

Rapaport, ʿAmir, 'Yeḥidat Haʾazanot 8200: Kakh ha-Hol Hitḥil' (Eavesdropping Unit 8200: This is How it All Began), *NRG-Maʿariv*, 14 October 2008, available at: http://www.nrg.co.il/online/1/ART1/798/764.html (accessed 15 December 2013) (Hebrew)

Raz, Avi, *The Bride and the Dowry: Israel, Jordan, and the Palestinians in the Aftermath of the June 1967* War, New Haven, CT, and London: Yale University Press, 2012

Raz Krakotzkin, Amnon, 'Galut be-Tokh Ribonut: Le-Bikoret "Shelilat ha-Galut" ba-Tarbut ha-Yisraelit (Exile within Sovereignty: Towards a Critique of the 'Negation of Exile' in Israeli Culture), *Teʾoria u-Vikoret* (Theory and Criticism), 4 (Autumn 1993), pp. 23–55 (Hebrew)

Rehovot Archive, available at: https://commons.wikimedia.org/wiki/File:PikiWiki_Israel_1515_Rehovot_3_%D7%93%D7%9E%D7%95%D7%99%D7%95%D7%AA_%D7%9E%D7%90%D7%A8%D7%92%D7%95%D7%9F_%D7%94%D7%A9%D7%95%D7%9E%D7%A8.jpg?uselang=he (accessed 25 August 2013)

Rogan, Eugene L. and Avi Shlaim (eds), *The War for Palestine: Rewriting the History of 1948*, Cambridge: Cambridge University Press, 2007

Rolef, Susan Hattis, *Political Dictionary of the State of Israel*, New York: Macmillan, 1987

Rozen, Minna, 'The Position of the *Mustaʿrab*s in the Inter-Community Relationships in Eretz Israel from the End of the 15th Century to the End of the 17th Century', *Cathedra*, 17 (October 1980), pp. 73–101 (Hebrew)

Rynhold, Jonathan, 'Peace and Security in the 2006 Israeli Elections', *Israel Affairs*, 13 (2) (2007), pp. 384–400

Saban, Ilan, 'Kol (du-Leshoni) Boded ba-Afeilah?' (A Lost Bilingual Voice in the Dark?), *ʿIyunei Mishpat: Tel Aviv University Law Review*, 27 (1) (2003), pp. 109–38 (Hebrew)

Saban, Ilan, 'Deeply Divided Societies: A Framework for Analysis and the Case of the Arab-Palestinian Minority in Israel', *New York University Journal of International Law and Politics*, 36 (2004), pp. 885–1003

Saban, Ilan, 'Appropriate Representation of Minorities: Canada's Two Types Structure and the Arab-Palestinian Minority in Israel', *Penn State International Law Review*, 24 (2006), pp. 563–94

Saban, Ilan and Muhammad Amara, 'The Status of Arabic in Israel: Reflections on the Power of Law to Produce Social Change', *Israel Law Review*, 36 (2) (2002), pp. 5–39

Said, Edward, *Orientalism*, Harmondsworth: Penguin, 1995

Sayigh, Yusif A., 'Dispossession and Pauperisation: The Palestinian Economy under Occupation', in George Abed (ed.), *The Palestinian Economy: Studies in Development under Prolonged Occupation*, New York and London: Routledge, 1988, pp. 259–86

Schwarb, Gregor, 'Vestiges of Qaraite Translations in the Arabic Translation(s) of the Samaritan Pentateuch', *Intellectual History of the Islamic World*, 1 (1–2) (2013), pp. 115–57

Sebeok, Thomas Albert, *Current Trends in Linguistics: Linguistics in South-West Asia and North Africa*, Paris: Mouton, 1970

Segev, Tom, *1967: Israel, the War, and the Year that Transformed the Middle East*, New York: Picador, 2008

Shafir, Gershon, *Land, Labor and the Origins of the Israeli–Palestinian Conflict, 1882–1914* (Berkeley, CA: University of California Press, 1996

Shafir, Gershon and Yoav Peled, *Being Israeli: The Dynamics of Multiple Citizenship*, Cambridge: Cambridge University Press, 2002

Shapira, Anita, *Land and Power: The Zionist Resort to Force, 1881–1948*, Stanford, CA: Stanford University Press, 1992

Shavit, Jacob, *Jabotinsky and the Revisionist Movement, 1925–1948*, New York: Routledge, 1988

Sheffer, Gabriel and Oren Barak, 'The Study of Civil–Military Relations in Israel: A New Perspective', in ibid. (eds), *Militarism and Israeli Society*, Bloomington, IN: Indiana University Press, 2010, pp. 14–42

Shenhav, Yehouda, 'The Jews of Iraq, Zionist Ideology, and the Property of the Palestinian Refugees of 1948: An Anomaly of National Accounting', *International Journal of Middle East Studies*, 31 4 (1999), pp. 605–30

Shenhav, Yehouda, 'Ethnicity and National Memory: The World Organization of Jews from Arab Countries (WOJAC) in the Context of the Palestinian National Struggle', *British Journal of Middle Eastern Studies*, 29 (1) (2002), pp. 27–56

Shenhav, Yehouda, *Ha-Yehudim ha-ʿAravim: Leʾumiyut, Dat, Etniyut* (The Arab Jews: Nationalism, Religion, Ethnicity), Tel Aviv: ʿAm ʿOved, 2003 (Hebrew)

Shenhav, Yehouda, 'Me-ʿolam lo Haytah ha-Leʾumiyut Modernit – ve-Ḥilonit: ʿAl Hakhlaʾah ve-Ṭihur etsel Bruno Latour' (Nationalism was Never Modern – and Secular: On Purification and Hybridity in the Thought of Bruno Latour), *Teʾoria u-Vikoret* (Theory and Criticism), 26 (Spring 2005), pp. 75–88 (Hebrew)

Shenhav, Yehouda, *The Arab Jews: A Postcolonial Reading of Nationalism, Religion, and Ethnicity*, Stanford, CA: Stanford University Press, 2006

Shlaim, Avi, *The Iron Wall: Israel and the Arab World*, New York: W. W. Norton, 2001

Shlaim, Avi and William Roger, *The 1967 Arab–Israeli War: Origins and Consequences*, Cambridge: Cambridge University Press, 2012

Shohamy, Elana, *Language Policy: Hidden Agendas and New Approaches*, New York: Routledge, 2006

Shohat, Ella, 'Sephardim in Israel: Zionism from the Standpoint of its Jewish Victims', *Social Text*, 19 (Autumn 1988), pp. 1–35

Shohat, Ella, 'The Invention of the Mizrahim', *Journal of Palestine Studies*, 29 (1) (1999), pp. 5–20

Shohat, Ella, *Taboo Memories, Diasporic Voices*, Durham, NC: Duke University Press, 2006

'Siyum Kurs Morot-Hayalot: Maḥzor Yud-Alef' (Upon Finishing the 11th Session of the Soldier-Teachers Course)', *Ḥamanit: Biṭaʾon Ḥeil ha-Modiʿin* (Ḥamanit: The Israeli Military Intelligence Journal), 15 (August 1990), p. 20 (Hebrew)

Snir, Reuven, 'Ha-Shirah ha-ʿAravit: Gan Naʿul' (Arabic Poetry is Blocked in Front of Israeli Jewish Students), *Bitaʾon ha-Morim le-ʿAravit* (Israeli Journal of the Teachers of Arabic and Islam), 3 (December 1987), pp. 15–19 (Hebrew)

Snir, Reuven, 'Yehudim ke-ʿAravim: Matsav ha-Meḥkar' (Jews as Arabs: The Status of Research), *Ruʾaḥ Mizraḥit: MEISAI Electronic Journal*, 2 (Summer 1995), pp. 9–18 (Hebrew)

Snir, Reuven, *ʿArviyut, Yahadut, Tsiyonut: Maʾavak Zehuyot bi-Yetsiratam shel Yehudei ʿIraq* (Arabness, Jewishness, Zionism: A Struggle of Identities in the Literature of Iraqi Jews), Jerusalem: Yad Yitzḥak Ben-Zvi Institute for the Study of Jewish Communities of the East, 2005 (Hebrew)

Snir, Reuven, '"Ana min al-Yahud": The Demise of Arab-Jewish Culture in the Twentieth Century', *Archiv Orientální*, 74 (2006), pp. 387–424 (Hebrew)

Snir, Reuven, 'The Arab Jews: Language, Poetry and Singularity', *Qantara.de*, 18 December 2009, available at: http://en.qantara.de/wcsite.php?wc_c=9132 (accessed 14 November 2012)

Soshuk, Levi and Azriel Eisenberg (eds), *Momentous Century: Personal and Eyewitness Accounts of the Rise of the Jewish Homeland and State 1875–1978*, Cranbury, NJ: Cornwall Books, 1984

Spivak, Gayatri Chakkravorty, 'Can the Subaltern Speak?', in Bill Ashcroft, Gareth Griffiths and Helen Tiffin (eds), *The Postcolonial Studies Reader* (New York: Routledge, 1995), pp. 24–8

Spolsky, Bernard, 'Language in Israel: Policy, Practice and Ideology', in James. E. Alatis and Tan Ai-Hui (eds), *Georgetown University Round Table on Language and Linguistics*, Washington, DC: Georgetown University Press, 1999, pp. 164–74

Spolsky, Bernard and Robert Cooper, *The Languages of Jerusalem*, Oxford: Clarendon Press, 1991

Spolsky, Bernard and Elana Shohamy, *The Languages of Israel: Policy, Ideology and Practice*, Clevedon: Multilingual Matters, 1999

Steinschneider, Moritz, *Jewish Arabic Literature: An Introduction*, Piscataway, NJ: Gorgias Press, 2008

Steven, Stewart, *The Spymasters of Israel*, New York: Ballantine Books, 1986

Suleiman, Yasir, *A War of Words: Language and Conflict in the Middle East*, Cambridge: Cambridge University Press, 2004

Suleiman, Yasir, 'Charting the Nation: Arabic and the Politics of Identity', *Annual Review of Applied Linguistics*, 26 (2006), pp. 125–48

Swirsky, Shlomo, *Israel: The Oriental Majority*, London: Zed Press, 1989

Tajfel, Henri (ed.), *Differentiation between Social Groups: Studies in the Social Psychology of Intergroup Relations*, London: Academic Press, 1978

Tessler, Mark, *A History of the Israeli–Palestinian Conflict*, Bloomington, IN: Indiana University Press, 1994

The Military Dictionary, Darby, PA: Diane Publishing, 1987

Trumper-Hecht, Nira, 'Constructing National Identity in Mixed Cities in Israel: Arabic on Signs in the Public Space of Upper Nazareth', in Elana Shohamy and Gorter Durk (eds), *Linguistic Landscape: Expanding the Scenery*, New York: Routledge, 2009, pp. 238–52

Uhlmann, Allon J., 'Policy Implications of Arabic Instruction in Israeli Jewish Schools', *Human Organization*, 70 (1) (2001), pp. 97–105

Uhlmann, Allon J., 'The Field of Arabic Instruction in the Zionist State', in James Albright and Allan Luke (eds), *Pierre Bourdieu and Literacy Education*, New York: Routledge, 2008, pp. 95–112

Uhlmann, Allon J., Arabic Instruction in Jewish Schools and in Universities in Israel: Contradictions, Subversion, and the Politics of Pedagogy', *International Journal of Middle East Studies*, 42 (2) (2010), pp. 291–309

US Department of Defense, *The Dictionary of Military Terms*, New York: Skyhorse Publishing, 2009

US Joint Military Terminology Group, *The Military Dictionary*, Darby, PA: Diane Publishing, 1987

Vashitz, Yoseph, *The Arabs in Eretz Yisrael*, Tel Aviv: Sifriyat ha-Poʿalim, 1947 (Hebrew)

Vashitz, Yoseph, *The World of the Bedouins*, Givʿat Ḥavivah: Institute for Arabic Studies, 1976 (Hebrew)

Versteegh, Cornelis, *The Arabic Language*, Edinburgh: Edinburgh University Press, 2001

Weinreich, Max, *History of the Yiddish Language*, New Haven, CT: Yale University Press, 2008

Wikimedia, 'Haganah', available at: https://commons.wikimedia.org/wiki/File:Hahagana.jpg?uselang=he (accessed 25 August 2013)

Wikimedia, 'IDF', available at: https://commons.wikimedia.org/wiki/File:IDF_Symbol.svg?uselang=he (accessed 25 August 2013)

Williams, Michael C., Words, Images, Enemies: Securitization and International Politics', *International Studies Quarterly*, 47 (4) (2003), pp. 511–31

Yaʿari, ʿOdeda, *Kavei Govah: Sipuro shel Deni Agmon* (Contour Lines: The Story of Deni Agmon, the Commander of the Mistaʿaravim Unit (Tel Aviv: Beit ha-Palmach, 2006) (Hebrew)

Yaari, Avraham (1984) 'Hashomer Learns Sheepherding', in Levi Soshuk and Azriel Eisenberg (eds), *Momentous Century: Personal and Eyewitness Accounts of the Rise of the Jewish Homeland and State 1875–1978*, Cranbury, NJ: Cornwall Books, pp. 75–9

Yakobson, Alexander, 'Miʿuṭ Leʾumi bi-Medinat Leʾom Demoḳraṭit' (A National Minority in a Democratic Nation-State), in Elie Rekhess and Sarah Ozacky-Lazar (eds), *Maʿamad ha- Miʿuṭ ha-ʿAravi bi-Medinat ha-Leʾom ha-Yehudit* (The Arabs in Israel: The Status of the Arab Minority in the Jewish Nation-State) (Tel Aviv: Dayan Center, 2005), pp. 19–26 (Hebrew)

Yakobson, Alexander and Amnon Rubinstein, *Israel and the Family of Nations: The Jewish Nation-State and Human Rights*, Milton Park: Routledge, 2008

Yellin, Avinoʿam, 'Le-Horaʾat ha-Safah ha-ʿAravit be-Vet ha-Sefer ha-Tikhoni ha-ʿIvri – 1939' (About Teaching Arabic in the Hebrew High Schools –1939), in Jacob M. Landau (ed.), *Horaʾat ha-ʿAravit ke-Lashon Zarah* (Teaching Arabic as a Foreign Language), Jerusalem: School of Education of the Hebrew University and the Ministry of Education and Culture, 1961, pp. 75–83 (Hebrew)

Yunai, Yosef (ed.), *ʿAravit be-Vatei Sefer ʿIvriyim: Osef Mismakhim* (Arabic in Hebrew Schools: A Collection of Documents), Teʿudah: Israel Ministry of Education and Culture, 1992 (Hebrew)

Zohar, Zion, *Sephardic and Mizrahi Jewry: From the Golden Age of Spain to Modern Times*, New York: New York University Press, 2005

Index

increased involvement in Arabic studies, 114–17
work with head teachers, 121–2
Sharoni Arabic–Hebrew dictionary, 113–14

Zaken, Motti, 221
Zakin, Dov, 149
Zamiri, Aryeh, 104
Ze'ev, Herbert, 194, 197, 198, 199
Ze'ira, Eli, 109, 112
Zionism
'Conquest of Labour', 24, 25
'Conquest of Land', 25
'Conquest of Language', 25
differentiation from Arab culture, 6
Hebrew, 88
influence on Arabic studies, 5, 25–6, 27
'new Jew', 23, 24
relationship with Arabic, 25–30, 39–40
separation through integration, 24, 25
Zionist immigration to Palestine, 21–5
Ziv, Michael, 51, 62, 64, 92, 94, 99
Zore'a, Giyora, 193

Lightning Source UK Ltd.
Milton Keynes UK
UKOW02f0230300816

281776UK00001B/8/P

9 781349 463787